# Death of a Dream

## HISTORY OF CUBA
### ELUSIVE QUEST FOR FREEDOM

## PEDRO ROIG

INSTITUTE FOR CUBAN AND
CUBAN-AMERICAN STUDIES

UNIVERSITY OF
Miami

**DEATH OF A DREAM: A HISTORY OF CUBA**
Second Edition by Alexandria Library Publishing House, MIAMI
Copyright© 2008 by Pedro RoigA

ISBN: 978-1495289606
alinaroig@bellsouth.net  or  Pedro Roig
1350 SW 57 Ave., Miami, FL 33144

Library of Congress number 1-108767601

Cover illustration: Paisaje Cubano, 1933 by Marcelo Pogolotti

# DEDICATION

To the beloved memory of my father Pedro Roig, historian, attorney and educator, who taught me the wisdom of tolerance, justice, freedom and has been the inspiration of my life.

"Remain united, pay the soldiers
and take no heed of the rest"
Emperor Septimus Severus to his sons.

# TABLE OF CONTENT

# FOREWORD

The Cuban revolution has produced a vast literature. Since the rise of Fidel Castro to power in 1959 a variety of books on the Cuban economy, politics, history, foreign relations, have been written, many in an attempt to explain Castro's rise to power. Some have emphasized the U.S. role in Cuba's history as an explanation for Castro anti-Americanism. Others have tried to blame Cuba's pre-Castro's economic conditions for a major revolution in the island. Still others, more recent ones, have tried to assess the successes and failures of Castroism's 50 years rule over the Cuban people.

"Death of a Dream" belongs to this last category. Pedro Roig is eminently qualified to write a critical appraisal of Castroism and its impact on Cuba. Historian, educator, attorney and for the past five years, Director of the Office of Cuba Broadcasting that manages Radio/TV Marti, Roig has been intimately involved in Cuban affairs. His vast experience and keen understanding of events in Cuba has helped him produce a brilliant, analytical work that enriches our understanding of Cuba.

Organized in chronological order, the book delves into key events in Cuban history. The British occupation of Havana in the 1860's; the wars for independence; the 1933 revolution and finally the Castro revolution with its two initial momentous events the Bay of Pigs fiasco and the Missile Crisis, are some of the topics discussed.

For the Bay of Pigs, Roig has searched Soviet as well as Cuban and U.S. sources and has written a coherent analysis of the events that led to the disaster. The author points to the fact that the fundamental premise of hiding the U.S. involvement, doomed from the beginning, the possibilities of a successful operation. The magnitude of such enterprise made it impossible to fake the U.S. commitment in the planning, training, arming and delivery of the Cuban Brigade to the Bay of Pigs but cut short, the needed military resources for victory, like the critical control of the air over the beachhead.

On the missile crisis, Roig has found several wonderful nugget of information, including a memo from Robert Kennedy written while the Brigade was running out of ammunitions in which the

Attorney General calls for U.S. direct involvement in Cuba, warning that the Soviets would eventually bring nuclear missiles into the Island if we fail to act. Another nugget of information is the assertion of the Soviet Ambassador in Washington, Anatolyn Dobrynin, that all along during the crisis, Khrushchev was bluffing and that the Kremlin leadership would have never gone to a nuclear war over the missiles in Cuba.

With the sharp mind of a prosecutor, Roig points to the issue of the Spanish political heritage, the army as the arbiter of power, the U.S. meddling in Cuba's internal affairs and the failure of Castro's revolution. For Roig the Cuban youth "is living in the shadows of hopelessness looking for a place to bury the decaying corpse of the revolution".

"Death of a Dream" is an extraordinary book that provides much insight into the values, psychology and behavior of the Cuban people. For those interested in understanding what happened in Cuba, Pedro Roig's book is a must.

**Jaime Suchlicki**

**Emilio Bacardi Moreau Professor of History, University of Miami, November 2008**

# INTRODUCTION

To write a book on Cuba, at a historical crossroad when the Revolution of 1959 is fading into oblivion and the road ahead seems shrouded in the unfathomable events of the future, is an especially appropriate time to look back and offer the lessons of the past for the coming generations. Still, the need to create a narrative posed a challenging process of selection in which, the chronological order coexists with the thematic unity to offer the readers a comprehensive synthesis of Cuba's history. All care possible has been taken to verify every fact.

Cuba had a historical beginning as a military base in charge of providing protection to the gold being transported to Spain from Mexico and Peru. This garrison mentality has not changed. Cuba has remained throughout the centuries a military base, governed by generals whose wishes have reigned supreme. It is also a historical fact that from Columbus to Castro, Cuba has been free from military controlled governments for just 36 years.

Sugar was for Cuba the driving force of economic wealth and industrial development. It was also the agent of slavery with its horrible quota of pain, suffering and humiliation to hundred of thousands of African men and women. In this brutal setting, religion and music became the melancholic sanctuary to care for their mutilated self-esteem, and to feed the spiritual needs of loneliness and desperation. One of the major contributions to modern music was made by these African slaves who combined their homeland instruments and rhythms with European hymns. It was a magnificent tran-cultural event and the genesis of what became the world-renowned Cuban music.

Cuba was among the first regions in the world to be impacted by the Industrial Revolution. In 1817, sugar mills began using steam engines. By 1841, grinding, boiling and evaporation processes were combined into a single machine. It was a remarkable achievement. Cuban sugar barons took full advantage of the United States market demand, placing Cuba as the top producer of sugar in the world. By the beginning of the War of Independence in 1868, the island colony was wealthier than Spain, its decaying master.

Madrid was the wrong political model, a dysfunctional

"teacher" where the leading politicians had a profound inclination for grandiose speeches and self-deception, a burning need to behave like a great power, and a national obsession with their brief and shining past, despite Spain's industrial backwardness and widespread poverty. From the Spanish decadent political society, Cubans learned about bureaucratic corruption, dogmatic intolerance, "caudillismo" (warlord syndrome), messianic leadership, a malformed judicial system, an inept administration and the authority of the military as arbiter of power and violence. It was, indeed, the wrong recipe for creating a pluralistic and functional democracy.

The War of Independence left a confused legacy of an inconclusive revolution cut short by the American intervention. The Cubans believed they were about to win the conflict even though that premise has been bitterly debated by military historians. Furthermore, the fierce and terrible struggle created among the political elite the need for a violent nationalistic revolution as a way to conquering, by blood and sacrifice, Cuba's glorious destiny. A revolutionary mythology was born from the ashes of the War of Independence. Castro did not create this dysfunctional formula. He found it and articulated the anger, turning it into a passion. He knew that the army was the arbiter of power, so he wiped out the old one and built a new army, framed in the doctrine of loyalty, discipline and obedience to him. Backed by an efficient security force, Castro implemented the Marxist dogma that provided an alliance with the Soviet Union, a nuclear power engaged in a worldwide confrontation with the United States. Castro's international vision was predicated on the premise that in the Cold War, the Soviet Union was to prevail over the hated "Yankees" and bury the market economy.

The "Maximo Leader" was wrong. Castro's ideological vision was mistaken. It all came crashing down in 1991 when the Marxist dogma collapsed and the Soviet Union disintegrated, but in the early 60's, the Cold War was very real. Castro's relation with Washington deteriorated swiftly and, eventually, led to the Bay of Pigs tragedy and the October 1962 Missiles crisis, in which, the Russian Premier, Nikita Kruschev, bluffed his way into a potential nuclear confrontation with the U.S. It was during those frightful hours that Castro displayed the apocalyptic nature of his dogmatic devotion.

Blessed with extraordinary good fortune, Castro emerged from this confrontation as a victorious international figure.

In February of 2008, the dying dictator, still entrenched in the decrepit Marxist dogma, transferred the absolute power to his brother Raul while he went on writing incoherent thoughts, telling the people that what failed was everything except his vision that communism was the right path to the well being of the nation. It is evident that Cubans paid a terrible toll for this revolutionary madness.

The island, 90 miles away from the U.S. shores, is blessed with fertile soil, good harbors, and beautiful beaches, a delicious subtropical climate touched by light and color, and the warm hospitality of an enterprising people in love with life. A truly quasi paradise land, with a promise of wealth and happiness that was transformed into a nightmare of oppression and misery. Why did it turn out to be so? In this book we search for the answers. A most difficult task in which we look for the roots of the Cuban collective behavior, the values, beliefs and the fortuitous events that has framed the historical path of a tragic island that remains, like five centuries ago, a military base governed by generals.

**Pedro Roig**

# CHAPTER I

# A THEOCRACY IS BORN

*To understand Cuba we must understand Spain....*

*THE INQUISITION – SOCIAL MOBILITY - VICTORY AND
RELIGIOUS PERSECUTION – ENTER CHRISTOPHER
COLUMBUS – THE NEW WORLD – THE HAPSBURG
DYNASTY IN SPAIN.*

The marriage of Ferdinand and Isabella in 1469 heralded the Golden Age of Spain.  He had been the King of Aragon, she the Queen of Castile, and their Spain a nation of shepherd-warriors. Out of this royal union of two cousins was born the Spanish National State, the first in Medieval Europe.

Isabella was a remarkable monarch -beautiful, brave, intelligent, well educated, friendly and incorruptible.  She was also dedicated to Catholicism, deeming it her sacred duty to place a devoted Nation-State under an all-mighty monarchy at the altar of the Roman Church.  Ferdinand was an efficient administrator, shrewd politician, cosmopolitan aristocrat and great warrior.  Reserved, cold and distant, he was the very model of a Renaissance prince.[1]

Ferdinand and Isabella formed a task-oriented partnership based on mutual respect.  Together, they elevated the throne, established a powerful centralized government, led a victorious army and united Spain (with Castile as the dominant partner).  But their successful union's most far-reaching impact was the alliance between Church and State, which from this point on became one and the same.  The Crown reinforced the clergy's power in exchange for the Church's commitment to strengthen national union, preserve social stability and encourage the loyalty of the people while the Church gave the Monarchy the legitimacy to govern in the name of God and to rule by Divine Right.  This close alliance of Church and State framed the cultural and political life of Spanish society for the next 400 years, a relationship that would significantly impact her colonies.

Isabella and Ferdinand faced a monumental task in their quest to forge a Nation State.  The Spanish Peninsula was an ethnic, racial and religious mosaic in a land divided by several mountain ranges that made internal communication extremely difficult. Dry, poor soil comprised two-thirds of the country, requiring dutiful irrigation for a modest yield. The earliest recorded settlers were the Iberians, the Celts and the Basque. Intercourse between the first two groups created the Celtibers of the Central Meseta. The Basque remained mostly isolated in the northern mountains, where their eventual conversion to Catholicism gave them a well-earned reputation as the most militant religious people in Spain.

The Celts settled in rainy northwest Galicia and Asturias, among forested mountains beside the sea, primarily as shepherds and fishermen. In 711 AD, when Arab-Berber Armies crossed the Straits of Gibraltar and conquered most of the Peninsula in the name of the prophet Mohamed, a few surviving nobles of the fallen Visigoth Kingdom — led by King Pelayo, the folklore hero of Asturias — rallied the rugged shepherds and defeated the Muslims at Covadonga in 718. The victory marked the beginning of the Spanish Reconquest.[2]

The northeastern regions of Aragon and Catalonia were like their king, Ferdinand, enterprising, cosmopolitan and ever eying the Mediterranean Sea for trade partners and new ideas. Their harbors and hamlets had been vital gateways for the ancient Greeks and Romans, and Barcelona, "the Spanish March," had been the strong frontier outpost for Charlemagne's Franco-Germanic Empire. In the Thirteenth Century, this magnificent city was a rich trade center rivaling Genoa and Venetia.

From the arid, dusty soil of Castile sprang a society of warrior shepherds, uncompromising, frugal and honor-minded like their beloved queen Isabella. These Iberian and Celtic settlers had fought the Carthaginians, Romans and Visigoths. Against the Moors, Castile became the driving force of the "Reconquista," and the birthplace of El Cid, Don Quijote, the Holy Inquisition and the Spanish language.

Valencia, "the Garden of Spain," was an extension of Catalonia, with a mild climate and powerful Muslim heritage. By the Fourteenth Century, it had developed a sophisticated irrigation system to make the land rich and fertile, yielding several crops a year (Valencia oranges were highly valued in the Mediterranean market.) The region plays a major role in the great Spanish epic, *El*

*Cid*, when the legendary hero retakes it from the Moors in 1099. For the next 500 years, the Moors of Valencia remained in their *"huertas"* growing olives, rice, onions and wheat, and manufacturing oil, wine and flour. The victorious Christian nobles initially saw the economic advantages of religious tolerance toward these hard-working Muslim farmers.

To the south of Spain lies fabulous Andalusia. The Arabs called it Al Andalus, and it was a true Muslim society in character and culture. Cities like Seville, Cordoba and Granada are living testimony of the deep-rooted Moorish tradition, where Africa and Spain meet. The Moors were industrious, sensuous, friendly and proud. They loved music and were highly superstitious. Their farms exhibited carefully irrigated crops, while their aristocracy cultivated artists, scholars, poets and philosophers, making the region the best and most diverse center of knowledge in the Middle Ages. Given the standards of the period, Andalusia was open and modern.

In this multi-ethnic and multi-cultural Spanish society, the Jews were a dynamic force. "The people of the book," as they were called in antiquity, had settled the peninsula in Roman times. As agents of economic development, they endured centuries of cyclical religious tolerance followed by periods of hostility that sometimes became brutal persecution. In 1391, a pogrom was launched against the Hebrews of several cities, from Toledo to Barcelona. Thousands of Jews converted to Christianity to avoid torture and execution. The new converts were called *marranos* (swine), and church leaders never accepted them as true Catholics. Nevertheless, the Jews of medieval Spain prospered as merchants, bankers and administrators in the service of the nobility and kings for another one hundred years.

## THE INQUISITION

That Isabella and Ferdinand fulfilled the daunting goal of national unity speaks volumes about their leadership abilities (and less about the fairly docile aristocracy). But there was a price to be paid: the Church's insistence on its pound of flesh. The Church had been a decisive instrument in welding the various races and regions into one formidable, obedient whole, loyal to, and trusting in, their monarchs. The clergy had the heart of the realm; now they wanted its soul.

To preserve the dogmas of faith, the Church instituted the Holy Inquisition tribunal for identification and punishment of acts of heresy.[3] Ferdinand and Isabella, cementing the alliance of Church and Monarchy as joint powers in affairs of state, instituted it in Spain. The history of Spain thus became the story of a theocracy that would shape her destiny for more than 400 years.

The Holy Tribunal punished heresy, not sins, a significant difference, with profound influence on socially accepted behaviors and ethics. For instance, an individual could be married under the Sacraments and still enjoy a sexual liaison without fear of prosecution. According to Church rules, an extramarital affair is a capital sin, but the Inquisition ignored these violations. Charles V's affair with Barbara Blomberg — his Dutch mistress and the mother of his illegitimate son, Juan de Austria — did not stop the crusade against heretics. Even the clergy indulged in violations of chastity vows without fear of the Tribunal (a Spanish priest's relationship with his *barragana* [mistress] was an accepted institution).[4] Such flaunting of religious laws with impunity was to be exported to the American colonies, reinforcing a deep-rooted indifference to rules. The ethical void carried over into the secular arena, creating a corrupt government bureaucracy, promoting a moral double standard and encouraging an unhealthy disregard for moral codes. This socially accepted pattern of misconduct was one of the worst, most unexpected and longest-lasting legacies of the Inquisition.

In 1480, a Dominican friar, Tomas de Torquemada, was appointed Inquisitor General. An incorrigible fanatic who rejoiced in the prosecution of his indisputable dogma, he became the most feared man in the realm. Torture became widely used in extracting confessions from accused heretics. Thus, the roots of a totalitarian state ruled by a symbiotic clergy and monarchy became firmly entrenched in a nation that cherished the epic-heroic quest for honor and glory in the name of God.

Spain's shepherd-warrior society had tenuous ties to Fifteenth Century European feudal tradition. The Spanish military aristocracy was impacted by 700 years of intermittent wars against Muslims and among its own peoples, which resulted in erosion of rigid class stratification. By plundering the wealth of their enemies, hundreds of Spaniards managed to purchase a horse and sword to become mounted soldiers. These *caballeros (The Knights)* automatically joined the lower echelons of the aristocracy, prospering with the fortunes of war. With sword, courage and good fortune determining their new social status, the *Reconquista* reinforced the fluid relationship and upward mobility of successful warriors.

The peasants-turned-noblemen were sensitive about their hard-won promotions. Any reminder of their humble origins was denied, with manual labor especially despicable. Only Moors and Jews, who filled "low-status" jobs such as builders, farmers, moneylenders and merchants, carried out the manual labor. Sixteenth Century Spanish society was characterized by aversion to menial work, especially among the nobility to which everyone aspired.[5]

## *VICTORY AND RELIGIOUS PERSECUTION*

In 1457, Granada — the last Muslim stronghold in the Iberian Peninsula — agreed to pay Castile an annual tribute. By this time, Granada was rich and cultured, but militarily impotent. Granada paid this humiliating ransom for ten years, until the bold and unwise Emir Ali abu-al-Hassan made the fatal decision to discontinue the tribute. Soon after, Isabella and Ferdinand's ascension to the throne of Castile, they demanded resumption of payments. Granada again refused to pay. After Ali's death, his son Boabdil reaffirmed his father's refusal to pay the tribute. Isabella and Ferdinand marched to war at the head of a 30,000-man army. The bloody fight lasted 11 years. It was during this period that Christopher Columbus first asked the Spanish Monarchs for financial assistance for his search for a western sea-route to China and Japan. He would have to wait, however, until the siege of Granada to end. On January 2, 1492, Ferdinand and Isabella entered Granada in triumph, completing the Spanish Reconquista. It had taken 781 years to evict Islam.

Even after the fall of Granada, Muslim culture continued to have a powerful influence on the beliefs, values and behavior of the people of Andalusia. A multitude of Arab words entered the daily language of the Spaniards and Portuguese. The word *ojala,* which communicates one's wish for a positive outcome, is commonly used without awareness of its Islamic content: "O Allah". The cockfight, so popular in Ibero-America, came by way of Seville. The desire for magical solutions rooted in Near Eastern culture blossomed in Muslim Spain and never left. Superstition and magic remained especially powerful in Andalusia and traveled with the Spaniard to the American colonies.

After the conquest of Granada, the Inquisition turned on the Jews. Isabella and Ferdinand initially resisted Torquemada's request to unleash the hateful tribunal on a community that included some of their closest advisors. The Queen's confessor, Fray Hernando de Talavera, was the son of a converted Jew. Isaac Abrabanel was a member of Ferdinand's inner circle of advisors. Luis de Santander, a converted Jew, was his finance minister. Fernando del Pulgar, also a converted Jew, was Isabella's secretary. King Ferdinand himself had Jewish blood in his veins.[6] But anti-Semitism was a popular issue among the lower social strata, and the upper class saw the immediate benefit of under-pricing and confiscating Jewish property. Thus, the monarchs acquiesced to Torquemada.

On March 31, 1492, three months after their victory at Granada, Ferdinand and Isabella signed the Edict of Expulsion, "physically driving from Spain any Jew who would not accept immediate conversion."[7] More than 150,000 went into exile. Their properties were sold cheap and their lives ruined. The destruction of Spanish Jewry was not only a crime, it was a financial disaster, depriving Spain forever of its best bankers and traders.

With the Jews gone, the focus of the Inquisition fell on the Moslems still living in Andalusia. These enterprising, hard-working people had developed modern irrigation and tillage techniques, creating the best farmland — Spain's "food basket" — on the Iberian Peninsula. In 1499, Isabella and Ferdinand ordered the Moslems to either be baptized or go into exile. Thousands left Spain, while many others converted to Christianity and became known as "Moriscos."[8] They remained in Spain for four generations, until 1611, when they were either massacred or expelled. For religious fanatics, it was a glorious event, for the wiser, a human tragedy. For Spain, it was another costly mistake. Its best farmers and laborers were, like the Jews before, also gone forever. The Spanish Catholic Church was triumphant. It was the co-protector of the kingdom. The clergy and the state had forged an indisputable theocracy. New ideas that could challenge this symbiosis were banned or punished. "For good or ill, Spain chose to remain medieval, while Europe, by the commercial, intellectual and Protestant revolutions, rushed into modernity."[9] This was a marginal concern, however, at the time. Spain was relishing the fruits of victory. There were new lands to be conquered.. Isabella was now willing to listen to Christopher Columbus.

## ENTER CHRISTOPHER COLUMBUS

In the will he made before his third voyage to America, Columbus named Genoa, Italy, as his birthplace.[10] The city-harbor of his first 22 years was a well-established commercial center, where veteran sailors, mapmakers and ship-builders worked with enterprising activity. Marco Polo's tales of wondrous kingdoms in China and Japan flourished in its citizens' imagination, Columbus among them. Having had no formal schooling, he taught himself to read and write in Spanish, and mastered the letters. At 14, he joined a sailing crew and began his extraordinary life as a sailor.[11]

In 1476, while on a voyage to Lisbon, Columbus' ship was sunk by French pirates. He survived by hanging on to a floating oar then swimming ashore at Lagos, Portugal. It was a providential landing for the 25-year-old seaman. King Henry the Navigator had made Portugal the exploration hub of Europe and perhaps the world. His legacy was paying off in rich cargoes of slaves, pepper and gold dust from Africa.[12] Columbus and his brother, Bartholomew, settled in Lisbon and opened a marine chart business. Christopher married Felipa Muniz, the daughter of a powerful Portuguese family,[13] and often participated in the ongoing explorations and discoveries of the African coast.

It was during these years of seafaring adventure that Columbus learned of a letter by famous Florentine astrologer Paolo del Pozzo Toscanelli advising King Henry that a short sea route to India and China lay due west. The letter included a maritime chart of the route. Columbus wrote to Toscanelli for more information. Toscanelli replied with encouraging words and a new chart (which Columbus carried on his first voyage).[14]

Columbus initially approached King John II of Portugal, who appointed a committee of scholars to review his proposition. Their negative assessment was not over the roundness of earth (by then most learned people knew the planet was round), but about the distance separating Europe from Asia. After the Portuguese rejected his petition, Columbus traveled to Spain, where Isabella and

Ferdinand were near Granada fighting the last campaign of the "Reconquista."

Columbus' negotiations with the Spanish monarchs and their advisors proved long and boring, but with the war over, and a large monetary investment from Ferdinand's finance minister — and baptized Jew — Luis de Santander, Isabella authorized the joint venture with Columbus. The popular notion that the queen sold her jewelry to pay for Columbus' voyage is false. Isabella was the nucleus around which all investors secured participation. She also pledged support from the newly created nation-state.

"Spain was capable of deeds of epic proportions in 1492. The Spain of the year 1000 could never have colonized the New World. The Spain of 1800 would have been equally impotent, but in 1492, that nation stood at the pinnacle of her destiny; she exerted herself to create the golden movement and she was able to follow through."[15] On April 7, 1492, three months after their victory march into Granada, Isabella and Ferdinand signed the Capitulations of Santa Fe, by which they assigned Columbus the rank of Admiral of the Sea, with full authority over any lands he discovered, plus a percentage of the revenues.

In the early morning of August 3, 1492, the *Santa Maria*, *Nina* and *Pinta* cast off from Palos de la Frontera, with Christopher Columbus and 83 crewmen aboard. The Admiral was 41 years old, a tall, thin man with graying hair and blue eyes. His first destination was the Canary Islands, a familiar spot he had sailed to before. From there, Columbus set his course due west into the unknown. He was searching for the northeasterly trade winds. The three ships sailed for several weeks in good weather. But without sighting land, the crew became restless and anxious and demanded he return home. Understanding the gravity of the situation, Columbus promised to turn back if land was not spotted soon. On October 5, birds began flying above the ships, signaling that land was near. On October 17, 1492, the *Nina*'s lookout, Rodrigo de Triana, saw the sandy island of Guanani (San Salvador), located in the Bahamas Archipelago. They had been sailing for 33 days from the Canary Islands.

## THE NEW WORLD

It is currently fashionable to debate whether other sailors from Europe might have reached America, certainly a feasible possibility. But what makes Columbus' voyage unique and monumental is that he was the first to return to Europe with the news. His second major contribution was a clearly charted route for future round trips, "both the best sea passage from Europe to North America and the best passage back".[16] Future sailors were to follow Columbus' route for the next 400 years.

It was in the Bahamas that the Admiral learned from the natives of a larger island due south. On October 21, Columbus spotted the northern coast of Cuba. The next day, he entered the Bay of Bariay (in Oriente Province) and landed with his men. Columbus was certain he had reached Cypango (present-day Japan) though the natives called the island "Cuba." The admiral named it "Juana" after the princess daughter of Isabella and Ferdinand.

In Cuba, Columbus dispatched two crewmen in search of gold. What they found was tobacco. Rodrigo Jerez of Andalusia and Luis Torres of Murcia were the first Europeans to see natives smoking through their nostrils. The Indians had mastered the process of growing, drying, fermenting and rolling tobacco leaves. Incorporated into cigarettes, cigars and snuff tobacco, it soon became very popular in Europe — and one of Cuba's main sources of income.

Disappointed at not having found gold, Columbus left Cuba on December 4. The next day, he sighted the mountains of present-day Haiti-Dominican Republic, which he named Hispaniola. It was on this island that the Europeans found gold nuggets and gold dust. They also lost their flagship, the *Santa Maria*, grounded on a reef. In Hispaniola, Columbus established the New World's first European settlement. He built a small fort called "Natividad," left 39 men with food and provisions, and named Diego de Arana their leader. On January 16, 1493, Columbus sailed from Samana Bay back home toward Spain.

On March 15, 1493, one hundred and ninety three days after his departure, Columbus reached Palos harbor. Ferdinand and Isabella gave him a grandiose royal welcome and named him Governor General of the territories he had taken in the name of the Spanish Monarchy. Six months later, he departed Spain on a second voyage, with 17 ships and 1,200 men. On this trip he discovered Puerto Rico, Jamaica and the Lesser Antilles. Revisiting Cuba, he explored the southern coast from Oriente to Bahia de Cortes in Pinar del Rio. But with the caravels leaking, ships' rigging tattered, supplies low and crew showing signs of mutiny, Columbus decided to turn back. "A pity, if he had gone only fifty miles farther, he would have discovered that Cuba was an island."[17] On his second voyage, Columbus introduced the sugar cane crop to the Caribbean Islands.

By this time, other sea captains and explorers were taking Columbus' sea route to the west. In 1497, John Cabot, serving the English King, reached Canada. Two years later, Americo Vespucci sailed with Alonso de Ojeda to the New World, which would, by fortuitous circumstances, one day bear his name: America.[18] Vicente Pinzon, the *Nina*'s captain on Columbus' first voyage, explored the coast of Brazil and discovered the Amazon River. A veteran of Columbus' second voyage, Juan Ponce de Leon, conquered Puerto Rico in 1508, founded San Juan in 1511, and discovered Florida in 1513. Pedro Menendez de Avilez established the first recorded European settlement in North America in present day St. Augustine.

As they compiled their geographical data, these exploring captains began to question Columbus' belief that they were actually sailing the China Sea. The great admiral died in 1506 in the unshaken conviction that he had reached the fabulous land of Marco Polo's stories. The debate ended in 1520 when Ferdinand Magellan rounded the southern tip of South America and sailed into the great ocean he named "the Pacific". Months later, Magellan reached the Philippine Islands, where he was killed by native warriors. Juan Sebastian del Cano completed Magellan's voyages around the world, proving that Columbus had discovered a new and unknown continent, which lay between Europe and Asia.

## THE HAPSBURG DYNASTY IN SPAIN

Queen Isabella's final years were saddened by the mental illness of her daughter, Juana, who in 1496 had married Austria's Philip "the Handsome," son of Hapsburg emperor Maximillian I, bringing the house of Austria into the Spanish Royal Dynasty. Their son, Charles V, was later crowned King of Spain and Emperor of Germany. In her will, Isabella asked to be buried beside her beloved Ferdinand in whatever place he chose. On November 26, 1504, the

Queen died in the old palace of Medina del Campo. Her daughter "Juana the Mad" became Queen of Castile, with Ferdinand regent of the realm. Ferdinand outlived Isabella by 12 years, remarried to 18-year-old French princess Germain de Foix, and died in 1516 (a death reportedly hastened by his effort to fulfill his marital duties to the young princess).[19] Isabella and Ferdinand were buried side by side in the Cathedral of Granada, a most fitting resting-place, where their "Reconquista" had been victoriously fulfilled. They had achieved their political goals. Spain was united, a New World had been discovered and was in the process of being conquered; Catholicism reigned supreme in both dominions, and the Spanish *Tercios* established their reputation as the best, most feared fighting force in Europe. But the seeds of decline and ruin had also been sown. The Church's intolerance to ideas contrary to Catholic dogma fatally delayed Spain and her colonies' march into modernity.

# CHAPTER I

## *A THEOCRACY IS BORN*

---

[1] Nicolo Machiavelli, the advocate of duplicity determination and courage in the quest for power in his classic book *The Prince*: "We have in our time Ferdinand of Aragon, the present King of Spain. He can almost be called a new prince, because he has risen, by name and glory, from being an insignificant King to being the foremost King of Christendom". Nicolo Machiavelli, *The Prince* (Hertforshire: Editor Wordsworth Reference, 1993), 173.

[2] The Visigoth Kingdom was originally ruled by Christian Arian Kings until the conversion of King Reccared to Catholicism in 589. Arian-Christians who did not believe in the doctrine of the Holy Trinity and were condemned at the Council of Nicaea in 325.

[3] The Inquisition was not founded by Spanish Kings and was not limited to Spain, but the Spanish Inquisition was the most mentioned by its enemies.

[4] John A. Crow. *Spain* (Berkeley: University of California, 1895), 113.

[5] Jordi Nadal. *España en su Cenit:1516 -1598*. (Barcelona: Critica, 2001), 39.

[6] Americo Castro. *España en su Historia* (Barcelona: Cristianos, Moros y Judíos, 1983), 517.

[7] Paul Johnson, *A History of the Jew* (New York: Harper and Row, 1985), 232.

[8] Beatriz Comella. *La Inquisición Española* (Madrid: Ediciones Rialp, 1999), 70.

[9] Will Durant. *The Reformation. A History of European Civilization from 1300-1564* (New York: Simon and Schuster, 1957), 220. For a detailed study of the subject matter, see Benzion Netanyahu. *The Origins of the Inquisition in the Fifteenth Century Spain* (New York: Random House, 1995).

[10] Some historians like Salvador de Madariaga emphasize their belief in Columbus' Jewish ancestry.

[11] Durant, op cit, 259

[12] Daniel Boorstein. *The Discoverer* (New York: Vintage Books, Random House, 1983), 224.

[13] Julio Le Riverand. *Historia Económica de Cuba* (Barcelona: Ediciones Ariel, 1972), 11.

[14] Ibid.

[15] Crow, op cit, 158-9.

[16] Boorstein, op cit, 233.

[17] Ibid, 240.

[18] Americo Vespucci was the first to call the newly discovered continent Mundus Novous (New World).

[19] Crow, op cit, 163.

# CHAPTER II

# SPAIN: THE GLORY AND THE RUIN

*THE NATIVE POPULATION – THE FIRST SETTLERS – THE COLONIAL ADMINISTRATION – CHARLES V, THE PROTESTANT REFORMATION AND THE JESUITS – SPAIN'S FAILURE TO DEVELOP A RELIALABLE MANUFACTURING AND BANKING SYSTEM – PHILLIP II: FROM RICHES TO RAGS – HAVANA AS A NAVAL BASE – TOBACCO AND COFFEE.*

For 15 years after Columbus discovered Cuba, it, remained forgotten. As late as 1508, there were lingering doubts about whether Cuba was an island or part of a continent. The governor of Hispaniola, Fray Nicolas de Ovando, ordered an expedition to find out the truth. The task of navigating the coastline lasted eight months. At the end, it was positively charted as a large narrow island.

## THE NATIVE POPULATION

At the time of the European explorations, Cuba's indigenous population was almost a Stone Age society composed of three main groups: the Guanahatabey, Siboney and Taino. The Tainos were the most advanced and were highly proficient at polishing stone to make axes and other utensils. They built houses from palm tree leaves (resembling present day *bohíos* or farm dwellings), arranging them in a weaved pattern that protected the inside from rain and heat. These houses were grouped around an open area called *batey*, where religious ceremonies and *areitos* (parties) were held. Each family had its piece of land called *conuco,* where they grew corn, yucca, sweet potatoes and tropical fruits. They knew how to use fire to cook food, such as the yucca-based *cassava*, which early Spanish settlers used as a bread substitute. The natives complemented their diet with fish, crab, *jutías* (a rodent) and barbecued iguana meat. In America, the Old World discovered what would be some of the most widely used staples of modern times: potatoes, corn, chocolate and tobacco. They also discovered syphilis, the deadly disease that entered Europe with returning sailors who had indulged in sexual intercourse with the native females.[1]

## *THE FIRST SETTLERS*

In 1509, Ferdinand ordered inquiries into the practicality of finding gold in Cuba and recommended an expedition to the unexplored island. Two years later, Diego Velazquez, a rich landowner in Hispaniola and veteran soldier of the Catholic Monarchs' campaign, landed on the eastern tip of Cuba and founded Baracoa, the first permanent settlement on the island. An Indian chief who had fled from Hispaniola to Cuba, Hatuey decried the Spaniards' abuses and launched a rebellion that lasted for four months. He was captured and burned at the stake.

Slowly, the Spanish soldiers began to march inland and, in November 1513, established a second settlement, the village of Bayamo, beside Cuba's largest river, the Cauto. Velazquez' men were looking for gold and were finding small deposits of the precious metal. They forced the Indians to do the searching and mining.[2] However, there was little gold to be found in Cuba.

Once the western regions of Cuba had been explored, the Spaniards established five other towns: Trinidad, Santi Spiritus, Puerto Principe, Havana and Santiago de Cuba. Together with Baracoa and Bayamo, this made a total of seven settlements.

As had been the practice in Hispaniola, Velazquez ordered the distribution of land and Indians known as *encomiendas*. Since the discovery, Isabella had decreed that the Indians were to be free. They also had the right to be paid and converted to Christianity. In practice, the Indians were abused and forced to do the manual labor so distasteful to the Spaniards. The *encomiendas* were abolished in 1542. By then the Indian population had been nearly wiped out, and slaves from Africa performed the hard labor. Since few Spanish females went to the New World, the early male settlers established sexual liaisons with the native women, finding them to be attractive and docile. In turn, a female native gained status by mating with the conqueror. Miscegenation became the norm in the Spanish colonies. The village priest encouraged marriage with the female natives. Although some settlers did wed to form legitimate families, the majority chose out-of-wedlock relationships, remaining faithful to one woman and fathering illegitimate offspring. Within a few generations, the children of Spanish fathers and Indian mothers were being assimilated into the social circle of their fathers. It was the best doorway into the world of the Conqueror.[3]

In Cuba, as in most of Spanish America, colonizers belonged to the lower class (less than five percent were from the upper class). They were rough, uneducated, violent and contemptuous of authority. They came to this faraway land seeking wealth and social status. The first few villages became safe havens from a hostile environment. Land ownership and subjugation of indigenous people were prerequisites for social and financial success, and both were readily available on the island. Slaves — first native, later African — came to be the labor force. At first, Indian females satisfied the Spaniards' sexual needs, but as years went by and Spanish women began arriving in large numbers, they became the preferred partners for marriage.

In a society born of miscegenation, whiteness became an issue, particularly to the common settler seeking a higher social status. Whereas in Spain purity of blood had to do with Jews and Muslims, in America it was the Indians and blacks. In later years, a newly arrived Spaniard, no matter how boring, illiterate or poor, could feel socially superior to a wealthy America-born *creole* suspected of having mixed blood. The issue of whiteness became so important that it prompted the need to secure an official document from the crown identifying the bearer as being of pure white blood. In some cases, certification of whiteness had to be bought.[4]

## *THE COLONIAL ADMINISTRATION*

Immediately after the conquest of Cuba, Governor Diego Velazquez — invested with almost full authority over the island's political and financial affairs — began the process of organizing the government bureaucracy needed to manage the new colony. The *Oficiales Reales* and their deputies were responsible for collecting taxes, keeping the royal accounting books, and judging commercial disputes and contraband cases.

The *cabildos,* composed of councilmen, *regidores* and *alcalde*, who served as the main judge, ran the town.[5] Velazquez colonized the island for the Spanish crown, contributed money and supplies to the Herman Cortez expedition, which sailed from Santiago de Cuba in 1518 to conquer the Aztec Empire of Montezuma, and witnessed the beginning of Cuba's colonial decline as its settlers rushed to the gold mines of Mexico. Velazquez died in 1524.

In 1535, Hernando de Soto arrived in Cuba with the rank of governor and an order from Emperor Charles V to settle Florida. De Soto moved from Santiago to Havana, built a small castle named La Fuerza, and appointed his wife, Isabella de Bobadilla, governor of Cuba, the first woman in the New World to hold such power. De Soto recruited more than 1,000 residents and departed for Florida in 1539. The combination of hostile natives and swarms of mosquitoes doomed the expedition. It was a total failure. Twenty years later, Cuba's population was estimated at 600 Spaniards, 800 African slaves and 5,000 Indians, altogether fewer than 7,000 inhabitants on the island.[6]

It was the gold rush in Mexico and Peru that devalued Cuba's role to that of a humble, non-profitable military outpost. The Aztec and Inca empires had been conquered by the first half of the Sixteenth Century, and their huge gold and silver deposits made Spain the wealthiest kingdom of this period. The few settlers who remained in Cuba turned to raising cattle and pigs or growing tobacco and sugar cane. To pay for the troops stationed there, the Crown ordered a subsidy known as the "Situado de Mejico" to be financed by New Spain's vice royal treasury. The *situado* would remain Cuba's main source of steady income for years to come.[7]

## CHARLES V AND THE PROTESTANT REFORMATION

In November 1517, 17-year-old Charles V was crowned King of Spain. The Flanders-born regent (as an infant he spoke Dutch) was linked by blood to two of the most powerful monarchies in Europe, and so united three major European dynasties. On his maternal (Juana "The Mad") side, he was Isabella and Ferdinand's grandson, and inherited a united Spain plus its American colonies, as well as Sicily, Sardinia and Naples. As the son of Phillip the "Handsome" and grandson of Maximilian Hapsburg, Austria was his, as well as a preferential status toward the elective office of Holy Roman Emperor. From Mary of Burgundy, Phillip's mother, he inherited Flanders, the Frenche-Comte and Artois.[8] Enriched by gold from Mexico and Peru, and enhanced by the military might of the Spanish *tercios*, Charles was the dominant monarch of Europe. "His first enterprise, after putting down a rebellion in was to drive the French out of Italy. By 1525 he had succeeded."[9]

But Charles lived in times of sweeping cultural change, and the challenges to his political power and religious belief became the central issues of his 40-year reign. The very autumn of Charles' coronation, an Augustinian monk, Martin Luther, posted his 95 Propositions on the door of the All Saints Church at the University of Wittenberg, thus initiating the Protestant Reformation. The Spanish Church, faced with the challenge to Roman Catholic dogma, entered a critical stage. When attempts at conciliation failed, the Pope condemned Luther for heresy. Many German nobles endorsed the Reformation and the struggle took on a political dimension.

In other parts of Europe, the Reformation continued to diversify. John Calvin preached total obedience to Scripture and stressed the concept of Predestination, the belief that every life has been predetermined by God and, more radically, already destined to be saved or damned. A sure sign of eternal salvation was earthly success, best won through hard, efficient work. Thus a strong work ethic accompanied Calvinist reform. "The Calvinist acceptance of work as a dignity instead of a curse, of wealth as a blessing instead of a crime, of republican institutions as more responsive than monarchy to the political ambitions of the business class, contained ingredients diversely welcome to many elements in the population."[10] In later years, the Mayflower would take Calvinist doctrine to the English colonies in North America, where the Puritan-Calvinist pilgrims shaped the social, political and economic culture of the United States.

In Holland, land of the fiercely independent Dutch and one of the jewels in Charles' crown, Calvinism gained considerable momentum in becoming an important faith. This was a disturbing challenge for the young Emperor. At first Charles tried to negotiate peacefully with the Protestant leaders, but his efforts failed. A few powerful families and a wealthy bourgeoisie that rejected state intrusion into their religious affairs controlled the Dutch Oligarchy.[11] What followed was the beginning of a long and often savage religious war in which the Spanish infantry won renown as the best, most reliable force in battle. The courage and endurance of these shepherd-soldiers became legend, as well as their cruelty.

In response to the Protestant challenge, one member of the Spanish high nobility, Ignacio de Loyola, founded the Society of Jesus in 1540. The Jesuits trained and molded their members in a frugal environment that demanded obedience and discipline on physically fit bodies. They became the ideological vanguard of the Counter-Reformation.

The Jesuits founded some of the most prestigious schools in Spain's American colonies. Their outstanding teachers molded and trained many young members of the local elite in mathematics, philosophy, theology and the Greek classics.[12] But despite the new curriculum, the Jesuits remained a dogmatic, intolerant and militant society. Their motto was direct and simple: "a la mayor Gloria de Dios" (to God's greatest Glory).

The Jesuits can be credited with reshaping the Catholic Church message in Europe, keeping Poland, Hungary, Belgium and the southern German principalities under the spiritual leadership of the Pope. More than all the troops that fought the religious wars, the Jesuits were the Counter-Reformation's finest soldiers, and Ignacio de Loyola one of the most influential men of his time.

## SPAIN: FAILURE TO DEVELOP A RELIABLE MANUFACTURING AND BANKING SYSTEM

During Charles V's reign, Spain was the master of Europe. It was a glorious, but brief, time for her courageous yet intolerant people. Spanish soldiers, poets, painters and novelists blossomed in a burst of genius that formed a true Golden Age. The Spanish State was a casualty of her inability to articulate and foster a sound economic system within a multi-cultural society held together by a powerful monarchy and a militant church. Spain had the opportunity and the wealth for such a task, but the leadership could not develop a reliable agricultural infrastructure, capable of extensive cultivation, nor a reliable banking system. Spain's leadership failed to create a modern economy, whereas England was rushing into capitalism and adapting to changing market realities by "making property and money" the sources of influence and wealth.[13]

A glaring example of Spain's failure was the unrealized potential of the textile industry in a nation of shepherds. In 1394,

Catherine of Lancaster brought from England a flock of Merino sheep as part of her dowry to Henry III of Castile.[14] The Merinos were one of Europe's best breeds in quality and beauty of their fleece. Their arrival marked the beginning of a great demand for wool to serve the manufacturing needs of Flanders, then growing into a textile emporium. England and Spain were the two main suppliers of quality wool to the European market. However, while England realized the economic benefit of establishing its own textile industry, Spain failed to further the initial manufacturing efforts begun in Avila, Segovia, Soria, Alcala and many other cities.[15] It was easy to sell wool at a good price in a growing market as long as manufacturers demanded the raw material. But in the long run, the Spanish ruling elite was incapable of redirecting the economy from a supplier of wool to a textile-producing nation, another crucial misstep on the road to poverty.

An inept and corrupt administration of the wealth coming from America was a major contributing factor to the economic chaos. The Spanish elite could not develop a balanced and productive agrarian economy, failed to promote a manufacturing industry able to meet market demand, and missed the opportunity to create a banking system that would manage and supply the capital needs of a rich and expanding nation. These faults were dutifully transposed to the administration of the colonies, thus sowing the seeds of much of Hispanic America's bureaucratic and political maladies, many of which exist today.

With most of Europe changing from a manorial to a cash economy, a financial revolution was underway. Many of the Jewish families persecuted and expelled from Spain in 1492 had become the most successful bankers in Amsterdam, where they sought refuge. What difference they might have made in Spain's financial handling of the huge treasure coming from America is one of history's great debates. It can be argued that in a rapidly changing economy, few experts understood the danger of inflation created by the huge influx of gold and silver. As a result, the Crown had to raise taxes and borrow money to pay for its religious wars and the overpriced luxuries bought in foreign markets.[16] In this financial madness, the treasures of Mexico and Peru ended up in the vaults of bankers in Genoa and Amsterdam. America's gold and silver became the seeds of European capitalism.

In 1556, Charles abdicated the throne in favor of his 29-year-old son, Phillip II. The 56-year-old warrior retired to a monastery in Yuste, some 120 miles west of Madrid, at the time a marginal village. He died in August 1558, having seen the glory of victory in battle, but also failing to defeat the Protestant Reformation. Under Charles V, Spain achieved the pinnacle of power and splendor. It also began the process of decline and decay.

## PHILLIP II: FROM RICHES TO RAGS

Charles V's son, Phillip II, was born in Valladolid in 1527. Educated by priests who taught him the catechism of eternal salvation, the young king grew into an unflinching Catholic, loved by Spaniards. "The very air around him buzzed with prayers and admonitions against the wicked heretics. Philip's son developed the mind of a rigorous fanatic."[17] In 1560, he transferred the capital from Toledo to Madrid and ordered the building of El Escorial, a somber, monumental structure that would house a royal palace, monastery, library and mausoleum. Most of the cedar wood used in the construction came from Cuba.

Phillip was proud, reserved and polite, but humorless. He loved music, art and literature. He married three times — Princess Maria of Portugal, Mary Tudor, Queen of England, and Elizabeth of Volois, princess of France — and was thrice widowed. He promoted his half brother, Don Juan de Austria, the natural son of Charles V and his Dutch mistress, to the rank of commander of the combined navies of Mediterranean Christendom in the decisive victory against the Muslim fleet at Lepanto.

Phillip's heaviest burden was the brutal Dutch war of independence, sparked by the Protestant Revolution during his father's reign, which was to continue intermittently for more than 80 years. Spain lost the wealth of America on the battlefields of Flanders. "By 1600 no less than 40% of the Spanish government's income was earmarked for the service of the old debts."[18] When Elizabeth I of England sent aid to the Dutch, Phillip went on the warpath. He organized "the Invincible Armada" to dethrone Elizabeth and restore Catholicism to the English people, a major tactical mistake since Spanish Naval doctrine was predicated upon a fight with the Turks in the Mediterranean using ramming galleys in the engagements. Spain was late in "accepting the logic of gunned warships."[19]  The Spanish warships sailed on May 1588 under the command of the Marquis of Medina-Sidonia, an irresolute admiral. "The Spanish ships were better" for close-in fighting than for cannonading at a distance, even though the galleons that constituted the backbone of the Spanish fleet were stoutly built vessels... But they were clumsy to maneuver and could not successfully return the fire of the nimbler English ships. The English however were unable to sink the Spanish galleons by gunfire alone. The major disaster to the Armada was due to storms".[20]  Its defeat crushed Phillip II, though he fought tenaciously for ten more years.

In 1596, the Crown finally admitted that the Treasury was bankrupt.[21]  Phillip died two years later at El Escorial, looking out from his austere room to the high altar of the Church. He was succeeded by the shy, indecisive, monkish Phillip III who recognized his own incompetence at giving orders, and so empowered his favorite advisor, the Duke of Lerma. The glory of Spain was fading fast. The Crown could only pay its armies and navy "by virtue of loans made by bankers and private speculators, many of them foreigners."[22] In the 1630's, Spain could field an army of 300,000 soldiers, by the 1700's it could only pay for 50,000 men.[23] The final blows were dealt to Phillip IV by the Dutch navy's defeat of the Spanish at the 1639 Battle of Downs, and the French army's crushing victory at Rocroi in 1643.

The last of Spain's Hapsburg kings was the half-idiot Charles II. Known as "the Bewitched," he misruled Spain for 35 years. "When Charles II came to the throne in 1676 eveything was lost. He had not the ghost of a chance to redeem Spain from her wretchedness... the dream was dead".[24] By the end he nominated Phillip of Anjou, grandson of French king Louis XIV, to succeed him on the Spanish throne, inaugurating the Bourbon Dynasty.[25]

On the surface, everything seemed in order. The Spanish perception was one of greatness, power and importance. The bitter truth, yet to be faced, was that Spain was militarily impotent, economically bankrupt and socially resentful. Spanish philosopher Jose Ortega y Gasset wrote: "The same old words and ideals were still repeated, but they no longer stir the heart. Nothing new was undertaken in the realm of politic, or science, or morality... Castile was transformed into the very opposite of her old self: she became suspicious, narrow, sordid, bitter."[26]

## HAVANA AS A NAVAL BASE

By the dawn of the Seventeenth Century, Spain was having trouble protecting the commercial sea route with its American colonies. During this period of hardship and neglect, Havana was a modest settlement of fewer than 200 Spaniards, no match for French, English and Dutch ships lying in wait for the gold and silver being transported to Spain. The small town was burned by French pirate Jaques de Sores in 1555. In 1628, Dutch pirate Piet Heyn seized the entire gold and silver convoy in the Bay of Matanzas.

During Spain's long and costly wars in Europe, the Crown ordered the fortification of Havana's harbor, where the gold and silver galleons from Cartagena and Veracruz could merge into a powerful, navy-protected fleet.

The next three decades saw an accelerated rate of development in Havana as many people settled in the growing military outpost that offered protection, jobs and business opportunities in the supplying and refitting of the fleet, construction of fortifications and the needs of thousands of sailors.[27]

Juan Bautista Antonelli, a fortification engineer and master of defense, built El Morro and La Punta castles at the harbor entrance. Havana became a secure anchorage, and her economic and social life revolved around the fleet. Her trading partners were Cartagena, Veracruz, Seville and the Canary Islands. In 1595, Havana gained city status with a population of more than 4,000 (10,000 if one included surrounding hamlets from Mariel to Matanzas, half the island's inhabitants). The other half, who lived in the mostly isolated eastern region, raised cattle and pigs and traded with whomever wanted to buy their meats and hides. They also engaged in contraband with the English, Dutch and French colonies.[28]

Havana's merchants primarily provided services for transient sailors, always under the watchful eye of the corrupt bureaucracy. They traded in food, tobacco, rum and women. Guesthouses, small eateries, taverns and brothels flourished in an environment of lust, drinking, gambling and fighting. Quietly, slowly, but surely, a more stately society began to emerge, as merchants, craftsmen, masons, carpenters and farmers rose to prominence in the expanding city.

## *TOBACCO AND COFFEE*

Tobacco was Cuba's main industry during the Seventeenth Century. Columbus took it with him to Europe when he returned from his first journey, where within a few brief years; it became a market success and the most coveted product of the Americas. Tobacco growers or *vegueros* located their farms or *vegas* close to exporting towns such as Havana, Trinidad, Bayamo and Manzanillo and later moved into the Pinar del Rio region, "where they began to cultivate the tobacco of the special quality, aroma and taste associated with the Vuelta Abajo."[29]

By the beginning of the Eighteenth Century, tobacco had become Cuba's most profitable business until the hard-pressed Spanish treasury decided to regulate the trade through a monopoly known as *estanco del tabaco* (tobacco price and market control). A rebellion by the *vegueros* was crushed; the tobacco monopoly became firmly entrenched in Cuba. Many *vegueros* turned to smuggling. In 1817, the old tobacco monopoly was abolished, but by then sugar had become the dominant industry in the island, even though Cuba's tobacco remained a profitable and popular commodity. By 1850, the island was "the acknowledged master of the tobacco industry and a Havana cigar being the supreme pleasure after dinner in a self'confident London or New York"[30]

Coffee probably was used by the Arabs in the Thirteenth Century and was taken to Europe 200 years later, from where it traveled to the American colonies and spread successfully in the tropical regions. Coffee grows best at elevations above 1,000 feet on well-drained soil. By the Eighteenth Century, coffee was an important European commodity, and the French colony of Haiti the leading world producer. For centuries, coffee was grown marginally in Cuba, mostly for household consumption. All of this changed abruptly when the Haitian coffee industry was destroyed by the slave revolt.

Thousands of French growers and their families fled to Cuba's shores where they settled and began cultivating and marketing their coffee but, by 1840, production began to decline due to the expansion of the sugar industry, a sharp drop in prices, destructive hurricanes and higher U.S. import duties.

# CHAPTER II

## *SPAIN: THE GLORY AND THE RUIN*

---

[1] Hugh Thomas. *Cuba: The Pursuit of Freedom* (Harper and Row. New York. 1971), 21.

[2] Levi Marrero. *Cuba Economía y Sociedad* (Madrid: Editorial Playor, 1974), vol. 2, 5.

[3] Ricardo Herren. *La Conquista Erótica de las Indias* (Barcelona: Editorial Planeta, 1991), 101.

[4] Manuel Tuñon de Lara, *Estudios sobre el siglo XIX Español* (Madrid: Editorial siglo XXI de España, 1984, 247.

[5] Calixto Maso. *Historia de Cuba* (Miami: Ediciones Universal, 1976), 15.

[6] Ibid, 45.

[7] Ibid, 57.

[8] Nadal, op cit, 12.

[9] William Mc Neil. *The Pursuit of Power* (The University of Chicago Press, 1982), 91.

[10] Durant, op cit, 615.

[11] Nadal, op cit, 105.

[12] Four hundred years later, Cuba's Marxist dictator, Fidel Castro, was in his youth trained and educated by the Jesuits.

[13] Simon Schama. *History of Britain* (New York: Talk Miramar Books. Hyperion, 2000), 241.

[14] Crow, op cit. 124

[15] Ibid, 125

[16] Levi Marrero, op cit, 265.

[17] Crow, op cit, 168.

[18] McNeil, op cit, 110.

[19] Ibid, 101.

[20] Ibid.

[21] Levi Marrero, op cit, 266.

[22] McNeil, op cit, 103.

[23] Ibid, 111.

[24] Crow, op cit, 226.

[25] The Hapsburg's colonial bureaucracy was administered mostly by "Creoles". The male issues of the "conquistadores", born in America. The Bourbon kings changed this policy by appointing Spanish-born officials, replacing the old Hapsburg practice.

[26] José Ortega y Gasset. *La España Invertebrada* (Editorial Espasa Calpe, Madrid, 1921), 51

[27] 27 Levi Marrero, op cit, 152.

[28] Ibid, 166.

[29] Thomas, op cit, 25.

[30] Ibid, 134.

# CHAPTER III

# CUBA IN ECONOMIC AND POLITICAL TRANSITION

*THE FIRST SUGAR BONANZA – THE BRITISH CAPTURE HAVANA – THE U.S. BIRTH OF FREEDOM IN AMERICA – THE FRENCH REVOLUTION AND THE IMPACT ON THE POLITICAL CULTURE OF SPANISH COLONIES – CUBA'S CREOLE ARISTOCRACY – THE COLLAPSE OF THE SPANISH MONARCHY – CUBAN LOYALTY TO SPAIN.*

## THE FIRST SUGAR BONANZA

Cuba and sugar are tied inseparably in history. Soon after Columbus took sugar cane on his second voyage, the crop, initially grown on the outskirts of Havana, began sharing in the commercial life of the island along with tobacco, beef and hides.

The Portuguese were the first to embark on large-scale production of sugar, introducing the *trapetto* to Brazil (*trapiche* in America).[1] They were able to integrate all the right elements for success: plenty of fertile virgin land, control of the source of slaves from local Indian and African enclaves, investments from Amsterdam bankers and the Dutch fleet.

Realizing the growing demand for sugar in the rich European market, Dutch traders went straight to the production sources. Professor Brion Davis, a leading authority on slavery in the Western World, wrote: "The Dutch temporarily capture Salvador (Brazil's capital)... and in 1630 seized Brazil's largest producing region, Pernambuco."[2] During their brief military occupation of Pernanbuco, the Dutch learned from the Portuguese settlers how to farm and grow sugar cane. With the financial support of their powerful banking system, they soon developed new sources of sugar in the Lesser Antilles, providing French and English settlers in the Caribbean Islands with investment capital for crops, equipment and slaves. "The Dutch, who had achieved naval dominance on the Caribbean, even supplied the British with African slaves, at bargain prices, and refined and marketed British grown sugar in

39

Amsterdam."[3] All the Dutch merchants needed were warehouses and ships. "To some extent, this trade was directed by Sephardic Jews, who had found refuge in Holland from the Spanish and Portuguese Inquisition."[4] The banking and financial revolution was underway. In England and France, there was "a conscious collaboration between rulers and their officials on the one hand and capitalist entrepreneurs on the other… the rise of French and British overseas enterprise registered and reflected the relatively smooth cooperation between business mentality and political management that came to prevail in those countries."[5]

The sugar business boomed. London coffee houses were bustling by 1652 and Paris' famous cafes by 1672. Many European cities followed in the coffee craze. The bitter taste of coffee was sweetened with sugar from the Caribbean colonies, creating a huge demand for both commodities. By the last decade of the Seventeenth Century, the British Sugar Islands were worth more in the total balance than the 13 North American colonies. According to professor Brion Davis: "The British planters in the Caribbean became far richer than their cousins in the North American wilderness… The West Indes became the true economic center of the New World."[6] From 1503 to 1600, the price of sugar in the European market rose 600 percent.[7]

Cuba did not benefit from the early sugar bonanza in proportion to its size and potential. Once again due to Spanish Colonial restrictions and bureaucrats, they failed to effectively promote the sugar industry's development in Cuba at a time of great demand, one major reason being that unlike England, Holland and France, the Spanish home market was miserably poor[8]. Sugar was a luxury well beyond the meager buying power of the average Spaniard. A rich market was needed to spark the Cuban economy, and Spain's trade monopoly was far from it.


## *THE BRITISH CAPTURE HAVANA*

In May 1756, the Seven Years' War began. England and France engaged in a struggle for overseas colonies, markets and military supremacy. It was a truly worldwide conflict, fought in North America, Europe, the Caribbean and India. It was England's most successful war of the Eighteenth Century; in America known as the French-and-Indian War, it was considered a prelude to the American

Revolution.

In January 1762, the enlightened Bourbon King of Spain, Charles III (1759-1788), decided to join the war on the side of his cousin, Louis XV, the King of France. It was a costly mistake. On March 5, 1762, a formidable fleet of warships, troop transports and supply vessels sailed from Portsmouth, England, toward Havana. The commander of the British forces was George Keppel, third Earl of Albemarle. Leading the fleet was hardened veteran Sir George Pocock.

Protected by the castles El Morro, La Punta and La Fuerza, Cuba's capital city had a population of more then 40,000. It had 3,000 veteran soldiers, 3,000 civilian militiamen and 600 African slaves, who were promised their freedom in exchange for fighting in defense of the city. There were 14 warships anchored in the harbor.

The British fleet sailed through the Old Bahamas sound reaching the small fortification at Cojimar, 15 miles east of Havana, on June 6. Several ships opened fire on Cojimar's defenses, overwhelming it. The next day, British troops began landing on Cuban soil. Their second-in-command, Gen. George Elliot, advanced on and captured the village of Guanabacoa despite a spirited defense led by Cuban-born *creole* Jose Antonio Gomez, who had armed his men with *machetes*.

Cuban Captain-General Juan del Prado Portocarrero tried to block the harbor by sinking three ships in the entrance's narrow channel. It was a senseless decision since the Spanish warships were also bottled up there. The unchallenged British vessels took control of the seaboard approaches to Havana.

On July 1, the British army — though suffering from tropical diseases like malaria and dysentery — advanced on Havana's main defenses. On the night of July 30, they detonated a mine under El Morro's thick walls and stormed the fortress through the opening. The fight was fierce. Don Luis de Velazco, El Morro's commander, was fatally wounded in the chest. The old castle was captured. The British guns then turned on the city itself. On August 14, Havana surrendered. The siege took 65 days. The eastern region of Cuba, meanwhile, remained under the administration of Lorenzo Madariaga, the governor of Santiago de Cuba.

The 11-month British occupation of Havana proved to be an

economic bonanza for Cuba. The ports of New York, Boston, Philadelphia, Charleston, Liverpool and Bristol became Havana's trade partners. Hundreds of commercial ships sailed to the newly conquered city, where tariffs had been abolished under the new administration. English and American merchants sold manufactured goods, horses, cloth, foodstuff, equipment and slaves at lower prices than ever before, and in turn, bought sugar, tobacco, molasses and rum.

When the Seven Years War ended in 1763, Havana was returned to Spain in exchange for Florida. A victorious England now ruled a powerful worldwide empire that included Canada and India. Upon its return to Havana, the Spanish government was determined not to lose it again. El Morro, La Punta and La Fuerza were repaired, and construction of the castles La Cabaña, El Principe and Atares begun. Havana was transformed into the most powerful military stronghold in America.

The result of the brief British occupation of Havana marked the beginning of the great economic growth that took place in Cuba over the coming years. At first, it was modest and hesitant, reflecting Spain's concern about rich North American and British merchants doing business in their Cuban colony. But the commercial inducement grew overwhelmingly, beginning with lower prices, bigger profit margins and better quality of products, steadier supplies, improved shipping service and more available credit. The Spanish bureaucracy benefited from a high trade tariff that provided substantial revenues to the crown, the greedy captain generals and their corrupt entourage. To be named captain general of the Cuban colony was a financial windfall in which personal fortunes were made in a few short years. Slowly but surely, Cuba became the most valuable prize in the personal inventory of the Spanish generals.

The Spanish government took notice of the business and revenues being opened to the exhausted treasury by its Cuban colony. It introduced a series of economic reforms, lifting the restraints on commerce and opening new ports in Spain, such as Barcelona and Santander, to trade with Cuba.

## *THE BIRTH OF FREEDOM IN AMERICA*

In 1776, the American Revolution began, laying the

groundwork for a new independent republic. Several philosophers inspired the revolution, chief among them Seventeenth Century English political thinker John Locke. Locke's premise on individual rights reaffirmed the belief that governments derived their power from the consent of the governed.[9] His ideas were a direct challenge to the European monarchies, which made God the source of their power. The American Declaration of Independence stressed the general principles of human rights: "We hold these truths to be self-evident that all men are created equal, that they are endowed by the Creator with certain unalienable rights; that among these are life, liberty and the pursuit of happiness…"

These untested ideas and institutions became the most compelling subject among the political and intellectual elite of Europe and the New World. "There was much to admire during the 1780s and early 1790s as the American Revolution was proceeding healthily from stage to stage, accomplishing its goals."[10] In 1791, the Bill of Rights was added to the Philadelphia Constitution.

At the outbreak of the American Revolution, France seized the opportunity for revenge against England by entering the conflict on the rebels' side. Hoping to take back Florida, Spain did the same and sent significant financial and military aid from Cuba. Even the wealthiest ladies of Havana pawned their jewelry to help fund the Revolution. During the war, Louisiana governor Bernardo de Galvez recovered Florida for Madrid, and Cuba continued to enjoy an economic boom.

The American War of Independence and birth of the United States had a powerful impact on Cuba's economic development. When North America closed its sugar and molasses market to England's Sugar Islands in the Caribbean, Cuba quickly filled the void, and the United States became its best market. In 1850, the United States imported 39% of Cuba's sugar crop. Fifteen years later, it increased to 65% (with Spain accounting for three percent). By 1877, the United States was taking in 82% of Cuba's total sugar production.

### THE FRENCH REVOLUTION AND THE IMPACT ON THE POLITICAL CULTURE OF SPANISH COLONIES

In 1789, the French Revolution erupted in the streets of Paris, transforming the political course of Europe and the world. Philosopher Jean Jacques Rousseau provided the philosophical framework — as well as the urgency, energy and indignation. "Liberty, Equality and Fraternity" became the battle cry of the bourgeoisie, the peasantry and the proletariat alike.

The French Revolution shared with the American both an idea of freedom and an appeal to the heart. The difference was in the meaning. America's founding fathers felt that freedom meant the individual's right to speak openly, without fear of government reprisal, even against the majority opinion. It included the pursuit of individual wealth and personal happiness. The French Revolution, on the other hand, stressed national unity and the "Common Good," as preached by Rousseau in his book, *The Social Contract.* The Common Good concept was at the core of the fight for freedom and equality, expressing the best interest of the popular majority. Consequently, individual interest was anathema to the revolutionaries. Their "Common Good" reflected the General Will, which gave them the right to demand obedience from the individual citizen. Rousseau was specific in his political dogma: "Whoever refuses to obey the General Will shall be constrained to do so by the whole body; which means nothing else than that he shall be forced to be free."[11] Maximilian Robespierre and the Jacobin party became the driving forces of this radical political ideology.

The critical question remained: who defined the Common Good? According to Rousseau, the virtuous revolutionaries would interpret the best interest of the people. They knew what had to be done and how best to do it. This was a fatal flaw in thinking, but one fashionable among many European and most Spanish American intellectuals. The guillotine became the emblem of justice and virtue. Robespierre stated, "The revolution is the despotism of Liberty against Tyranny...."[12] The radical philosophy made for tragic contradictions — Justice and Crime, Freedom and Oppression — resulting in a bloody orgy of hatred and violence. It also spawned a fertile breeding ground for monstrous tyrannies. Gates of terror opened in the name of the People, and worse still, spawned a fierce secular crusade. Future tyrants could cite Liberty and Social Justice as the cause of their oppression.

Whereas the American Revolution developed in calibrated steps that gave individual rights center stage, the French Jacobins wholeheartedly believed they were the virtuous representatives of the Common Good. Saint-Just, the most radical of the Jacobins alerted to be on guard because the enemies of the revolution were trying to "stir-up pity...but virtuous citizens owe them nothing but inflexible justice and the blade of the guillotine."[13] Virtue, truth and revolution became the patriotic slogan of violent demagogues that took root in Hispanic America.[14] The French Revolution projected a giant shadow over Spain and its America — especially powerful was the influence of Jean Jacques Rousseau and the Jacobins on the intellectual elite and emerging political leadership. Its ideological dogmas came in different colors, but they promoted the same culture of violence, intolerance, demagoguery and terror.

## CUBA'S CREOLE ARISTOCRACY

Haiti was the New World's richest colony and the largest producer of sugar and coffee. Inspired by French Revolution ideals, the slaves of Haiti revolted against their French masters in 1790. Their actions were swift, bloody and decisive. The destruction of plantations had a dramatic effect on the market, causing the price of commodities to skyrocket. Sugar went from 5 to 36 pesos per arroba (25 pounds). More than 30,000 French planters, their families and many skilled employees of African ancestry fled to Cuba, taking with them technical expertise on sugar and coffee production marketing. The impact of the Haitian Revolution on Cuba's economy was monumental.

During the Haitian slave rebellion, Don Luis de las Casas was named Captain General of Cuba. It was a fortunate choice. Las Casas joined a new generation of well-educated, financially shrewd, aristocratic Creoles in shaping the social and economic life of the colony.

Las Casas reflected the modern thinking of the late Charles III, for many historians the best of the Spanish Bourbon monarchs. Within the restrictions of the ever-present Church, Charles managed to create a sizeable opening for enlightened institutions, of which the most typical was the Society of the Amigos del Pais (Friends of the Country). In 1764, he authorized 16 Basque noblemen of the Amigos del Pais Society to encourage agriculture, industry, commerce and arts and science.[15]

In Cuba, the Amigos del Pais Society was under the leadership of Francisco de Arango y Parreño and a remarkable generation of enterprising young creoles. To study the new technology of sugar production, Arango and the Count of Casa Montalvo traveled to Portugal, England and some of the British sugar islands. By a stroke of fortune, they arrived in England at the outset of the Industrial Revolution, when the new steam engine was establishing its reputation as a premier machine of the Modern Age. Arango and Montalvo immediately understood the steam engine's potential for powering the sugar mills and increasing production. With the financial cooperation of Arango's cousin and Montalvo's son-in-law, the Count of Jaruco, one of the new machines arrived from the Reynolds firm.[16]

The sugar aristocrats also established the Agricultural Consulate and the Development Board to look into planning and financing new agro-industrial projects. For the rich Creoles, this was the beginning of their Golden Age, when many of the wealthiest families in Cuba received titles of nobility. "The established, wealthy, marital related families of Calvo, Penalver, O'Reilly, Montalvo, Arango, Herrera, Pedroso, Recio, Nunez del Castillo and O'Farrill monopolized Havana's society and government for more than a century."[17] Some of these families made a point of showing off their wealth in frivolous expenditures that proved ruinous in later years, when a natural disaster struck plantations and the price of sugar fell.

In 1878, Jose Pablo Valiente, the first of Cuba's outstanding comptrollers or *intendentes*, was appointed by Charles III. It was an administrative position introduced in Spain by the Bourbon Dynasty that carried a great deal of power and influence because it reported directly to the monarch. The *intendente* was involved in several areas of the administration, regulating commerce, agriculture and justice, but its most important duty was to collect taxes and custom tariff payments.

Pablo Valiente was a brilliant promoter and manager who accelerated commercial growth by means of a formula, which by reducing custom tariffs, caused a major increase in trade volume, and, in turn, state revenues. In the first year, custom revenues rose from 498,000 to 865,000 pesos, and within five years, topped the one million peso mark.[18]

To supply the growing sugar industry, the creole "sacarocracia" pleaded for unrestricted slave trade. Their lobbying efforts paid off on February 28, 1789, when the King of Spain issued a royal decree authorizing Cuban residents to buy slaves from any market for a period of two years, on condition that only the ports of Havana and Santiago be used.

## TABLE I
## NUMBER OF SLAVES ENTERING THROUGH HAVANA
### (1790-1820)

| Years | Number of Slaves |
|---|---|
| 1790-94 | 27,501 |
| 1795-99 | 23,015 |
| 1800-04 | 38,230 |
| 1805-09 | 14,728 |
| 1810-14 | 28,193 |
| 1815-19 | 89,785 |
| 1820 | 4,122 |
| | 225,574[19] |

The sugar planters further recommended elimination of customs tariffs on machinery and material needed to modernize the sugar industry[20] and Arango promoted the production of rum and cane sugar.[21] The administration of Luis de las Casas was a time of successful planning and implementation. New roads, bridges, aqueducts and hospitals were built, and Cuba's first newspaper, *El Papel Periódico*, started publishing.

## *THE COLLAPSE OF THE SPANISH MONARCHY*

On the eve of the French Revolution, Charles III died and was succeeded by his 64-year-old son Charles IV. The new king was inept, dissolute and unintelligent. His Italian princess-wife, Maria Luisa, was unable to suppress her sensuality, becoming enamored with a 25-year-old royal guardsman, Manuel Godoy, who was promoted to Spanish Prime Minister. Viewing his mother's lover as a threat to his hereditary rights as future king, Prince Ferdinand plotted to get rid of Godoy.[22] Their partisans fought in the streets of Madrid; chaos reigned. Charles IV abdicated the crown in the name of his son, Ferdinand VII, but soon rescinded his decision. The Spanish monarchy was in distress.

In Paris, Napoleon Bonaparte seized the opportunity to reinforce his continental blockade against Britain by placing Spain under his direct control. He invited Maria Luisa, Ferdinand, Charles IV and Godoy to meet him at Bayonne. During the meeting, the Spanish royal family quarreled bitterly — a most pitiful sight. Napoleon decided to replace these unworthy, unreliable allies with his brother Joseph as King of Spain. The French armies, already in the Peninsula, carried out Napoleon's orders.

On May 2, 1808, Madrid awoke to fighting in the streets. Under attack, soldiers from the French garrison opened fire on the people. The Spanish War of Independence was underway, with the Spaniards refusing to accept the new French king. The Spanish American Colonies became confused. Who was in charge? Who was the lawful monarch? What should be done? Whom to obey? All they knew was that the Spanish monarchy had collapsed. "It was not that the Americans rose against Spain; it was that Spain fell away from America."[23]

Soon, most of the Spanish colonies declared their independence: Argentina on May 25, 1810 (the Buenos Aires Cabildo); Mexico on September 16, 1810 (the "Grito de Dolores"); and Venezuela on July 5, 1811 (the Caracas Congress). It was to be a hard-fought struggle. Simon Bolivar and Jose de San Martin became war heroes who led their people to victory. In the end, Cuba, Puerto Rico and the Philippines were all that remained of the once great Spanish empire.

### CUBAN LOYALTY TO SPAIN

Three major factors kept Cuba in the Spanish fold: fear of a Haiti-style slave revolt, second, the close ties between the "sugar aristocracy" and the Spanish nobility, and the island's healthy economy.

The memory of thousands of refugees arriving from nearby Haiti had a great impact on Cuban society for most of the Nineteenth Century, as living testimony of the swift and bloody demise of the French plantation system in the once richest colony in America.[24] According to Professor Brion Davis: "The Haitian Revolution reinforced the conviction (especially of slave holders) that slave emancipation in any form would lead to economic disaster as well as the slaughter of whites... The very word "Santo Domingo", which English-speakers used to refer to the doomed French colony of Saint-Domingue, evoked at least a moment of alarm and terror in the minds of slave holders throughout the hemisphere."[25] The best guarantee for the continued social and financial well-being of Cuba's planters, merchants and slave traders was the Spanish army stationed there.[26]

Cuba's wealthy sugar creole, the *sacarocracia*, had close financial and political ties with the highest level of power in Spain.[27] These included Gonzalo O'Farril, Charles IV's Minister of War; the Count of Santa Cruz de Mompox, a business partner of the powerful Manuel Godoy, the Queen's lover; Vicente de Quesada y Arango, Marquis of Moncayo and Captain General of Andalucia and Castilla la Vieja; and the Marquis' nephew, Andres Arango, second-in-command of the Spanish army at Bailen (site of the great victory over the French Imperial Forces). Another influential creole was Jose de Zayas, chief of Ferdinand VII's Royal Guard during the king's triumphant march into Madrid.[28] It was during this difficult and bloody struggle when Spain was fighting Napoleon's army that Cuba sent more than $200,000 to help in the war effort.[29] Never again would the sugar aristocracy enjoy as much influence over Cuban affairs as between 1790 and 1834. After that, the army and the greedy generals became the dominant political force in Spain, and would remain so for the next 150 years.[30]

The third barrier to Cuba's revolutionary fervor was its thriving economy. Despite some difficult moments — such as a fluctuation in the price of sugar, and a temporary closing of the market because of protectionist wartime policies — the economy was thriving. A sense of confidence prevailed among sugar planters.[31] Despite the political chaos in Spain and its bloody struggle against Napoleon, Cuba remained loyal and became known as "the ever faithful," even after most other Spanish American colonies had won independence.

# CHAPTER III

## *CUBA IN ECONOMIC AND POLITICAL TRANSITION*

---

[1] A Sicilian wooden roller mill used to grind sugar cane.

[2] David Brion Davis. *"Inhuman Bondage"*. *The Rise and Fall of Slavery in the New World*. (Oxford University Press, 2006), 111.

[3] Ibid

[4] Hugh Thomas. *The Slave Trade* (New York: Simon and Schuster, 1997), 159.

[5] Mc Neil, op cit, 150.

[6] Brion Davis, op cit, 112

[7] Marrero II, op cit, 320.

[8] England yearly consumption of sugar was 6.7 kilograms per capita while Spain was limited to 1.18 kilograms. Moreno Fraginals. *El Ingenio*. (Editorial de Ciencias Sociales, La Habana, 1978), Vol. II, 105.

[9] John Dunn. *The Political Thought of John Locke* (Cambridge University Press, 1995), 124.

[10] Susan Dunn. *Sister Revolutions. French Lighting, American Light* (New York: Fober and Fober Inc., 1999), 11.

[11] Ibid, 64.

[12] Ibid, 118

[13] Ibid, 119.

[14] One hundred and seventy years later, Fidel Castro would rule Cuba, insisting that he was the flesh and blood embodiment of the "Common Good" and the "Will of the People."

[15] Richard Herr, *Spain a History*. Edited by Raymond Carr (New York: Oxford University Press, 2000), 181.

[16] Moreno Fraginals, op cit, vol. I, 74.

[17] Knight F.N. "Origins of wealth and the sugar revolution in Cuba. 1750-1850," *Hispanic American Historical Review*, 57. (1977), 23.

[18] Jacobo de la Pezuela. *Diccionario Geográfico, Estadístico, Historia de la Isla de Cuba*. (Madrid, 1863), Vol III, 381.

[19] Marrero, op cit, vol. 9, 37.

[20] Discurso sobre la Agricultura en la Habana y medios de fomentarla: Obras del Excmo. Senor Francisco de Arango y Parreno (Havana, 1888), 78-9.

[21] Ibid, 91-2.

[22] Raymond Carr. *Spain: 1808-1975* (Oxford: Clarendom Press, 1982), 83.

[23] Carr, Ibid, 102.

[24] Hugh Thomas, 89.

[25] Ramiro Guerra, *Manual de Historia de Cuba* (Madrid: Editorial Playor, 1975), 225.

[26] Brion Davis, op cit, 159

[27] Moreno Fraginals, op cit, vol. 2, 121.

[28] Ibid.

[29] Jorge García de Arboleda. *Manual de la Historia de Cuba* (Havana, 1859), 46.

[30] In 1976, Francisco Franco, the fascist dictator, died and the Spaniards began the march towards democracy and modernity.

[31] Hugh Thomas, op cit, 89.

# CHAPTER IV

# SUGAR, SLAVERY AND THE BIRTH OF CUBA´S NATIONAL CONSCIENCE

Cuban sugar production remained a small enterprise for more than 250 years. By 1760, it had reached a modest yield of 5,500 tons per year.[1] Spanish laws prohibited Cuba from trading with foreign markets and, as a poor metropolis, it lacked domestic demand for sugar.[2] As the last chapter pointed out, the 1762 British occupation of Havana changed all that. The financial elite profited from the free trade, experiencing firsthand the potential for wealth from the North American sugar and molasses markets.

## THE SUGAR PLANTATION

Before the British occupation of Havana, Cuba had some one hundred sugar plantations, mostly near the capital.[3] The machinery at the mills had not changed much in two centuries and consisted of three vertical wooden rollers, designed to crush cane stalks and extract the sugar juice or *guarapo.* The juice was poured into the *casa de calderas* (boiler house) then boiled in five open copper kettles of decreasing size, mixed with vegetable ash. This triggered an alkaline reaction that improved product quality. The boiling house converted the *guarapo* into syrup, which was brought to the *casa de purga* (purging house) and poured into molds or hogsheads, often made of clay for cooling and settling. After several weeks, the finest sugar crystals rose to the top of the mold and the viscous portion, or molasses, sank to the bottom. The molasses was then used to make rum or second-class sugar, known as *cucurucho* or *raspadura.*

The typical sugar plantation was divided into three sections: the cane field or *canaveral*; the areas reserved for animal pasture, wood and vegetables; and the *batey,* the actual production complex, which included mills, shops, service facilities, owner's house, free laborers' houses and slave quarters or *barracones.*[4] The hardest task for the plantation was the harvest or *zafra.* Slaves cut the cane stalks with machetes, picked them up by hand and hauled them onto ox carts. The whole process was known as *corte, alza, y tiro*. The cane fields had to be rotated with other crops or fertilized. The penalty for not doing so was a sterile piece of land within 30 years of continuous harvesting.

Just before the slave revolt of 1791, Haiti was the leading sugar producer in the world, yielding 78,696 tons a year. Jamaica was second with 60,900 tons, and Cuba third with 16,731 tons.[5] That year, England and France controlled 78.75% of the entire European sugar market, of which Britain consumed 80% of her imports and resold the remainder, while the French used 18% and re-exported 82%.[6] Sugar was France's most profitable commercial export.

Contrary to a conscious effort by London and Paris to provide credit, ships, equipment and slaves to their sugar-producing colonies, Spain could not satisfy the basic needs of Cuba's sugar industry. It had no sugar refineries. Spain's deficiencies gave Cuban planters an opportunity to fill the vacuum with their own resources. The *sacarocracia* took full advantage of Cuba's optimal potential to become a major sugar producer. They invested in refining technology and became the only colony able to sell refined sugar directly to Europe and North America. The credit for this achievement belongs to the planters, who had the vision and financial resources to fill the vacuum left by the metropolis.[7] "The island's sugar development transformed the creole landowner into an economic modern man, creating the most solid and illustrious bourgeoisie class in all of Latin America."[8]

After 1793, Cuban society began to accelerate into a powerful sugar-producing economy, but since the same old mills were still in operation, the higher yield came not from a greater production capability, but from an increase in the number of mills. For Cuba's sugar economy, the true agent of economic change came with the Industrial Revolution, which coincided with market demand and planters' willingness to invest huge amounts of capital in the new technology. Cuba was among the first regions on earth to be impacted by the Industrial Revolution, particularly its sugar production and transportation.

In 1817, Cuba's first successful steam engine began driving three iron horizontal rollers at a Matanzas sugar mill. The machine was manufactured in England (by Fawcett Preston and Company).[9] In 1812, responding to the needs of Europe's beet-sugar producers,

Edward Howard patented a steam engine to evaporate liquid. The Howard machines began being used in Cuban sugar mills in the early 1830s. In 1841, a milestone in Cuban sugar production occurred with installation of the Derosne Engine in La Mejia, a plantation-mill near Limonar in Matanzas. The Derosne combined grinding, boiling and evaporating in a single machine[10]. To complete the cycle of sweeping change in the manufacturing process, a revolutionary piece of equipment was introduced in Cuba in 1849. It was the Centrifugal machine manufactured by the Cail Company, the Industrial Revolution's answer to the process at the *casa de purgas* of separating sugar crystals from molasses.[11] A year later, the Anglo-American factory of Benson and Day held an exhibition of their Centrifugal in Regla. It was an instant success, and its use became an industry standard. The machine "converted the juice as soon as it left the rollers into a clear, loose, dry and fine sugar."[12]

The Industrial Revolution also impacted Cuba's backward, convoluted transportation system. The sugar aristocracy took full advantage of the steam locomotive and invested aggressively to create a modern railroad network among sugar-producing regions and ports. In 1838, the first train began traveling the 45 miles between Havana and Guines. Spain's enterprising island colony enjoyed the use of steam-powered trains long before Spain itself and the rest of Latin America, reducing the transportation price of sugar from 12 pesos in 1830 to 1.25 pesos by 1840. By 1860, Cuba had more than 400 miles of railroad tracks.

In 1792, Cuba's 14,600 tons of sugar exports came from 473 plantations, about 30 tons per factory. One hundred years later, 470 factories yielded 625,000 tons, an average yield of 1,330 tons per factory.[13] Compared with the average per-factory yield of other sugar-cane producing regions, the result was striking. "British West Indian exports in that year (1894) produced in 1,046 factories could have been produced in 100 factories in Cuba. Barbados' exports, produced in 440 factories, could have been produced in 20 Cuban factories. Jamaica's, produced in 140 factories, could have been produced in eight in Cuba."[14]

## *SLAVERY*

Slavery was a major institution among ancient civilizations of the Near East, Greece and Rome, China, Africa and Pre-Columbia America. But by the Fifteenth Century, it had taken a definite form. Whereas slavery had once been exclusive to no particular race, by now Africans had become its preferred target.

The first New World territory to engage in widespread slave trading was Brazil, followed by the Caribbean Sugar Islands of France and Britain. Spurred by demand for sweetened coffee, tea and chocolate, sugar became Western Europe's most lucrative tropical crop during the capitalist expansion of the late Seventeenth and Eighteenth Centuries. It was during this first New World sugar boom that the Dutch Merchant Marine moved simultaneously into the sugar and slave trades, controlling nearly half the slaves being shipping from Africa to Brazil, and sugar from Brazil to Europe.[15]

The result of market demand was a massive labor deficit in sugar production and the need to supply sugar plantations with African slaves. Some 350,000 slaves were shipped to Brazil in the latter half of the Seventeenth Century.[16] Between 1680 and 1776, Haiti received more than 800,000, while Jamaica, between 1700 and 1786, took in 610,000.[17] From 1763 to 1789 (after the British occupation of Havana), Cuba received 30,875 African slaves.[18]

On Cuba's sugar plantations much of the hard labor was carried out during the harvest season or *zafra,* which lasted around six months, starting in late November or early December.[19] The day began at 3 am After the slaves said their Hail Mary's, they started cleaning the mill and ancillary facilities. At daybreak, they divided up into groups and marched into the fields, where they cut the cane and loaded the ox carts that took the cane to the sugar factory. At noon, they had lunch and rested for an hour.

A typical diet consisted of six to eight ounces of meat, usually jerked beef or codfish, and four ounces of rice. The daily ration also included six to eight plantains or *boniatos.*[20] At other times, the slaves ate rice, yucca, corn and the always-handy cane juice. "It's possible that the slaves in Cuba ate a little better than their cousins in Virginia."[21]

At 1 pm, the slaves resumed cutting cane until 8 pm, when the bells rang and the workday ended. Dinner was basically the same as lunch. During harvest time, the slaves worked 16-hour days, including night shifts in the sugar factory. This monstrous, inhumane demand was imposed on the slaves after working the fields from sunset to sundown. The result was a very tired human being, prone to make mistakes and suffer painful injury or even die. In many instances, slaves were horribly burned by the boiling sugar syrup.[22]

There were a number of eyewitnesses to the slaves' cruel treatment. They said they looked "quite worn out."[23] One British merchant-planter, testifying at an inquiry on slavery in the House of Commons, stated: "The labor which I have seen exacted from the slaves in Cuba would have been quite fatal to Europeans if that amount of labor had been exacted from them in that climate."[24]

The African male was physically strong and resourceful, possessing a "remarkable reserve of toughness. African women made superb cooks, nurses, wet nurses and mistresses."[25] A slave's yearly quota of clothes, his *esquifación,* consisted of two pair of pants *(lienzo de canamazo),* a jacket *(bayeton),* a blanket and a nightcap. Few slaves had shoes.[26]

During the long days of work, the slaves sang songs from their African homelands, mixed with Spanish and French hymns. The beautiful transcultural rhythms they created formed the genesis of what became world-renowned Cuban popular music. Their preferred instruments were the bongo, kettledrum, maraca, stick, gourd and cowbell, which, when combined with the trumpet, produced the deep cadence of the "Conga," and when accompanied by guitar, was enjoyed by Creole society as the Son, the most typical Cuban beat.

Many slaves had been farmers and warriors in their native lands. Brave and proud, many rebelled against captivity, several even committing suicide. Others escaped into the dense woods and mountains. Some of those who escaped with women formed communities called *palenques,* where they raised families and lived for generations as free people.

From the beginning of the slave presence in the New World, Spanish law provided two ways for a slave to win his or her liberty. One was the *manumision,* wherein either the slave-owner or the king granted him freedom. The other was the *coartacion* by which slaves could buy their freedom through their own initiative. In 1817, close to 340,000 people of African descent lived in Cuba, of which nearly 225,000 were slaves and some 116,000 free.[27]

## THE BIRTH OF CUBA'S NATIONAL CONCIENCE

Jose Agustin Caballero in the classrooms of San Carlos Seminary College sowed the seeds of Cuba's national conscience. From his academic pulpit, Agustin Caballero stimulated critical debate while proposing a change in curriculum of the archaic scholastic models (a Medieval Christian theology-philosophy that inflexibly and "infallibly" combined Biblical dogmas with Aristotelian metaphysics)[28] and reform of Cuba's colonial administration. Indifferent to material wealth, the young priest enjoyed research, critical inquiry and teaching. Jose Marti called him "the father of the poor,"[29] because he always gave to the needy out of his own pocket. An uncorrupt teacher in a corrupt medium, Caballero called for political reform in Cuba and "never hid his feelings, or feared being alone in his opinions."[30] He was the teacher and mentor of Felix Varela who revered his memory. On the need to publish Caballero's work, Varela wrote: "Let us do what we must so that Caballero lives on, not only in the indelible memory of his virtues, but in the salutary influence of his doctrine."[31]

Felix Varela was the first Cuban thinker to believe in independence and to conceive of a democratic government in a clear, systematic manner. As a professor at San Carlos Seminary College, he framed the emerging ideals of Cuban national identity. A saintly priest, he also taught by the example of his dignified life, yet he was a radical teacher in the quest for freedom. Jose Antonio Saco and Jose de la Luz y Caballero were among his enlightened students. In the classroom, they felt the rumble of a growing nationalism that would eventually shape Cuba's identity. In 1821, Varela was appointed delegate to the Spanish "Cortes" or legislative chamber in Madrid. While there, he witnessed the military rebellion that forced Ferdinand VII to accept the liberal Constitution of Cadiz curtailing the king's power. At the legislative assembly, Varela proposed the abolition of slavery, defended the independence of Spain's former South American colonies, and — after Ferdinand VII took back the mantle of absolute power — sided with the legislators who voted for the king's removal.[32]

Varela fled to the United States, where he joined the New York Archdioceses. As a priest, he worked with the thousands of immigrants seeking new opportunities and became Vicario General.

In 1850, he retired to St. Agustine, Florida, where he died three years later. Of Varela, Jose de la Luz y Caballero wrote, "Whenever one thinks of the island of Cuba, he will think with veneration and affection of he who first taught us to think."[33]

Jose Antonio Saco is one of Cuba's most influential political writers of the colonial period. Born in Bayamo in 1797, Saco studied at San Carlos college-seminary under Father Varela. A skeptic and pessimist, he differed from his teacher in a belief that Cuba was not yet ready to form an independent government.[34] He also doubted that Spain would grant Cuba autonomy and permit it self-government under Spanish sovereignty, writing, "Those who wish Cuba to have a government like Canada's are chasing a Chimera."

Saco was a brilliant writer and polemicist, with a sober, concise style. He ran the *Cuban Bimonthly Magazine*, through which he criticized the colonial regime's economic, social and political actions while influencing the younger generation of creoles. The government punished him with banishment to Trinidad. Captain-General Miguel Tacon personally told Saco that "the banishment order was due to his enjoying too much influence over Havana's youth."[35]

In general, the Creole patrician class to which Saco belonged was conservative and pessimistic about the surrounding society's high level of ignorance and illiteracy.[36] Yet for all his skepticism about Cuban independence and autonomy, Saco contributed to the concept of Cuba as a separate state from Spain. He opposed its annexation by the United States a la Texas (following independence from Mexico), writing, "Annexation ... would eventually cause the destruction and disappearance of the Cuban nationality." In another piece, he wrote, "It's about closing my heart to all hope and becoming the executioner of my native land."[37] Nevertheless, the man whose brilliance helped forge national identity did not answer the call to independence of the Ten Years War. Throughout his life, Saco remained unflinching in his profound socio-political pessimism.

Jose de la Luz y Caballero (born in Havana in 1800) studied alongside Saco at San Carlos seminary under Father Varela, whom he succeeded as Philosophy chairman. Luz y Caballero shared with his friend, Saco, an innate pessimism concerning their colonial society's ability to remake itself into an independent republic. He was greatly influenced by Latin America's terrible experience with tyranny, citing "the tragic state of excitement and disorder presented by the new republics."[38]

Luz y Caballero traveled throughout Europe and the United States, associating with such luminaries as Longfellow, Walter Scott and Michelet. He was a prominent figure in the Economic Society of the Friends of the Nation and collaborated with Saco on the *Cuban Bimonthly Magazine*. But it was his apostolic teaching that placed him among the Nineteenth Century's most notable Cuban teachers.

In 1848, Luz y Caballero founded El Salvador school in Havana, where he reaffirmed the reformist thinking of his teachers. His disciples were among the leaders of the Ten Years War: Ignacio Agramonte, Manuel Sanguily, Perucho Figueredo and Rafael Maria de Mendive, Jose Marti's future teacher. As part of the most distinguished pre-revolutionary generation, Luz y Caballero agreed with Saco that the Cubans of their day were not ready for independence. Schools were needed in a land where only seven percent of children received educations. Luz y Caballero considered education a prerequisite of independence. He wrote: "Once we get the education, Cuba will be ours."[39]

In reviewing the works of Agustin Caballero, Felix Varela and Jose de la Luz y Caballero, Princeton University professor Warner Fite made a comparison of North American and Cuban philosophies of the time. "I doubt if we could show as much interest in abstract philosophy ... as these volumes show for Cuba," Fite wrote. He described Varela as someone who "writes like John Stuart Mill and the English empiricists," and considered Jose de la Luz y Caballero "a noble and impressive figure."[40]

Cubans had a passion for poetry, at which some were good, few excellent and most mediocre. But the importance of poetry in this period was the emphasis on Cuban themes, where the: "emerging soul found its best expression. Poets such as Fornaris and Juan Napoles Fajardo ("El Cucalambe") eulogized the Indian past and used Indian themes to attack oppression and foster a love for the island's tradition. As the century progressed, the bellicosity of Cuban poetry increased, especially between the 1830's and the wars for independence of the 1860's."[41]

Jose Maria Heredia, Gabriel de la Concepcion (Placido), Jose Jacinto Milanes, Juan Clemente Zenea and Gertrudis Gomez de Avellaneda stood out among their fellow poets. What was extraordinary in this case was the interaction and personal involvement among teachers and students, which transmitted ideas, values and concepts from generation to generation, commencing with Agustin Caballero all the way to José Martí. With them, Cuba began thinking about liberty.

# CHAPTER IV

## *THE SUGAR INDUSTRY AND THE BIRTH OF CUBA´S NATIONAL CONCIENCE*

[1] Moreno Fraginals. *Ingenio,* op cit, Vol. I, 41.
[2] Ibid, Vol II, 101.
[3] Ibid, 15.
[4] Ibid, vol. II, 74.
[5] Ibid, 41.
[6] Ibid, 43.
[7] Ibid, 25.
[8] Moreno Fraginals. *Azúcar, Esclavos y Revolución.* (Revista de la Casa de las Américas, 1968) num, 50, pg. 36
[9] Ibid, 207.
[10] Moreno Fraginals. *Ingenio.* Vol II, 219.
[11] Ibid, 233.
[12] Hugh Thomas. *The Slave Trade,* op cit, 118.
[13] Williams, op cit, 362 -363.
[14] Ibid, 369.
[15] Hugh Thomas. *The Slave Trade,* 136.
[16] Ibid, 219.
[17] Williams, op cit, 145.
[18] Ibid
[19] Moreno Fraginals, op cit, Vol II, 36.
[20] Bando de Gobernación y Policía de la Isla de Cuba. Don Gerónimo Valdez, Gobernador y Capitán General. Habana 1842. Reglamento de Esclavos, Artículo 6.
[21] Hugh Thomas. *Cuba,* op cit 179.
[22] Ibid, 175.
[23] Moreno Fraginals, op cit, 33.
[24] Hugh Thomas. *Cuba,* op cit, 136.
[25] Ibid, 137.
[26] Ibid, 179.
[27] Rafael Estenger. *Sincera Historia de Cuba.* (Editorial Bedout, Medellin, 1974), 127.
[28] Will Durant. *The Story of Philosophy. Simon and Schuster.* (Touchstone, New York, 1961), 102.
[29] Marti Obras Completas. (Editorial Lex, La Habana), 799.
[3] Roberto Agramonte. *José Agustín Caballero y los orígenes de la Conciencia Cubana.* (Universidad de la Habana), 28.
[31] Ibid
[32] Calixto Maso. *Historia de Cuba.* (Ediciones Universal, Miami, 1976), 143.
[33] Raimundo Menocal. *Orígenes y Desarrollo del Pensamiento Cubano.* (Editorial Lex, La Habana, 1945), Vol I, 173.
[34] Guerra. Manual, op cit, 409.
[35] Ibid, 343.
[36] Ibid, 345.
[37] Ibid, 498.
[38] Ibid, 410.
[39] Agramonte, op cit, 21.
[40] Ibid
[41] Jaime Suchlicki. Cuba: From Columbus to Castro. (Charles Scribnes's sons, New York, 1974), 68.

# CHAPTER V

# SPAIN: THE ARMY AS ARBITER OF POWER

### THE CREOLE LINKS WITH FERDINAND VII – ENTER THE SPANISH ARMY - THE UNITED STATES AND THE ANNEXATION MOVEMENT IN CUBA.

During Spain's years of war against Napoleon's armies, the Spanish Parliament took refuge in Cadiz, a port whose wealth was based on the Spanish colonies' trade. From there, it reaffirmed its support for Ferdinand VII and proclaimed a revolutionary Constitution framed in the failed French model. "A military accident stationed the first liberal parliament (1810) in Cadiz, the only town with a liberal society ... where the test of status, even for nobles (who invested in trade) was wealth."[1]

After Bonaparte's defeat in 1815, however, European kings took up the task of reestablishing political order, profoundly altered by the French Revolution. To preserve the divine right of kings and their own absolute power, the monarchs forged the Holy Alliance. That year, Ferdinand VII returned triumphant to the Spanish throne, and with dust still on his boots, abolished the Liberal Constitution of Cadiz. He rejected the notion of sharing government and resumed ruling in the old despotic tradition.

### THE CREOLE LINKS WITH FERDINAND VII

The king's return proved quite beneficial to Cuba's economy, then in the process of expanding. Ferdinand VII had strong bonds with the creole aristocracy, who had eased his dark days of exile with generous and opportune financial aid[2]. In 1815, he named Alejandro Ramirez as Fiscal Comptroller in Cuba, inaugurating one of its most notable and successful administrations. Because of his talent, honor and accomplishments, Ramirez may be considered one of the best officials Spain had in Cuba. One of his more important appointment achievements was the naming of his old friend and fellow creole aristocrat, Francisco de Arango y Parreno, permanent advisor of the Counsel of the Indies, in charge of landowners' rights on the island.

From his very arrival in Cuba, Alejandro Ramirez used all of his influence with Madrid to break up the monopolies that were obstructing free trade. The King responded to his requests by decreeing the Regal Order of February 10, 1818, authorizing Cuban ports to open trade with the rest of the world. The move had spectacular results. In three years, the colonial administration's revenues increased from 2,272,000 to 4 million pesos.[3] Ramirez was a uniquely honest administrator. Although millions of pesos passed through his hands, he died a poor man.

Another royal decree fostered migration colonization by Spaniards, including poor Canary Islanders who settled in Cuba to work the small farmlands the King gave them. The 1819 founding of Cienfuegos by Louisiana emigrants was the result of this policy, acting on the advice of the Cuban aristocracy, closely bound to the Spanish Crown. Cubans saw their island less a colony than a province of Spain, and Spanish Royalty felt a preferential relationship with Cuba's aristocracy. "No other Creole society of the Spanish colonies enjoyed a position close to the Cuban elite in the Eighteenth Century through the start of the Nineteenth."[4]

This special Cuban-Spanish relationship began to unravel with the outbreak of the first successful army revolt against the King, led by Gen. Rafael Riego. On January 1, 1820, Riego — at the head of a powerful army stationed in Cadiz — disobeyed the king's order to embark toward and fight the rebellious Spanish Colonies in America. Instead, he proclaimed the liberal Constitution of 1812, and marched with his troops to Madrid. Ferdinand VII yielded to Riego's forces and agreed to share power with the Cortes[5]. This marked the first of the military uprisings, or *pronunciamientos*. From this point on, military meddling in the affairs of the State became a hallmark of Spanish politics.

In Vienna, the bastion of reactionary Europe, the Holy Alliance[6] decided to intervene in Spain. On April 23, 1823, French monarch Louis XVIII, acting on behalf of the Alliance, ordered the army to restore Ferdinand VII as the absolute King of Spain. General Riego was captured and executed, the Courts disbanded, and the King's enemies viciously persecuted, imprisoned or killed.

It was a terrible time for people seeking freedom in Spain. Father Felix Varela, deputy to the Cortes from Cuba, proposed a government for the island based on full autonomy. He also cast his vote against the return of absolutism. With Ferdinand back in power,

Spanish authorities went after Varela. He fled to the United States.

A consequence of the Holy Alliance's intervention in Spain was the fear in England and the United States that European powers were willing to transfer Spain's last possessions in the Caribbean — Cuba and Puerto Rico — to France. This concern prompted London to seek an understanding with Washington, which became the prelude to the Monroe Doctrine.

The Catholic malcontents rallied around the leadership of the king's brother, Don Carlos, the heir to the Spanish throne since Ferdinand was childless. Then Ferdinand married again. The new queen, his fourth, Maria Cristina of Naples, was a cheerful, beautiful young woman who filled the palace with dancing and laughter and gave Ferdinand a daughter, the future queen Isabel II. Near the end of his life, the king found joy in living. He worked to remove the old Salican law that denied Spanish princesses the crown, reestablishing the Pragmatic Sanction that guaranteed Isabel the throne. In September 1833, Ferdinand VII died, and his widow, Maria Cristina, became Regent of the Realm in the name of her infant daughter, the future Queen Isabel II.

## ENTER THE SPANISH ARMY

Isabel's uncle, Don Carlos, rejected both Maria Cristina's regency and his niece's right to the crown. Carlos claimed the Spanish throne for himself, marking the beginning of the Carlist Wars.[7] To protect Isabel's position as future queen, Maria Cristina formed an alliance with her late husband's political adversaries, specifically the Army Gen. Baldomero Espartero, the dominant power at the time.[8] The regent and the infant queen became so dependent on the army for survival that when Espartero, a man of humble origins and liberal ideas, demanded a constitution and return of the Cortes. Maria Cristina could only yield.

In 1834, Espartero named Miguel Tacon Captain General of Cuba. The 60-year-old veteran despised the Creole elite, who reminded him of the South American aristocracy that had led the armies of independence. He surrounded himself with merchants and slave traders who became profitable partners for the governor. By the time he left the Cuban colony in 1838, Tacon was a very rich man.[9] The governorship of Gen. Miguel Tacon signaled a radical departure from a close relationship between Madrid and the island's

Creole elite to one of suspicion and open hostility, a status that lasted until the end of Spain's dominion in the island, 64 years later. From Tacon onward, Cuba became a rich colony to be exploited, especially by the Spanish military.

As a whole, the Creole aristocracy was better educated than the Spanish *peninsulares*[10], but their financial interest was firmly rooted in the reactionary, despotic regimes of Charles IV and Ferdinand VII. This political paradox had a profound impact on Cuba's future when their differences grew first into rivalry, and later open hostility. "Cuba was for the majority of *peninsulares* not a province but a conquered colony."[11] With the Spanish merchants allied with the generals, the Cuban aristocracy lost influence in Madrid and began looking for a political alternative. For some Cubans, annexation to the United States became an attractive option. At the time, Cuba was wealthier than Spain and Cuban revenues provided the salaries of most Spanish ministers. Income from Cuba was one of the few guarantees of debt repayment that Madrid could offer its London bankers.[12] Even the powerful Rothschild banking institution requested Spanish loans be secured by revenues from Cuba.[13]

Many of Spain's largest fortunes had their roots in the rich island colony. The Catalan Juan Guell invested his Cuban revenues in the cotton industry of Barcelona. Pablo de Espalza, founder and first president of the Banco de Bilbao, made his money from Cuba as financial advisor to the Queen Mother and other members of the nobility. Antonio Lopez, Marquis of Comillas, became a self-made millionaire from the shipping trade with Cuba. It was said that captain general after captain general would return to the poor peninsula with their pockets lined with bribe money to embark on well-financed political careers.[14]

### THE UNITED STATES AND THE ANNEXATION MOVEMENT IN CUBA

On July 4, 1776, the United States of America was born. At first it was an idea for freedom enshrined in the Declaration of Independence. By 1779, with the outcome of the revolution still uncertain, stories of the American Revolution became the most compelling political issue in Europe and the Spanish American colonies. "People applauded the Revolution across the sea as the most important event since Columbus' discovery of the New

World."[15] When on April 30, 1789, George Washington took oath as the new Republic's first president, he was about to lead a form of government never before undertaken.

The challenges were astronomical. The Founding Fathers had to preserve a fragile union, formulate an acceptable body of laws, establish a judicial system, develop a democratic institution of government, and protect the civil, religious and political rights of individual citizens. They were successful and, in the process, built a nation more interested in institutions that could get the job done than in abstract philosophical debate.

Over the next 60 years, the young republic purchased the Louisiana territory, fought the British again (1812), became one of the leading nations of the Industrial Revolution, proclaimed the Monroe Doctrine and expanded westward to the Pacific. In 1836, Texas declared independence from the political chaos engulfing the Mexican government. Nine years later, the Republic of Texas requested and received annexation into the Union. In the ensuing war with Mexico over Texas, the victorious Americans claimed the vast territories north of the Rio Grande.[16] By the mid-Nineteenth Century, the United States was poised to become a major industrial and commercial world power.

The possibility of the Holy Alliance restoring to Spain her former colonies in America prompted President James Monroe to announce on December 2, 1823, in his annual message to Congress, that the New World was closed to further European colonization. The Monroe Doctrine proclaimed that any attempt by a European power to conquer any of the newly independent Hispanic-American Republics was to be regarded as an act of war against the United States.[17] The Doctrine stressed that the United States would not interfere with existing European colonies. Cuba was to remain a Spanish Colony. Echoing the United States and fearing the Holy Alliance's intentions in Latin America, Great Britain committed her powerful naval fleet to enforce the bold, unilateral and unexpected U.S. foreign policy initiative.

The Texas model had a great impact on Cuban political debate, clearly blueprinting the four necessary steps for annexation: first, a war of Independence; second, the creation of a republic (Texas was officially recognized by France, England and the United States, among other nations, and exhibited a tri-color flag with a lone star wanting and waiting to join the stars of the American Union); third, a request from the citizens of the independent republic for annexation to the United States; and fourth, approval by the U.S. Congress of the annexation request.

The Cuban elite was caught in a political dilemma. They had lost their special relation with the Spanish monarchy; moreover, the island's status had changed from a loyal province to an exploited colony. Spain was poor and rapacious. While Cuba's best trade partner was now the politically stable and free North American Union, common sense as well as economic well-being pointed to annexation as a favorable option for many rich Creoles.

The Cuban issue entered the American Republic's political debate early on. In 1801, George Morton, interim U.S. consul in Havana, wrote in an official report: "The wealth and importance of this Spanish Colony has increased during the few years that it has been open to the American trade in a most astonishing degree." [18] In 1805, Thomas Jefferson, third president of the United States, pointed to the strategic need of acquiring Cuba. "The possession of which was necessary for the defense of Louisiana and Florida... it would be an easy conquest." [19] In 1809, with Spain under Napoleon's imperial grip, Jefferson wrote President James Madison: "He (Napoleon) will consent to our receiving Cuba into our Union... and I would immediately erect a column in the southernmost limit of Cuba and inscribe on it a Ne Plus Ultra as to us in that direction." [20] Madison was clearly in favor of acquiring the island at the first convenient opportunity. [21]

In 1853, the U.S. ambassador to England, France and Spain met in Ostende, Belgium, to discuss Secretary of State Marcy's directive regarding a secret negotiation to purchase Cuba from the Spanish government led by General Baldomero Espartero and Regent Queen Maria Cristina.

Other Cubans took their separatist quest to South America, where in 1825, two Creole leaders, Jose Agustin Arango and Jose Aniceto Iznaga, met in Lima with Simon Bolivar. The "Libertador" expressed his sympathy and desire to help the Cuban independence effort, but by the time the new Latin American Republics met at the 1826 Pan American Conference in Panama, Spain had agreed to recognize her former colonies' independence. With new priorities taking center stage in the region, Cuba would have to wait. On this issue, Bolivar wrote Colombian patriot Jose de Santander: "It is more important to have peace than to liberate the islands..."[22]

In March 1843, the fear of a slave rebellion took center stage when slaves on several Matanzas plantations revolted. It was a brief but fierce fight. With reinforcement from Havana, the uprising was crushed. Many slaves were killed in the struggle or executed on the spot after their capture. On December 24, 1844, more than 4,000 people, mostly free Negroes and slaves, were arrested in Matanzas and charged with sedition. Those suspected of being the leaders were tied to a ladder and whipped until they confessed and named their accomplices. Seventy-eight were shot and more than a hundred tortured to death.[23] For Professor Brion Davis: "Slavery has always depended, ultimately, on physical power, and Caribbean planters, no matter how small their numbers, could always summon armed troops who had no compunctions about mass slaughter."[24]

Yet the issue of Cuba's breaking loose from Spain remained a priority of a large segment of the Creole population, especially after the Republic of Texas's admission into the American Union (1845). Gaspar Betancourt Cisneros, Miguel Teurbe Tolon, Cirilo Villaverde, Joaquin de Aguero, Jose Armenteros, Narciso Lopez and his brother-in-law Francisco de Frias, the Count of Pozo Dulce, spearheaded the political option for annexation.

The Venezuela-born Narciso Lopez became the foremost military leader of the annexationist movement. In his native land, he had fought with the royalist armies against independence. In 1823, Lopez married Dolores Frias, the Count of Pozo Dulce's sister. Later in Spain, he joined the Carlist War on the side of Queen Isabella II and General Espartero. His superior officer and friend, Geronimo Valdez, was named Captain General of Cuba, and Lopez was rewarded with a top administrative post on the island. But when Gen. Ramon Narvaez gained control of the Spanish government in Madrid, Espartero's friends where summarily fired from their posts and Lopez became a political outcast.

In 1848, Lopez became involved in the conspiracy known as "Mines of the Cuban Rose." When the Spanish police discovered the plot, Lopez was forced to escape to the United States, where he began to organize a military invasion of Cuba. It was during this time that Narciso Lopez had the idea for a Cuban flag. During a meeting in 1849 at the home of Miguel Teurbe Tolon, he proposed the need for the future independent Republic to have its own banner.

Lopez drew his design on a piece of paper. Teurbe Tolon provided it its shape and color, and his wife, Emilia, sewed it together. The new flag had a single white star like that of Texas on a red Masonic triangle with three blue and two white stripes.

With the financial assistance of U.S. southern slave's planters, Lopez organized an invasion force that assembled on the island of Cozumel, near the Yucatan peninsula. Before departing on their mission, Lopez issued a proclamation: "The Star of Cuba ... will emerge beautiful and shining on being admitted with glory into the splendid North American constellation where destiny leads it."[25]

On May 19, 1850, Lopez landed his forces and took Cardenas, capturing the small Spanish garrison there. He raised the new flag on Cuban soil for the first time. Of his 610 men, only five were Cuban. Lopez soon realized that the promised popular reaction to his cause was not forthcoming, and, under pressure from the Spanish army, he and his men withdrew and returned to Key West.

New Orleans welcomed Lopez as a hero, and, with renewed enthusiasm and financial aid from Southern pro-slavery planters, he organized a 400-man expedition with Mexican War veteran Col. William L. Crittenden and 44 Cubans.[26] The small army landed in Bahia Honda, near which a large Spanish force that had been alerted was waiting. Over the next few days of intense fighting, the invading expedition was defeated. Colonel Crittenden and 50 of his men were captured and executed at Plaza Mayor in Havana. Days later, Lopez was betrayed by a local peasant, captured and, on September 1, 1851, executed by *garrote*, a slow, agonizing, suffocating death. (Some years later, Jose de los Santos Castaneda, the peasant from Canarias who had betrayed Lopez and handed him over to authorities, was shot and killed through a window while playing pool in a Havana billiard hall by Nicolas Vignaud, who fled to New Orleans.)

Narciso Lopez died a hero and martyr. A few weeks before his final expedition landed in Cuba, Joaquin Aguero and Jose Armenteros, trying to coordinate military action with Lopez, led an uprising in central Cuba. On July 4, 1851, Aguero proclaimed Cuba's independence near Puerto Principe. On August 12, Armenteros took up arms in Trinidad. Both efforts failed and their leaders were executed by firing squad. So ended the direct military attempts at Cuba's annexation to the U.S.

# CHAPTER V

## *SPAIN: THE ARMY AS ARBITER OF POWER*

[1] Carr. *Spain*, op cit, 51.
[2] Guerra. *Manual*, op cit, 253.
[3] Sagra, op cit, 285.
[4] Juan Casanova Codina. *O Pan, O Plomo* (Madrid: Editorial Siglo Veintiuno, 2000), 57.
[5] Juan Pablo Fusi and Jordi Palafox. *España: 1808-1996. El Desafío de la Modernidad* (Madrid: Editorial España,1997), 30.
[6] Austria, Prussia, France and Russia.
[7] Carr. *Spain*, op cit, 151.
[8] Fusi y Palafox, op cit, 47.
[9] Hugh Thomas. *The Slave Trade*, op cit, 194.
[10] Guerra. *Manual,* op cit, 318.
[11] Ibid.
[12] Carr, *Spain*, op cit, 171.
[13] Hugh Thomas, op cit, 196.
[14] Ibid, 155.
[15] Dunn. op cit, 9.
[16] Mostly Apache and Comanche lands.
[17] John Basset Moore, A. *Digest of International Law* (Washington, 1906), Vol. 6, 401-3.
[18] Herminio Portel Vila, *Historia de Cuba en sus Relaciones con los Estados Unidos y España* (Miami: Mnemosyne Publishing Inc.,1969), Tomo II, 131-2.
[19] Ibid, 142.
[2] Ibid, 158.
[21] Ibid, 164.
[22] Hugh Thomas, op cit, 103.
[23] Vidal, Morales y Morales, *Iniciadores y Primeros Mártires de la Revolución Cubana* (Havana, 1931), Vol 1. 335.
[24] Brion Davis.
Brion Davis. *Inhuman Bondage*, op cit, 122
[25] Hugh Thomas, op cit, 216.
[26] Guerra. *Manual*, op cit, 492-3.

# CHAPTER VI

# *THE TEN YEARS WAR (1868-78)*

In 1865, a ray of hope for political reform appeared in Cuban society when the Spanish government authorized the election of a commission to address reforms on the island. The commission was known as the "Junta de Información" and some of Cuba's most prominent were elected members, including Jose Antonio Saco, Miguel Aldana and Francisco de Frias, Count of Pozo Dulce. The Junta's deliberations in Madrid generated great expectations, and some important political reforms were adopted, but early in 1867, reactionary forces in Madrid overturned all of the reforms and disbanded the Junta. A year later, the landed aristocracy of the eastern provinces of Cuba took up arms against Spain. The war was to last for ten years.

The region was ideal for a rebellion thanks to its topography, racial and social composition, and distinct cultural traits. Oriente had two important mountain ranges that traversed the entire southern and northeastern portions. Cuba's largest river, the Cauto, flows from these mountains into the gulf of Guacanayabo. Furthermore, Oriente is covered by an almost impenetrable forest, and the high rainfall rate keeps the forest permanently dense. Another factor that facilitated organization of an armed revolt in the region was its racial composition. In 1860, more than 92% of the population was creole,[1] and most blacks had been free for several generations. For Professor Phillip A. Howard: "Many 'cimarrones' (runaway slaves) who were longtime residents of Oriente, joined the revolutionaries. The rebels took advantage of the struggle of the 'cimarrones' against reenslavement. Not only the 'palenque' (the hidden mountain village of the runaway slaves) served as rebel camps and hospitals; but the 'cimarrones' also allowed their secret trade with Jamaica, Haiti and Santo Domingo to be converted by rebels into channels for obtaining weapons and war material."[2] According to Cuba's 1869 census (see Table II), only one out of every five people living in the island, or 20 percent of the population, lived in the Eastern Department.

## TABLE II
## DISTRIBUTION OF CUBAN POPULATION
## IN 1869*

|  | Whites | Free Blacks | Slaves | Total Blacks | Asians | Total |
|---|---|---|---|---|---|---|
| Western Dept. | 600,840 | 141,677 | 300,989 | 441,834 | 33,449 | 1,076,753 |
| Central Dept. | 48,634 | 14,061 | 14,887 | 28,950 | 340 | 77,924 |
| Eastern Dept. | 113,702 | 83,189 | 47,410 | 130,599 | 631 | 244,932 [3] |

Oriente was isolated from the administrative center of power in Havana. Overland communication was primitive and dangerous, and the sea-route lacked reliable schedules. Raising cattle and selling beef and hides were the first business in the region. Coffee and a modest sugar production came later. From early colonial times, the main business clients of the settlement were French, English and Dutch buccaneers. As the European powers established their Caribbean possessions, Jamaica, Haiti and the rest of their colonies became steady commercial partners, an illegal practice in light of the prohibition on trade with foreign countries by Spanish monopolies. The response of the "Orientales" was a vigorous and flourishing contraband network that did business even in times of war.

In three and a half centuries of virtual isolation, the people of Oriente developed distinct cultural and financial traits. They were loyal and warm toward family and associates, rough and prone to fight when provoked, inclined to ignore colonial authority and its rules, sensitive to perceived abuse, and highly influenced by French literature and Afro-creeds and music. They loved poetry, dancing and sensual pleasures. Honor-bound within their close-knit society, they were patriarchal and traditional in social values. Their business acumen made them the main suppliers of meat and hides in the Caribbean basin.

Since the sugar industry's development was marginal, the Africans' experience in Oriente was also different. The dense woods and mountain ranges encouraged the formation of African communities that included escaped slaves. Black men and women enjoyed a family environment, enduring together the joys and hardships of daily life. In such a setting, these free and proud people were able to care for their children, breaking the dehumanizing effect of slavery on the family. The village of El Cobre, with its copper mines and Virgin Sanctuary, is illustrative of the type of community founded by runaway slaves. Many black officers and soldiers of the revolutionary army flourished in a community that revered work and human dignity. The Cebrecos, Rabi, Crombet, Banderas, Moncadas and Maceos blossomed in this environment of family love and freedom.

Finally, Oriente received a steady flow of political refugees from Haiti and Santo Domingo. When war broke out, refugees contributed to its early successes as military instructors and top officers. Foremost among them was Dominican-born Máximo Gomez.

By 1868, the Eastern Department was ripe for revolution. The people of the region were ready for a fight. Spanish arrogance, abuse and greed accelerated the clash with the Orientales and sparked the rebellion. Oriente became the cradle for the War of Independence.

## 1868: SPAIN'S POLITICAL AND INSTITUTIONAL CRISIS

For Spain, 1868 also proved a milestone in the long, painful process of decay, poverty, corruption and violence. Since 1834, a succession of Army generals took the government's helm. Gen. Espartero headed the Progresista Party, General Ramon Narvaez, the Moderados, General Leopoldo O'Donnell, the Liberals. Generals Francisco Serrano and Domingo Dulce were also active in politics and, when not in power, plotted against those who were. O'Donnell, Serrano and Dulce had been captain generals in Cuba and contributors to the worst tradition of graft and greed. In 1848, Serrano married Maria Antonia Dominguez, a beautiful, rich Cuban-Creole and successful Madrid socialite.

Spain's economic and political crisis took a turn for the worse in 1866, when artillery sergeants at San Gil Barracks in Madrid revolted against General Narvaez' government and were crushed. More than 200 were killed or executed. By the summer of 1868, discontent had spread to every area of the nation, fueled by a catastrophic food shortage.[4] The British and French banks stopped lending and ceased operations in all major Spanish cities. The boom in railroad construction came to a halt. Three years of low rainfall devastated the already precarious agricultural infrastructure. In most regions, there was hunger, famine and high unemployment.

The people's anger turned against Isabel II and her government.

On September 17, Gen. Juan Prim landed in Cadiz and began the revolt that toppled the Monarchy. Gen. Serrano joined the uprising and marched his army toward Madrid. At the bridge of Alcolea, Serrano defeated the loyalist forces. Isabel II escaped to France,[5] and Prim and Serrano entered Madrid. Prim became the dominant figure of the new regime. They were aided by a substantial economic recovery, sparked by a rush of British investment in mining and increased demand for Catalonian cotton and textiles. Seeking political stability, the generals sought establishment of a constitutional monarchy. After difficult negotiations, Gen. Prim found the new Spanish king in the Italian Royal House of Savoy; his name, Amadeo. "On the day Amadeo arrived in his new kingdom, he was greeted with the news that Prim had been shot in Madrid; his death was a catastrophe for the monarchy he created."[6]

## THE UPRISING AND FIRST CUBAN CONSTITUTION

In August of 1867, Francisco Vicente Aguilera, one of the richest and most respected men on the island, formed the Committee of Bayamo with the goal of planning the coming war. One of the revolutionary movement's leaders, Carlos Manuel de Cespedes, rose to prominence. The rich, handsome, cosmopolitan scion of an illustrious Creole family, de Cespedes received a law degree from the University of Madrid. He showed himself to be quite brave. During a conspirators' meeting, de Céspedes concluded a speech, saying, "The power of Spain is decrepit and worm-eaten. If it appears still strong and great, it is because for over three centuries we have regarded it from our knees. Let us rise."[7]

On October 10, 1868, at an out-of-the-way sugar mill called La Demajagua, Carlos Manuel de Céspedes freed his 30 slaves and proclaimed Cuba's independence, inviting the former slaves to join the revolution. That same day, a small force of his attacked the village of Yara but was repelled. De Céspedes regrouped his men and, with reinforcements from important rebellion leaders, successfully attacked Bayamo, where the Revolutionary Army entered in triumph on October 20. It was in Bayamo during this time of great hope and celebration that Pedro Figueredo wrote the Cuban National Anthem, a hymn that echoed the will to fight for freedom or to die in the struggle.

Death of a Dream

*Al combate corred Bayameses*
*Que la Patria os contempla orgullosa*
*No temáis una muerte gloriosa*
*Que morir por la patria es vivir.*

To the Battle Bayameses!
Let the fatherland proudly observe you!
Do not fear a glorious death,
To die for the fatherland is to live!

It was at this early stage that many of the future leaders of the 1895 War of Independence joined the rebellion.

Upon learning of the eastern uprising, Captain General Francisco Lersundi ordered two columns to recapture Bayamo. The Cuban rebels under Dominican Generals Máximo Gomez and Modesto Diaz defeated both forces. In November 1868, the central city of Camaguey joined the fight for independence, led by Ignacio Agramonte. Agramonte, a young, romantic, cultured, charismatic and daring patrician attorney, became one of the most successful leaders of the revolution.

Early in 1869, Gen. Blas Villate, Count of Valmaseda, defeated the Cubans at El Salado near the Cauto River and recaptured Bayamo. The Cubans moved into the think mountain cover and began fighting as guerrillas. Before Bayamo fell, its citizens burned their homes and whole families moved to mountain bases. Thousands of peasants, white and black, joined the revolutionary army. It was to be a long and bloody fight. In February 1869, the eastern part of Las Villas province rebelled and entered the war.

On April 10, 1869, delegates from the three fighting provinces gathered in the village of Guaimaro, Camaguey. Out of this assembly came the first constitution of the Republic of Cuba in Arms. Like the U.S. Constitution, it divided the government into three branches, the Executive, Legislative and Judicial. The flag designed by Narcisco Lopez became the national emblem. And the House of Representatives elected Carlos Manuel de Céspedes President of the Republic, which was acknowledged by the Benito Juarez government in Mexico.

On the issue of freeing the slaves, the new revolutionary government hesitated out of fear of antagonizing the rich sugar planters in the West. But Agramonte managed to introduce into the new Constitution its Article 24, which proclaimed "all inhabitants of the Republic to be absolutely free." Fearful of giving the president too much power, the Legislative Chamber, led by Agramonte, approved its right to overturn presidential decisions and to dismiss the president and commander-in-chief.

In Madrid, the government tried to find a peaceful solution to the conflict and named Domingo Dulce — husband to the Cuban Countess of Santovenia — as Captain General of Cuba. Upon his arrival, Dulce offered amnesty to prisoners and a pardon to the rebels in the field. The "Peninsulares" considered Dulce's peace negotiation a betrayal. "The powerful and cohesive group of influential Spaniards was firmly entrenched in their loyalists' convictions."[8]

"El Cuerpo de Voluntarios" (the civil militia of Peninsular volunteers) — organized 15 years earlier to fight Narciso Lopez' invasions — was converted by rich merchants into an active force of intolerance, repression and fear. By 1869, the Volunteers numbered more than 20,000 infantry and 3,500 cavalry.[9] The merchants paid for their uniforms and equipment and provided them paid jobs.

On January 21, 1869, the volunteer civil militia rioted in Havana, launching into a violent rampage. They roamed the streets shouting slogans against Domingo Dulce and the rebels. Early on that evening, their fury turned against the mostly Cuban patrons of the Villanueva Theater who had applauded at the mention of Céspedes' name on stage. It was a savage attack on innocent civilians that ended in the deaths of 14 people and the wounding of 27 others. The police had stood by during the attack afraid to intervene.

Captain General Domingo Dulce tried to work out a deal with the Volunteers by enacting harsher measures against the rebels. This failed. On June 5, 1869, the Volunteers rioted again in Havana, forcing Dulce to resign his post. The forces of intolerance became the real power of the unfortunate colony. On December 20, 1870, Gen. Juan Prim was shot to death in Madrid, his assassins never found. Antonio Caballero de Rodas, who replaced Dulce, upon arriving in Havana, established a political alliance with the Volunteers. "The cities, and above all Havana, were run by the Spaniards. Some were absentee planters, others rich merchants narrowly bound to Catalonian commercial interests."[10]

With each report of an heroic effort by the Cubans fighting in the eastern provinces, the Volunteers became even more violent and vengeful. The peak of infamy was reached when, on November 27, 1872, eight University of Havana medical students were sentenced to death.[11] The eight were part of a group of 40 students charged with scratching a glass ornament on the tomb of a leading Spanish journalist killed in Key West in a duel with a Cuban revolutionary. The Volunteers demanded severe punishment. The court sentenced five students to six months' incarceration, but that was not enough for the Volunteers. Enraged by the tribunal's ruling, they took to the streets of Havana chanting "death, death." To appease the Volunteers, a second trial was hastily convened, and the new tribunal sentenced eight of the students to death by firing squad.

## SPANISH MILITARY STRATEGY IN CUBA AND POLITICAL CHAOS IN MADRID

At the time of the 1868 war in Cuba, the generals remained arbiters of political power in Madrid. Spain was a deeply divided society in permanent institutional and financial crisis. Though large, the army was badly trained, poorly paid and quick to rebel. The soldiers were drilled in the narrow confines of the barrack patios, and most units never took part in tactical field maneuvers. A military analyst of this period wrote, "No war can be properly fought without a good army, and there can be no good army in the midst of a disorganized society. Nor can there be any organized society that it is not well constituted. Spain is a nation in critical and constant state of restructuring. Its army is always being remade. In this state all wars have found it. This is why no war, not even the War of Independence, was well fought."[12]

The war in Cuba was a burden on the impoverished Spanish economy, but despite the recurrent political and financial crisis, Spain made a remarkable effort to field an army of 97,495 men, 3,700 horses and 36 pieces of artillery.[13] (These figures do not include the several thousand-man "volunteer militia".)

While trying to contain the war to the eastern regions of Cuba, the Spanish government continued its rapid descent into chaos. On February 11, 1873, King Amadeo I abdicated. After ruling for two years and two months, he found Spain "ungovernable."[14]   The following day, the Courts proclaimed the Spanish First Republic, inaugurating one of the most confusing political periods in modern Spanish history.

The Republic lasted ten months and, in those ten months, had four different administrations.  Estanislao Figueras presided for the first four months and failed.  Francisco Pi y Margall governed for a little more than 60 days, during which time the Barcelona council proclaimed the Catalonia Republic, followed by Seville, Granada, Valencia and Cartagena.   The Spain forged by Isabella and Ferdinand was falling apart.  The Swiss Cantons became a rough model.  The city of Jaen rebelled against Granada, and Utrera against Seville.  Chaos reigned.  Nicolas Salmeron oversaw the Republic for a few days.  Emilio Castelar followed him. The great orator of his generation wrote, "There were days in that summer (1873) when we believed our Spain was completely dissolved ... similar to what occurred at the collapse of the caliphate of Cordova..."[15] On the night of January 2, 1874, Manuel Pavia, Captain General of Madrid, dismissed the Cortes and formed a provisional military government headed by Gen. Francisco Serrano. The generals were back in power.

## THE CUBANS' MILITARY STRATEGY AND POLITICAL DIVISIONS

After the loss of Bayamo, the Cubans' response was flexible use of military resources adapted to the island's topography and climate. Small and mid-sized forces using swift maneuvers would make hit-and-run raids on targets of opportunity and then pull back to their forest bases. Yellow fever, malaria and other tropical diseases were the rebels' best allies, causing more casualties than bullets.

During this phase of the war, some of the wealthiest planters who initially led the uprising began yielding their commands to younger officers.  These included men of African ancestry who had earned the troops' respect and admiration in combat.  Cuban national pride blossomed with tales of courage and sacrifice.

On May 11, 1873 the revolution suffered a terrible loss:  Ignacio Agramonte's death in battle.  The dashing Agramonte was one of the Cuban army's best commanders and the folklore hero of Camaguey.

He led by charging at the head of his cavalry, and his soldiers loved him. Saddened by the news of Agramonte's death, Céspedes began looking over his top commanders for a suitable replacement to lead the forces in Camaguey. His decided on Gen. Máximo Gomez, a hardened veteran and a master at guerrilla warfare. Gomez assumed command on July 9, 1873, and became the leading advocate for invading the rich sugar plantations in eastern Las Villas, Matanzas and Havana provinces. His strategy faced spirited opposition — in particular from Gen. Vicente Garcia.

The simmering antagonism among rebel commanders reached an institutional boiling point when, on October 27, 1873, the House of Representatives dismissed Carlos Manuel de Céspedes as president of the Cuban Republic in Arms. Enrique Collazo, a veteran of the war, wrote, "The deposing of Céspedes is the culminating act of the Cuban revolution and the point of departure for our misfortunes..."[16] Denied the protection of a military guard, Céspedes was killed by Spanish forces at San Lorenzo farm. He had fought to the bitter end, a lone and gallant fight that befits his heroic role. Salvador Cisneros Betancourt became the new president.

Céspedes' dismissal was followed by a serious crisis between Washington and Madrid when the rebel supply ship *Virginius*, sailing under the U.S. flag, was captured by a Spanish gunboat off the coast of Jamaica. The *Virginius* was taken to Santiago de Cuba with 175 men aboard. All were courts martial and sentenced to death. Early on November 4, 1873, Pedro de Céspedes (brother of Carlos Manuel de Céspedes), Gen. Bernabe Varona and William O'Ryan were shot along with 53 other men. More executions were planned when the British frigate *H.M.S. Niobe* sailed into Santiago harbor, and her captain, Lambton Lorraine, threatened to turn his ship's guns on the city if the executions were not stopped. This quickly executed initiative saved 122 lives. Seeking to avert a conflict with Britain and the United States, the Spanish government spared the lives of the remaining prisoners.

Saddened by the news of Céspedes' death, and in the midst of Cuba's presidential crisis, Gen. Máximo Gomez launched a military offensive that produced some of the best rebel victories of the war. The first was La Sacra, where Gomez, leading the crack cavalry regiments of Camaguey, broke the Spanish infantry's defense and inflicted heavy losses. On December 2, 1873, Gomez and his cavalry overtook Col. Vilchez' column at Palo Seco. The fierce battle that ensued left 500 dead, including the battalion commander.[17]

On January 30, 1874, Gen. Gomez met with top rebel commanders at the San Diego base to discuss the invasion of western Cuba. Generals Calixto Garcia, Vicente Garcia and Antonio Maceo, and President Salvador Cisneros Betancourt, among others, attended the meeting. Gomez got the point quickly. He needed Gen. Antonio Maceo, 500 of his infantry from Oriente and his veteran cavalry from Camaguey. Gen. Vicente Garcia opposed the invasion, but the rest of the rebel leadership was in favor. With his marching orders still fresh, Gomez began the westward march.

The Spanish commanders in Camaguey got hold of the Cuban plans and tried to intercept and engage the invasion forces. On February 9, the two forces met at "El Naranjo," where they fought for ten hours, both sides sustaining heavy casualties. The following day, as the Spaniards were returning to their base, the rebels attacked again at "Mojacasabe," inflicting serious losses on the retreating column. Manuel Sanguily, a seasoned veteran and intellectual, wrote: "No other battle of the war was more heroic than El Naranjo."[18]

A few weeks later, the two forces met again, this time at "Las Guasimas". The crack cavalry of Camaguey and the hardened infantry from Oriente routed out the 4,000-man column under the command of Gen. Manuel Arminan.[19] Las Guasimas, the largest battle of the Ten Years War, was a tactical victory for the rebels, but yet a strategic setback. The Cubans' war supplies were depleted at El Naranjo and Las Guasimas. Máximo Gomez wrote. "The invasion would probably suffer some delay as a result of these hard-fought battles."[20] The march to the West had to be postponed. During the campaign, Antonio Maceo showed great courage, tactical genius and leadership.

In Spain, Arsenio Martinez Campos, an intelligent and ambitious general, gathered his loyal troops at Sagunto and, on December 1874, restored a constitutional monarchy, proclaiming Alfonso de Borbon king. Alfonso, the 16-year-old son of Isabel II, was a cadet at Sandhurst Military Academy in England. He took the throne of an exhausted nation fighting on two fronts, the Carlist rebellion in the North of Spain and the war in Cuba. Antonio Canovas Del Castillo, the able and powerful conservative leader, was named president of the government.

Meanwhile, Máximo Gomez was taking advantage of the rainy season to rest and re-supply his troops. In the first week of January 1875, he launched the invasion of the west. The rebels were initially successful, advancing into the rich Santi Spiritus region, where they burned 83 plantations and freed the slaves,[21] but the offensive was cut short. Divided by petty regionalism, strategic differences and personality clashes, the rebel leadership could not coordinate the military effort. The government recalled large numbers of Gomez's troops, supplies failed to arrive, then Gomez himself was ordered back. The invasion was called off, and by the last week of May, Gomez began the trek back to his eastern bases.

Another source of concern of both conservative Cubans and Spaniards on the island was the large and increasing number of blacks fighting in the rebel army. The Spanish colonel Adolfo Jimenez Castellano wrote that by the end of the war, almost half of Cuban forces were former slaves who had joined the struggle for independence.[22]

The issue of Maceo's African ancestry was negatively portrayed by both Spanish "integristas" and conservative Cubans claiming that Maceo's goal was establishment of a black republic along the lines of the Haiti model. Maceo brought the matter up with rebel authorities: "I have known for some time that … a small circle exists which indicated that it did not wish to serve under my command because I belong to the colored race … since I form a not unappreciable part of this democratic republic, which is founded on the principles of liberty, equality and fraternity, I must protest energetically that neither now nor at any other time am I to be regarded as an advocate of a Negro Republic.... The men who act in the manner I have described can never form part of the country for which we are fighting…"[23]

In such an atmosphere of controversy, personal rivalry, persistent indiscipline and confusion, events continued to deteriorate for the revolution. Gen. Calixto Garcia was captured, and Gen. Vicente Garcia staged a military coup at Las Lagunas de Varona, in which he demanded the resignation of President Salvador Cisneros Betancourt, dismissal of the civil assembly and creation of a military government. Máximo Gomez called the action "a military mutiny."[24] By now the rebel leadership was hopelessly divided. On this issue

Gomez wrote: "I pity Cuba's luck, her sons may lose her."[25]

## THE COLLAPSE OF REVOLUTION

By January 1, 1875, Spain was once again a monarchy, and Martinez Campo's unexpected ascendancy both in political and military affairs made it inevitable that he would be called upon to end the war in Cuba. On November 3, 1876, the new military governor, Martinez Campos, arrived in Cuba with an expeditionary force of 26,000 men.[26] The Spanish Army swelled to more than 100,000 regular soldiers and 80,000 "volunteers".[27]

Upon his arrival, Campos implemented a policy of military offensive with the promise of reforms. The first political measure intended to undermine revolutionary army morale was a decree made public on January 13, 1877, pardoning all Cubans who would desert the rebel forces. He also made it unlawful to take reprisals against rebel soldiers taken prisoner and ordered field commanders to treat all surrendering Cubans with respect. Bribery was also used. Intransigent rhetoric was replaced by a conciliatory tone. It worked. The Spanish offensive moved from West to East like a counter invasion. Las Villas province was first and was captured on March 20, 1877. Martinez Campos announced that the Central Department had been pacified, even though a fair number of rebel troops continued to operate there. As the offensive entered Camaguey, the Captain General sent peace offers to the rebel commanders in the region.

On February 10, 1878, the Spanish military leader met at his "El Zanjon" base with members of Camaguey's Central Committee to propose peace terms. With some slight modifications, the rebels verbally agreed to end the war. No document was signed, but a truce was called.[28] The peace terms offered by Martinez Campos granted Cuba political reforms similar to Puerto Rico's, a general amnesty that included army defectors who joined the rebels and freedom for the slaves fighting for independence. Most of the Cuban leadership accepted the Zanjon Agreement.

After accepting the peace offer, Máximo Gomez sailed on a Spanish ship to discuss the Zanjon treaty with Antonio Maceo. When Gomez' ship entered Santiago de Cuba's harbor, a large crowd gathered by the dock to see the veteran war leader. The next day, the hero of Palo Seco and Las Guasimas met with Antonio Maceo his beloved lieutenant. Gomez stressed the hopelessness of continuing the war. Maceo was of a different opinion. Just the day before, his forces had defeated the San Quintín battalion at San Ulpiano.

Unable to persuade Maceo to disarm, Gomez returned to Santiago de Cuba where he boarded the Spanish gunship *Vigia* for Jamaica. Distraught at the failure of the heroic war effort, Máximo Gomez retired in Santo Domingo with his family.

A few days later, Maceo requested a meeting with Martinez Campos. The two met on March 15, 1878, at Los Mangos de Baragua. The Spanish General reiterated the El Zanjon peace terms accepted by the Camaguey committee and a majority of rebel commanders. Maceo expressed strong opposition to the accord and his willingness to continue the struggle for independence. A disappointed Campos complained that he would not have accepted Maceo's invitation to meet had he known that peace negotiations were not on the agenda.[29] The meeting — known in Cuban history as the "Baragua Protest" — adjourned with the understanding that hostilities would resume on March 23. It was a futile effort, but the dream of freedom was very much alive. The spirit of Don Quijote was riding with the rebels to a final impossible fight. It lasted for seven more weeks. Finally, the undefeated warriors, led by a Cuban of African decent raised from the bosom of the Oriente peasantry, accepted the fact that the war of independence had collapsed. On May 10, 1878, Antonio Maceo sailed aboard the Spanish warship *Fernando el Católico* for Jamaica and a long exile.

The Spanish welcomed peace. With a war debt of 46 million pesos, Spain's treasury was on the brink of bankruptcy,[30] and the nation had suffered terrible casualties, mainly among the illiterate peasant-soldiers, stoically brave and fiercely devoted to their hamlets, virgins and saints.

## TABLE III
### SPANISH ARMY CASUALTIES IN CUBA
#### (1868-1878)

| | |
|---|---|
| Officers killed in combat or from disease | 919 |
| Soldiers killed in combat or from disease | 54,495 |
| Wounded, disabled or ill, repatriated or discharged | 15,234 |
| **Total casualties** | 70,648 [31] |

Eastern Cuba was depleted by war, hunger and disease, but the long, bloody struggle had turned the rebel soldiers into formidable guerrilla fighters. The war became the Cubans' foremost military training camp, where many leaders of the next war developed their fighting skills.

## TABLE IV

| Ranks | War of 1895 | Veterans of 10 Years War who fought in the 1895 war |
|---|---|---|
| Major General | 26 | 24 |
| Division General | 32 | 19 |
| Brigadier General | 81 | 38 |
| Total No. of Generals | 139 | 81[32] |

Along with the heroic deeds and bloody sacrifices were also disturbing questions regarding Cubans' performance within the rules of a civilian government. The first two presidents of the Republic in Arms were deposed, and bitter disputes among rebel leaders poisoned the fragile framework of consensus building, compromise and institutional government. They were difficult tasks in the midst of a brutal war. Yet it was also clear that despite their noble ideals, the rebels failed in a crucial area to be bound by their own rules. The unruly and often chaotic Spanish political heritage was quite evident in the rebels' deplorable performance in government.

In the military theater of operations, the Cubans, while excelling in guerrilla warfare, lacked strategically cohesion, which seriously limited their offensive capability. The western sugar plantations had been spared the rebel torch, and the best opportunity for victory was probably lost as a result of King Amadeo's abdication and the subsequent collapse of the First Republic, throwing a prostrate Spain into the grips of political disintegration.

In the end, Spain prevailed, at a desperate cost of men and money, but witnesses to the fierce fight entertained no illusions about a lasting peace in Cuba. A few months after the Zanjon Treaty was secured, Governor Joaquin Jovellar wrote, "The country as a whole is in favor of the rebels, and from the roots of this war, another will grow."[33]   Gen. Martinez Campos also clearly understood the prospect of a future war. He wrote, "They didn't need to have government jobs at the time of their uprising, and now they're seasoned soldiers. If there are no great generals among them, they are what they need to be most, outstanding guerrilla fighters."[34]

The war that ended in 1878 had a higher purpose: to strengthen the roots of Cuba's national conscience. The heroic deeds of so many men and women blossomed in the next generation's boundless pride and commitment to Cuba's independence. As historian Ramiro Guerra writes, "A country is essentially a historical being, a moral entity with a past and a future. It must have a heritage of glory and heroism, of epics and legends. There aren't a single strong people or a robust nationality in which those elements are lacking. Before 1868, Cuba did not have them, at least not nearly enough of them. The greater part of its heritage stemmed directly from the Ten Years War, very rich and impossible to surpass. After El Zanjón, despite its unfavorable outcome, Cuba possessed a grand patriotic tradition to be revered and loved."[35]

# CHAPTER VI

## *THE TEN YEARS WAR (1868-78)*

---

[1] de la Pezuela, op cit, 247

[2] Phillip A. Howard. *"Changing History"*. *Afro-Cuban Cabildos and Societies of Color in the Nineteenth Century."* (Louisiana State University Press. Baton Rouge, 1998), 112

[3] Carlos Sedano y Cruzat. *Cuba desde 1850 a 1873*. (Madrid, 1873), 152-153

[4] Fusi y Palafox. *España*, op cit, 37.

[5] Ibid, 75

[6] Carr. op cit, 319.

[7] Antonio Pirala. *Anales de la Guerra de Cuba*, 3 Vols. (Madrid, 1896) Vol. I, 249.

[8] Octavio Delgado. *The Spanish Army in Cuba, 1868-1898: An Institutional Study*. (Colombia University, 1980), 102.

[9] Pirala, op cit, 385.

[10] Daniel R. Handrick. *Ejercito y Política en España: 1868-1898*. (Editorial Tecnos, Madrid, 1981), 177.

[11] Maso. *Historia de Cuba*, op cit, 264.

[12] Delgado, op cit, 129.

[13] Ibid, 90.

[14] Fusi y Palafox, op cit, 80.

[15] Emilio Castelar. *La España Moderna. Critica Internacional*. (June 1893), 192-3.

[16] Juan J. Casasus. *Calixto García*. (Editorial Moderna Poesía. Miami, 1981), 93.

[17] Pirala, op cit, 819.

[18] Raul Roa. *Aventuras, ventures y desventuras de un Mambí en la lucha por la independencia de Cuba*. (Editores Siglo XXI. Mejico, 1970), 58.

[19] Delgado, op cit, 111.

[20] Máximo Gómez. *Diario de Campaña del Mayor General Máximo Gómez*. (Cieba del Agua. Talleres Centro Superior Tecnológico, 1941),

[21] Fernandez Almagro, op cit, Vol. 1, 322.

[22] O Pan o Plomo, op cit, 141.

[23] Philip S. Forner. *La Guerra Hispano/Cubano/Americana y el Nacimiento del Imperialismo Norteamericano*. (Akal Editor, Madrid, 1975) Tomo I,

[24] Gómez, op cit,

[25] Ibid

[26] Pirala, op cit, 362. Tesifontes Gallego. *La Insurrección Cubana Madrid*. (Imprenta Central, 1897), 48.

[27] Ramiro Guerra, op cit, 378.

[28] Emilio Bacardi Moreau. *Cronicas de Santiago de Cuba*. (Editorial Brogan, Segunda Edición, Madrid, 1972), Vol. VI, 201.

[29] Bacardi, op cit,

[30] Tesifontes Gallego, op cit, 58.

[31] Ramiro Guerra. *Guerra de los Diez Años*. (La Habana: Cultura S.A., 1956), 378.

[32] Rafael Soto Paz.

[33] Pirala, op cit,

[34] Guerra, op cit,

# CHAPTER VII

# BETWEEN THE WARS (1878-1895)

*THE DAWN OF CUBA'S POLITICAL PARTIES –*
*BEAUROCRATIC CORRUPTION – THE AUTONOMIST PARTY –*
*CUBAN AFRICAN RELIGION – RACIAL PREJUDICE – THE*
*END OF SLAVARY – THE INDUSTRIAL REVOLUTION IN*
*CUBA – TRANSFORMATION OF THE SUGAR INDUSTRY AND*
*THE DAWN OF THE CUBAN BOURGEOISIE – JOSE MARTI,*
*THE APOSTLE OF CUBAN INDEPENDENCE – PRELUDE TO*
*WAR.*

Once peace was attained, the Spanish nation declared Martinez Campos a hero. The fragile monarchy he had proclaimed at Sagunto was further strengthened by his Cuban victory. He was at the time the only Spanish leader with enough power to implement modest reforms in the hostile environment of the powerful Spanish clique in Cuba. In January 1879, Cuba was granted the right to have political parties, an electoral system, freedom of the press and its own deputies in the Spanish "cortes" (legislatives assemblies). In 1881, the Spanish Constitution of 1876 was promulgated for the island, including the civil right to assembly in public places and the code of civil and criminal procedure.

But the Royal Decrees of 1825 and 1878 combined to give special power to the military governors in Cuba to regulate and even suspend constitutional rights in the event of a perceived security threat.[1] This special power became the principal tool of economic and political control for the Captain General, the bureaucracy, and Spanish financial and commercial oligarchy.[2]

### THE DAWN OF CUBA'S POLITICAL PARTIES

The seven months of Martinez Campos' postwar governorship marked a creative and dynamic period in Cuba's political life. Two of the most prominent parties of the colonial period were founded: the Liberal Party, comprised mostly of Cubans who believed in the right to self-government, and the Union Constitutional, mostly

Spaniards in favor of integration of Cuba as an Spanish province. Over time, the parties became popularly known as the "Autonomists" and "Integrationists."

The Autonomist party was founded on August 3, 1878, by a group of prominent attorneys, journalists, planters and businessmen. It included José Maria Gálvez, Eliseo Giberga, José Antonio Cortina and Rafael Montoro. The Autonomists believed in Cuba's right to self government within the Spanish monarchy and in a local, administrative mandate to legislate and implement laws, including trade tariffs and customs regulations that would respond to the will of residents as freely expressed in multi-party elections. Their model was Canada's political system, a successful structure of localized self-government within the British Commonwealth.[3] The Autonomists also supported the abolition of slavery, proposing "immediate abolition without pecuniary compensation."[4]

On August 16, 1878, the Constitutional Union "Integristas" party was founded. From the outset, it was a party of the entrenched Spanish Oligarchy, its president the Count of Casa More, one of the wealthiest men on the island. Members included a select group of bankers, merchants, tobacco growers and high-ranking bureaucrats. Their popular base was rooted among Spanish laborers, clerks and craftsmen. Their aim was to integrate the island as a Spanish province, enjoying special customs regulations with Spain to protect their profitable, privileged trade and to further commercial ties with the United States.

## BEAUROCRATIC CORRUPTION

The powerful leadership of the Constitutional Union (UC) became the engine that drove Madrid's political and economic decisions regarding Cuba. The UC had large interests to protect and large amounts of money with which to influence lobbyists and corrupt bureaucrats. The first opportunity for business came after El Zanjón, when Cuba was required to cover war expenses. In 1867, Spain's debt totaled 7 million pesos; by 1876, it had grown to more than 128 million. The Spanish oligarchy recognized a financial windfall and established the Banco Hispano Colonial. A loan was negotiated with Madrid[5] by which the bank was to make payments to the Spanish government in increments of 15 to 25 million and at an interest rate of 12% plus 40% of any increases in customs-income from the amount recorded at the time of the loan's signing. The loan was secured by Cuban customs revenues. Banco Hispano Colonial received daily installments of $35,500 from the island's fiscal revenues.[6] Such an outrageous loan was arranged to the detriment of growth and internal development in Cuba.[7]

Another source of friction and discontent with the Cubans was the various maritime laws known as *cabotaje*, which provided custom-duty exemptions on products transported in Spanish ships to Cuba. The wheat trade illustrates the arrangement. Cargo purchased in New York was shipped to the Spanish port of Santander and back across the ocean to Havana at a cost of $8.79 per barrel, while the shorter direct route — New York to Havana — cost $11.46 due to high maritime and custom tariffs.[8]

## TABLE V
## SHIPPING TARIFF

| Wheat | Ship | Dollars per barrel |
|---|---|---|
| From Spain | Spanish | $2.00 |
| From Spain | Foreign | $6.00 |
| Foreign | Spanish | $8.50 |
| Foreign | Foreign | $9.50 [9] |

As a result, ship owners, merchants and corrupt bureaucrats made large profits, while the people in Cuba could scarcely afford to eat bread because of the prohibitive price.[10] Antonio Lopez, a leading Constitutional Union figure, future Marquis of Comellas and owner of the Transatlantica shipping line, was a direct beneficiary of *cabotaje* law. Through his influence in Madrid, Lopez managed to get Spanish soldiers and materiel shipped during Cuba's War of Independence. Trasatlantica collected yearly revenue of $720,000 from the island's budget.[11]

The personal gains of the few powerful business brokers dominated the island's political status. "All attempts at reforms were blocked by those with interest in the Cuban connection, slave traders, merchants, shippers, wheat exporters and industrialists who, limited by restricted internal demand, needed a protected colonial market. These groups welcomed Cuba's being ruled by special laws as this precluded serious parliamentary discussion of the island's problems."[12]

The electoral process was rigged from the start in favor of the Constitutional Union. Voting for a deputy to the National Assembly (cortes) demanded a fiscal contribution of 25 gold pesos.[13]    In addition, Spanish merchants could assign their surplus business payments to their clerks and other low-paid employees in favor of the Constitutional Union at the polls. They were labeled "Occasional Associates." In the first election of 1879, still under the spell of the Zanjón accord, the Cubans elected 14 deputies to the "cortes" out of a total of 24, but as the Spanish oligarchy began applying the restrictive rules and regulations, the number of Cubans elected declined sharply. In 1881, there were only 10 out of 24; by 1884, only four.[14]

**TABLE VI**
**Cuba's Revenues 1889-1890 (in pesos)**

| | |
|---|---|
| Customs | 14,971,300 |
| Taxes | 5,818,600 |
| Lottery | 3,104,026 |
| Old Debts | 1,608,900 |
| Other | 312,550 |
| | 25,815,376 [15] |

While Cuban revenues were accounted for, expenditures reflected the predatory nature of the colonial administration. This unfair distribution of island revenues fueled Cubans' perception of being exploited. For example, revenues for 1884 were $27,261,200, out of which $14,811,340, or well over 50%, went to fund Spanish army and navy expenses.[16] Most of the rest covered bureaucratic salaries and the Ten Years War debt, leaving less than 4% for Cuba's social needs and infrastructure development. Expenses for that year reached $38,166,008 creating a $10,904,888 deficit.[17]

## THE AUTONOMIST PARTY

The Autonomist party leadership fought the fiscal injustice and related corruption in public forums, even under government duress and intimidation. Eliseo Giberga spoke of Cuba's right to regulate its own commercial and political life. The popular and wealthy Jose Antonio Cortina provided financial aid to educate the poor and assailed the shameless corruption riddling the colonial bureaucracy. Miguel Figueroa became a leading anti-slavery advocate. Party president Jose Maria Galvez and secretary Antonio Govin insisted that autonomy was not only the best political formula for Spanish sovereignty in Cuba, but also the only peaceful one.

Rafael Montoro was among the most eloquent public speakers of his generation, acclaimed in both Cuba and Spain as a brilliant orator for his clarity, coherence, substance and debating skills. Montoro's speeches framed the Autonomist cause. "In the Peninsula," he proclaimed, "the representative government was established some years ago and has survived with great problems and peril... While in Cuba ... has ruled a regime based on the absolutism of military governments and the systematic disavowal of human and citizen rights."[18]

On the issue of self-government and loyalty to Spain, Montoro wrote, "Autonomy in Cuba holds no dangers for the Spanish nation, as it has not for the British nation in her free and prosperous colonies."[19] Montoro was adverse to violent political upheaval. "Revolutionary radicalism has caused all the great disasters that depress the modern world."[20] Stressing his party's doctrine, he wrote, "The doctrine of liberal and progressive democracy has as a base the recognition and guarantee of the human condition, with all its rights and all its necessary freedoms."[21]

Cuba's political life began after El Zanjón, and it was not an auspicious beginning. The Spanish oligarchy clung to its privileges and applied a set of restrictive rules, censorship, unfair voting criteria and dishonest behavior at the polls to ensure the election results — all of it designed to retain their grip on power. The Autonomists accepted the challenge as the only window to a peaceful political process. In public forums, they denounced slavery, unfair customs tariffs, an outrageous budget, intolerance and corruption were deeply rooted in the powerful Spanish oligarchy.

The Autonomists' role and impact on Cuba's governance has been the subject of heated debate. For Marxist historian Raul Roa, the Autonomists were the party of ... the counter-revolutionaries ... the bourgeoisie ... the neo-annexationists."[22] For Manuel Sanguily, revered patriot of the Ten Years War, the Autonomists were, during those uncertain years, the party of the Cubans.[23] According to

Sanguily, the obstacles to self-government were overwhelming, yet, despite the odds, the Autonomists had a tremendous impact on Cuban society. "The Autonomists' objectives were sterile in their dreams for changes, but they were extremely effective in reaching and transforming the Cuban spirit."[24]

A great thinker of his generation, Enrique Jose Varona has provided one of the most poignant statements regarding the period. Just after the Zanjón peace treaty he wrote: "A defeated ideal is not easily replaced. There is always a transition period, in which your people go about like a group of pilgrims in unexplored regions, looking at a rallying point they don't know if they will ever reach." During this confusing political period, the Autonomists provided a sense of hope, direction and goals, but entrenched business privilege and profound corruption proved to be unconquerable forces. In the end it was an impossible quest, and with the Autonomist failure, Spain lost its best chance of avoiding a bloodbath, economic ruin and national disaster awaiting it in a just few short years.


## CUBAN-AFRICAN RELIGION

Slaves were being shipped to Cuba from practically everywhere in West Africa, from the shores of Senegal, the forests of Angola, from the coastal fringes, to hundreds of kilometers inland. The largest group of Africans in Cuba, and the one most studied by scholars, is the Yoruba from southwestern Nigeria. In Cuba, they were called the Lucumi.

The second most important African group is the Carabali, their name derived from the port of Calabar, their shipping point in southeastern Nigeria. They were most numerous in the province of Havana and the cities of Cardenas and Matanzas.[25] The third relevant group was the Congolese tribes, found mostly in eastern Cuba, particularly the cities of Guantanamo and Santiago.[26] The Africans' arrival had a significant impact on the island's social and economic structure.

To understand Cubans, one must understand the African contribution. Eminent Cuban anthropologist Lydia Cabrera said, "You cannot understand our people without understanding the Negro. This influence is more evident today than in colonial times. We do not enter far into Cuban life without encountering the African presence." Their cultural influence is most apparent in Cuban religious beliefs, its hauntingly beautiful music, sensual dance and the will to survive in a hostile environment.

In this dehumanizing and brutal setting, the ancestral heritage of the African warriors and traders was partially destroyed by confinement and enslavement. They had to adapt and conform to their master's culture and, since they came from many different regions with diverse languages and dialects, communication was difficult, reinforcing a sense of isolation and loneliness. "A small compensation for the suffering of slavery was a sharpening of the religion sentiment."[27]

In Cuba, the dominant African religion was the Lucumi or "Regla de Ocha," better known as "Santeria." Its deities are known as "Orichas". Olodumare is the supreme god,[28] but the responsibility of dealing with believers falls on a group of powerful Orichas, such as the beautiful Ochun, goddess of love, water and rivers. It is believed that Chango, god of thunder, fire, music and dance, was the fourth king of the Yorubas, deified as a god after his death. Yemaya, goddess of the sea and motherhood, is among the most respected Orichas.

In the Lucumi religion it is believed that Obatala, a great force in the Lucumi pantheon and a favorite of the mighty Olodumare, took part in the creation of the Universe. His son Elegua is the key to all Lucumi initiation rites. Elegua's name must be uttered at the start of any religious invocation to other Orichas; and he can tell the future. His enemy is his brother, Ogun, another son of Obatala, punished by their father to eternal labor and, thus, the deity of ironworkers. Ogun is prone to violence and knows all human secrets. His help is needed for developing inner-strength. Babalu Aye watches over the infirm. He can also see the future, but his rites are complex and seldom evoked.[29]

Isolated under the cruel yoke of slavery, the Yorubas adapted their religious beliefs to those of their masters and, in the process of syncretism with Catholicism, developed their own Afro-Cuban Lucumi pantheon. Obatala is also Jesus of Nazareth or the Virgin of Mercy, Chango is Santa Barbara, Ochun is the Virgen of Cobre and the patron of Cuba, Yemaya is the Virgen of Regla, Babalu Aye is Saint Lazarus, and Elegua is the Nino de Atocha.[30]

The second religion of African origin was the Congolese religion of "Palo Monte Mayombe," known in Cuba as "Brujería," a mystical rite devoted to the care and protection of family and friends. It allowed women and men to perform as priests, also referred to in the Afro-Cuban rites as "Nganga," "Paleros," or "Mayomberos." There is a deep devotion to the ancestors' spirits and the belief that those spirits can help family and harm enemies after an elaborate ritual is conducted, presided over by the Nganga.[31] In Cuba, the Congolese belief would later be influenced by the well-defined Lucumi religion.

The third important religious belief on the island was the "Carabali's Abakua Secret Society". A tribe from the Bantoide trunk of the Ibibios branch, the Efik, took the Abakua rites to Cuba. The Efik were successful warriors, fishermen and merchants who conquered, and settled, the shores along the Calabar Gulf.[32] Once captured and sent to Cuba, these tough warriors formed the Abakua Secret Society to help and protect members and inflict harm on their tormentors if need be. They practiced witchcraft and were known in Cuba as ñañigos.[33]

The Efik share with most of the Bantoide tribes the belief in one good god and one evil one. The beating of the sacred drums, the Ekue, brings forth the voices of the spirit. The Abakua rite takes place in an isolated room, "the room of mysteries" or Sacred Sanctuary, where members receive the blessed message of the beckoned god. During carnival, the ñañigo appeared completely covered from head to toe to conceal their identity from the rest of the world and danced to drumbeats along the festival route. The ñañigos were feared and frequently persecuted by authorities. Like the Congos, the Carabali were also influenced by the Lucumi pantheon and the syncretism with Catholicism.

On sugar plantations during the years 1850-1860, African slaves could be classified by place of origin:

**TABLE VII**

| ORIGIN | % OF SLAVE TOTAL |
|--------|------------------|
| Lucumi | 34.52 |
| Carabali | 17.37 |
| Congo | 16.71 |
| Ganga | 11.45 |

| | |
|---|---|
| Mina | 3.93 |
| Bibi | 2.84 |
| Others | 13.18 [34] |

## *RACIAL PREJUDICE*

The importance of the race issue on the island is well documented in newspaper articles, political debates and contemporary literature. Cuba's best known novel of the period, Cirilo Villaverde's *Cecilia Valdes*, has as central theme the tragic love affair between a wealthy Creole and a beautiful girl of African ancestry. Having slaves at the bottom of the social ladder reinforced the prejudice against people based on the color of their skin. "Free blacks and mulattos suffered from widespread social discrimination, including limited access to public gatherings and prohibitions on interracial marriage... An African 'stain' continued to stigmatize the Cuban descendants of slaves."[35]

The 1862 census shows that of a total population of 1,359,238, there were 729,957 whites, 368,550 slaves and 149,226 free persons of African Ancestry[36] called *libertos*, mostly mulattos. Even some members of the Creole elite who demanded an end to slavery evinced deep prejudice. In 1889, Antonio Maceo visited the island, were he met with several war veterans. During the trip, Maceo tried to schedule a meeting with the president of the Autonomist party, Jose Maria Galvez. Galvez turned down the request. In his memoirs, Spanish General and Governor Camilo Polavieja stated: "Mr. Galvez did not meet with Maceo, nor did he wish to be part of his conspiracy. (He) told me, touching his cheeks... 'You know Maceo is a mulatto'."[37]

Yet despite the manifest social prejudice, Cubans of African ancestry were opening new roads in the difficult route to freedom, respect and economic self-sufficiency. By 1862, fewer than half of the slaves worked on sugar plantations The majority lived and worked in cities, towns and farms. Many became skilled carpenters, shoemakers, tailors, blacksmiths and barbers, while women became maids, hairdressers, midwives and seamstresses. Some enlightened masters taught their slaves to read and write, who, in turn, passed this valuable knowledge on to their own children.

## TABLE VIII
### Distribution of Slave Population by Place of Residence, 1862

| Residence | Males | Females | Total | % |
|---|---|---|---|---|
| Sugar Plantation | 109,709 | 62,962 | 172,671 | 47% |
| Town | 37,014 | 38,963 | 75,977 | 21% |
| Stock-raising farm | 20,414 | 11,100 | 31,514 | 9% |
| Coffee Plantation | 14,344 | 11,598 | 25,942 | 7% |
| Small Farm | 14,253 | 10,597 | 24,850 | 7% |
| Tobacco Farm | 11,622 | 6,053 | 17,675 | 5% |
| Ranch (Hacienda) | 4,220 | 2,698 | 6,918 | 2%[38] |

In the eastern provinces, where the majority of free Afro-Cubans lived, some 23,700 worked on small farms, 15,500 grew tobacco, and 7,400 lived on ranches or stock-raising farms.[39] Free colored Cubans represented more than 16% of the population, and the best educated, such as Juan Gualberto Gomez and Miguel Coyula, were acutely aware of the political and social issues of their time. Some of them had lived briefly in the United States and were shocked by the racial hatred and violence in the South. Eventually, Cubans of African decent would become a militant force against annexation.

## THE END OF SLAVERY

The abolitionists' victory in the U.S. Civil War (1860-1865), along with Britain's anti-slavery prohibitions, made of slavery a dying institution in the Western Hemisphere; in Spain and its colonies, abolitionist triumph was preceded by a campaign in which both Spanish and Creole intellectuals played an active role. On April 2, 1864, the Abolitionist Society was founded in Madrid, with the avowed purpose of ending slavery.[40]

Slavery proponents claimed that abolition would adversely affect the production of sugar, the main cash crop in the West Indies.[41] In 1872, Cuban and Puerto Rican slave owners created the Overseas League Against the Reformation of Slavery, but, by then, the abolitionist movement had enlisted a majority of the most powerful figures in Spanish politics of the time, including Emilio Castelar and Francisco Pi y Margall. The latter, who led the Spanish partisans of Federalism, was a profound writer with a clear understanding of the human right issues. Castelar, the greatest speaker of the Spanish courts, offered his incomparable talent to the cause of abolition, while Pi y Margall devoted many articles to that of freedom.

The slave issue in Cuba faced a dramatic contradiction. The slaves who fought for independence were freed thanks to a clause in the El Zanjón peace treaty, while those who continued working for their masters remained slaves. In an effort to redress this situation, in 1870, the courts granted approval to the so-called Law of Free Birth, which declared free all children of slave parentage born after September 1868.

By the end of the 1870s, most of the sugar plantation leadership were of the notion that slavery was an obsolete institution whose dismantling was long overdue. On February 13, 1880, the Law of Patronage was proclaimed. Stating that slaves would remain for a limited time under the "tutelage" or "patronage" of their former masters, the law of patronage marked the official beginning of abolition.

For four years, the "patronaged" were to be trained and paid a small stipend. Families had to be fed and kept together. In essence, the "patronage," or wardship, was to "provide masters with indemnification in the form of labor and provide the slaves with tutelage."[42] At the time there were some 200,000 slaves in Cuba. A quarter was freed in 1884 according to age and starting with the oldest. Over the next three years, all "patronaged" were freed. By 1888, slavery had come to an end.

## TRANSFORMATION OF THE SUGAR INDUSTRY AND THE DAWN OF THE CUBAN BOURGEOISIE

The war years saw profound and lasting socio-economic changes on the island. Exigencies of the world sugar market — especially the widespread U.S. use of packaged white granulated sugar (an innovation of entrepreneur Henry O. Havemeyer and marketed by the American Sugar Refining Company) — increased crop demand and accelerated the industry's modernization.

The solution was for sugar mills to increase production and reduce labor costs by introducing more mechanical equipment. Plantation owners with enough capital reserves could buy needed machinery and pay workers' salaries, but those lacking money and financial credit were forced to sell their plantations. Large investments became essential for survival in the sugar industry.

Transformation of Cuba's sugar economy revolved around three distinct production roles: the large modern industrial milling complex, called "Central", the "colonies" or large cane growing farms and a salaried labor force. Modernization and concentration of the central milling process led to the development of the "colono" system. The "colono" was an independent cane grower who farmed land he either owned or leased. Under this arrangement, the "Central" owner entered into a contract with the "colonos" to cultivate a certain amount of cane. The "colonos" paid operation costs and, in turn, received a percentage of the profit from the harvest from the "Central" owner.

This sophisticated economic formula put the different stages of sugar production in the hands of the salaried worker, the "colono" and the industrial-plant investor, with the common financial incentive of being efficient and to cooperate with each other.[44] "By 1887, one-third to two-fifths of Cuba's sugar was grown within the "Colono" system, and the percentage was increasing every year."[44] By 1895, there were more than 15,000 colonos in Cuba. Their hard-won wealth would allow them to join the growing middle class.[45]

Responding to the Cuban sugar industry's labor needs, the Madrid government offered free passage to poor Spanish peasants, in exchange for the promise of one year's work on the island. Between 1882 and 1894, more than 224,000 Spaniards, desperately poor, made the transatlantic journey.

Another consequence of the sugar industry's transformation to a central system was the profound change it had on Cuba's social hierarchy, further precipitated by a sudden drop in prices in 1888. In the following years, U.S. investors launched a major push into the island's sugar commodity. Atkins and Company was among the first to acquire the failed plantations of the sacarocracy families who had defaulted on their debts. Other American merchants and private investors followed and bought their way into the Cuban sugar business.

Many of the old families lost land holdings and were forced to sell, declare bankruptcy, or join the U.S. corporations as minority partners. The result was the collapse of the landed aristocracy.

97

During this period, old aristocratic families lost their status at the top of Cuba's social hierarchy. A few of them survived the financial crisis but could not overcome the disintegration of their status as Cuba's most influential class.

The emerging bourgeoisie formed the new upper strata, and the noveau riche became the dominant social class. This revolutionary departure from the stratified European tradition was more in line with the North American ideal of fluid mobility based on individual ability to generate wealth. There were also important changes taking place in the labor force. The end of slavery created a boom in salaried workers, and the new technology created a demand for skilled labor. It was the dawn of modernity in Cuba.

## THE INDUSTRIAL REVOLUTION IN CUBA

The new technological developments sweeping across Europe and North America were present in Cuba at early on. Steamships first came to the island in 1819, with the vessel *Neptuno* opening the Havana-Matanzas shipping lane.[46] By 1823, three steamships linked the northern Pinar del Rio coast with the capital. In 1841, steamships also connected the ports of Santiago de Cuba, Casilda, Cienfuegos and Batabano.[47] This modern form of navigation greatly reduced travel and shipping time between Cuban ports. A voyage from Matanzas to Havana that once took more than two days was reduced to six hours.[48] Important steamships also connected the large production regions in Cuba with U.S. ports.

The first successful steam machine used in a sugar mill began driving a three-iron horizontal roller at a Matanzas plantation in 1817. Sugar industry modernization gained momentum in 1850 with introduction of the Benson and Day "Centrifugal Machine," which could separate sugar crystals from molasses.[49] By 1894, Cuba was the world's largest and most technically advanced sugar producer.

Another industrial innovation that reached Cuba early was the railroad. The first train ran in 1838 between Güines and Havana. By 1894, a remarkable railroad network linked the major *centrales* with embarkation points throughout the island. The industrial revolution came very early to this tropical island, albeit still the colony of a decrepit empire.

Other important sources of U.S. cultural influence in Cuba came through education, immigration and tourism. Impressed with the technological and political achievements of the young Republic, many wealthy Creoles sent their sons to study in North America, with St. Mary College in Baltimore and Fordham in New York among the preferred institutions.[50] These young people took back with them to Cuba the American cultural values, fashions, political beliefs, financial practice and sports appreciation.

An early critic of the trend, Captain General Jose Gutierrez de la Concha, wrote: "Many have sent their sons to the American Union, causing grave damage to their ties of family and nationality... (and) they returned with new habits, ideas and dangerous affectations."[51] Other travelers wrote of the upper class preference for North American governesses to teach their children the English language.[52]

The immigration issue worked both ways. Hundreds of North Americans settled in Cuba, while thousands of Spaniard and Cuban families moved to the United States in search of jobs or freedom from political persecution. Seeking proximity to good harbors, many Americans purchased properties near Cardenas or Matanzas, establishing settlements with strong American character.[53]

In the second half of the Nineteenth Century, Cuban migration to the United States included all social classes on the island. Professionals and laborers, rich and poor alike were the first to migrate to the northern shores. High U.S. custom tariffs precipitated the exodus. The American economic crisis of 1857, combined with the Civil War (1860-1865), led Washington to levy a protectionist tariff on foreign goods, including the coveted Havana Cigars. Almost one-third of Cuba's tobacco exports to the United States were affected. To overcome the tariff barrier, several cigar factory owners relocated their operations to Key West and Tampa. To these factories came the cigar makers and their families. Between 1860 and 1880, thousands of Cuban laborers settled in Florida.[54] Key West's Cuban population grew from 2,800 to 18,000 and Tampa's increased from 2,000 to 23,000.[55]

The North American settlers impacted other regions of the island as well. "The district of Holguin, of which Gibara is the port of entry, can boast a higher English-speaking society than any other foreign place of equal size and note."[56] Also in Oriente, near

Santiago de Cuba, the Bethlehem Steel Corporation created the Juragua Iron Company. Pennsylvania Steel operated Daiquiri's manganese and nickel mines, while the Sigua Iron Company opened up mining production. "In one year, 1892, more than $875,000 worth of iron was shipped to the United States form Santiago de Cuba."[57]

By 1875, Cuba was the favorite destination of thousands of North Americans, mostly sick people seeking the pleasant fresh winds of the mild winter. They came in droves from October to April, with Charleston, South Carolina and New York their main ports of departure. Havana was the transit center through which they rapidly moved to their chosen spas. Among the most popular were Madruga, San Antonio and Santa Maria del Rosario. The American visitors discovered many other beautiful sites that they celebrated upon their return home, such as Guines, Alquizar, Limonar and Guanabacoa.[58] In 1891, the Foster-Canovas agreement was negotiated, giving Cuba preferential access to the U.S. market in exchange for Spanish tariff concessions on U.S. manufactured goods. The result was spectacular, and another wave of investors rushed to the island. Among the most prominent, the New York firm of Perkins and Walsh acquired the largest sugar plantation in the world, the Constancia; the American Refining Company bought the Trinidad Sugar Company; and other New York investors backed the huge sugar operation in the Sancti Spiritus region. As a result, Cuba's sugar production increased from 632,000 tons in 1890 to one million tons four years later.

By 1894, the last year of peace, Cuba was solidly anchored to the U.S. market. The main urban centers were linked by telegraph (telephone service would be introduced in 1889), while the Spanish American Power Company of New York lit the Havana nights. New technology brought electricity, gas, water pumps, generators, building materials, steel, cloth, sewing machines, woven wire mattresses, bicycles, elevators and every innovation available to the American consumer. Cuban society was enjoying the utilitarian ideal of vitality, modernity and progress.

It was also a time of great contradiction. With the island still the colony of a backward Spain, some Cubans became wealthy while others remained desperately poor. More than 90% of people were illiterate. Social frictions between Cubans and Americans rose to the surface. The U.S. cultural influence in Cuba was vast, but the differences, fueled by the language barrier, increased tensions. For some North Americans raised in the puritan tradition, most Cubans had lax moral standards and a propensity for lascivious behavior. Cubans, on the other hand, considered the average American arrogant and vulgar.

It was obvious that Cuba had found and joined its natural market, soon to be the largest and wealthiest in history. But America was also a racist society, and Cuba had a large population of African ancestry that had already fought for their individual rights and were prepared to fight again. As the Nineteenth Century came to an close, Europe was riding the wave of imperialism, and the United States was just getting on board. The doctrine at the time was "The White Man's Burden" to help the worlds less fortunate races.

In 1893, the New York Stock Exchange crashed. A year later, a glut in the sugar market plunged the price to below two cents a pound. Panic seized the island. Washington rescinded the 1891 Foster-Canovas sugar tariff concession to Cuba, and in 1894, Congress passed the Wilson-Gorman act with its higher custom tariffs. In New York, a young Cuban intellectual concluded that the time had come for a new War of Independence. Jose Marti was knocking at the door of history.

While the American influence was increasing, a group of Cuban exiles from the United States returned to Cuba beginning in 1883 to organize the first Protestant Congregations in the country. The earliest examples were the Baptists (1883), Episcopalians (1883), Methodists (1883) and Presbyterians (1890). The Spanish Government granted religious toleration in Cuba in 1886. The Baptists had the largest presence by 1895, when Protestant leaders joined the armed independence struggle. Some of them had conspired against Spanish rule as early as 1892. Some 2,000 Cubans were attending Protestant services by 1895. The largest churches were in the cities of Havana and Matanzas.[59]

## *JOSE MARTI*

If Cuba could be known by any other name, that name should be Marti. During the terrible years of defeat, confusion and exile, this poet of love and life was the wise political counselor, the steady and pragmatic leader who overcame rivalries among the Ten Years War veterans, raised funds for the coming fight, framed the goals of a civil society and rallied Cubans for war in the best liberal tradition of social justice and individual freedom. "Let us march toward the true Republic," Marti wrote, "and place around the star on the new flag this formula for love triumphant, with all and for the good of all."

Jose Marti was born in Havana on January 28, 1853. His father, Mariano Marti, was a rough, illiterate, and underpaid army sergeant from Valencia. His mother, the caring and wise Leonor Perez, was the daughter of an army lieutenant from the Canary Islands. Jose was the couple's oldest child and only son. He shared the household with five sisters, two others having died in infancy. Poverty was the family's constant companion, a fact he addressed directly. "We were poor, very poor," he wrote.

Marti's childhood education began at San Anacleto School, where he met his lifelong friend, the wealthy and noble Fermín Valdez Dominguez. At 13 he enrolled in Rafael Maria de Mendive's school, a turning point in his life. Mendive, a former student of Jose de la Luz y Caballero, was also a liberal thinker committed to Cuba's independence. He became the adolescent Marti's role model and father figure. In a letter to Mendive he wrote: "If I have the strength to face so much, I owe this to you alone. Whatever I have of good and tenderness, I owe it to you,"

While the war raged in the east, a scuffle broke out in a Havana street between Marti's friend Fermín and a group of Voluntaries,[60] which led to Fermín's arrest. A search of his home produced a letter, signed by Marti and Fermín, criticizing a Cuban friend for joining the Spanish army. Both were put on trial. Marti assumed full responsibility for the letter, and when Fermín was sentenced to six months in prison, Jose, age 16, received six years of hard labor. Chained at the ankle, Marti toiled in the stone quarry of San Lazaro. Family friends interceded, and on January 15, 1871, Marti was deported to Spain. He had a ring made from his iron chain, which he wore thereafter. The inscription read "Cuba."

With much financial difficulty, Marti completed his high school education and enrolled as a law student at the Central University of Madrid. He then transferred to the University of Zaragoza, where he got his law degree. While in Spain, Marti witnessed the fall of the monarchy and the political convulsions of the First Republic. His hopes of peaceful reform for Cuba were soon dashed as neither liberal nor conservative, with a few notable exceptions, were willing to change the brutal and corrupt colonial system. After a brief visit to Paris, Marti traveled to Mexico, where he settled in 1875.

While in Mexico, Marti began writing the prestigious *Revista Universal*. He soon became well known in Mexican literary circles. Poet-journalist Luis G. Urbina (1859-1928) wrote, "Justo Sierra, Gutierrez Najera, and I would occasionally run into him taking a stroll with his alter ego, Manuel Mercado. Marti had a dream, a splendid dream. He spoke of mankind, of the world around it ... and the Cuban Revolution. His faith was boundless ... his love of beauty knew no limits." Eminent Mexican poet and diplomat Amado Nervo (1870-1919) said, "I met him. I let my spirit gorge on his resplendent verse, and I listened to the patriot ... Jose Marti has a gift, a charisma ... he made me believe in freedom."

In Mexico, Marti met his future wife, Carmen Zayas Bazan, the daughter of a wealthy aristocratic cattle rancher from Camaguey. In 1877, he visited Havana briefly then traveled to Guatemala with letters of recommendation from Fermín's father to the president. In Guatemala, Marti taught history and literature at the Normal School, head-mastered by his Cuban friend, Jose Maria Izaguirre. His students included Maria Garcia Granados, the beautiful 20-year-old daughter of the former president of Guatemala. Maria possessed a tender charm mixed with a delicate melancholy. She played the piano and sang in the intimacy of her family and friends. Her sensible soul was attracted to the poet, the dreamer of hopes and love. He frequently visited her home and spent long hours in the warmth of her family gatherings. But Marti was already engaged to Carmen and felt duty-bound to fulfill his commitment. He later recalled their sad farewell in a memorable poem. "Like burning bronze/ the farewell kiss/ it was her forehead, the one/ I had loved the most in my life."

Marti returned to Mexico, married Carmen then resumed his teaching job in Guatemala. A few weeks later, Maria Garcia Granados died. Deeply saddened, Marti attended the funeral. Maria's memory inspired one of his best-known poems, "La Niña de Guatemala" ("The Girl of Guatemala"). Marti had a son with Carmen, but the marriage failed. She wanted a household where stability and a steady income were important ingredients in a loving, caring relationship. Marti could provide neither. By 1884, he was totally committed to Cuba's independence.

The culture of Marti, so admired by his contemporaries, is fundamentally Spaniard. Upon meeting the young revolutionary in Madrid, liberal politician Cristino Martos told him, "Cuba is not big enough for your people and mine. Yet you continue to be Spaniard ... drenched in Hispanicism the way a sponge absorbs water. And in your admirable prose, and in your ingenious verses, are Cervantes and Teresa de Jesus, Quevedo, Pi Margal and Bequer." Marti may have been rooted in Spain, but he momentously chose to be Cuban — and to fight for its independence.

From 1881 to 1895, Marti lived in New York City, a center of Cuban dissent from which he launched his revolution. His nationalist sentiment was part of mainstream Nineteenth Century thought. Marti's idea of "patria"[61] (fatherland), which runs throughout his writings, represents a vision of Cuba's past and future liberty. Of his profound belief in freedom and equality, he remarked that politics is the way to lead the diverse racial segment of society into the harmony of justice for the welfare of all."[62]

Marti's political thoughts were influenced by English philosopher Herbert Spencer's view of government. He said as much at the opening of the Pan American conference in New York when referring to the former Spanish colonies in Latin America struggling to overcome the cycles of despotism and chaos. "These countries should walk with Bolivar on one hand and Spencer in the other."[63] Spencer proposed that private property and the civil right of the individual citizen are the fundamental roots of a law-abiding free society. "Industry makes for democracy and peace ... patriotism becomes a love of one's country rather than a hatred of every other ... the status of women rises, and the emancipation of women becomes a matter of course. Superstitious religions give way to liberal creeds whose focus of effort is the ennoblement of human life and character on this earth... History ceases to be a record of personalities and becomes the history of great inventions and new ideas. The power of government is lessened, and the power of productive groups within the state increases, there is a passage from equality in subordination to freedom in initiative, from compulsory cooperation to cooperation in liberty... the State exists for the benefit of the individuals."[64]

Marti promoted Cuba's nationalism at every opportunity and urged others to do likewise.[65] He frequently spoke of the inevitability of Cuba's independence, believing that freedom — as he wrote General Máximo Gomez — was a precious prerequisite of government.[66] In a memorable speech, he said, "If in the affairs of my homeland I could pick one good above all others ... this would be the one I'd choose: I want the first law of our Republic to be the respect of Cubans for the dignity of men."

In the Autumn of 1891, Marti was invited by a group of Cubans in Tampa, Florida to be guest speaker at a fundraising event for the independence cause. He took the train to Florida, opening up one of the most rewarding periods of his life when he addressed cigar workers in Tampa and later Key West. On the night of November 26, Marti surpassed even himself speaking to the humble Creoles gathered at the Liceo Cubano about Cuba's suffering. A sense of hope and determination to free the fatherland charged the gathering. The deeply moved cigar workers committed themselves to Marti's vision of liberty. From their humble paychecks sprang the funds for a revolution.

On January 5, 1892, Marti reorganized the different factions of Cuban exiles into a single group he named "the Cuban Revolution Party," persuading his followers to contribute one-tenth of their earnings to the cause.[67] In this well-thought-out political organization, Marti's revolutionary ideas coalesced into three main objectives: to bring the younger generation into the party, accrediting it inside and outside Cuba; to collect the funds to pay for the fight; and unite leading veterans in a common military effort.

The new organization was made up of a delegate, advisory committees and associations that had previously been revolutionary clubs. Marti was named Delegate. In August 1892, the party leadership authorized his visit to Máximo Gomez, then living in Santo Domingo, to offer him his former post of Commander in Chief.[68] That meeting and Gomez' acceptance marked a turning point in Marti's efforts to unite Cubans. When Antonio Maceo in Costa Rica agreed to the plan submitted by Marti, the foreseen struggle became a viable effort, with all of the preliminary work complete.

## THE PRE-WAR U.S. NAVY

Shortly after the end of the Civil War in 1865, the U.S. Navy began a rapid decline in quality and availability of long-range fighting ships to the point that, according to Secretary of the Navy William C. Whitney in 1880, "it did not have the strength to fight nor the speed to run away."[69] The debate over building an inter-ocean link in either Nicaragua or the Panama isthmus heightened awareness of a neglected Navy in need of an urgent rebirth.

In 1890, U.S. Naval War College president Captain A.T. Mahan published his classic thesis, *The Importance of Sea Power in History*, which held that, since antiquity, only the nations that possessed powerful navies ultimately prevailed in war. The premise had immediate impact and incited debate in the United States and abroad. Kaiser Wilhelm II "ordered a copy of Mahan's book to be placed on every ship in the German Navy." The rebirth of the U.S. Navy began hesitantly and reluctantly, but Secretary Whitney lobbied Congress and began constructing what later became known as "The New Navy." Two prototypes, the heavy-armored cruisers *USS Maine* and *USS Texas*, were built. In 1890, Congress authorized construction of three battleships, the *Indiana*, *Oregon* and *Massachusetts*. The *Iowa* joined them two years later. The ships were finished between 1895 and 1897, just in time for the Spanish-American War. Without their heavy guns and thick armor, the U.S. could not have waged a successful war in Cuba. The New Navy made the difference, proving Mahan's thesis.

## PRELUDE TO WAR

By September 1894, Marti had managed to raise about $58,000. With these funds available, he then proceeded to organize a military expedition known as "The Fernandina Plan."[70] The plan called for three large swift ships — the *Lagonda*, *Amadis* and *Baracoa* — to be contracted in the United States. Each would be loaded with weapons, ammunition and some 200 men and then depart Fernandina port near Jacksonville, Florida. The *Amadis* would pick up Antonio and Jose Maceo, along with Flor Crombet in Costa Rica, and take them to Oriente (Eastern Cuba). The *Lagonda* would carry Serafin Sanchez and Carlos Roloff to Las Villas in central Cuba. The *Baracoa* would take Jose Marti to Santo Domingo, pick up Máximo Gomez and land them near Santa Cruz del Sur in

Camaguey province. The western provinces would simultaneously rise up under the leadership of Julio Sanguily and Jose Maria Aguirre. It was a sound military plan, but on the very eve of the invasion, an indiscretion by Col. Fernando Lopez Queralta alerted Spanish agents and doomed the mission. The details were disclosed to President Cleveland's government, which ordered the immediate confiscation of the Cuban ships and war material.[71]

A telegraph reporting the material's seizure surprised Marti in New York on January 10, 1895. Marti was devastated by the loss of three years of painstaking fundraising among the humble cigar workers and the revolutionary clubs. In Cuba, the sudden exposure of the plan caused a major commotion. Conspirators on the island had no notion of the magnitude of war preparations. "So often punished by deceptions, they became aware of their own power and a faith more vibrant than ever surged from that disaster."[72]

Spanish authorities were even more surprised, having always dismissed Marti as a mad and visionary poet. It was a time of crisis and supreme danger for conspirators on the island. Marti faced the most decisive test of his leadership: what to do next. Party funds were almost exhausted, but he believed that the hour for action could not be delayed any longer. On January 29, 1895, just three weeks after the seizure of the three ships at Fernandina, he signed the order to begin the War of Independence. Juan Gualberto Gomez, the Afro-Cuban intellectual and Marti's coordinator in Cuba, received the order and confirmed that the military leaders on the island accepted the date for the uprising.

In preparation for war, Marti wrote a letter to Gen. Antonio Maceo analyzing why the Fernandina plan had failed. Maceo requested $6,000 to arm and fund an expedition.[73] Marti said he could only supply $2,000, which was all he had. Maceo insisted that $3,500 was the least amount with which to organize a well-equipped 20-man expedition.[74] Gen. Flor Crombet, engaged at the time in a bitter personal dispute with Maceo, said he could organize such a landing with less than $2,000.[75] Pressed for time, Jose Marti decided to give $2,000 to Crombet. Maceo was resentful but still went along with the plan. The issue may have been at the root of Maceo's later problem with Marti. Máximo Gomez also wrote Maceo, "As you well know, everything the Party Delegate has ordered and directed has been rational, fair and urgent... In the instant that I send you these lines, the cable tells us that there is gunsmoke in Cuba, and that on those lands falls the blood of our comrades ... There is no other path for us than to depart wherever we can and however we can ..."[76]

On February 24, 1895, the War of Independence began as planned. Once again the Cubans retook the battlefield. In New York, Jose Marti, the peace-loving poet, was ready to wield the "machete" of freedom. "Now let us give a human and gentle dimension to the sacrifice," he wrote. "For we must make war viable and unshakable ... I will lift up the world. But my only desire would be to stick there, to the last tree, to the last fighter: to die quietly. For me the hour has come."

February 24, 1895, signaled Marti's hour. The uprising failed in the western provinces, while in Oriente it was massive and simultaneous. The date is remembered as the "Grito de Baire" ("Cry of Baire") from the town where the Lora brothers began the fight, when in fact the whole region answered the call to arms. From Manzanillo, Bayamo, Holguin, Tunas, Jiguani, Baracoa, Guantanamo, Santiago and Baire, the veteran warriors rallied to the Independence army. They included experienced commanders: Guillermo Moncada, Jesus Rabi, Quintin Banderas, Pedro (Periquito) Perez, Jose Manuel Capote and the new generation led by Alfredo Justiz, Juan Maspons, Mariano Corona, Guillermo Fernandez Mascaro, Sanchez Vaillant, Jose Miro Argenter, Rafael Manduley, Enrique Brooks, and hundreds of others — old and young, rich and poor, black and white. The lone-star flag of Cuba flew proudly in their hands. In their midst, 65-year-old patrician Bartolome Maso rode his war horse as he had in the old days when he fought alongside Carlos Manuel de Céspedes. Maso was the steady hand that kept the flame lit until the arrival of Maceo, Gomez and Marti.

# CHAPTER VII

## *BETWEEN THE WARS (1878-1895)*

[1] Poderes Omnímodos

[2] Marta Bizcarrondo y Antonio Elorza. *Cuba y España. El Dilema Autonomista 1878-1898.* (Editorial Colibrí, Madrid, 2001), 71.

[3] Rafael Montoro. *Discursos y Escritos.* (Editorial Cubana. Miami, 2000), 38.

[4] Luis Estévez y Romero. *Desde el Zanjón hasta Baire: Datos para la Historia Política de Cuba.* (La Habana: Tipografía "La propaganda Literaria", 1899), 54.

[5] The Hispanic Colonial Bank

[6] Mildred de la Torre. *Autonomismo en Cuba 1878-1898.* (Editorial de Ciencias Sociales. La Habana, 1997), 71.

[7] Maria del Carmen Barcia. *Elites y Grupos de Presión. Cuba: 1868-1898.* (La Habana, 1998), 24-28.

[8] Rafael Montoro, op cit, 197 – 198.

[9] Moreno Frajinals, op cit, Vol II, 140.

[10] Bizcarrondo and Elorza, op cit, 127.

[11] De la Torre, op cit, 71.

[12] Angel Smith and Emma Davila. *The Crisis of 1898.* (Mc Millan Press LTD, 1999), 68.

[13] In later years it was reduced to $5.00 gold pesos

[14] Bizcarrondo and Elorza, op cit, 206.

[15] Montoso, op cit, 176.

[16] De la Torre, op cit, 71.

[17] Ibid

[18] Rafael Montoso, op cit, 37.

[19] Ibid, 38.

[20] Ibid, 41.

[21] Ibid

[22] Roa. *A Pie y Descalso*, op cit, 132.

[23] Manuel Sanguily. *La Lucha política en Cuba. Los Unos y los Otro.* (Imprenta de Soler Álvarez y Cia. La Habana, 1889), 42.

[24] Manuel Sanguily. *Defensa de Cuba.* (Oficina del historiador de la Habana, 1948), 35.

[25] Ely. *Cuando Reinaba.*, 474.

[26] Ibid., 476.

[27] Daniel Boorstin. *The National Experience*, (Vintage Books, New York, 1965), 192.

[28] Isabel y Jorge Castellanos. *Cultura Afrocubana.* (Ediciones Universal. Miami, 1992), Vol III, 18.

[29] Ibid

[30] Ibid, 138.

[31] Ibid, 140 – 141.

[32] Ibid, 210.

[33] Ibid

[34] Moreno Fraginals, op. cit, Vol II, 9.

[35] Rebecca J. Scott. *Slave Emancipation in Cuba. The Transition to Free Labor: 1860-1899.* (University of Pittsburg Press, 1985), 8-9.

[36] Ibid, 7.

[37] Marques de Polavieja. *Relación Documentada de Mi Politica en Cuba: LO que Vi, lo que Hice, lo que Anuncié.* (Madrid. Emilio Minuesan, 1898), 94.

[38] Scott, op cit, 12.

[39] Ibid, 8.

[40] Juan M. Aidaud de la Sartre. *La Primera Republica Española. Historia y Vida.* (Extra 3, Madrid, 1974), 44.

[41] Ibid, 47.

[42] Scott, op cit, 123.

[43] These developments are summarized in Harry F. Guggenheim, The United States and Cuba, a Study in International Relations (New York, 1934) and Robert F. Smith, The United States and Cuba, Business and Diplomacy, 1917-1960 (New York, 1961)

[44] Hugh Thomas, op cit, 276.

[45] Ibid, 277.

[46] José Maria de la Torre. *Lo que Fuimos y lo que Somos. O la Habana Antigua y Moderna.* (La Habana, 1857), 171.

[47] José García de Arboleya, *Manual de la Isla de Cuba; compendio de su historia, geografía, estadística y administración.* (La Habana, 1859), 215.

[48] Francisco González del Valle. *"Antecedentes y Consecuencias de la Dominación Inglesa".* Cuaderno de Historia Habanera No. 12. (La Habana, 1937), 216.

[49] Moreno Fraginals, op cit, 233.

[50] Marrero Fraginals, op cit, 106.

[51] José G. de la Concha. *Memorias sobre el Estado Político, Gobierno y Administración de la Isla de Cuba.* (Madrid, 1853), 63.

[52] Ely, op cit, 682-685.

[53] Richard R. Madden. *The Island of Cuba: Its Resources, Progress and Prospects.* (London, 1849), 83; Herminio Portel Vila. *La Decadencia de Cardenas.* (Estudio Económico, La Habana, 1929), 34-36.

[54] Jean Stubbs. *Tobacco on the Periphery. A case Study in Cuba labor History, 1860-1958.* (Cambridge Eng., 1985), 19-20.

[55] Perez , op cit, 66.

[56] John Glanville Taylor. *The United States and Cuba, Eight Years of Change and Travel.* (London, 1851), 165.

[57] Pérez, op cit, 60.

[58] Levi Marrero, op cit, 81.

[59] Marco Antonio Ramos. *Panorama del Protestantismo en Cuba.* (Editorial Caribe, San Jose, 1986), 107-136.

[60] pro Spanish Militia fanatics

[61] Patria means Fatherland

[62] Fernando Ortiz. *Cuba, Marti and the Race Problem.* (Phylon III, 3rd Quarter 1942), 268.

[63] Manach, op cit, 146.

[64] Durant, op cit, 286-287.

[65] Nuestra America (Jose Marti). Selected Writings, pg.143

[66] De Marti a Máximo Gómez. (Cartas Políticas, septiembre 1892), 104.

[67] Mañach, op cit, 56.

[68] Máximo Gómez. *Diario de Campaña*, 273.

[69] Barbara W. Tuchman. *The Proud Tower: 1890-1914*. (Ballentine Books, New York, 1996), 132.

[70] Benigno Sousa. *Máximo Gómez: El Generalísimo*. (La Habana: Editorial Trópico, 1936), 148.

[71] Horatio S. Rubens. *Liberty: The Story of Cuba*. (New York: Brewer, Warren and Putman, Inc., 1932), 73-76

[72] Manach, op cit,

[73] José Luciano Franco. *Antonio Maceo: Apuntes para una Historia de su Vida.* Manach, op cit,

[74] José Luciano Franco. Antonio Maceo: Apuntes para una Historia de su Vida. (3 Vols) (La Habana, Municipio de la Habana, 1951), Vol. II, 95.

[75] Emilio Roig de Leuchsenring, Antonio Maceo: Ideología Política, Cartas y Otros documentos. 2 Vols. (La Habana: Municipio de la Habana, 1950) Vol. II, 15.

[76] Manach, op cit, 146.

# CHAPTER VIII

# *THE WAR OF INDEPENDENCE: (1895 – 1898)*
# *THE FIRST PHASE: SECURING THE*
# *EASTERN PROVINCES (1895)*

*THE UPRISING – THE RETURN OF CUBA'S LEADERSHIP –*
*THE "MEJORANA" MEETING AND THE DEATH OF JOSE*
*MARTI – MACEO'S VICTORY AT "PERALEJO" – THE CUBAN*
*GOVERNMENT IN ARMS.*

## *THE UPRISING*

The war began on February 24, 1895. Initially, the news did not cause much alarm in Madrid, which assumed it to be a new "little war" doomed to certain failure. The Spanish press appeared optimistic about a quick solution to the conflict. A *LondonTimes'* Madrid correspondent cabled the newspaper on February 28: "The government reports from Havana that its troops have defeated a party of *bandoleros*, killing their leader, Manuel Garcia. The insurrection in the village of Baire has been totally liquidated[1].

The British journalist issued a new report on March 4: "The Cuban Autonomists' concur with the government that the uprising is of no major political importance. Spanish Captain-General Emilio Calleja evidently believed that his 16-thousand troops were adequate to quell the new uprising. Even so, an expeditionary force of 9,000 sailed from Spain, and constitutional guarantees were suspended on the island[2]."

On January 31, 1895, with his orders for the uprising already given, Marti left for Montecristi in Santo Domingo intending to join Gen. Gomez. On February 25, they learned of the uprising from "Mayia" Rodriguez, who had been in the capital. Anxious to ensure his participation, Marti wrote Maceo the next day. The following weeks saw feverish preparations, aided by Santo Domingo president Ulises Hereaux (Lilis), who supplied 2,000 pesos.

On March 25, Marti drafted the Manifesto of Montecristi,

signed by himself and Máximo Gomez. In it they renewed the basis for the new independent Republic, forged on the bloody fields of the Ten Years War. The Manifesto was a balanced exhortation that avidly sought a national consensus. "War is not in the serene view of those who today represent it ... the insane victory of one Cuban party over another, or even the humiliation of one mistaken group of Cubans... the war that has resumed in Cuba is not the cause for jubilation that might embark toward thoughtless heroism but for the responsibilities that should concern the founders of nations."

Marti preached warfare without hate and urged the conciliatory coexistence of all residents in a peaceful and free nation. In the Montecristi Manifesto, committed democrat Marti condemned the two endemic evils of Hispanic America: ignorance and caudillismo. He rejected fear of the black man as promoted by intransigent Spaniards. "Another fear they perhaps seek to validate today, with the pretext of prudence and cowardice, the foolish fear, never justified in Cuba, of the black race. The Cuban black has no schools of ire, just as in the war he did not have a single flaw of earned superiority or insubordination. On their shoulders securely rode the Republic, only those who hate the black see hatred in the black."

In the Montecristi Manifesto, Marti also extended a friendly hand to the Spaniard, with the sadness of one who loves his roots and wishes to embrace them in the new and free Republic. "More than saluting him in death, the revolution hopes to welcome him in life." Finally, the Manifesto made a serene and dignified call for unity and generosity in the fight for Independence.

"Today, in proclaiming from the threshold of this beloved land the spirit and doctrines that produced and advance this whole and humanitarian war that once more unites the Cuban people, invincible and indivisible, let us be fair in invoking, as guides and helpers to our people, the magnanimous founders, the identical work of two generations, jointly making the declaration for the common responsibility of representing them, and in proof of the unity and solidarity of the Cuban revolution, the delegate of the Cuban Revolutionary Party, created to order and aid the actual war, and the General in Chief, elected by all active members of the Liberating Army." Montecristi, March 25, 1895. Jose Marti and Máximo Gomez.

## *THE RETURN OF CUBA'S LEADERSHIP*

On March 25, Antonio Maceo, his brother Jose, Agustin Cebreco, Flor Crombet and 17 others left Costa Rica aboard the steamship *Adirondack*. This was the expedition organized by Crombet with Marti's $2,000. The ship was en route to New York, but the captain agreed to sail near Oriente so that the Cubans could disembark in small boats. But at the last moment, the captain could not fulfill his promise and instead took the group to Fortune Island, a British colony in the Bahamas. There the captain arranged for a friend to procure a boat for the Cubans. A *goleta*, a type of rugged sailboat, was hired for 100 dollars in U.S. coins. The group sailed on April 1 in a stormy sea and landed in Duaba Beach near Baracoa, just before the *goleta* capsized and sank. The expedition's courage and determination had prevailed. Finally, 17 years after his last departure from the battlefield, Antonio Maceo returned to lead his countrymen in their struggle for freedom.

Spanish authorities soon detected the Maceo party and mounted a relentless and ferocious persecution. In the ensuing fight, Flor Crombet was killed and a few others were captured, but most insurrectionists escaped in different directions. Maceo and three men lived for days on sour wild oranges before being rescued by the rebel forces of Pedro (Periquito) Perez. The following day, Maceo took command of the Cuban army in Oriente province. His brother Jose and Agustin Cebreco were also rescued. An outstanding group of military leaders were now safe at their bases.

On the same day that the Maceo expedition was landing in Cuba, Máximo Gomez and Jose Marti began their journey. A crooked ship's captain deceived them and stranded them on Inagua Island. But by April 5, the small group of six secured a promise from the captain of the German steamship *Nordstream* to take them close to Oriente and allow them make the final approach in a small boat. The landing took place on April 11, 1895, at Playita, a small beach between Guantanamo and Baracoa in eastern Cuba. Marti described it in his diary, "They lower the boat. Raining hard as we push off. Set course wrong. Conflicting opinions in the boat. Another downpour. Rudder lost. We get on course. I take forward oar. Salas rows steadily. 'Paquito' Borrero and the General help in the stern. We strap on our revolvers. Steer towards clearing. Moon comes up red ... we land on a rocky beach ..."

The group moved quickly inland into the wooded mountains. Two days later, aided by a local farmer, they reached the safety of Felix Ruanes' base. On April 25, Jose Maceo, already in command of Oriente's eastern military district, greeted the Gomez-Marti party with a moving and vibrant embrace, the veterans and the poet sharing the historic moment. After so many years of toil and hardship, Marti was back in his beloved Cuba fighting side by side with the soldiers of freedom that he had, more than anyone else, placed on the battlefield. Jose Maceo presented Marti with a beautiful white horse and took him to meet his brother Antonio.

While the principal revolutionary leaders were secure in the rebel bases, the Spanish Prime Minister Antonio Canova Del Castillo put Martinez Campos in command of the army in Cuba and arranged for the deployment of 7,000 troops to the island. Martinez Campos, the general that negotiated the end of the Ten Years War at El Zanjón, landed at Guantanamo, where he received a hero's welcome, with bands and cheering crowds lining the narrow streets[3].

## THE MEJORANA MEETING AND THE DEATH OF JOSE MARTI

On May 5, Marti, Gomez and Maceo met at the old sugar mill of La Mejorana. After the initial greetings, Gomez and Maceo sat alone for a short time, presumably to discuss Gomez' imminent march into Camaguey and the invasion of the western provinces[4]... Marti soon joined them and the three men retired behind closed doors to discuss formation of the Cuban government in arms. What was actually discussed at the meeting is unknown, except for Marti's account in his last diary. Although Marti mentioned no discussion of military issues, the conjecture is that Gomez and Maceo reviewed such matters during their short conference.

According to Marti's diary, he and Maceo disagreed on the composition of the government. "Maceo had other thoughts on government – a general's junta... I cannot unravel Maceo's conversation. Are you staying with me or leaving with Gomez? He talked, interrupting me as if I was the continuation of the bickering government and its representative. I see him hurt. He says to me 'I love you less than before' because of the Flor (Crombet) expedition and the moneys[5]." Maceo was hurt, but he was also trying to avoid the mistakes of the Ten Years War, in which the civilian government hindered the military campaigns with its meddling in the conduct of that war. Maceo favored a junta headed by Gomez to lead the fight without interference from a civilian group[6]. What position Gomez took is unknown, for he does not mention the meeting in his diary.

Based on the available evidence, it can be assumed that Gomez supported Maceo, since the Maceo plan was similar to Gomez' 1884 plan. Maceo's position ultimately prevailed, and Marti accepted the army's independence from the future civilian government and agreed to return to the United States to raise funds for the war effort.

Related to the formation of a government was the question of the Cuban Army command structure. Maceo, basing his authority on the 1868 Cuban Constitution, insisted that he should be the Cuban Army's commander in Oriente province since that had been his position at the end of the Ten Years War. This demand was also accepted. After the meeting, the three leaders had lunch with some of Maceo's troops. Maceo again raised the question of government formation and Marti expressed his disagreement with a junta form of government. Right after lunch, Maceo departed with the bulk of his forces, leaving a small escort to stay with Gomez and Marti. That night, Marti slept with a heavy heart and "sad ideas."[7] These conflicts were to haunt Cubans to day.

The following morning, "abysmally dismayed" — Gomez wrote in his diary — with Maceo's conduct, Gomez and Marti were met by Maceo's soldiers, who again took them to his base. In this second meeting, Maceo asked them to excuse his behavior the day before and introduced them to his troops[8]. After about three hours, Gomez and Marti left Maceo's headquarters and headed toward Manzanillo, where Gen. Bartolome Maso was stationed. On May 13, they camped on the plains of Dos Rios, where the rivers Cauto and Contramaestre meet. Maso arrived with his cavalry, and Marti addressed the troops, who responded with enthusiastic "vivas" to Marti, Gomez and the fatherland. This would be Marti's farewell speech. He wrote his Mexican friend, Manuel Mercado, concerned about the growing expansionist mood in North America. "It is my duty ... to prevent, through the independence of Cuba, the U.S.A. from spreading over the West Indies and falling with added weight upon other lands of Our America. All I have done up to now and shall do thereafter is to that end... I know the Monster because I have lived in its lair — and my weapon is only the slingshot of David."[9]

On the morning of May 19, news reached Gomez of Spanish troops in the vicinity, commanded by Colonel Ximenez de Sandoval. The general decided to go out in search of the enemy, but, unable to find any trace, returned to his base at Dos Rios. It was a radiant day for Marti. He was finally in the thick of the struggle, putting an end to the vicious remarks regarding his absence from the Ten Years War's bloody battlefields. He was there among veterans and young soldiers, sharing their fight and its danger.

Suddenly, shots rang out. The Spanish force had discovered Gomez' trail and was fast approaching the Cuban camp. A defensive perimeter was hastily formed, while part of the cavalry headed by Gomez and Maso charged at the enemy. A spirited fight ensued. Just before mounting his horse, Gomez pleaded with Marti to stay at the base. It was a confusing situation. What prompted Marti's decision to ride is unknown. He mounted his horse, invited his aide, Angel de la Guardia, to follow him and galloped out to join the fight. Nobody knows his last conscious thoughts during his brief and lonely charge. A few minutes into the ride, he was struck by a fusillade and killed. Cuba's Apostle of Independence died "de cara al sol" ("facing the sun").

With Jose Marti's death, the revolution lost its inspired missionary of goodwill and love, fully committed to the democratic principles of both civil and individual rights. Marti had inspired a vision of self-reliance and heroism. He was dearly missed as the Cubans embarked, with faulty charts, on the adventure of freedom.

## MACEO'S VICTORY AT PERALEJO

Hard pressed for time as the rebellion threatened to spread across the island, Martinez Campos decided to take up the first offensive against Antonio Maceo's forces in Oriente, planning to deal with Máximo Gomez later. Campos took the field with several columns to attack Maceo near Bayamo[10]. The Captain General departed the port of Manzanillo at the head of 1,500 troops. Two other columns were to march from Tunas and Santiago to join the campaign against Maceo, a force of over 5,000 altogether.[11] The rebels assembled nearly 3,000 men in position to prevent the joining of the marching columns.[12]

At dawn on July 13, 1895, Maceo deployed his infantry along the plains of Peralejos, 10 miles from Bayamo. The cavalry was kept in a rear position as reserve. They awaited Campos' column. Maceo planned an ambush to crush the Spaniards with a fusillade and a cavalry charge. But the Spaniards did not arrive as expected; instead, Gen. Fidel de Santocildes, Campos' second in command, suddenly appeared with 500 men behind the insurgent's lines. Maceo, who was personally in command of the rebel cavalry, immediately realized the danger and charged the advancing Spaniards, gaining time to redeploy his infantry to face the oncoming column.

Here was the Cuban hero at his best, proving once more his tactical genius and leadership. Maceo was pure courage with a brilliant mind. His rapid response overcame a dangerous attack, as he swiftly directed difficult maneuvers with precise instructions until his forces encircled Campo's column.

Spanish newspaper correspondent Andres Ollero reported on the battle at Peralejos: "Our soldiers, in fact, were soon attacked from every direction, and Gen. Santocildes, at the head of his column, broke the enemy's lines several times and advanced, only to be encircled again. Both the regulars and the rebels fought fiercely and in the midst Santocildes was killed."[13]

According to eyewitnesses, Gen. Campos remained calm and in control of his beleaguered troops, he gathered his forces in hollow squares, using wagons for protective breastwork, and he personally directed the defenses.[14] The fierce fight lasted more than four hours until the rebels began running out of ammunition. Late in the afternoon, the Spaniards broke through the Cuban encirclement and reached the safety of Bayamo's forts, which the captain general entered in shock and disbelief.

From Peralejo, Maceo marched to the Santiago region. On August 30, he learned that his brother Jose, lying in a rebel field hospital with acute sciatica, was about to be attacked by Col. Canella's 900-man force based in Guantanamo. Maceo immediately mobilized Agustin Cebreco's crack troops, who marched at top speed to the aid of the bed-ridden general. The following day when Antonio Maceo arrived in Sao del Indio, he found his sick brother riding a horse alongside the vanguard of

Cebreco's troops. The bitter, bloody fight lasted more than nine hours. In the afternoon, the Spaniards began to disengage and struggled back into Guantanamo. The two Cuban brothers embraced each other with the deep affection that was a trademark of the Maceo household. Antonio believed Jose to be the bravest of the brave among the rebel chiefs, often remarking that were Jose to have been there, he could have captured Campos at Peralejos.

A few weeks after Peralejo, Martinez Campos, Spain's best politician-general, wrote Prime Minister Canovas about the war and his reluctance to carry on a brutal extermination campaign against the independence-minded Cubans. "We could concentrate on the families of the countryside in the towns but ... the misery and hunger would be terrible. I would then have to give rations, which reached 40-thousand a day in the last war. It would isolate the country from the towns but it would not prevent espionage, which would be done by women and children. Perhaps we will come to this, but only in a last resort, and I think I lack the qualities to carry through such a policy.

Among our present generals, only Weyler has the necessary capacity for such a policy, since only he combines the necessary intelligence, courage and knowledge of war. Reflect, my dear friend, and if after discussion you approve the policy I have described, do not delay in recalling me. We are gambling with the destiny of Spain; but I retain certain beliefs and they are superior to everything; they forbid me to carry out summary executions and similar acts. The insurrection today is more serious and more powerful than early in 1876. The leaders know more and their manners of waging war are different from what it was then... Even if we win in the field and suppress the rebels, my loyal and sincere opinion is that, with reforms or without reforms, before 12 years we shall have another war."[15]

The war in the eastern provinces was not going well for the colonial government, and the rebels were beginning to implement plans for invading the western provinces. Following Marti's death, Gomez marched into Camaguey province, where most Cubans — particularly older, upper class families — opposed the war.[16] For more than a month, Gomez stayed close to the provincial capital, making a wide circle around it and firing on the outskirts of the city every night.[17] This operation was called the "Circular Campaign," and it was one of Gomez' finest military feats.

## THE CUBAN GOVERNMENT IN ARMS

By the end of the summer of 1895, Cuban delegates began gathering at Jimaguayu, in Camaguey province, to discuss the new Constitution of the Republic and formation of a rebel government. Each of the five army regions or corps sent four representatives, 20 in all. Each article in the Constitution was debated until a final consensus was reached. Marti's vision of checks and balances prevailed, but with a special provision granting the commander in chief full authority over military matters. The Jimaguayu Constitution created a government council headed by the president of the Republic, with powers to levy taxes, issue paper currency and request and approve loans.

The delegates elected Salvador Cisneros Betancourt, the aristocrat patriarch from Camaguey, as president, with Bartolome Maso as vice president. There were also the Secretaries for War, Interior, State and Treasury. Gen. Máximo Gomez was appointed Commander in Chief and General Antonio Maceo second-in-command or Lieutenant General. Tomas Estrada Palma was named the Cuban Government's official envoy in Washington. The Cuban rebels were following political precedent set by previous revolutions to clearly frame their objectives and establish governmental institutions. Now came the most difficult task: winning the war for Cuba's independence. With this goal in mind, Gen. Gomez sent letters to Gen. Maceo in Oriente with instructions for organizing an invasion force and joining him in Camaguey, as soon as possible, for the invasion of the sugar emporium in the western provinces.

# CHAPTER VIII

## THE WAR OF INDEPENDENCE (1896-1898)
## THE FIRST PHASE: SECURING THE EASTERN
## PROVINCES (1895)

---

[1] London Times. March 1, 1895 pg. 5

[2] Fernandez Almagro, op cit, 236

[3] José Ibañez Marín. *General Martines Campos*. (Madrid, 1908), 388.

[4] Benigno Sousa. *Ensayo Histórico Sobre la Invasion*. (Habana, Imprenta Ejército, 1948), 26.

[5] Martí. *Ultimo Diario*, op cit, 42.

[6] Emilio Roig de Leuchsenring. *Ideario Cubano: Antonio Maceo* (La Habana, Municipio de La Habana, 1946), 86. Maceo expressed his position at La Mejorana in a letter writen to Manuel Sanguily.

[7] Martí, op cit, 41.

[8] Gomez, op cit, entry of May 5, 1895, pg. 373

[9] Martí. *Obras Completas*. Vol I, 271-3

[10] By June 1895, there were 52,000 Spanish soldiers in Cuba fighting between 6,000 to 8,000 revolutionaries. G. Maura Gamazo. *Historia Crítica del Reinado de Don Alfonso XIII*. 2 Vols. (Madrid, 1925), 235.

[11] Fernández Almagro, op cit, 246.

[12] José Miró Argenter. *Cuba: Crónicas de la Guerra*. (La Habana: Editorial Lex, 1945), 65-66.

[13] Andrés F. Ollero. *Teatro de la Guerra*. (Madrid, 1898)

[14] Ibid

[15] Fernandez Almagro, op cit, 246-247.

[16] Letter from Salvador Cisneros Betancourt to Bartolomé Masó, Souza, Ensayo, pg. 27-28

[17] Emory W. Fee. *Ten months with the Cuban Insurgents*. (Century Magazine, June 1898), 304.

# CHAPTER IX

# THE WAR OF INDEPENDENCE (SECOND PHASE 1896-1897). THE INVASION OF THE WESTERN PROVINCES

*THE FALSE RETREAT AND THE ADVANCE INTO HAVANA AND PINAR DEL RIO PROVINCES – A TRAIL OF BURNING SUGAR FIELDS – MARTINEZ CAMPOS OUT, WEYLER IN – WEYLER'S MILITARY OFFENSIVE – THE DAWN OF U.S. IMPERIALISM – THE YELLOW PRESS – THE ELUSIVE VICTORY – SPAIN'S MILITARY COMMITMENT IN CUBA – THE DEATH OF ANTONIO MACEO – THE DESTRUCTION OF THE SUGAR INDUSTRY – ONE FOURTH OF THE SPANISH SOLDIERS DIED IN CUBA – THE ANARCHISTS AND THE DEATH OF CANOVAS DEL CASTILLO – WEYLER: BACK TO SPAIN.*

On October 20, 1895, at historic Mangos de Baragua, in Oriente, Antonio Maceo assembled the forces that were to march into the Western provinces, the heart of the sugar industry, which in the 1894 harvest had for the first time reached the one million ton mark and was the cradle of the greatest North American investment. By the time Antonio Maceo left his stronghold in Oriente, he had 1,403 men, mostly cavalry, but as they moved westward their ranks began to swell with the addition of independence-minded Cubans.

The invading contingent crossed most of Camaguey in 21 days without meeting Spanish forces and on November 28, approached the old Spanish palisade called La Trocha located between the towns of Jucaro and Moron. The next day, very early in the morning, Maceo feigned an attack on Moron, and while the Spaniards rushed troops to defend that town, the rebel forces made their way through a pass a few miles south without sustaining any losses. That same night, Maceo met Gen. Máximo Gomez, who had been in las Villas since October 30. Together their forces numbered some 2,600.[1]

On December 2, 1895, the invasion columns had a brief encounter with a large enemy force under Gen. Alvaro Suarez Valdez at La Reforma in Central Cuba. Winston Churchill, a lieutenant on leave from the British Army, was riding with Suarez Valdez and witnessed the skirmish. Here is how Churchill described the action. "Our force was fired upon by concealed Cubans. Gen. Suarez Valdez ordered an attack. The Spaniards displayed their traditional courage under fire; the skirmish came to be known as "The Battle of La Reforma."[2] This brief encounter was heralded by the Spaniards high command as a great military victory.[3] La Reforma was one of the first army reports issued during the invasion of the Western provinces.

The Spanish government and later historians accepted such reports at face value, though usually exaggerated and, in some cases, even fabricated. Eventually inaccurate, the information made it impossible for headquarters to know the strength and whereabouts of the rebel forces at any given time. Both Martinez Campos and later Valeriano Weyler suffered from the same misleading reporting. So outrageous and fantastic were these field reports of Cuban losses, that, according to a North American professor living in Cuba who took the time and trouble to compute the numbers, 395,856 Cubans had been killed, 726,690 wounded and 451,100 taken prisoner.[4] This was out of a total population of fewer than 600,000 males on the island. The Spanish government continued receiving inaccurate reports for the remainder of the war.

The next day, the invasion column moved into the mountainous region of Sancti Spiritus, where they rested, were re-supplied by the local peasantry and explored feasible routes for the westward march. The strategic maneuver seemed to confuse the enemy. Gen. Jose Oliver, a seasoned and able commander, believed that the Cubans had been defeated and forced to take refuge in the mountains and that a raid into the rich sugar region of Cienfuegos would be entirely too difficult for the rebels.[5] Martinez Campos shared this view. He felt strongly that at long last Gomez and Maceo had been stopped. Now was the time to entrap and wipe them out. He ordered several battalions to march into the area and gain control of mountain passages while other forces were to advance into rebel positions. The Cuban forces were about to be encircled and destroyed, so believed the Spaniards.

Concerned with their situation, Gomez and Maceo searched for a way out while engaged in a bloody rear guard fight. Early on December 15 they found it, in the plains of Mal Tiempo near Cienfuegos. The 600-man force of Col. Narciso Rich, spotting the approaching rebels, began organizing for the battle. Riding at the head of the column, Maceo spotted the enemy force and quickly realized the need to attack before they could complete their deployment. He ordered his bugleman to sound a cavalry charge. The whole column sprang into action wielding machetes and rushed forward in a head-on attack.

When Gomez heard the bugles, he raced forward, "like in Palo Seco, and overwhelmed the strongest Spanish position."[6] The fight was brief but fierce. The Spaniards held on for a few desperate minutes, but the horsemen pressed on with the attack and broke the Spaniards' ranks. One eye witness wrote: "In honor of the Spanish Army, I must declare that neither before nor after during the war I saw their soldiers lose their moral and break ranks."[7] The battle of Mal Tiempo was a decisive turn of events. The rebel forces had broken through and were now at the gates of Cuba's sugar emporium. Suddenly and unexpectedly, the Spanish colonial system was shaken to its very foundations.

After Mal Tiempo, the revolutionary army, reinforced by a light brigade of 700 men from Las Villas, commanded by a young doctor named Juan Bruno Zayas, headed northwest toward Matanzas Province, which the Cubans reached on December 20. Matanzas was, after Havana, the richest and most densely populated province in Cuba.[8] Martinez Campos, eager for a victory after the Mal Tiempo fiasco, took personal command of the forces in the provinces to try to stop the Cubans from going any further by concentrating a large number of troops in the city of Colon. Campo's objective was to trap the Cubans between the Hanabana River and Colon and finish them off once and for all in a decisive battle. When Martinez Campos finally arrived in Colon, the Cubans had not only crossed the Hanabanilla River, but had also bypassed Colon.

On December 23, 1895, the rebel forces attacked and entered the town of Coliseo. Just as the Cubans were leaving, General Martinez Campos was arriving. There followed an intense exchange of fire between the Spanish front lines and rebel rear guard, but Martinez Campos decided not to pursue the Cubans. He was content to have possession of the city. For Martinez Campos personally, Coliseo was a humiliating political upset. Not only did he have to publicly admit the Cuba's presence in Matanzas after having made assurances that the Cubans would not leave Las Villas, but more importantly, his failure to prevent the Cubans from destroying Matanzas' vast agricultural wealth.

From Coliseo, Martinez Campos continued on to Havana, where he ordered the concentration of all available forces, plus several pieces of artillery, on a line following the railroad from Matanzas city to Union de Reyes.[9] Such a concentration of troops along a very narrow, flat region, crisscrossed by railroads, was impassable for the Cubans. Fortunately for the invaders, Gomez learned of the Spanish plan from Cuban informants working on cargo and passenger trains traveling between Havana and Matanzas provinces.[10]

## THE FALSE RETREAT AND THE ADVANCE INTO HAVANA AND PINAR DEL RIO PROVINCES

Gomez and Maceo met on the night of December 23 to discuss the new situation and it was at this meeting that they conceived the most brilliant maneuver of the invasion, what would be later called the "False Retreat." The plan consisted of turning back towards Las Villas to fool the Spanish military leaders into thinking that the Cubans were headed back east. To this effect, the invaders quickly turned eastward. At the same time, the Cubans made sure their trail was well noticed. They also left the railroads untouched for the plan was to draw as many Spanish troops as possible into Las Villas so as to leave Matanzas unguarded and facilitate the invasion of Havana Province.

The move was a success as Campos ordered the transfer of most of his troops in Matanzas to Las Villas, commandeering all available trains and ships for this purpose. Indeed, Campos was so convinced that the rebels had been stopped that on December 29, he assured his government in Spain that the negative reports had been a false alarm. Campos cabled Madrid that the Cubans were fatigued and were retreating to Las Villas[11] but, that same day, the Cubans had already turned back and were marching westward.

The invasion of Havana province, in theory impossible, turned out to be the easiest for the Cubans since Camaguey. The heavy movement of Spanish troops to Las Villas as a result of the "False Retreat" contributed much to the Cubans' success. Besides, most of the Spanish troops in the province were needed to protect the city of Havana and its sugar mills. Still, eight Spanish columns (more than 10,000 men) were available for combat duty, and, with the existing railroad facilities, could have made it extremely difficult for the invaders. Instead, the Spanish high command fell into a paralysis. Between January 2 and January 7, the invading forces conquered a string of 11 towns and a number of important cities, including Guira de Melena, almost without resistance.[12]

On their way they took hundreds of weapons and thousands of rounds of ammunition from the captured towns, while hundreds of Cubans joined them everywhere. When the invaders came as close as 12 miles from Havana, the Spanish authorities panicked and issued orders to barricade the city out of fear of an imminent attack.[13]

News of the worsening situation was reaching Spain, and some newspapers were demanding Martinez Campos' recall. *El Heraldo de Madrid* editorialized: "What is happening is truly inconceivable. It is incomprehensible how experienced generals ... can be fooled in the way they are being fooled. It is beyond amazement... it is stupefying. Of course, the government must realize that this situation cannot be tolerated."[14]

On January 7, Maceo and Gomez divided their forces at Hoyo Colorado on the border between Havana and Pinar del Rio provinces. Maceo took 1,560 men to Pinar del Rio, while Gomez stayed in Havana with a little more than 2,000. As the rebels took town after town along Pinar del Rio's northern coast, the reception was tumultuous with hundreds joining their cause.[15] Maceo's march was made easier by Gomez who stayed in Havana province with the remainder of the Cuban forces preventing the Spanish from reinforcing and stopping Maceo in the narrow province of Pinar del Rio. A large Spanish force under the command of Gen. Ramon Echague left the city in pursuit and met the Cubans at Las Taironas, seven miles away from the city of Pinar del Rio. The rebels fought the Spaniards for over two hours, with both sides claiming victory.

Finally, on January 22, 1896, Antonio Maceo, at the head of the invasion forces, reached Mantua, the westernmost town of the island. The Cubans had accomplished a great strategic victory, unthinkable just three months before. The rebels, averaging about 3,000 men, had marched across some 1,200 miles of territory guarded by almost 140,000 Spanish soldiers. The first of the direct and indirect results was accomplishment of the invasion's foremost objective: bringing the war to Cuba's sugar emporium. Furthermore, Spain's most respected general, Arsenio Martinez Campos, had been forced to resign as a result of having been completely outmaneuvered by Gomez and Maceo.

## A TRAIL OF BURNING SUGAR FIELDS

The impact of the invasion was fully realized by all. *The Review of Reviews* not only acknowledged it, but also predicted a possible victory by the patriots. "The Cuban insurgents, whose field of action until recently had been confined to the eastern and central districts (of Cuba), have written the past few weeks — under the remarkably brilliant leadership of General Gomez, with the dashing cooperation of Maceo and his troops, carried the war into the province of Havana... their marching and counter-marching has been one series of surprises to the Spanish, and the revolution has gained much new headway... If the patriots can avoid risking too much in open battles with the great Spanish army now in Cuba, they are practically sure to win."[16]

Spanish historian Fernando Gomez wrote: "... since the arrival of Marti, Gomez and Maceo, the insurrection grew stronger until the disaster of the invasion of the west occurred, which extended the war throughout the island as if it were a huge trail of burning powder.[17] Gomez' huge trail of 'burning powder' had a devastating effect upon the economy of Cuba. It completely wrecked the island's sugar economy. The Cuban sugar harvest dropped from over 1,400,000 tons in 1895 to only 225,000 tons in 1896."[18]

The events in Cuba were closely watched in Germany, the largest beet sugar producer and keenest competitor of "colonial" cane sugar. The *Hamburger Nachrichten* of the great German port, Hamburg, issued the following report concerning the conditions of the Cuban sugar industry (as quoted by the *Literary Digest*): "... having devastated Matanzas, the rebels entered Havana and Pinar del Rio... wherever they came, the harvest was burned in the fields, laborers who continued to work were fired upon, the railroads were destroyed and telegraphic communication interrupted. Only a very small portion of the harvest of sugar cane can be saved. Of the 361 *centrales* (sugar mills) in Cuba, only 32 are working now. The rest have been forced to shut down, partly because the harvest is destroyed, partly for fear of attacks. The planters have endeavored to obtain the permission of Máximo Gomez to carry on their work, but it has been refused. Unless the government manages to quell the rebellion soon, the fields cannot be tilled, and there is no hope for a harvest next year."[19]

Last but not least, even the extremely pro-Spanish *Diario de la Marina* recognized the seriousness of the situation: "... to the gravity of the advancement of the insurgent bands headed by Gomez and Maceo into these western zones, must be added the fact that they have not only reached the West but, in doing so, have devastated the entire territory that is Cuba's granary." The *Diario* ended its remarks with the not so rhetorical question: How could it have happened? "...the advancement of the rebel forces, divided into large columns headed and flanked by numerous cavalry troops, through the vast network of columns posted by our army to stop them, is a motive for amazement."[20]

The effects of the invasion nearly ruined Spain, not only because of the loss of Cuba's commercial assets after the destruction of the island's rich sugar cane fields, but, most importantly, by the fact that Spain had to spend literally "every penny and every man" in its effort to keep Cuba, as Prime Minister Canovas had once promised its people.

On October 5, 1895, The *Economist* magazine published this report on Spanish financial difficulties: "... Spain had been forced to go to the European money markets for the first time since the beginning of the war to obtain the necessary funds to finance the war."[21]

## MARTINEZ CAMPOS OUT, WEYLER IN

Finally, the success of the invasion of the Western Provinces meant the end of Spain's most respected general, Arsenio Martinez Campos. Having been completely outmaneuvered by Gomez and

Maceo, Martinez Campos was forced to resign. On January 20, 1896, he telegraphed Canovas: "I have failed. The responsibility is mine. The government has in no way restricted my action, neither political nor military."[22]

The architect of the "Peace of Zanjón" was thoroughly defeated. Here was a man who had dearly understood the urgency of political reform in Cuba as a way of avoiding a much bigger conflict. While captain general of Cuba in 1879, Martinez Campos, pushed for reform, advising his government of the need to take the Cubans' deep grievances seriously. As he wrote Canovas: "If we want to avoid Spain's future ruin we need to enter openly in the realm of the liberties."[23] His advice was not taken seriously and the Cubans went back to war. With the sugar economy destroyed, Spain stubbornly marched into a bloody and bitter disaster. To succeed Martinez Campos as captain general of Cuba, Canovas chose Valeriano Weyler y Nicolau, Marquis of Tenerife.

During the final months of his administration, Grover Cleveland, U.S. President pressed on with his offer to mediate a peaceful end to the conflict, including full autonomy "while preserving for Cuba the sovereignty of Spain."[24] The offer was rejected. The Spanish leadership exhibited remarkably poor political timing. A year and a half later, Madrid granted full autonomy to Cuba, but by then, it was too late to make a difference, with Cleveland gone from the White House and public opinion and the Yellow Press calling for direct military confrontation with Spain over Cuba.

Cleveland's offer to mediate a peaceful settlement might have made a difference; the fact that it was not even explored tells the story of a feeble government, incapable of implementing a promising initiative. For Spain it was another lost opportunity to avert the looming disaster and improve channels of political and economic cooperation with the leading industrialized nation of the world.

## WEYLER'S MILITARY OFFENSIVE

On January 25, 1896, Valeriano Weyler sailed from Barcelona to Havana, where he arrived on February 10 to be welcomed by the pro-Spanish population.[25] The new captain-general was quick to realize the severity of the insurrection. In an address to the crowd gathered in front of the Governor's Palace, Weyler said, "I shall not hesitate to punish with all the most rigorous sanctions those who in any way help the enemy cause... for the time being I shall disregard all political considerations. My mission is to end the war. I have come to uphold Spanish sovereignty ... as long as the war goes on. I will ignore all political distinctions. Only Spanish political ideas will be allowed. I condemn all other political factions and in my opinion there are only two major political groups on the island. Those who are in favor of Spanish rule and the separatists... they can be easily told apart. There are those who love Spain, and those who fight against her."[26]

Weyler lacked an attractive personality. He was dry, uncommunicative, lean and "very short."[27] He dressed carelessly and looked rather vulgar, but he was a reflective, resourceful commander, able to satisfy his thirst and hunger in the field with a tin of sardines and a pitcher of wine.[28] Weyler's first report to Canovas clearly reflected the revolution's success in its main military objective: to cripple the economic wealth of the Western provinces. "The day after my arrival they prevented milk coming in (to Havana)... the insurgents had been burning everything in their path and were not sparing anything ..."[29]

For the conduct of the war, Weyler assembled a small group of trusted officers. He believed in the principle of the military offensive. As he saw it, the Spanish battalions had not pulled together but had acted like a disorganized team with no definite strategy for dealing with the insurrection. Weyler sought first to try to isolate Maceo in Pinar del Rio by fortifying a new north-south line (*trocha*) between Mariel and Majana.

Gerardo Castellanos, author of *La Trocha de Mariel a Majana*, said, "The trocha began at Mariel on the northern coast. Its full 40 kilometers length was a maze of bunkers, blockhouses and fortifications, protected by veritable networks of barbed wire and manned by large numbers of soldiers."[30] The Mariel *trocha* was specifically designed to trap Gen. Antonio Maceo in Pinar del Rio Province. As Weyler admitted later, "I had to worry more about Maceo than I did about Gomez, even though Gomez was the higher ranking of the two. Maceo's daring had a great effect among people of his race, and the high risk operation which he had undertaken showed, in my opinion, that Maceo would attempt even more risky actions than he had... at any rate, that is where pacification had to begin."[31]

Weyler chose Gen. Juan Arolas to command the defense perimeter from Mariel to Majana with a force of 12,000 riflemen, reinforced by 26 pieces of artillery.[32] The *trocha* between Jucaro and Moron ran north south at the narrowest point in Camaguey province. The line was built in 1871 during the Ten Years War. It had 33 small forts of the kind known as blockhouses, guarded by large numbers of troops and patrolled constantly. There were also sentries or scouts posted between them[33].

Weyler's initial scheme to isolate Maceo in Pinar del Rio was thwarted by the rebel leader. In a bold drive, Maceo returned to the Havana neighborhood before Weyler could initiate his plan and joined forces with Gomez. The two warrior-leaders of the revolution embraced one another. The troops cheered while the band played the national anthem.[34] In the following weeks, Gomez and Maceo marched into Matanzas province. These maneuvers seem to confuse the Spaniards as to the rebels' intent. Assuming they were moving back to Oriente, Weyler fell into the triumphalist pattern so typical of senior Spanish officers during the war in Cuba. On March 8, 1896, Valeriano Weyler issued a communiqué announcing that the Western provinces were now under army control and that the rebels were in full retreat. It read, "Our troops have chased the rebels, caught up with them and defeated them on the field. The remnants of their army are now thoroughly demoralized and are retreating toward the East."[35]

A Spanish merchant who lived in Havana at the time, Luis Goicochea, made the following entries in his diary: "March 13, the Governor General Weyler had promised the sugar growers that by the middle of March (1896) conditions would allow them to begin the long process of manufacturing this year's output. March 18, General Weyler is beginning to pull dossiers out of the filing cabinets. That sort of desperate effort to make up rebel defeats out of thin air brought about Martinez Campos' discredit and ultimate downfall."[36]

On March 15, Maceo's forces fought their way through the yet to be completed Mariel Majana *trocha*. For the second time, the Cuban hero was invading Pinar del Rio. By moving into the mountains of El Rosario, he hoped to pin down large numbers of Spanish troops, which would allow Gomez to take the offensive in Las Villas Province and his brother, Jose, in Oriente.

Antonio Maceo established his defensive position in the mountains of El Rubi and waited for Weyler's attack, which began on April 14. Several Spanish columns converged on the rebel strongholds from different directions. It was a bloody and brutal affair. On the April 26, Weyler ordered a full-blown assault on Maceo's mountain force, which culminated on April 30 in the "Cacarajicara" battle. It lasted from early in the morning until sunset, when the Spanish battalions retired to their bases. Here the veteran infantry from Oriente, mostly soldiers of African descent, under the command of Juan Ducasse, became the decisive factor in holding back the Spanish attack in the dense, rugged mountains. The onset of the rainy season hampered further major military operations.

## *THE DAWN OF U.S. IMPERIALISM*

By the end of the Nineteenth Century, the United States was rapidly becoming an urban nation, with farmers looking for jobs in city factories and new waves of immigrants flooding urban centers like Chicago, New York and Detroit. These farmers and immigrants were a ready source of cheap labor. America was turning fast into an economic colossus that surpassed England in manufacturing output. Its national markets were linked with factories and raw material sources in an efficient continental railroad network linked by more than 170,000 miles of track, equal to the rest of the world put together.

Among the principal agents of industrial development were ready capital, talented and often ruthless entrepreneurs, huge sources of raw material, a large labor pool, excellent communications system, technology, inventions and the federal government as a facilitator of economic growth and modernization. In 1866, the U.S. continental telegraph system was linked to Europe by an underwater cable across the Atlantic Ocean, greatly accelerating the spread of business and other news among the world's industrial powers.

In the midst of such unprecedented economic growth, some

American workers joined trade unions to pressure management for better wages, hours and working conditions. The American Railway Union, led by Eugene V. Debs, and the American Federation of Labors (AFL) under Samuel Gomper fought for the workers' share of the industrial wealth. Bitter fights broke out in factories, streets and parks, such as the Pullman and Homestead strike and the bloody confrontation in Chicago's Haymarket Square. Boom and recession cycles reinforced the lack of job security, which hit bottom during the depression of 1893, but, all in all, American workers at the time were experiencing a rise in earnings and standard of living. In general, the American labor leadership's goal was not to overthrow the capitalist system, like their dogmatic European counterparts, but to allow workers a share in the enormous wealth being generated by the market economy.

As the western frontier officially closed in 1890, American expansionists began looking for new markets overseas. It was the dawn of "American Imperialism," which came to age with a profound difference to the European powers engaged in a race to grab new lands and colonies in Africa and Asia. The Americans set their sights and resources into finding a suitable spot in Central America for an inter-oceanic canal, acquired strategic Pacific islands (Hawaii and Samoa), promoted a commercial open-door policy with China and claimed the Caribbean Basin as within their commercial and political sphere of influence.

In the best Mahan theory, the United States was ready to project preeminence as a major naval power. "To overcome the handicap to an American navy of the long and dangerous sea voyage between the Atlantic and Pacific coasts and to command the most strategic interior line of sea communication in the Western Hemisphere, a canal must be built across the isthmus of Central America under United States control. To protect the approaches to the canal, the United States must prevent foreign powers from acquiring or developing new naval bases and coaling stations in adjacent waters and must meanwhile acquire and develop bases of its own in the Pacific and the Caribbean. Above all, the United States must build a modern navy."[37]

One of the first signs of a major change underway in U.S. foreign policy toward the Caribbean was the British-Venezuelan crisis of 1895. When gold mines were discovered in the Esequibo

Region on the British Guiana-Venezuela border, both nations laid claim to them. London was prepared for a war over the border dispute when the United States stepped into the arena, requested a mediator role, invoked the Monroe Doctrine and threatened to side with Venezuela and use force if necessary. The British were stunned. How did the United States dare to stand up to the most powerful empire on earth?

U.S. Secretary of State Richard Olney was direct and to the point: "Today the United States is practically sovereign on this continent, and its fiat is law... (America's) infinite resources combined with its isolated position render it master of the situation and practically invulnerable as against any or all other powers."[38] Lord Salisbury, Queen Victoria's Prime Minister, took four months to answer the Americans. A clever, experienced aristocrat at the pinnacle of power, he was more concerned with other foreign issues, in particular, the German challenge to Britain in South Africa's Transvaal region.[39] After a few harsh notes rejecting U.S. demands, and heavily influenced by Kaiser Wilhelm II's anti-British policy, Lord Salisbury took a sharp turn to settle the growing dispute with the Americans. As a result, Great Britain, in the zenith of her power, wisely agreed to an arbitration settlement ending the Venezuela crisis.

London made an historic decision. The United States was to be regarded as a friend, commercial partner and desirable ally in world affairs. Britain's Foreign Minister declared, "The two nations are allied and more closely allied in sentiment and interest than any other nations on the face of the earth. While I should look with horror upon anything in the nature of a fratricidal strife, I should look forward with pleasure to the possibility of the stars and stripes and the Union Jack floating together in defense of a common cause sanctioned by humanity and justice."[40] As a goodwill gesture to Washington, London dismantled her pro-Madrid policy in the Cuban war and dissuaded other European nations from providing aid to Spain. By this time, the United States had become the supreme power in the Western Hemisphere, with its brand of imperialism on the rise.

## THE YELLOW PRESS

The people of the United States and their press closely watched the events in Cuba. For years no foreign event had aroused and sustained the American public's interest like the Cuban Revolution did. It came at a time when the young industrial nation had found a new mode of mass communication in the form of several daily newspapers engaged in a historic race for circulation, in which the public received a daily doses of exaggerated and distorted tales of sensationalist news that sold millions of copies to avid readers.

The biggest circulation duel was between two New York titans, Joseph Pulitzer (*The World*) and William Randolph Heart (*The Journal*), who clearly understood from the start the human drama of Cuba's war. Moreover, most Americans sympathized with the Cubans' quest for independence from a corrupt, often brutal colonial power. The arrival of Valeriano Weyler fueled the bloody stories and inflamed American public opinion against Spanish dominion over Cuba.

Among the many gathering places for journalists covering the Cuban War, the two favorites were the lounge at the Hotel Inglaterra in Havana and the Peanut Club in New York. At his Broadway office, Jose Marti's Harvard grad friend, Horatio Rubens, legal advisor to the rebel Junta, met every afternoon with dozens of journalists, providing them complementary peanuts along with news of the war. At Havana's Hotel Inglaterra, reporters mingled with diplomats, merchants, writers and rebel sympathizers, sharing horror stories to feed American readers' thirst for scandal and sensationalism. At the informal and fashionable lounge, rum was king and Daiquiri the preferred tropical mix.

Many of the journalists were famous even before their Cuba assignment. Among them were novelist Stephen Crane, author of *The Red Badge of Courage* (1895) (a Civil War story about a Union recruit's psychological reaction to the suffering and fear of war); George Bronson Rea, a pro-Spanish journalist for the *New York Herald*; Richard Harding Davis, a gifted and powerful storyteller, handsome and witty Philadelphian, and popular member of the glamorous eastern seaboard society, who wrote for Hearst's *Journal* and who years earlier, while living in Santiago de Cuba as a guest of reputed "Daiquiri" inventor Jennings Cox, wrote the novel *Soldier of Fortune*; Frederic Remington, the famous sculptor-painter of the American West noted for his cowboys, Indians and horses, who illustrated the *Journal*'s war stories; and Sylvester

Scovel of *Pulitzer's World*, who had the privilege of interviewing rebel Commander-in-Chief Máximo Gomez.

Shortly after Weyler's arrival in Cuba, the *Journal* devoted a special Sunday feature to the captain general: "Spain ... has at last played her trump card and sent on the field of battle ... her most ferocious and bloody soldier... There is nothing to prevent his carnal, animal brain from running riot with itself in inventing tortures and infamies of bloody debauchery."[41] A *World* feature story presented a fearful record of Spanish atrocities claimed to have been committed in the province of Pinar del Rio under Weyler's command, and catalogued some 200 victims with names and places of residence. The editor claimed to have in his possession a stack of eyewitness affidavits confirming his correspondent's statements.[42] These stories were in many cases exaggerations, fabrications, or outright rebel propaganda; however, American journalists spread them for their own benefit in the profitable circulation war.

But Weyler's war was very real and controversial. On October 21, 1896, the captain general issued his most brutal order, a decree known in Cuba as "La Reconcentración" (Reconcentration). The military objective behind it was to deny the rebels their source of support among the peasantry. In Pinar del Rio province, which had a population of 275,000, some 140,000 peasant men, women and children were interned in "Reconcentrados" camps, where by November 1897, 53,000 had died from starvation or illness.[43]

The order was implemented from West to East until it encompassed the whole island. The towns of Colon and Union de Reyes in the Matanzas province illustrated the horrible human suffering of Weyler's war policy. In Colon, of a population of some 15,000 inhabitants, 9,851 were forced into the camps, 2,148 of them dead by November 1897. In Union de Reyes' 10,000 population, 4,448 were interned in the camps, and 1,122 died by the same date.[44] According to Spanish historian Conde de Romanones, more than 300,000 mostly peasant Cubans died as a direct consequence of Weyler's Reconcentration policy.[45]

Curiously, New York newspapers seemed slow to grasp the terrible human drama of Weyler's order. The *Journal* and *Sun* failed to mention it for weeks. The *World* was the first to realize the magnitude of a decree that forced civilian peasants into troop-guarded areas, a *World* editorial, almost a month after the order was given, predicted dire results: "A whole province will be depopulated by hunger and disease... General Weyler orders these people to go to the towns where even now there exists a scarcity of food, and leave their fields, which are still yielding enough food to feed all in the province... These people have no money and now, without food they will starve, and the results of such horrible conditions is indescribable."[46]

A *Journal* editorial the following day was perhaps inspired by the *World*: "The rural populations are given the choice of being murdered by the Spanish soldiers or of dying of starvation in the towns... This is wholesale murder, not war."[47]

### THE ELUSIVE VICTORY [48]

On March 24, 1896, one of the largest expeditions of the war landed at Marabi, Oriente. It came aboard the 1,000-ton steamship *Bermuda*, piloted by Captain Johnny "Dynamite" O'Brien, a daring blockade runner, and carried more than 1,200 rifles, two Hotchkiss cannons, nearly one million rounds of ammunition, medical supplies and numerous war materiel. Gen. Emilio Nunez was in command of the expedition, which included Major General Calixto Garcia, one of the revolution's legendary leaders. Over six-feet tall, with a fair reddish complexion and long white mustache, Calixto Garcia was nearly 60 at the time of his return to Cuba. As a military commander, he had a different tactical approach. He was one of the few Cuban generals who believed field artillery an essential offensive weapon.

Garcia's arrival created a bitter dispute with Jose Maceo over the issue of who should command the Oriente Military Department, which included all rebel forces of Camaguey and Oriente. The crisis had a racial undertone, fueled by President Salvador Cisneros Betancourt, who never lost a chance to show his dislike for the Maceo brothers. To settle the issue, Commander-in-Chief Gomez invoked Garcia's military seniority, but Jose Maceo remained resentful until his death in combat three months later.[49]

On July 6, 1896, at "Loma del Gato," Gen. Jose Maceo was mortally wounded while leading a charge against enemy lines. This was a great loss to the Cubans since Jose Maceo was regarded to be the bravest of rebel leaders and was dearly loved for his warmth and incredible courage. The news of Jose Maceo's death reached Gomez headquarters three days later. There was a mood of profound sadness in the rebels' camp. Like his father before him and all his brothers except Antonio, Jose Maceo had died a heroes death.

While in Pinar del Rio, Antonio Maceo left his Rubi mountain stronghold with 300 crack veterans and began the dangerous march to Cabo Corrientes in westernmost Pinar del Rio. Their mission was to receive and protect a large expedition led by Gen. Juan Rius Rivera, an attorney, Puerto Rican native and veteran of the Ten Years War. Among the new arrivals was Francisco Gomez Toro, Máximo Gomez's eldest son. Rius Rivera brought official word of Jose Maceo's death, which deeply saddened Antonio.

By September 18, military supplies were secured, but Weyler planned to capture and destroy Maceo's forces on their way back to the mountains. More than 8,000 Spanish soldiers in four columns maneuvered to encircle the rebels. The situation grew critical and, on October 4, the bloodiest encounter of the war was fought at "Cejas del Negro." In a ferocious battle, the Spaniards stood their ground with their ancestral fatalistic tenacity, their generals in the front ranks. Only the battle-trained skills and sheer courage of Maceo's veterans allowed them to break through the encirclement. A few days later, the rebels were back in the mountains with most of the Rius Rivera expedition.

Nine months after Weyler's arrival in Cuba, the Spaniards took the offensive in the Western provinces, while the Cubans attacked fortified towns in the East. On October 17, Calixto Garcia's guns, under the command of Charles Dana Osgood, began shelling the town of Guaimaro, protected by eight forts and several blockhouses. It took 11 days to demolish and storm the gallant defense, during which Weyler failed to relieve it. Guaimaro finally fell while Commander Osgood was killed in the siege.[50]
October proved a good month for the rebels. Maceo had rescued and secured the Rius Rivera supply expedition. Calixto Garcia had demolished with his few guns the fortified town of Guimaro. And the filibustering steamship *Dauntless*, piloted by John O'Brien, landed near Nuevitas, Camaguey, with a large cargo of war materiel. Upon learning that Weyler had put a price on his head, the

60-year-old New Yorker, O'Brien, slipped into Havana, left his calling card in the Governor's palace and withdrew without a trace. In this expedition came Frederic Fuston, a young man who was to be Calixto Garcia's artillery commander.

## SPAIN'S MILITARY COMMITMENT IN CUBA

At the outbreak of war, there were 20,197 Spanish soldiers stationed in Cuba.[51]   This number proved insufficient.  As the rebellion spread from Oriente to the western provinces, the need for massive reinforcements became the top priority of the Antonio Canovas government.  The rebels' main strategic objective had been achieved with the destruction of the sugar economy.  In March 1895, the first of 12 expeditions made the journey from several Spanish ports to Cuba.

### TABLE IX

| Expedition | Date | Troops |
|---|---|---|
| 1 | March 1895 | 8,302 |
| 2 | April 1895 | 7,252 |
| 3 | May 1895 | 3,418 |
| 4 | June 1895 | 2,668 |
| 5 | July 1895 | 9,193 |
| 6 | August 1895 | 26,835 |
| 7 | November 1895 | 24,173 |
| 8 | January 1896 | 8,667 |
| 9 | April 1896 | 21,463 |
| 10 | July 1896 | 7,241 |
| 11 | November 1896 | 36,836 |
| 12 | January 1897 | 18,568 |
| Two battalions from Puerto Rico | | 1,450 |
| | | **176,066** [52] |

In February 1898, the last contingent of 7,186 men landed on Cuban soil,[53] bringing to the total to 203,449 (including the original garrison) and making it the largest European army ever to cross the Atlantic to America.  Angel Castro, the father of communist dictator Fidel Castro, came from Galicia during this reinforcement phase to fight against Cuba's independence.

The Spanish army of the 1895-1898 war was equipped with the best rifle in the world, the Mauser; however, its soldiers were poorly trained. "Taking no time for aiming, the Spanish infantryman often fired his rifle with the stock in his armpit rather than at the shoulder, and he always fired high. When attacked, a Spanish column invariably formed an anachronistic hollow square and banged away with ineffective volleys."[54] In time, some units overcame these deficiencies but, overall, still remained a courageous but poor-performing, inefficient fighting force.

With the Spanish treasury in ruins, the quality of troop rations and health care was infamous, but worse for morale was the mechanism by which sons of wealthy Spaniards could buy draft-deferments to avoid serving overseas. Spanish law allowed cash payments called "redemption" of around 2,000 pesetas. A draftee could transfer his military duty to a recently discharged soldier, who, for cash payment, would reenlist in his place.[55] There is no doubt that for the Spanish people, this was a poor man's war. But by the fall of 1896, at the onset of the dry season, Spain was in the process of committing to the war in Cuba "el ultimo hombre y la ultima peseta" (the last man and the last penny).

On November 8, the Spanish army began the advance into Maceo's defenses in four columns. It was rough terrain covered with thick woods and underbrush called *manigua*. Maceo handpicked his Afro-Cuban's veterans who could in mid-battle move swiftly to new trenches and maintain steady fire. The Spaniard's advanced into the Rubi mountains was painful and bloody. On November 18, the Spaniards broke off the attack and moved to their bases. The operation was heralded as a great victory, and Queen Maria Cristina rewarded Weyler with the noble title of Duke of Rubi.

Prior to the attack on his stronghold, Maceo received instructions from Máximo Gomez to meet him in Las Villas Province to address the sensitive question of President Salvador Cisneros Betancourt's meddling in military affairs. In addressing the crisis, Maceo decided to cross the Mariel Trocha and join his commander-in-chief.

Pedro Roig

## THE DEATH OF ANTONIO MACEO

On December 4, 1896, under cover of a cloudy night, Antonio Maceo and 20 of his most trusted officers crossed in a boat the mouth of the unguarded Mariel Harbor at the very end of the *trocha*.[56]    The following day, they were met by the forces of Ricardo Santorious and Baldomero Acosta. By eight o'clock on the morning of December 7, 1896, Maceo arrived at the San Pedro rebel base, where more than 400 cavalrymen greeted the black hero of the Cuban Revolution.[57]    Weyler, in the meantime, was still looking for Maceo in Pinar del Rio.

Several planning sessions were held the following morning. Most of the province rebel leaders attended. That morning, Maceo decided to raid the town of Marianao, a capital suburb.    The following day, he ordered all available local horsemen to assemble in the camp for the attack.  This was Maceo at his best, a superb and daring commander who could grasp the psychological and political impact of a daring raid so close to Havana, with a humiliating twist for Weyler, who was still looking for him in Pinar del Rio.  Maceo's risk-taking combat style tells us a great deal about his ability to command.  It was heroic in the epic tradition.  The ethos of his youth was rooted in the Ten Years War concept of courage and honor, bound by the idea that the leader's place was at the head of his men in the forefront of battle.

Around midday, Col. Juan Delgado brought news of an enemy force nearby road.  Maceo immediately dispatched a search patrol. Francisco Cirujeda, a 44-year-old veteran from Valencia, led the Spanish force.  At the front of the Spanish column came the 90 Cuban horsemen known as the "Peral Guerrilla," followed by a 365-strong Spanish regular infantry and 24 Cubans from the Punta Brava Guerrilla bringing up the rear.[58]  At one o'clock in the afternoon, Maceo had lunch with his aides, drank the customary cup of coffee and retreated to his hammock for a nap, unaware that the search patrol had failed to find the approaching enemy.

Around 3 o'clock, the Spanish surprised the San Pedro camp. Their vanguard swept the sentries and moved on the rebel camp. Some 40 Cubans led by Alfredo Justiz, Baldomero Acosta and Juan Delgado, reacted swiftly with a spirited counterattack.    The Spaniards retreated behind stone fences by Guatao road.  After the initial surprise, the Cubans regrouped and deployed along the enemy line of fire.

With bullets flying overhead, and enraged by the security's failure, Maceo took about 10 minutes to get into uniform, secure his weapons and prepare his horse, then rode with 45 of his most trusted veterans to personally assess the situation. The Spanish attack had been stopped and was well under control, so the "Bronze Titan" decided to charge the center of Cirujeda's line. A wire fence stood in the way and Maceo ordered it cut. Someo of his horsemen dismounted and approached the fence. "This is looking good," Maceo told his officers. Just then a volley of rifle fire coming from behind a wall struck him in the face and neck. He remained on his horse for a few seconds, lost grip of his machete and fell to the blood-soaked ground. The Cuban legend had been killed. The invasion's hero, the victor of Peralejo, Mal Tiempo, Cejas del Negro, and dozens of bitter fights, the eldest of the brothers and last of the Maceo lions was dead. Cuba had lost its best tactician and beloved commander. It was a devastated loss to the Cuban war effort

Francisco Gomez Toro, Máximo Gomez's son, was killed in the same action -- an unexpected Spanish victory since Weyler was still looking for Maceo in Pinar del Rio but one nevertheless celebrated by Spanish authorities. It was the worst blow to the Cuban Revolution since the death of Jose Marti. On December 16, 1876, while Máximo Gomez received the unconfirmed news of his son "Pancho" and Maceo's death. Ten days later, the news now official, completely devastated the old warrior.[59] The following day, he wrote Maceo's widow Maria Cabrales, "Weep, weep, Maria for both, for you and for me, since for this unhappy old man, the privilege of relieving his innermost grief by letting go a flood of tears is not possible."[60]

## THE DESTRUCTION OF THE SUGAR INDUSTRY

Immediately after Maceo's death, Weyler began a race against time to crush the rebel forces before mid-May, when the rainy season began, The captain general had the regular army, plus 86,628 Spanish civilian volunteers[61] integrated into local militias, more than 300,000 fighting men in an island the size of Tennessee. But despite this massive force the Spanish Army could not prevent the burning of the cane fields and the continuous destruction of the sugar industry. This was the main goal of the 1895 invasion of the

Western provinces and remained the primary strategic objective of the Cuban revolution. The following numbers speak for themselves.

## TABLE X

| Year | Sugar Production |
|------|------------------|
| 1895 | 1,004,264 tons |
| 1896 | 225,221 (the year of the Invasion) |
| 1897 | 212,051 (the year of Weyler's offensive)[62] |

From the beginning of the war, Máximo Gomez's fundamental objective was the destruction of the sugar industry, a goal the Cubans had failed to achieve in the Ten Years War. In August 1895, he stated, "I firmly believe that Spain will not leave Cuba while it produces enough to pay her army and parasites."[63] In November 1896, Gomez issued a general order, direct and to the point: "All plantations, sugar cane and railroad connections must be destroyed."[64] It is obvious that despite the massive effort in men and money, the Spanish Army failed in its most urgent task, to protect its main source of revenue, the sugar industry. Sugar output fell more than 75% in 1896 and kept on falling while Weyler was telling Madrid that he had pacified the West and sugar production could resume. The 1897 sugar crop was even worse that the year before.

Gomez knew that to defeat the Spanish Army without a decisive battle, tropical disease, fire and time were his best weapons. While waiting for Weyler in Las Villas in January 1897, he wrote Tomas Estrada Palma, "No sugar crop must be made this winter under any circumstances or for any amount of money. It is the source from which the enemy still hopes and dreams of obtaining his revenues. To prevent that had been and shall be our program."[65]

On September 5, *El Heraldo de Madrid* published an interview with the wounded Gen. Federico Gasco. It was the day he arrived from Cuba after 22 months of fighting the rebels in Pinar del Rio and Havana province. He said, "The enemy is very active in the Western Provinces... when after a great deal of hardship you think you are about to force a battle, the rebels simply vanish in the woods... we must believe that the end of the war is not achievable unless the Western Provinces are truly pacified."[66]

After Maceo's death, one of Weyler's main objectives was to capture or kill Máximo Gomez, who had been in Las Villas province since January. The captain general had an available force of 40,000 soldiers. At 60, Valeriano Weyler was still a model of tenacity and willpower in pursuit of his military objectives. His nemesis, Gomez, was at 63 a master at guerrilla warfare. Few military commanders had endured so much physical stress and been so successful at his age. Gomez decided to challenge Weyler in the Sancti Spiritus region and relayed the plan to his officers. "The hour has come to fight with absolute tenacity. Don't waste men ... or horses and make use of the night. In these circumstances 20 men can easily conquer one thousand." [67]

## ONE FOURTH OF THE SPANISH SOLDIERS
## DIED IN CUBA

The Cuban forces were divided into small detachments. Gomez carefully selected a group of 250 horsemen and the Reforma Farm as his command post. Moving furtively, with swarms of enemy troops looking for his whereabouts, Gomez changed camps 337 times always keeping within a 25-mile radius. Sometimes marching ahead of the pursuing Spaniards and other times at their rear, Gomez maneuvered for over six months with the express purpose of exhausting the enemy without a fight. La Reforma was the most important military victory of Gomez's career. He knew that yellow fever and malaria were killing Spanish soldiers by the thousands. The numbers again speak volumes.

## TABLE XI
## OFFICER AND SOLDIER DEATHS 1895-1898

| Causes of Death | Officers | Soldiers | Total |
|---|---|---|---|
| In Combat | 61 | 1,314 | 1,375 |
| Due to Wounds | 82 | 704 | 786 |
| Yellow Fever | 313 | 13,000 | 13,313 |
| Other diseases | 127 | 40,000 | 40,127 |
| During the sea voyage | | 60 | 60 |
| **TOTAL** | **583** | **55,078** | **55,661**[68] |

From its large supply of men, mostly poor illiterate peasants, Spain paid the staggering price of losing over 25% of those who made the transatlantic voyage to Cuba. By comparison, U.S. losses in World War I were fewer than 52,000, the Korean War, 34,000, and Viet Nam, 58,000. One in every four soldiers never returned to their families in Spain. With tens of thousands in hospital beds, it was obvious from a statistical standpoint that Weyler's army was going through a process of uncontrollable deterioration. Given the available data, one wonders why 1898 is referred to in Spanish history as the "year of the disaster." Most of the 55,661 soldiers had died before 1898 when the United States entered the war in April, the majority of the 300,000 civilian concentration camp victims were dead before 1898, and both Cuba and Spain were in ruins. Why then is it called the "year of the disaster?" Perhaps it was the year of the unbearable humiliation at the hands of the Americans and a wake-up call from the national addiction to fantasy and demagoguery. Andalusian poet Antonio Machado said it best: "It was a time of lies and infamy."

In August of 1897, time began running out for Valeriano Weyler. Two unrelated developments triggered the end of his command in Cuba. The first was the murder of Antonio Canovas del Castillo, the head of the Spanish government and a staunch supporter of Weyler's tactics. The second was Calixto Garcia's victory in Tunas, the first major urban area conquered by the rebels when their light artillery destroyed the Spanish defenses.

## THE ANARCHISTS AND THE DEATH OF
## CANOVAS DEL CASTILLO

Canovas was the arbiter of Spain's political life and mastermind of the "Restauracion"[69] and also the architect of the "Disaster." His death in the San Sebastian beach resort at the hands of Miguel Angiolillo, an Italian anarchist marked the end of the war hardliner cabinet. Queen Maria Teresa Hapsburg asked the Liberal Praxedes Mateos Sagasta, a sworn political foe of Weyler's, to form a new government.

At the time, anarchism was at the height of its strength among the radical revolutionaries of of Europe during the period known as "La Belle Epoque," which lasted from the turn of the century to the start of World War I (1914). Its philosophy of indiscriminate terror directed against the political and financial establishment was responsible for the assassination of six heads of state: France's President, Sadi Carnot, King Humberto of Italy, Empress Elizabeth of Austria, U.S. President William McKinley (shot in 1901 after the Spanish-American War), and Spanish Premiers Antonio Canovas and Jose Canalejas. It was Frenchman Pierre Joseph Proudhon who conceived the term "anarchy" as a stateless society. For Proudhon, government of any kind was the worst enemy of humanity and an instrument of exploitation and degradation.

His Russian disciple, Michael Bakunin, added the need for violence, assassination and terrorism, with dynamite as the weapon of choice. Contrary to Karl Marx's doctrine of a proletarian revolution in industrial societies, Bakunin believed that poor agricultural economies such as Spain and Russia could begin the revolutionary process of overthrowing the bourgeoisie. The Anarchist philosophy traveled to Latin America with some of the European immigrants, especially Italians and Spaniards, but as the doctrine began losing its ideological appeal, what remained was a call for violence with dynamite as a political tool and assassination as a weapon of fear against the state. Cuba, too, received its anarchistic quota, who considered urban terrorism as an acceptable means of achieving their political goals.

The second event that hastened the end of Weyler's command in Cuba was a major tactical defeat. Equipped with five pieces of artillery, on August 28, more than 1,300 rebels, under the command of Calixto Garcia, laid siege to the fortified city of Tunas in Oriente province.[70] The city was protected by several forts, garrisoning 800 regular army soldiers and 200 volunteers with two pieces of artillery. The siege began at dawn with a barrage from the rebels, led by Gen. Mario Garcia Menocal, future third president of the Republic. Once their artillery demolished the forts, the rebels charged into the center of town. After two days of heavy fighting, the Spanish commander surrendered. The rebels seized 1,200 rifles and more than one million rounds of ammunition. It was the first time that the Cubans had captured a mayor urban center. Garcia's victory in Tunas caused a commotion in Spain and was terrible news for Weyler's apologists.

Pedro Roig

## WEYLER: BACK TO SPAIN

In Madrid, the liberal press and politicians renewed their criticism of Weyler in Cuba. On September 11, the *Heraldo de Madrid* published an editorial: "Without the effort of the government to hide the truth ... lying with news of victories and pacification of their exclusive fabrication, the loss of Victoria de las Tunas would not have hit the public spirit with such a deep impression... The people had been able to measure the magnitude of the farce to which it had been exposed. To attain such a poor result, has Spain given 200,000 soldiers and thousands of millions of pesetas."[71]

The new Sagasta government was quick to address the issue of a political formula to end the war. On October 4, Sagasta told *Pulitzer's World*, "We shall reverse completely the policy of the last two years in Cuba, beginning, naturally, with the recall of Weyler... The Liberal party is prepared to grant to Cuba all possible self-government, a broad tariff and every concession compatible with the Spanish sovereignty..."[72] The following day, Sagasta also told the journal's reporters: "The only thing I can say is that I will fulfill my program, establish autonomy in Cuba, and recall Weyler." [73] On October 10, the *Heraldo de Madrid* accused Weyler of being militarily incompetent and a corrupt administrator.[74] Within ten days and under heavy pressure from the new government, Valeriano Weyler had resigned his command in Cuba, saying that he was against Sagasta's policy of granting autonomy to the Cubans.[75] The news that Weyler was returning to Spain created a major commotion on the island among the radically pro-war "Cuerpo de Voluntarios" and the Constitutional Union Party.

Weyler's successor was Gen. Ramon Blanco, a moderate who assumed his post with a clear mandate to end the war by political accommodation. Assessing the military situation in Cuba, Blanco wrote Sagasta: "Upon my arrival, I found that the army was broken down by diseases and without the will to go on in the struggle."[76] In his first official statement, Blanco made it clear that his top priority was to grant Cuba self-government and full amnesty for the political prisoners. On November 22, Sagasta announced a peace formula by which Cubans would have the right to elect their own autonomous government and a parliament with the power to draw up the island's budget. These broad political rights were granted within the context of Spain's sovereignty over Cuba. It was similar to President Cleveland's offer in 1896, which was at the time rejected by the war hawks in Madrid.

For the Cuban Autonomist party the reforms came too late. For the Cuban rebels, it was too little, for the Spanish "voluntarios," too much. Máximo Gomez, still fighting in "La Reforma," rejected Blanco's autonomy offer. The old warrior was certain that victory for the rebel forces was a matter of holding on to their weapons a while longer.[77] In Havana, the Union Constitucional party and the Voluntarios began organizing large demonstrations against General Blanco, shouting "down with Autonomy." [78]

Pedro Roig

# CHAPTER IX

## THE WAR OF INDEPENDENCE (SECOND PHASE 1896-1897)
## THE INVASION OF THE WESTERN PROVINCES

[1] Tomas Estrada Palma, editor. *La Invasión de Occidente. Partes Oficiales.* (New York: Imprenta América, 1896), 4
[2] The Times, London, December 9, 1895 pg. 6
[3] Miro, op cit, 143
[4] Henry H. Beck. *Cuba's Fight for Freedom and the War with Spain.* (Glove Publishing Company, Philadelphia, 1898), 212.
[5] Miro, op cit, 166.
[6] Ibid
[7] Manuel Piedra Martell. *La Campana de Maceo.* (La Habana, 1967), 62
[8] Murat Halstead. *Our Neighbors and Their Struggle for Liberty.* (Review of Reviews, April 1896), 430.
[9] Over 25,000 troops were stationed on this line. Rene E. Reyna Cossio. *El Lazo de la Invasión, 24-31 de Diciembre, 1895.* (Estudio Histórico-Militar. La Habana: Oficina del Historiador de la Ciudad, 1956), 18
[10] Ibid, 17.
[11] Ibid, 19.
[12] Miro, op cit, 285.
[13] Souza. *Ensayo*, op cit, 171.
[14] Miro, op cit, Vol I, 308.
[15] Ibid, 312.
[16] Murat. *Review of Reviews.* (New York, February, 1896),
[17] Fernando D. Gómez. *La Insurrección por Dentro.* (La Habana: M. Ruiz y Co., 1897), xiii
[18] Portel Vila, op cit, 116.
[19] The Literary Digest, New York, April 1896, pg.23
[20] Diario de la Marina, Habana, December 30, 1895, quoted in Souza, op cit, 215.
[21] The Economist, London, October 5, 1895 pg. 13
[22] Juan Ortega Rubio. *Historia de la Regencia de Doña María Cristina.* (Madrid, 1905) Vol II, 473-74
[23] Bizcarrondo and Elorza, op cit, 66.
[24] Grover Cleveland. *Fourth Annual Message.* December 4, 1896 FR.US, 1897 pg. 541
[25] Valeriano Weyler. *Mi Mando en Cuba.* ( Imprenta de F. González Rojas, Madrid, 1910), 120.
[26] Ibid, 122.
[27] Gabriel Cardona y Juan C. Lozada. *Weyler Nuestro Hombre en la Habana.* (Editorial Planeta. Barcelona 1997), 16.
[28] Julio Romano. *Weyler El Hombre de Hierro.* (Espasa- Calpe, Madrid, 1934), 30-31.
[29] Cardona and Lozada, op cit, 262.
[30] Gerardo Castellanos. *La Trocha de Mariel a Majana.* (Habana, 1947), 31.
[31] Weyler, op cit, 137.
[32] Ibid, 139.
[33] Manuel Piedra op cit, 47.
[34] Bernabe Boza. *Mi Diario de Guerra.* (Habana, 1924), 2.
[35] Weyler, op cit, 185.

[36] Luis Goicochea. *Diario* (Habana, 1921), 65-66.
[37] Russel F. Weigley. *The American Way of War*. (Indiana University Press. Bloomington, 1977), 177.
[38] Henry Kissinger. *Diplomacy*. (Simon and Schuster, New York, 1994), 38.
[39] Cecil, op cit, 287.
[40] Forrest Davis. *The Atlantic System*. (New York. Reynal Hitchcock, 1941), 58.
[41] Journal, February 23, 1896
[42] World, May 17, 1896
[43] Servicio Histórico Militar. Armario 6, Legajo 13, telegrama 73, of November 28, 1897 as cited by Octavio Delgado op cit. pg. 144
[44] Ibid
[45] Conde de Romanones, quote in Roig de Leuchsenring, Cuba no debe su Independencia a E.U. Habana, 1960 pg. 192
[46] World, November 18, 1896
[47] Journal, November 19, 1896
[48]
[49] Juan E. Casasus, Calixto Garcia. La Moderna Poesia, Miami, 1981, pg. 197
[50] Ibid pg. 218-219
[51] Antonio Carrasco Garcia. En Guerra con los Estados Unidos. Ediciones Almena, Madrid, 1998 pg. 185
[52] Ibid pg. 199. In this table, we showed the month were each expedition was officially completed.
[53] Ibid pg. 47
[54] Ivan Musicat. Empire by Default. Henry Holt and Company, New York, 1898 pg. 55
[55] Delgado op cit. pg. 154-156
[56] Piedra op cit. pg. 232
[57] Ibid pg. 236
[58] By the end of the War in 1898, there were 15,892 Cubans fighting in the Spanish payroll. Delgado op cit. pg. 275. They were known as "Guerrilleros"
[59] Gomez, Diario pg. 369
[60] GJA O'Toole, The Spanish War. Norton and Company, New York, 1896 pg. 76
[61] Cardona y Lozada op cit. pg. 196
[62] Moreno Fraginal op cit.
[63] Diario de la Marina. August 12, 1895
[64] Gomez. Diario op cit
[65] Correspondencia Diplomatica de la Delegacion Cubana en Nueva York durante la Guerra de Independencia de 1895 a 1898 (La Habana, 1943-1946) Vol. 2 pg. 241
[66] Heraldo de Madrid, September 5, 1897
[67] Souza, op cit. pg. 185
[68] Carrasco Garcia op cit pg. 250
[69] The Return of the Monarchy
[70] Juan J. Casasus. Calixto Garcia. La Moderna Poesia, Miami, 1981 pg. 235
[71] Heraldo de Madrid, Septiembre 11, 1897
[72] World. October 4, 1897
[73] Journal. October 5, 1897
[74] Heraldo de Madrid, Octubre 10, 1897
[75] Cardona y Lozada, op cit pg. 236
[76] Roig de Leuchsenring op cit pg.63
[77] Gomez, Diario, op cit pg. 406
[78] Almagro, op cit. p 438

# CHAPTER X

# *THE WAR OF INDEPENDENCE: THE THIRD PHASE(1898) THE U.S. ENTERS THE WAR*

*RIOTS IN HAVANA - THE USS MAINE – THE SPANISH AMBASSADOR'S EMBARRASSING LETTER – THE DESTRUCTION OF THE MAINE – OPPOSITION TO THE WAR – THE YELLOW PRESS DEMANDED WAR - SPAIN: NO WAY OUT OF THE DISASTER – THE PRESIDENT'S WAR MESSAGE – CONGRESS JOINT RESOLUTION, A PROMISE OF INDEPENDENCE – THE U.S. ENTERS THE CUBAN CONFLICT – GUANTANAMO BAY – THE U.S. INVASION OF CUBA – THE LAND ASSAULT (EL CANEY AND SAN JUAN HILL) – THE NAVAL BATTLE AND THE END OF THE WAR.*

## *RIOTS IN HAVANA*

On January 1, 1898, the new Autonomist government took office in Cuba with the formal investiture of Jose Maria Galvez as Prime Minister. The enemies of the reform initiative, led by the Union Constitutional party and some army officers, took to the street. "Down with Autonomy," "Down with Blanco," "Long live the Voluntarios." On January 12, the riots got out of control marking one of those fateful moments when the hands of destiny triggered a chain of events that dramatically altered the course of history. That day, the Havana paper, *El Reconcentrado*, published an article criticizing a close Weyler collaborator. The headline read "Flight of the Scoundrels." A group of army officers went on a rampage against the newspaper's office and other publications that supported autonomy or dared to print attacks on Valeriano Weyler. Angry mobs roamed the streets, chanting slogans and denouncing as traitors those in favor of a negotiated settlement of the war.

The American consul in Havana, Fitzhugh Lee, was an eyewitness to the level of violence. He telegraphed the State Department, "Mobs led by Spanish officers attacked today the offices of four newspapers here advocating autonomy."[1] Lee had previously urged Washington to send a battleship to protect

American lives and interests in Cuba. This time, however, it was President William McKinley who, shocked by the news that Spanish Army officers had led the riots against their own Captain General, ordered the Department of the Navy to deploy a warship to Havana.

## THE USS MAINE

The Key West-docked cruiser *USS Maine* steamed into Havana to a tragic fate. On January 24, at 11:00 in the morning, the *Maine* entered the narrow channel under the venerable watch of the Morro Castle and anchored in the assigned buoy number 5 close to the Spanish cruiser *Alfonso XII* and the Ward Line *Steamer City of Washington*.

Secretary of the Navy Richard Day and the top Spanish diplomat in Washington, Dupay de Lome, arranged for a friendly visit by the Spanish cruiser *Vizcaya* to New York. Fitzhugh Lee, a West Point graduate, nephew of Robert E. Lee, Civil War veteran of Chancellorsville, Gettysburg, and former Brigadier of the Confederate Army, had been appointed Consul General in Havana in 1896 by President Grover Cleveland, and maintained that post during the McKinley administration. The mustachioed Lee was now serving the Union in war-torn Cuba, where violence and political polarization made his job a very difficult and sensitive affair.

The first Sunday after his arrival, the *Maine*'s 52-year-old captain, Charles Sigsbee, joined Lee and a group of officers at the bullfights in Regla, where the famous matador Mazzantini ("El Torero") performed before a roaring crowd. They were provided a ringside seat and a detachment of Spanish soldiers for protection, a wise decision given the crowd's hostile anti-American attitude. Captain Sigsbee, an Annapolis graduate and Civil War veteran with extensive oceanographic expertise, was in charge of the 6,683-ton cruiser and its 354 officers and crew. The *Maine* was commissioned on November 5, 1895, along with her sister ship, the *Texas*.

Three days after the Spanish officer riots that sent the *Maine* steaming into Havana, the American Ambassador in Madrid, Gen. Stewart L. Woodford, met with Queen Maria Cristina. She discussed enforcement of sweeping reforms in Cuba, insisting that her government was interested in a peaceful settlement to the conflict. Woodford told the Regent Queen that the recent riots were a disturbing situation. "The mutiny in Havana does not look as if Marshal Blanco can control his own army. If he cannot control his own army, how can he hope to crush the rebels? And besides, I hear every day of mutinies and conspiracies that are threatened here in Madrid." Maria Cristina replied, "I will crush any conspiracy in Spain. Upon this you may rely. I believe that my government will keep peace in Havana and reduce army officers to obedience. I want your President to keep America from helping the rebellion until the new plan of autonomy has had a fair chance."[2]

McKinley appeared willing to accept Maria Cristina's request to give autonomy a "fair chance." In his annual address to Congress a few weeks earlier, the President clearly stated the need to give Spain a "reasonable chance to realize her expectations ...."[3] On this issue Woodford could inform the State Department, "the Spanish Minister of State is greatly gratified with the generous tenor of the President's message, and today authorized me to express his gratification to my government..."[4]

William McKinley was a cautious politician, naturally disinclined to make rash decisions. For a time it seemed likely that the Queen Regent would get her "fair chance." But it was not to be. In less than 30 days, the United States and Spain were at war.

## THE SPANISH AMBASSADOR'S EMBARRASSING LETTER

The American people's thirst for sensational news was incited by publication of a damaging letter from Spanish Ambassador Enrique Dupuy de Lome to his friend, *Heraldo de Madrid* Editor Jose Canalejas, expressing his criticism of William McKinley. Canalejas' secretary, Gustavo Escoto, a rebel sympathizer hired while the editor was visiting Havana, read the letter, smuggled it out of Cuba and went immediately to New York, where he gave the original to Junta leader Tomas Estrada Palma. Palma gave the letter to Hearst's *Journal* while the Junta's attorney, Horatio Rubens, took a copy to the State Department.

In the letter, the Spanish Ambassador wrote, "The situation here (in Washington) continues unchanged. Everything depends on the political and military success in Cuba... Until then we will not be able to see clearly and consider it to be a loss of time and an advance by the wrong road... The President has disabused the insurgents, who expected something else... in addition to the natural and inevitable coarseness with which the message repeats all that the press and public opinion had said of Weyler, it shows once more that McKinley is weak and catering to the rabble and also a low politician who wants to keep all his options open and stand well with the jingoists of the party. Nevertheless, as a matter of fact, it will only depend on ourselves whether he (McKinley) will prove bad and adverse to us."[5]

## *THE DESTRUCTION OF THE MAINE*

The yellow press reacted with incendiary headlines and damming editorials, denouncing De Lome's letter as an attack on the nation. The *Journal*'s front page read, "The worst insult to the United States in its history."[6]  Upon publication of his letter, Ambassador De Lome resigned his post and returned to Spain. He had been a very effective diplomat, well liked in influential Washington circles. He was also an arrogant aristocrat who in private showed negative feelings regarding the reforms proposed for Cuba.

Just as the De Lome scandal began to subside, a terrible explosion rocked Havana's harbor. On February 15, at 9:40 pm, the *Maine* blew up and sank, killing two officers and 258 men. The warship had come to protect the lives of American citizens after the Spanish army officers' riots three weeks earlier. Now it was resting at the bottom of the bay. What had happened?

In 1976, Admiral Hyman Rickover conducted an inquiry into the cause of the *Maine*'s demise. The result of his investigation, published in his book *How the Battleship Maine Was Destroyed*, points to an accident caused by coal spontaneously igniting in Bunker A-16 and the resulting fire spreading to the adjacent ammunition storage bunker, causing it to explode. It is a well-established fact that the bituminous coal used by the American Navy was highly volatile and ignitable by accidental combustion. Before and after the *Maine* disaster, several U.S. warships suffered from spontaneous fires in their coalbunkers, including the 8,200-ton armored cruiser *New York*. Another theory holds that a mine detonated under the ship's keel near Frame 18, on the port side, igniting the six-inch shell magazines and initiating a chain reaction that blew up the forward part of the ship, sinking the cruiser. According to this theory, there were two distinct explosions with a brief interval between them.[6]  Sigmund Rothchild was an eyewitness to the explosion. A passenger on the liner, *City of Washington*, anchored nearby; Rothchild was on deck facing the warship. "I looked around and I saw the bow of the Maine rise a little, go a little out of the water. It couldn't be more than a few seconds... then there came in the center of the ship a terrible mass of fire and explosion... the whole ship lifted out, I should judge about two feet. As she lifted out, the bow went right down."[8]

Some experts have valid reservations about Rickover's "accidental explosion" theory, pointing to the large hole beneath Frame 18 of the Maine's hull, where the keel metal was folded sharply into an inverted V, with the apex thrusting upward, suggesting an external explosion. A few days after the disaster, Spain and the U.S. sent naval experts to determine its cause. The American team concluded that it had been an external explosion that detonated the magazine.[9] The Spaniards arrived at the opposite conclusion, finding that the internal explosion was due to a tragic accident. By this time, the question of how it happened had become moot. The American press did not bother to seek a fair answer. They had already decided that Spain was guilty.

The Yellow Press was quick to unleash their lurid headlines. Two days after the *Maine* disaster, the *Journal* wrote, "The warship *Maine* was split in two by an enemy secret infernal machine."[10] America was aroused. The New York press broke the one million mark in sales,[11] fueling the nation's anger. The public's animosity toward Spain became so intense, it precluded any alternative to that of military conflict. Upon hearing that the *Maine* had blown up in Havana's harbor, William R. Hearst put it succinctly to his paper's editor, "This means war."[12] Before the *Maine* disaster the *Journal* averaged a little over 400,000 copies daily. Two days after the incident, the Journal sold 1,025,624 copies and 1,036,140 the following day (February 18)[13].

## *OPPOSITION TO THE WAR*

In the midst of the heated rush to military conflict, the fact that many influential Americans were opposed to the war with Spain was disregarded. First, among the anti-war's ranks was Thomas B. Reed, Speaker of the House of Representatives, regarded as the best parliamentarian of his time and one of the most powerful politicians in America. A Republican congressman from *Maine*, Reed "regarded the Hearst fabricated furor ... with contempt and Republican espousal of Cuba's cause as hypocrisy. He saw his party losing its moral integrity ... in response to the ignorant clamor of the mob. Without compunction he suppressed the resolution recognizing the belligerence of the Republic of Cuba."[14]

Another proponent of a negotiated settlement was John D. Long, Secretary of the Navy and former governor of Massachussetts. In a letter to his friend, the editor of the *Boston Journal*, Long wrote that America's political goals for Cuba could be achieved without war. "Do you realize the President has succeeded in gaining from Spain a concession upon every ground which he has asked ... except the last item of independence for Cuba... recalls Weyler, changed his *reconcentration* order, agreed to furnish food and order an armistice... I honestly believe that if the country and Congress had been content to leave the matter in his (the President's) hands, independence would have come without a drop of bloodshed as naturally as an apple from a tree."[15]

Most of McKinley's Cabinet shared Secretary Long's view of a negotiated settlement of the Cuban crisis. Former President Cleveland remained adamant against war with Spain. In a letter to Richard Olney he wrote, "I cannot avoid a feeling of shame and humiliation."[16] Even President McKinley felt duty bound to find a peaceful way out, but, by this time he had lost control of the national agenda. The kind, gentle McKinley was devoted to his sick and epileptic wife, Ida. "No more pathetic couple than the McKinley's ever dwelt in the White House ... when he was not working, he took no recreation but remained at her side."[17]

But McKinley was cautious enough to see the need to prepare the nation for the inevitable fight ahead. On March 6, he met with Joseph Cannon, Chairman of the House Appropriations Committee, and requested $50 million. He told the Congressman, "I must have money to get ready for war."[18] Congress unanimously approved it three days later.

156

## THE WELLOW PRESS DEMANDED WAR

The interventionist press pounded out daily demands that the nation's honor be upheld and that intervention was a clear imperative duty. The *Journal*, three days after the *Maine* sank, declared, "Intervention on behalf of Cuban Independence was our duty before De Lome wrote his letter, and it is our duty now... The prudent, proper and patriotic policy is to intervene in Cuba, not because an American warship has been destroyed in Havana's harbor by a suspicious accident, but because every dictate of national self-protection, every impulse of humanity compels such intervention.[19]

The *New York World* insisted that Cuba must be free and reiterated its preference for war to a dishonorable peace. In its many editorials after the destruction of the *Maine* it repeated: "Peace, but free Cuba. On general principles, Cuba ought to be free. What more is needed? ... The American people do not want war, but they do demand justice.... Cuba, as the scene of a remorseless and barbarous war of extermination, is a constant menace to us and a standing reproach to our civilization."[20] It was evident that McKinley could not check the public clamor for intervention, or resist the call for action by millions of American citizens.

In Spain the government was feverishly working to avoid war with the U.S. but also preparing for a fight with the US if diplomacy failed. In both countries the press began displaying the statistical strength of the Armed Forces with emphasis on the warships to be involved in the probable conflict. With their peculiar flair for fantasy and self-deception, most of the people in Spain entertained the idea of a possible victory. Demagogues like Romero Robledo, the powerful and greedy Spanish politician from the extreme right, fueled the belief that what was needed to defeat the Americans were the ancestral courage of the Spanish race.

### SPAIN: NO WAY OUT FROM DISASTER

But there were also a few voices of reason that clearly saw the abysmal differences in strength between the two countries. One of those lonely voices came from Admiral Pascual Cervera, the Commander of the Spanish Atlantic Fleet. Several days after the

Maine disaster he wrote to Minister of the Navy Segismundo Bermejo, "We do owe to our country not only our life, if necessary, but the exposition of our beliefs, ... I asked myself if it is right for me to keep silent, make myself an accomplice in adventures which will surely cause the total ruin in Spain. And, for what purpose? To defend an island which was ours, but belongs to us no more, because even if we did not lose it by right in war we have lost it in fact, and with it all our wealth, an enormous number of young men, victims of the climate and the bullets in the defense of what is no more than a romantic idea."[21]

On March 4th, Bermejo replied to Cervera that the American sailors were mostly "ill-trained mercenaries" that Manila-based Admiral Montejo could attack the USS West Coast from the Philipines, and that by the end of April all the Atlantic Fleet problems would be corrected, and Spanish ships concentrated in Havana against the US Navy.[22] Three days later, Admiral Cervera answered with a sober statement, "What we may reasonable expect is defeat, which may be glorious, but all the same defeat, which would cause us to lose the island in the worst possible manner".[23]

In Madrid, another voice was desperately trying to avoid the oncoming conflict with the US; that of a woman, mother and queen. Queen Maria Cristina Hapsburg-Lorena, a smart, cultured and beautiful widow and one of the ablest head of state in Europe, had advised all possible political reforms for Cuba except independence. She now requested mediation from the European Powers to find a peaceful settlement to the crisis. She first wrote to her uncle, the Austrian Emperor, and sent emissaries to Paris, Berlin and Moscow. Their answer was short and simple: England must be on board. Next Maria Cristina wrote a touching letter to her aunt, Queen Victoria, saying, "When the insurrection is nearly over, the Americans intend to provoke us and bring about a war... I cannot let my country be humbled by America ... I know how, with the greatest kindness, you always interested yourself in my poor fatherless son, for his sake I beg you to help me..."[24] but England was already committed to forging a durable bond with the US so the proposed European coalition fizzled.

McKinley and his cabinet read the final report of the Maine Court of Inquiry on Friday March 25. The Court of Inquiry put the blame for the explosion "on a submarine mine, which caused the partial explosion of two of her forward magazines. The Court was unable to obtain evidence affixing the responsibility for the destruction of the Maine upon any person or persons."[25]   On Monday March 28, McKinley sent the report to Congress with a message from the President, in which he requested, "deliberate consideration" on this issue. The last paragraph read, "I have directed that the findings of the Court of Inquiry and the views of this Government thereon be communicated to the Government of Her Majesty, the Queen Regent, and I do not permit myself to doubt that the sense of justice of the Spanish Nation will dictate a course of action suggested by honor and the friendly relations of the two governments"...[26]

But if McKinley had any doubts as to the need for military action, what sparked in his turn around seems to have been induced by the decision of Democratic leader and possible presidential candidate William Jennings Bryan who, in an unprecedented stand for an old anti-imperialist advocate, made a powerful call for war. "The time for intervention has arrived ... Humanity demands that we shall act".[27]  The Senate was for war, and in the House it was obvious that not even the Speaker "Tzar" Reed could control the call for intervention.  By the end of March, McKinley knew that his peace effort had failed and began the Constitutional procedures for the war with Spain.

### THE PRESIDENT'S WAR MESSAGE

On April 11, 1898, the President sends his war message to Congress. It began with a brief account of the Cubans' struggle for freedom and his predecessor Grover Cleveland's effort to bring about a peaceful end of the rebellion with the direct mediation of the US Government "on the basis of some effective scheme of self-government for Cuba under the flag and sovereignty of Spain."[28]  It next addressed the suffering of the Cuban people due to the brutal policy of *Reconcentrado*. "The peasantry, including all dwelling in the agricultural interior, was driven into the garrison towns, month by month the death rate increased in an alarming ratio.

The Maine incident was marginally addressed, pointing to the Naval Court of Inquiry's findings that "The destruction of the Maine was caused by an exterior explosion that of a submarine mine. It did not assume to place the responsibility that remains to be fixed".[29] The message concluded with a call for intervention in the Cuban conflict in the name of humanity and to end the serious injuries to America's trade and business in the island. "In view of these facts I ask the Congress to authorized and empower the President ... to use the military and naval forces of the United Stares as may be necessary for this purpose".[30] For the next eight days, the Congress debated on the issue of intervention and the political future of Cuba. The hottest question was the legal status to be given to the Cuban rebels. Should Washington recognize the Cuban Government in Arms? President McKinley's answer was emphatically no.

In his message to Congress, the President did not even mention Cuba's independence or give any indication that he was willing to acknowledge the existence of the Republic of Cuba. Instead, McKinley's emphasis was on the forcible intervention as a neutral to stop the war.[31] In another paragraph McKinley pointed to the need of "establishing a stable government" in the island.[32] The United States was marching to war with Spain over Cuba but avoiding the legal and political liabilities attached to the sensitive issue of recognizing a revolutionary government. In the President's view, "to commit this country now to the recognition of any particular government in Cuba might subject us to embarrassing conditions of internal obligations towards the organization so recognized."[33]

## CONGRESS JOINT RESOLUTION.
## A PROMISE OF INDEPENDENCE

But, Cuba's independence was a popular subject in America. After a heated debate, the Senate approved the J.B. Foraker amendment that proposed the immediate recognition of the Cuban rebel government. In the House, Speaker Reed opposed it and defeated the amendment. It was also made known to Congress that McKinley would veto any legislation that granted official recognition to the Republic of Cuba.[34] The U.S. government was on the verge of intervention in the conflict as a neutral force without acknowledging the existence of a Cuban political institution.

In such a confusion situation, it fell on Jose Marti's dear friend, Horatio Rubens, the task of finding an acceptable compromise between the opposing political views. Rubens, an experienced, skillful negotiator, swiftly began lobbying for an official U.S. disclaimer that in the approaching war with Spain, Washington was not seeking permanent control over Cuba, but to secure its independence. He proved to be good at finding common ground in a divided Congress when he gained the support of Henry M. Teller, senator from Colorado, a beet sugar-producing state, to present an amendment acceptable to the majority of both the Senate and House by which the United States officially and publicly promised independence for the Cubans, yet without formally granting recognition to the rebel government. The Teller amendment read: "The United States hereby disclaims any disposition or intention to exercise sovereignty, jurisdiction or control over said island except for the pacification thereof ... when that is accomplished, to leave the government and the control of the island to its people."[35]

During the final hours of the debate, House member Nelson Dingley, a Republican from Maine, introduced a last minute amendment that called for the right of Cuba to be free and independent. Congress approved it. On April 19, 1898, the Joint Resolution was adopted. It read: "...That the people of the island of Cuba are, and of right, ought to be free and independent ... demanding that Spain relinquish its authority and government in the island of Cuba ... directing the President to use the land and naval forces of the United States to carry this resolution into effect".[36] The following day, McKinley signed the Joint Resolution of Congress into law. Cuba's long and bloody struggle for independence was now officially recognized by its powerful neighbor to the North. Horatio Rubens had earned the gratitude of the rebel fighters in their heroic quest for nationhood.

## THE U.S. ENTERS THE CUBAN CONFLICT

On April 21, Pio Gullon, Spain's Foreign Minister notified Ambassador Woodford that Madrid had broken diplomatic relations with Washington. The American Ambassador requested his passport and left by train for Paris that same evening. From Havana, Captain General Ramon Blanco advised Madrid that the fleet of Admiral Cervera should immediately be sent to Cuba, adding: "Public spirit very high; great enthusiasm among all classes."[37] On April 24, Spain declared war on the United Stated, and McKinley ordered the Navy to blockade Cuban ports on the northern coast from Bahia Honda to Cardenas, and also Cienfuegos in the South. The President also called for 125,000 men to be assembled at army camps to prepare for war.

Admiral William Sampson, fleet commander, headed for Cuban waters to enforce the naval blockade of the island, to link with and coordinate military supply for the Cuban rebels and to wait for the disposition of Spanish Admiral Cervera's squadron. The American Atlantic fleet had four new battleships and several armored cruisers. The Spanish navy could count on three armored cruisers, the *Maria Teresa*, *Oquendo* and *Vizcaya*. They were fast, with good coal capacity and adequate punch for commerce riding. It also had a remarkably powerful ship in the Italian-built cruiser *Cristobal Colon:* "virtually it was a small battleship."[38] There was also the cruiser *Carlos V*. It had been re-fit for the fight ahead, but Spain's treasury was in ruins and the cruiser was barely ready for war. As a result, the *Cristobal Colon* was without her heavy guns, and the other three available cruisers, *Maria Teresa*, *Oquendo* and *Vizcaya* were having mechanical problems with their 5.5-inch guns that in Cervera's view were "practically useless on account of the bad system of their breech mechanism."[39]

In a letterer to Madrid, Admiral Cervera shows his pessimism: "The relative military position of Spain and the United States have grown worse for us, because we are reduced, absolutely penniless and they are very rich"…[40] Just before the outbreak of war, Cervera requested the preparation of a basic strategic plan of operation. What would be the main objective of his ships? The defense of the Peninsula, the Canary Islands or Cuba? "If I had this information … we could enter without vacillation upon the course we are to follow."[41] The answer was an outrageous mix of incompetence and sheer madness. The Spanish Minister of the Navy proposed to blockade the Atlantic seaboard of the United States.[42]

Cervera was quick to reply, with a sober analysis, of the available ships: "It seems to me that there is a mistake in the calculation of the forces we may have available…" He went on describing the various stages of unreadiness facing the fleet and summarized his view with a wake-up call: "In saying this I am not moved by a fault-finding spirit but only by a desire to avoid illusions that may cost us very dear." In the letter, the Spanish

Admiral suggested a course of action that was within the objective possibilities of the available forces: "As for the offensive, all we could do, would be to make some raids with our fast vessels, in order to do them as much harm as possible."[43] This was among the few strategic options available for the weaker Spanish Navy: to raid the American commercial shipping lanes and pick targets of opportunities on the eastern seaboard for swift raids to strike fear into the civilian population of a possible attack thus forcing the U.S. Navy to re-deploy their warships.[44]   Rear Admiral F.E. Chadwick did point to this possible course of action. "Had Cervera returned to Spain as he and his captains advised, awaited the Carlos V ... and placed aboard the Colon her 10 inch guns, he would have a squadron which would have given cause for thought to the American Government."[45]

For the Cuban rebels, American intervention decided the outcome of the war and signaled the end of Spain's dominion over Cuba.   It also accelerated the disintegration of the Cuban government in Arms that went swiftly from being a marginal civil institution to total oblivion. Among those Cubans fighting for Independence, there was a mixture of joy, apprehension and political confusion. The U.S. intervention meant victory over the old decrepit master, but it brought a new foreign army on Cuban soil and a Congressional Resolution that promised independence. This became the frame of reference for the island's political future.

In the elusive quest for their freedom, the Cubans were living the last chapter of the long and terrible war for Independence without having an effective, viable government. Maximo Gomez and Calixto Garcia, the top Cuban military commanders, were in full control.   Jose Marti's idea of a civilian leadership as the representatives of the revolution were just a dream. Both generals, Gomez and Garcia, exhibited deep-seated resentment against a civilian authority, rooted in the failed experience of the Ten Years War.[46]

With the United States entering the conflict, the strategic priority for Gomez and Garcia was to open channels of communications with the American armed forces to coordinate a joint military campaign. Maximo Gomez believed that with a large supply of weapons and food, together with a small American contingent landed in central Cuba, he could launch a victorious offensive.[47] The McKinley government was also looking into the feasibility of landing a 70,000-man army in Mariel, to fight the final battle at the gates of Havana.[48] All of these plans were abruptly changed when on May 19, Cervera's squadron anchored at Santiago de Cuba. For few faithfilled days, Cervera's senior officers proposed a dash for Spain or Havana.[49] The Admiral refused this advice, unknowingly deciding the final stage of the war in Oriente Province.

Captain Victor Concas, Cervera's chief of staff, recalled Santiago's supply shortage and the leadership's unreal expectations: "Although the city was in reality besieged by the insurgents, it was still able to obtain some vegetables ... The local Spanish authorities gave a banquet for Cervera and his men. The Archbishop of Santiago proposed a toast to the Admiral's anticipated attack on the U.S. Capitol in Washington D.C. The gesture was received with feverish enthusiasm by some and with profound sorrow by those who knew that our fate was already decided and that we were irredeemably lost."[50] The U.S. Navy spent some confusing days trying to confirm whether Cervera was really inside Santiago's harbor, but by May 28, the confusion was resolved and the American squadron was able to bottle up the Spanish ships.

This fortuitous event drastically changed U.S. war strategy. The Army and Navy were immediately re-directed to the eastern end of the island, were the decisive battles, both on land and at sea, were to be fought, shifting the main military scenario from Maximo Gomez's theater of operations in central Cuba to Calixto Garcia's command in Oriente. Chance was once more playing a prominent role in history. "Nothing could have been more fortunate for the Americans than Cervera's entrance into Santiago's harbor. His going there transferred the center of war from Havana to Santiago, eliminating from the contest that portion of the Spanish force occupying Western Cuba and causing the decisive struggle to take place where the Spaniards were specifically weak"[51]

Military historian John F.C. Fuller writes: "The port Cervera should have made was Cienfuegos ... there he would have been in railway communication with Havana ... and as Admiral Bonamico points out, the whole military resources (Spanish) could have been concentrated there with sufficient rapidity ... the result for Cervera

would have been the security of the squadron, the possibility of
holding in until the hurricane season and for Admiral Sampson, the
necessity of forcing the port with the greatest danger."[52] However,
the first major engagement of the war took place in a far corner of
the Pacific, where on May 1, 1898, the American Asiatic Squadron
under Commodore George Dewey sank the small Spanish fleet at
Manila Bay (Cavite), in the Philippine Islands. The "yellow press"
went on a victory frenz,y and Dewey became overnight a national
hero. A few days later, the U.S. Army shipped 5,000 men to claim
the Philippines as a prize of war.

In Cuba, the two top rebel commanders, Maximo Gomez and
Calixto Garcia, were issuing orders to coordinate their forces with
the American Army. In a letter to Bartolome Maso, Garcia clearly
stated: "I will help the Americans in all possible ways ...
unconditionally."[53] On May 1, General Garcia received Andrew S.
Rowan, who had come to Garcia's headquarters in the historic city
of Bayamo, to establish the military links between the U.S. forces
and Cuban rebels located in Oriente. On May 13, Maximo Gomez
sent Juan Joba, the American Consul in Sagua la Grande, to request
from the U.S. Navy a shipment of weapons and food for his
forces.[54] On July 3, a large supply expedition reached Gomez'
forces in Las Villas,[55] but by then the U.S. Army had landed in
Oriente and the decisive battles of the war were to be fought in and
around Santiago de Cuba.

## GUANTANAMO BAY

With the naval blockade of Cervera's squadron in effect, the
need for a nearby U.S. Navy-controlled anchorage for coaling
maintenance and supply became urgent. On June 6, in a combined
military operation with the Cuban rebels in the area, 400 U.S.
Marines landed at Playa del Este in Guantanamo Bay and after
three days of bitter fighting, one of Cuba's finest harbors was
secured. The Cuban forces under General Pedro (Periquito) Perez
were in full control of the region between Santiago and
Guantanamo and had completely isolated the Spanish Garrison of
6,000 men, commanded by General Parejas entrenched in the town
of Guantanamo, twelve miles from the bay. General Parejas failed
to challenge the permanent use of this vital anchorage by the U.S.
warships.[56] On June 16, General Perez was the guest of honor on

board the U.S. cruiser *Marblehead*, where the American officers paid tribute to the courage and fighting contribution of the Cubans in the Guantanamo Bay operation.[57]

By the time of the U.S. intervention in Cuba, communication technology had improved dramatically and President McKinley was able to have a direct link with his senior commanders. From the White House War Room, where several telephones and telegraph sets had been installed, the President was able to control important strategic and political decisions. The speed by which orders could be transmitted transformed the nature of command. This conflict also offered McKinley a golden opportunity to unite the nation and heal the wounds of the Civil War. Two senior ex-confederate officers, Fitzhugh Lee and Joseph "Fighting Joe" Wheeler, were commissioned in the invasion army. Thousands of blue and gray veterans fought side by side in Cuba and the President succeeded in bringing the nation closer together.

## THE U.S. INVASION OF CUBA

The sudden and fortuitous presence of Admiral Cervera's ships in Santiago de Cuba dictated the location where the army was to invade the island. The main target was to be the Spanish squadron.

The invasion forces under the command of General William Shafter were ordered to assemble in Tampa, Florida. On June 14, 1898, and after weeks of logistical confusion, 16,059 soldiers and 819 officers boarded the 48 transport ships. The force included four Gatlinguns, which were to play a key role in the fight ahead, plus field artillery. Eighty-nine journalists joined the force providing broad coverage to this popular war.

On June 19, while the invasion armada was on its way to Cuba, Gen. Garcia arrived at the small coastal hamlet of Aserradero where he was invited by Admiral Sampson to come on board the cruiser *New York*. Strategic options were discussed at this initial meeting. The following day, the U.S. troop transport arrived and a meeting between Sampson, Shafter and Garcia was immediately arranged. After heated discussions, Calixto Garcia's plan was adopted. Garcia proposed for the landing of the invasion force the beaches of Daiquiri and Siboney, 12 miles east of Santiago, and to fight the decisive battle at the gates of the old city. A Cuban contingent was shipped in U.S. transports and taken to Sigua beach, from where, led by General Demetrio Castillo Duany, they advanced and secured Daiquiri, which had been abandoned by the Spaniards in the face of the arriving force.[58]

At dawn on June 22, the American invasion of Cuba began, and by nightfall, over 6,000 soldiers had landed. The following day, the combined forces of Castillo and Wheeler took Siboney, where the remaining U.S. soldiers came ashore. To some military historians, the Spaniards should, and could, have made a decisive stand on the landing beaches since there were over 5,000 soldiers in the vicinity. "If General Linares (Santiago's commander) had ordered his forces to oppose the American landing, he might have dealt the "Yankees" one of the bloodiest defeats in their history. Even 300 men fighting from the fortified bluff above Daiquiri could have ranked and ripped the go-as you please amphibious assault,"[59] but Arsenio Linares, the Spanish commander, a brave but mediocre tactician, failed to seize the opportunity. This is an example of where outstanding commanders make a difference.

The following day, at the heights of "Las Guasimas," 2,000 Spanish soldiers had a brief but bitter fight with the Cuban vanguard led by Colonel Gonzalez Clave, together with the dismounted cavalry of Wheeler and Roosevelt. Fearing a flanking maneuver coming by the coastal road, Linares ordered his troops back into Santiago's outer defenses. Here, too, he missed another good opportunity since "Las Guasimas" was among the best defensive position in the area.[60] Dense vegetation and mountains covered most of the region, and the few roads turned into mud during the rainy season. For the average soldier, the natural environment was harsh and deadly. The United States was learning the hard facts of fighting in the hot, humid, mosquito-infested hills of this tropical island. With Yellow Fever about to strike the troops, the Americans needed to move swiftly to avoid a catastrophe.

The health of the troops became a serious concern, and Clara Barton, the founder of the American Red Cross, came with dozens of nurses to assist the sick and wounded soldiers as well as the desperately destitute civilians. Doctor Felipe Verenes was placed in charge of the medical facility. Clara Barton soon became a popular personality among the Cubans who greatly appreciated her humanitarian efforts. But, as the Americans and Cubans advanced toward Santiago, a disturbing and growing feeling of animosity began to develop between them. In Oriente, the rebels were mostly of African origin, without the academic training or skills for the complex siege of a fortified stronghold.

At the turn of the Nineteenth Century, the United States was fundamentally a racist society. Even in the more liberal northern cities, African Americans lived in segregated neighborhoods and schools. This was the time of the hateful and criminal activities of the KKK in the American South. Addressing this issue, historian Hugh Thomas wrote: "The sight of the Cuban rebels under Calixto Garcia appears to have disillusioned the U.S. forces. The American army was mostly white; the Cubans almost entirely Negro…Garcia was treated with contempt by Shafter who even suggested that, instead of battle, the Cuban soldiers should work as "Laborers."[61]

Gen.William Shafter was a tedious, insecure commander, a Civil War veteran who had spent most of his military career fighting Indians in the West. He weighed over 300 pounds, suffered from gouty arthritis and on many occasions had to be carried atop a wooden door by six soldiers. Shafter spent long hours gasping from the heat and humidity of the tropics. It was a pitiful sight.[62]

## THE LAND ASSALT (EL CANEY Y SAN JUAN HILL)

After "Las Guasimas," the American and Cuban forces advanced to the city's outer defenses and prepared for the attack. On July 1, Gen. Shafter decided on a two-prong assault, directed at San Juan Hill and the village of El Caney, which was defended by 520 men under the command of Gen. Joaquin Vara del Rey. General Lawton's division, over 5,000 strong, was ordered to take control of the fortified village. It was assumed that the task could be completed within two hours. The attacks began at daybreak, and, by late afternoon, the fight was raging. Both sides displayed uncommon valor. Vara del Rey, his two sons and several hundred officers and soldiers died a hero's death. Their determination to stand their ground greatly impressed the Americans; but, in spite of their valiant efforts, by nightfall, the American army captured El Caney. The attack on San Juan Hill began around eleven o'clock in the morning after a two-hour delay, waiting for Lawton's division still fighting at El Caney, which, according to Shafter's plan, was to join in the assault. Moving along the narrow trails, Generals Kent and Summer's forces began to approach the Spanish strongholds at San Juan and Kettle Hills (La Loma de la Caldera).

As the American soldiers began losing coverage of the dense vegetation of the foothills, Spanish firepower poured from their trenches, inflicting heavy casualties on the advancing men. The attack bogged down. For the most part, U.S. artillery was ineffective and out of range. In the early afternoon, the fight was turning ugly for the Americans. Heavily engaged, all along their line, it became obvious that decisive action was urgent. "Teddy" Roosevelt with the Rough Riders and the first dismounted cavalry brigade were just in front of Kettle Hill, when the order for a frontal assault was finally given. The men jumped forward and charged up the hill yelling and shouting. The black troopers of the ninth and tenth regiments joined in the attack. The future commanding General of WWI, John Pershing, was among the white officers leading the Afro American regiments charging the Spanish trenches. Kettle Hill was captured.

About a quarter mile southwest of Kettle Hill stood the blockhouse of San Juan Hill, where Kent's division and the Cubans led by Gonzalez Clavel were charging the Spanish trenches. U.S. artillery was rushed forward and shelled the Spanish lines, but it was Lieutenant John H. Parker, focusing the devastating fire of three Gatlinguns, that broke the Spanish stiff resistance. As the assault gained momentum, "General H.S. Hawkins with his erect figure and white hair, made an inspiring presence ... swinging his hat and calling out, come on, come on."[63] After a furious fight, the blockhouse at the top of the hill was captured and the surviving Spaniards retreated towards Santiago. The city was encircled and the water supply cut off.

The following day, Shafter received the casualty report and called a meeting of his seniors commanders. They had suffered severe losses and had yet to face the 3,600 men of Colonel Escario who had fought their way into the city. At the meeting, Shafter put forward the idea of abandoning San Juan and El Caney and retreating five miles back to high ground between the San Juan River and Siboney beach.[64] His top commanders did not agree and Washington rejected the idea of falling back. The soldiers dug in and waited for the looming fight soon to come.

## THE NAVAL BATTLE AND THE END OF THE WAR

With the possibility of being captured in the harbor if Santiago were captured, Captain General Blanco ordered Admiral Cervera's squadron to fight their way out. Blanco said: "If we should lose the squadron without fighting, the moral effect would be terrible, both in Spain and abroad."[65] On receiving the fateful order from Havana, Cervera recalled his officers and sailors who had been in the trenches to ready the ships for the encounter with the American battle fleet. No one fit for duty missed the roll call. They realized the odds and did not fail. For over three hundred of them, this was to be the ultimate sacrifice. At nine o'clock Sunday morning, Cervera's ships approached the narrow channel between El Morro and La Socapa. A gentle breeze, a sunny day, a quiet sea, out they came to meet their doom. Leading the way was the Admiral's flagship, the *Maria Teresa*, followed by *Viscaya*, *Cristobal Colon*, *Oquend* and at the rear the destroyers *Pluton* and *Furor*. The *Maria Teresa*'s Captain Victor Concas wrote: "From outside the conning tower … I asked leave of the Admiral and with that I gave the order to fire. The bugle gave the order to begin the battle … my bugles were the last of those which history tells were sounded in Granada; it was the signal that the history of four centuries of greatness was ended."[66]

After several weeks on blockade duty, the Americans were going about their Sunday routines when the guards saw the Spaniards moving out into the channel ready to do battle. The alarm gongs sounded for action. Up went the signal flag. "Enemy ships are coming out" a half-hour before Admiral Sampson, on the *New York*, had left the fleet for a meeting with Shafter at Siboney. Upon hearing the roaring guns, he ordered the *New York* back to join the fight.

The *Maria Teresa* came out at full speed and received the brunt of the U.S. Navy guns. It caught fire and ran aground. The *Oquendo* was badly damaged and also went ashore. *Vizcaya* was hit by the shells of five American ships and veered toward the beach, where it exploded. The two destroyers where swiftly sunk, but *Colon*, the best of the Spanish cruises, turned away until it ran out of her good quality coal. *Colon* lost speed and was shelled by the *Oregon*, *Brooklyn*, *New York* and *Texas*. By 1:15 p.m., she headed toward the coast near the Turquino River and struck her colors. Three hundred and twenty three Spanish officers and sailors were killed and 151 wounded. The Americans lost one sailor and one was wounded. A decisive victory.

For Spain, the war in Cuba was lost. The long, painful agony of her decrepit empire was over. With her navy sunk, the army isolated in the island and neither cash nor credit to keep on the fight, Madrid needed a negotiated settlement. It came quickly. On July 16, Santiago capitulated, and peace negotiations began in Paris, where on December 10, Spain signed a treaty transferring possession of Cuba, Puerto Rico and the Philippines to the United States. It was the rich and powerful young nation that joined Europe in the imperial race. The war marked a historical shift in U.S. foreign policy. Sometimes reluctantly, the young democracy began to break away from isolationism and into the international arena. Over the next 50 years, the United States would have fought and won two World Wars, and by the end of the Twentieth Century, have achieved superpower status and world hegemony without parallel in the history of the human race.

# CHAPTER X

# THE WAR OF INDEPENDENCE: THE THIRD PHASE(1898) THE U.S. ENTERS THE WAR

[1] Foreign Relations, January 1898 pg. 671

[2] G. J. O'Toole. *The Spanish War: An American Epic, 1898.* (W.W. Norton & Company, 1986), 113.

[3] Foreign Relaitons, January 1898, pg. XII

[4] State Department Archives, Vol. 132 Woodford-Sherman, December 7, 1897

[5] Trumbull White, United States in War with Spain. International Publishing, Chicago 1899, pg. 291-2

[6] Journal, February 11, 1895

[7] White, op cit, 310.

[8] U.S. Navy Court of Inquire (The Maine Explosion)

[9] Ibid

[10] Journal, February 17, 1892

[11] Joseph Wissan. *The Cuban Crisis as Reflected in the New York Press, 1895 – 1898.* (Columbia University Press, New York, 1934), 391.

[12] Edmond D. Coblentz and William Randolf Hearst. *A Portrait in his Own Words.* (New York. Simon and Schuster, 1952), 59.

[13] Wissan, op cit, 391.

[14] Tuchman, op cit, 149

[15] John Davis Long. *America of Yesterday: As Reflected in the Journal of Davis Long.* (Atlantic Monthly Press, Boston, 1923), 179-82.

[16] Millis, op cit, 161.

[17] John and Alice Durant. *The Presidents of the United States.* (Gache Publishing Co., New York, 1966) Vol. 2, 199.

[18] Morrison, op cit, 189.

[19] Journal, February 21 and 28, 1898.

[2] World, February 26, 1898

[21] Pascual Cervera y Topete. *From the English Translation to La Guerra Hispano-Americana.* (The English Collection of Documents was issued by the Government Printing Office in 1899, Washington DC), 30.

[22] Ibid, 31-32

[23] Ibid, 34

[24] *The Letters of Queen Victoria.* Third Series, 1886-1901. Edited by George Earle Buckle, London. (John Murray, 1930) Vol. 3, 326.

[25] Trumbull White, op cit, 313

[26] Ibid, 311

[27] Allen Reed Millet. *The Politics of Intervention; The Military Occupation of Cuba, 1906-1909* (Columbus, 1968), 124

[28] White, op cit, 324

[29] Ibid, 329

[30] Ibid, 330

[31] White, op cit, 328

[32] Ibid, 330

[33] Lewis L. Gould. *The Spanish American War and President McKinley.* (University Press of Kansas, 1982), 48

[34] Ibid, 50

[35] G. J. O'Toole, op cit, 171

[36] Enrique Collazo. *Los Americanos en Cuba.* (Editorial de Ciencias Sociales, Habana, 1972), 67

[37] G. J. O'Toole, op cit, 172

[38] Chadwick, op cit, 34-35

[39] Ibid

[40] Ibid, 94-95

[41] Ibid, 97

[42] Ibid, 98

[43] Ibid, 99

[44] G. J. O'Toole, op cit, 209

[45] Ibid

[46] Jose M. Hernandez. *Politica y Militarismo en la Independencia de Cuba: 1868-1933.* (Editorial Colibri. España), 54-56

[47] Maximo Gomez. *Diario de Campaña,* op cit, 409

[48] Jose M. Hernandez, op cit, 64

[49] G. J. O'Toole, op cit, 216

[50] Ibid, 217

[51] Sargent, op cit, Vol. I, 203

[52] J.F. Fuller. *Decisive Battles of the U.S.A.* (Da Capo Press, New York 1993), 340-341

[53] Collazo, op cit, 94

[54] Maximo Gomez. *Diario de Campaña*, op cit, 409

[55] Ibid, 414

[56] Chadwick, op cit, 356

[57] Foner, op cit, Vol. 2, 17

[58] Collazo, op cit, 86

[59] Leckie, op cit, 555

[60] Ibid, 557

[61] Hugh Thomas, op cit, 398

[62] G. J. O'Toole, op cit, 327

[63] Fuller, op cit, 352

[64] Chadwick, op cit, Vol. III, 109

[65] The Spanish American War: A collection of Documents Relative to the Squadron Operation in the West Indies, arranged by Rear Admiral Pascual Cervera y Topete. Washington: Navy Department, 1899,1899 pg.111

[66] Ibid, 127-128

# CHAPTER XI

# *FROM INTERVENTION TO INTERVENTION*

*A DECREPIT POLITICAL TEACHER – THE PROUD ARMY OF FREEDOM – GARCIA AND GOMEZ CLASH WITH A SHADOW GOVERNMENT – THE VETERANS' PAYMENT: A BITTER DIVISION – THE JOHN BROOKE ADMINISTRATION – THE LEONARD WOOD ADMINISTRATION – POLITICAL PARTIES, THE 1901 CONSTITUTION AND THE PLATT AMENDMENT – THE DECAPITATED INDEPENDENCE SYNDROME – THE ELECTION AND BIRTH OF THE REPUBLIC – IT FAILED IN THE FIRST ROUND – ESTRADA PALMA REQUESTED U.S. MILITARY INTERVENTION – VIOLENCE AS AN ACCEPTED POLITICAL FORMULA – CHARLES MAGOON AND THE SECOND U.S. INTERVENTION – ANNEXATION NO MORE.*

## A DECREPIT POLITICAL TEACHER

It was a time of economic misery and political confusion. While for Cubans the heroic fight was over, 400 years of Hispanic heritage remained very much alive and rooted in the Cuban psyche. Spain was Cuba's model of political behavior, a sort of decrepit teacher still living in the past. For centuries, Cubans learned about bureaucratic corruption, *caudillismo* (warlords), dogmatic intolerance, messianic leadership, a malformed judicial system and a deformed government administration.

At the turn of the century, Cuban society mirrored that of Spain, a divided semi-educated, unruly, exhausted and confused nation governed by a profoundly corrupt and inept political elite. Analyzing the political crisis of the period, Ortega y Gasset, a towering thinker of his generation, stated in his book *España Invertebrada*: "Spain, rather than a nation, is a cloud of dust remaining after a great people have galloped down the highway of history." This was Cuba's political frame of reference as it began the long, arduous march toward a free and independent republic. Within the inherited tradition was a deepseated distrust of the state. Professor Fernando Diaz Plaja wrote: "The Spaniard has an instinctive dislike of belonging to associations ... so the state, the one organization which one cannot help but belong to, is viewed with distrust. The state is an abhorrent body that is not considered the necessary link between the individual and society."

Another disturbing element of Spanish political heritage was a proclivity for political self-deception, a national obsession with a brief but glorious past feeding the collective need to behave like a great empire despite industrial backwardness, poverty and military impotence. The Spaniards were possessed with an absurd compulsion to impersonate the role of a first-rate European power. This genuine tendency for self-deception and distortion of reality became fertile ground for charismatic demagogues who nurtured the emotional needs embedded in the collective psyche, with the terrible consequence of human misery and political crimes.

Violence as a tool for addressing public grievances and a recurrent call to arms for settling political disputes is among the prominent traits of the old cultural heritage. There were 44 military rebellions (*pronunciamientos*) in Spain between 1808 and 1936. Compounding this, the Cuban political spectrum was profoundly and ferociously divided. The issue of independence was on everyone's mind. A powerful neighbor, with a different set of cultural values, was now the new master in full control of the government; the political future of the island was very much uncertain. The bitterly divided forces of independence had to face corrosive rejection by a large Spanish population, the thousands of Cubans who fought for Spain (*guerrilleros*), the autonomists and the annexationists for whom the possibility of Cuba's independence was unwelcome and even despised. It is obvious that Cuba's political heritage posed a huge challenge in the quest to build a modern nation-state. Over the next 58 years, Cubans would stage 20 armed rebellions.

## THE PROUD ARMY OF FREEDOM

They had fought long and well and felt they had fulfilled their soldier obligations against terrible odds. Most of the best rebel leaders had perished, and the revolutionary ideals of independence seemed to have been mutilated by the U.S. military occupation of the island. What was to be Cuba's political future? Article 4 of the "Joint Resolution" (the Teller Amendment) guaranteed independence. However, the arrogance of several U.S. commanders led by Gen. Shafter fueled resentment among Cuban veterans. An especially bitter pill was Shafter's order to deny Gen. Calixto Garcia's forces their hard-won right to enter Santiago after the Spanish capitulation on grounds of possible retaliation by the rebels against the Spaniards. "The entering of the Cuban troops into the city would not be tolerated for obvious fears of reprisal."[1]

This was an unfair assessment. There were isolated cases of reprisals, but the rebel forces that took control of dozens of towns and cities, such as Bayamo, Gibara, Manzanillo, Puerto Padre and Camaguey, kept the peace and protected lives and property. The fact remained, however, that most U.S. forces, harbored a deep-seated prejudice against the rebel soldiers who were more than 80% black, mostly illiterate and desperately poor. The Cuban revolutionary leaders were not invited to attend the Paris peace settlement, and on January 1, 1889, Maximo Gomez was not in Havana for the historic ceremony ending 400 years of Spanish rule in Cuba. "For many Cubans, American intervention, received with initial enthusiasm, quickly became a source of concern and anxiety... a foreign army had taken full command and was unwilling to even recognize the Cubans as valuable allies."[2]

For the cause of independence, these veterans were the best and only chance of ever reaching their objectives. The rebels lacked institutional cohesion and were deeply divided, but despite their pitiful appearance, they were capable of inflicting heavy damage on the island's economy. In the end, this would become the best weapon in the quest for independence. By this time, an epic war legend was entering the mainstream of Cuban folklore. The invasion of the western provinces was a catalyst for patriotic fervor and enthusiasm for Cubans. Under the successful leadership of Antonio Maceo and Maximo Gomez, a large degree of command and control was briefly accomplished, transcending regional loyalties of powerful local warlords. This important period was most revered by Cubans, overshadowing the profound maladies afflicting the revolutionary government throughout most of the heroic struggle for independence. By the time of the U.S. intervention in 1898, the Cuban army had been weakened by lack of a steady supply of weapons and food and a deeply divided leadership. And even though most troops and officers refused to fight outside their home regions, they were still a serious fighting force to reckon with, able to inflict heavy damage on the island's future economic revival, a key factor very much on the minds of New York investors and Washington politicians.

Such fear fueled an urgent need to disarm and disband the Army of the Revolution, one that was becoming a high priority for the first U.S. military governor of Cuba, Gen. John Brook, a likeable, well-meaning, efficient administrator.  The rebel veterans had not been paid for three and half years and had lost their properties in the terrible struggle.  Proud, penniless and facing starvation, they were now returning to their loved ones.  They needed to be paid, but, more than this, they needed jobs.  Soon these fundamental necessities developed into one of the most bitter and devisive issues of the post-war period.

On September 23, 1898, with Gen. Shafter recalled to the United States, Leonard Wood invited Calixto Garcia and his veterans to enter Santiago de Cuba at the head of his army; it was a glorious day for the cause of independence and vindication for years of sacrifice.  They received a hero's welcome.  It was also time to honor Maximo Gomez.  On February 24, 1899, the commander-in-chief of the Cuban army marched into Havana leading his cavalry. Thousands poured into the streets to cheer and salute the famous old warrior; Gomez had become a living legend.  It would be the final parade of the Army of the Revolution, a proud army that had blossomed from the humble roots of the people who forever were to remember them as the beloved icons of Cuba's nationalism.  It was a farewell parade for an army that on this date was fading into the pages of history.

## *GARCIA AND GOMEZ CLASH WITH A SHADOW GOVERNMENT*

Jose Marti's best hope of building a civil society in the narrow framework of a long and enduring military tradition was to establish a government managed by civilians. He preached the gospel of a democracy based on the rule of law. Marti wrote: "I wish the first law of our Republic to be respect for the full dignity of men."  But the generals had other ideas. Their experience with the quarrelsome and divisive civilian government in the previous war fueled misgivings about transferring control of the revolution to such an organization. In 1884, Marti clashed with Gomez and Maceo. "A Republic is not governed like a barrack." When they met again at "La Mejorana," the generals confronted Marti on the issue. Maceo insisted the military commanders be representatives of the Cuban people in arms. Marti felt sadly disappointed. He died a few days later in his lonely charge at Dos Rios.

The generals knew they needed to create the appearance of a governing body in the eyes of the world, especially the American public and press and Washington politicians. They believed this was their best chance of mustering American support and belligerence status. Thus, they formed a government in arms. The first president was Salvador Cisneros Betancourt. Cisneros clashed with Maximo Gomez and Antonio Maceo and was later replaced by the old patrician Bartolome Maso, who presided over the government in arms when the Americans entered the war. The official rebel representative in the United States was Tomas Estrada Palma, veteran, Quaker and teacher who did a first-rate job as a Washington lobbyist for the Cuban cause. His political goals were clear: independence from Spain and Cuba's admission into the American Union.

By the time of the U.S. intervention, the contempt of ranking rebel commanders for the government was apparent. When asked by Estrada Palma to convince the government council to align itself with him after the rebels captured Bayamo, Gen. Garcia swiftly and harshly rejected the idea: "When we agreed to fight with the Americans to expel the Spaniards, haven't we accepted their intervention as a matter of course?... we should no less ... concur with them that we do not have a government. The present Council of Government is incapable of fulfilling its institutional duties and does not have a reason to exist... you know that President Maso, despite his high rank in the Army, does not hide his lack of interest to be where he should be at this moment. A sad truth... let them spend their existence in full tranquility ... without disturbing any more the lives of those that are doing the fighting..."[3]

On August 13, the Government Council fired Gen. Garcia from his post as second in command of the Cuban Army. The order read: "(Garcia) abused military authority ... publicly countermanding orders given by the Government Council."[4] Garcia's reaction was solid proof that the Council of Government was a marginal organization, without real authority over the affairs of government or the war. "(I) reject the legality of the order of the so-called Cuban political government. This government has only two people, who cannot reach a quorum, and their actions are illegal."[5] The statement was made to a *New York Herald* reporter, dispelling publicly any pretense of a functional Cuban government in arms.

There were claims that refusal by the U.S. Administration to recognize the legitimacy of the Cuban Government contributed to the political instability and turmoil that followed. Evidence to the contrary indicates, however, that there was nothing of consequence to recognize. The Council of Government was a powerless shadow, a political charade that ended its functions at Santa Cruz del Sur, when on October 24, in an act of solemn wisdom, it officially concluded its existence. The next pressing issue was paying the officers and troops of the Cuban Army.

## THE VETERANS' PAYMENT: A BITTER DIVISION

During the invasion of the western provinces, officers and soldiers of the Cuban army were ordered paid for their service. Payment, however, was postponed so the money could be used to purchase supplies and weapons. The soldiers had to go three-and-a-half years without receiving any money. At the end of the war, the country was in ruins, and the Cuban army was penniless. The men and women who had fought for independence were literally starving. On this issue Maximo Gomez said the freedom fighters were: "in the saddest predicament that any man had faced in this world."[6]

With the Americans in control of the island's customs revenues, the main source of the administration's income, the country's military leaders began searching for a way to improve the desperate situation of their soldiers. A delegation headed by Calixto Garcia traveled to Washington where it was received at the White House by President McKinley. The two discussed the island's political future and payment of the war veterans. The delegation was divided as to the right amount. The majority thought that a bank loan to be paid later by the Republic would be a good solution, but Gen. Garcia was concerned a large loan might weaken the fragile economy of the independent nation.[7] During the White House meeting, the President asked how much money was needed, and Gen. Garcia replied: "three million dollars."[8] A heated discussion ensued, in which other delegates insisted the amount was not enough to mitigate the soldier's predicament, but McKinley refused to take the issue any further and ended the discussion. The three million was offered not as a loan, but as a grant. A few days later, Garcia fell ill and died of pneumonia.

During a visit a month later with Maximo Gomez, U.S. presidential envoy Robert Porter reconfirmed the Garcia-McKinley agreement of the three million. Gomez accepted the amount and met with Gen. Brook, U.S. military governor on the island, to work out the details of the arrangement and demobilization of the army. Maximo Gomez wrote the President. "It has been my pleasure to meet with your envoy Mr. Porter… I have been informed of your offer and feel satisfied."[9] How many soldiers were eligible for payment? This was a question that had to be answered before anything else. It would not be easy, however, as it had been an unconventional army for which keeping official records had been very difficult. There were charges of irregularities and favoritism, but with the cooperation of regional and local commanders, the veterans were eventually identified. In the end, their numbers were higher than expected — 33,930 – all of them eligible to receive $75.00, which they could pick up at one of the regional city halls. Weapons would have to be turned in at the same time.

The Army Assembly (Asamblea del Ejercito) disagreed with the arrangement. It has been formed at the Santa Cruz meeting where the Council of Government was dissolved. The group of officers had contacted some New York bankers led by C.M. Cohen to secure a 20 million dollar loan, a huge sum at the time. The bankers were to collect $7,600,000.00 up front and give $12,400,000.00 to the Cubans plus 5% interest for 30 years. Maximo Gomez flatly refused the loan on grounds that it would imperil the Republic's financial future.

The Army Assembly met in the Havana suburb of El Cerro. The Cerro Assembly was a tumultuous, emotional gathering that eventually fired Maximo Gomez from his post as Commander-in-Chief of the Army of the Revolution. In the unhealthy heritage of violent responses to a political crisis, some delegates demanded Gomez, the legendary hero of the war of independence, be executed. Gen. Jose Lacret volunteered to head the firing squad.[10] The people, however, were enraged at the dismissal and took to the streets in support of Gomez. The delegates eventually saw the light and resigned. The last vestige of the rebel military organization was no longer, leaving Maximo Gomez as the single most influential individual in Cuba. The war veterans were paid, but the bitter divided remained.

## THE JOHN BROOKE ADMINISTRATION

Washington lacked a clear political objective for Cuba after the war, which helps explain why John Brooke, the first U.S. military governor on the island, assumed command without a mandate. Brooke began his term by addressing what he understood to be the most urgent needs of the country. His priorities were security, feeding the hungry and bridging the growing gap with Cuban leaders. To help resolve the desperate famine situation, Brooke had 6 million food rations shipped to Cuba. To address the security issue, he named U.S. army officers as provincial military governors, and in Oriente, Cuban veteran soldiers were hired to patrol the countryside, initiating a practice that soon spread to other areas and led to the creation of the *Guardia Rural* (Rural Guard).

To build rapport with the rebel commanders, he named five Cuban Army generals civil provincial governors: Demetrio Castillo in Oriente, Lope Recio Loynaz in Camaguey, Jose Miguel Gomez in Las Villas, Pedro Betancourt in Matanzas and Juan Rius Rivera in Havana. The Brooke administration had four departments that were managed by Cubans, including Domingo Mendez Capote, the last vice president of the Cuban government in arms[11] during whose administration Church and State were separated.

On May 6, 1899, Brooke created Cuba's Supreme Court and the provincial courts or *audiencias*. He established *habeas corpus* but failed to introduce trial by jury. Initially, the Old Spanish law served to frame the legal system until it would be replaced by decrees and later by Cuban law. Brooke launched a massive sanitation program and conducted the 1899 census that showed a population of 1,572,797.

## TABLE XII
### Cuba's Population by Provinces
(1899 census)

| Pinar del Rio | 173,082 |
|---|---|
| Habana | 424,811 |
| Matanzas | 202,462 |
| Santa Clara | 356,537 |
| Puerto Principe | 88,237 |
| Oriente | <u>327,716</u> |
| | **1,572,845** |

Brooke was a Civil War veteran and the third highest-ranking officer in the U.S. Army at the beginning of the war. He proved to be a good administrator who delegated authority and worked well with the Cubans. This gentle governor established a close relationship with Maximo Gomez, consulted him on several issues, including veteran appointments in his administration, and treated the old general with utmost respect and dignity.

However, for some American officials, Brooke seemed too complacent and willing to give in to political pressures from the Cubans. Among leading critics was Leonard Wood. In a letter to his wife, Wood wrote: "I have a good deal of trouble with Brooke..."[12] To Roosevelt he said: "I am kept extremely busy doing all I can to preserve order and harmony in this part of the island, but the new order of things is not conducive to such conditions here."[13]

In the open American democracy, the people, and especially the political leadership, held different, and even opposing, views that were freely and passionately expressed in public forums. In Cuba's case, the debate was over the "Joint Resolution" promise for independence and the issue of whether Cubans were ready for self-government. In the summer of 1899, the anti-imperialist league requested an end to U.S. military occupation. It was followed by similar demands from the influential socialist Eugene Debs, social reformer Jane Adams and the Afro-American intellectual Booker T. Washington. Union leader Samuel Gomper stated: "Where has flown this great outburst of our sympathy for the self-sacrificing and liberty loving Cubans? It is not strange that now, for the first time, we hear that the Cubans are unfit for self-government..."[14]

Others in the United States had serious reservations about the readiness of the Cubans for self-government. Secretary of War Elihu Roots expressed his concern and the need to avoid the kind of turmoil that had led to perpetual revolution in Latin America.[15] Admiral Sampson believed the Cubans needed more time to learn how to behave in a democracy, and in an interview with the press, the arrogant Gen. Shafter stated bluntly: "Those people are no more fit for self-government than gunpowder is for hell."[16] George Barbour, head of Public Health in Oriente, warned: "To attempt to set them afloat as a nation during this generation would be a great mistake."[17]

But almost a year after the United States took control of the island, the question of what to do with Cuba, how to do it and when was still anyone's guess. Brooke's critics in Washington insisted that the military governor had surrendered to the divisive intrigues of emerging political factions[18] and had to be dismissed. On this issue, Wood added: "But dilly-dallying and talking politics will play the devil with people of this temperament... generations of misrule and duplicity have produced a type of man whose loyalty is always at the command of the man at the top whoever or whatever he may be. These men who a few months ago were fighting the Spaniards, are now intriguing vigorously against each other."[19]

It is obvious that Woods was also "intriguing vigorously" against Brooke. "Teddy" Roosevelt, by this time a powerful politician, wrote Secretary of State John Hay: "I most earnestly urge the wisdom of the President putting Major General Leonard Wood in immediate command of all of Cuba with a complete liberty to do what he deems is wisest..."[20] Finally, on December 13, 1899, 11 months after his appointment, Brooke was dismissed as Military Governor. The intrigues in Washington had prevailed. Brooke went into retirement having expressed serious doubts about Cuba's ability for self-government: "By my own observation ... I do not believe the time has yet come for this people to form a stable government."[21]

## THE LEONARD WOOD ADMINISTRATION

Leonard Wood was a hands-on, stern administrator who took command on December 20, 1899, with a clear mandate from President McKinley: "I want you to go down there to get the people ready for a Republican form of government. I leave the details of procedure to you. Give them a good school system, try to strengthen out their courts, put them on their feet as best as you can. We want to do all we can for them and go out of the island as soon as we safely can."[22] Wood included in his cabinet some of the most respected Cuban intellectuals and revolutionary leaders, including Enrique Jose Varona and two generals, Juan Rius Rivera and Diego Tamayo.

The mayors of the main cities were also from rebel army ranks: Gen. Porfirio Valiente in Santiago, Gen. Pedro "Periquito" Perez in Guantanamo, Gen. Manuel Plana in Bayamo, Gen. Gerardo Machado in Santa Clara, Gen. Juan Bravo in Trinidad, Gen. Carlos M. Rojas in Cardenas, and three prominent civilian leaders, Cesar Lancis, Santiago Garcia Canizares and Perfecto Lacoste as mayors of Pinar del Rio, Santi Spiritu and Havana, respectively. Some historians' argument that the revolutionary leaders were ignored or intentionally neglected by U.S. military authorities during the three years and five months of occupation is a clear-cut case of self-deception.

The newly arrived military governor set out immediately to tour the island under his command. He reorganized the educational system, with Alexis Frye heading the drive to teach Cuba's children. When the Spaniards left the island, there were 541 primary schools (65% of the population was illiterate). By the time Wood left Cuba in 1902, this number had risen to 3,800 schools providing instruction to 255,000 children of every race and gender. Child labor was prohibited.[23] To improve the quality of education, 1,500 Cuban teachers were sent to Boston, where they participated in a summer training program at Harvard University. Under Wood, 25% of the national budget was spent on education.

Another major accomplishment was the much-needed railway line linking Santa Clara with Santiago de Cuba. Since Santa Clara was already connected to Havana, the new railroad allowed the entire island to be linked, opening up virgin territory for agricultural production and commerce. William Van Horne, builder of the Canadian Pacific Railway, and Robert Flemming, a London banker, became the leading figures of the national railway that was completed on December 1, 1902. Before the trains reached Oriente, travel time between Santiago and Havana was 10 days, mostly by sea; it had now been shortened to a mere 24 hours.[24]

During the Wood administration, yellow fever, a recurrent and deadly disease, was eradicated. Cuban doctor Carlos J. Finlay's theory that the transmitter of the disease was the stegomyia mosquito was corroborated by a medical group headed by William Gorgas. Two doctors, Jesse Lazear and James Carroll, volunteered to be inoculated by the mosquito; Carroll survived, but Lazear died. Dr. Gorgas soon launched a massive sanitation program to eradicate the mosquitoes, with the result that Yellow Fever was eventually completely wiped out on the island.

New roads were opened, bridges built, Havana's streets paved and the Malecon (boardwalk) renovated. The water supply of major cities was greatly improved. Construction projects meant thousands of new jobs. Horse-drawn streetcars were replaced by electricity-powered streetcars (*tranvias*), ports were dredged and new piers built to facilitate overseas commerce. Some historians believe Leonard Wood to be the best head of government in Cuba's history.[25] However, for some Cubans at the time, he was an arrogant, highhanded Anglo-Saxon who wanted to refashion Cuba into a mirror image of American society and, eventually, make it a state of the American Union. On Wood's views on this issue, his friend "Teddy" Roosevelt wrote: "(Wood) believed that after a brief period of independence, which would satisfy the sentiment for theoretical liberty, the Cubans would voluntarily ask to be admitted to the Union. Annexation by acclamation had been his dream from the beginning."

## POLITICAL PARTIES, THE 1901 CONSTITUTION
## AND THE PLATT AMENDMENT

With the end of Spanish colonial rule, the Cuban leadership began to organize political parties for the promised elections that were to pave the way for an independent Republic but, none of the parties possessed national cohesion. They were mostly local or regional organizations without ideological commitment. Political loyalties were shifting affairs controlled by personal bonds and individual ambitions. There were dozens of small local organization. Within eight years, most of these organizations would disband, disappear or merge into larger parties, answering, in each case, the needs or fulfilling the political ambitions of the "cacique."[26]

On April 1, 1900, five months after his appointment, Wood

promulgated "The Election Law." Two months later (June 16), municipal elections were held throughout the island. The new electoral system excluded women and illiterate men. From 418,000 males of voting age, 200,630 could read and were eligible to vote. All veterans regardless of skin color or ability to read had the right to cast a vote. With the help of Maximo Gomez, the Nacionales of Alfredo Zayas won in Havana; the Republicanos of Jose Miguel Gomez carried Las Villas. Overall, the local bosses won in their municipalities.

Encouraged by the results, Wood called for a Cuban Constitutional Convention. He wrote Secretary Roots. "I am going to work on a Constitution ... similar to our own, my idea is to call a constitutional convention right away ... and, simultaneously, with the adoption of the Constitution, get a treaty that will bind (our) two countries and definitely state their relations."[27] This view was shared by McKinley, who, early in the U.S. occupation of the island, stated: "The new Cuba yet to arise from the ashes of the past needs to be bound to us by ties of singular intimacy."[28]

On September 15, elections for delegates were held, and on November 5, 1900, Cuba's first Constitutional Convention began framing the fundamental law of the island. The 33 delegates were among the best and brightest minds in Cuba. Within weeks, it became obvious that the underlying issue at the convention debates was the definition of the "singular intimacy" between Cuba and the United States. While it was clear that delegates were legally protecting the individual rights of citizens, it was also becoming obvious that the U.S. administration was concerned about Cubans' ability for self-government, prompting a decision to leave open the option of future intervention.

In June 1901, Secretary Root said: "The character of the ruling class is such that their administration of the affairs of the island will require the restraining influence of the U.S. Government for many years to come."[29] Whether their perception of Cuba's ability for self-government was right or wrong, the issue of U.S. intervention in Cuba's internal affairs became a source of deep resentment among Cuban nationalists. The fact remained that the new Constitution would guarantee citizens' freedom as never before in the island's history, though sovereignty remained still a myth.

Senator Orville Platt went forward with the administration's goals, and on February 25, 1901, authored a bill establishing the conditions for granting independence to Cuba. A few days later, the Platt Amendment was passed by the U.S. Congress. In April, a group of convention delegates traveled to Washington to plead for Cuba's sovereignty. The U.S. administration was cordial but unmoved. On March 2, the Platt Amendment was signed into law by President McKinley. There was strong opposition to the amendment in Cuba, but Wood insisted there was no room for negotiation. In a letter to Root, he wrote: "The time has come to state clearly the position of the government and to state it as an ultimatum of which there will be no further discussion."[30] Finally, a bitterly divided Cuban Constitutional Convention accepted the Platt Amendment and included it an appendage to the 1901 Constitution.

## *The Platt Amendment*

I.   That the government of Cuba shall never enter into any treaty or other compact with any foreign power or powers which will impair or tend to impair the independence of Cuba, or in any manner authorize or permit any foreign power or powers to obtain by colonization or, for military or naval purposes or otherwise, lodgment in or control over any portion of said island.

II.   That said government shall not assume or contract any public debt, to pay the interest upon which, and to make reasonable sinking fund provision for the ultimate discharge of which, the ordinary revenues of the island, after defraying the current expenses of government shall be inadequate.

III. That the government of Cuba consents that the United States may exercise the right to intervene for the preservation of Cuban independence the maintenance of a government adequate for the protection of life, property and individual liberty, and for discharging the obligations with respect to Cuba imposed by the Treaty of Paris on the United States, now to be assumed and undertaken by the government of Cuba.

IV. That all Acts of the United States in Cuba during its military occupancy thereof are ratified and validated, and all lawful rights acquired hereunder shall be maintained and protected.

V.   That the government of Cuba will execute and as far as necessary extend the plans already devised or other plans to be mutually agreed upon, for the sanitation of the cities of the island, to the end that a recurrence of epidemic and infectious diseases may be prevented, thereby assuring protection to the people and commerce of Cuba, as well as to the commerce of the southern ports of the United States and of the people residing therein.

VI. That the Isle of Pines shall be omitted from the proposed constitutional boundaries of Cuba, the title thereto being left to future adjustment by treaty.

VII.    That to enable the United States to maintain the independence of Cuba, and to protect the people thereof, as well as for its own defense, the government of Cuba will sell or lease to the United States land necessary for coaling or naval stations at certain specified points, to be agreed upon with the President of the United States.

VIII.    That by way of further assurance the government of Cuba will embody the foregoing provisions in a permanent treaty with the United States.

## *THE DECAPITATED INDEPENDENCE SYNDROME*

Cubans were now ready to embark on the difficult path of a liberal republic, with full political freedom and civil rights, but a decapitated independence. To the U.S. leadership, this was a necessary safeguard for internal peace and commercial stability, while for most Cubans, it was a painful blow to nationalistic pride.

There are few cases in Cuba's history where an issue has so completely dominated a period as The Platt Amendment has. The effect has clouded the important differences between liberty and independence. The 1901 Constitution provided the people with a set of civil rights never before implemented in the island, but article 3 of The Platt Amendment giving the United States the right to intervene in Cuba overshadowed this fundamental achievement. For the first time since the Spanish Conquistadores landed on the island, the people, through their elected delegates, had crafted the laws providing for a national government in which all basic political rights and freedoms of a liberal Republic were protected in the Constitution.

For some historians, however, the Platt Amendment was the principal cause of the Republic's maladies: "The Cubans remained disorganized and politically castrated, unable to reap the fruit of their labor. This had a ruinous effect on the development of a genuine national consciousness as the political system itself was designed and imposed by a foreign power."[31] Over the next century, there would be a huge outpouring of criticism led by the vitriolic Marxist dogmatic vision, while in recent times, a comprehensive assessment has advanced a wider, more complex set of cultural and political factors leading to the collapse of the liberal Republic.

One incisive argument is that of Professor Mary Catherine Crabb. She stated: "while the negative impact of the U.S. as imperial power during this time should not be ignored, I believe that this interaction of Cuban politics under the Platt Amendment is incorrect for the simple reason that it overlooks vital cultural continuities between the colonial and the early republican model of government."[32]

By the turn of the century, other countries were enjoying individual freedoms, yet lacked independence, which, considering cultural and geographical differences with Cuba, could serve as point of reference on the sovereignty issue. This was the case of Canada, Australia and New Zealand. As part of the British Empire, all three enjoyed autonomous democratic government but lacked state independence, which they would gain in due time minus the bitter display of grieving, fatalistic discourse centered on the political syndrome generated by a Platt Amendment.

## THE ELECTION AND BIRTH OF THE REPUBLIC

With the New Constitution and Platt Amendment in place, Wood called for presidential elections in Cuba on December 1901. Maximo Gomez, the beloved hero of the war and the first choice of the U.S. administration for president, decided not to run and instead supported Tomas Estrada Palma, Marti's successor as leader of the Cuban Revolutionary Party and former president of the government in arms during the Ten Years War. He had married the daughter of a Guatemalan president, settled in the United States in Central Valley where he became a Quaker and respected schoolmaster and rejoined the cause of Cuba's independence under the charismatic leadership of Jose Marti.

The other candidate was Bartolome Maso, legendary war figure who had joined Carlos Manuel de Cespedes in October 1868 and was president of the rebel government in 1898. Maso challenged Estrada Palma and offered his candidacy running on a platform of opposition to the Platt Amendment. Maso's main supporters were Salvador Cisnero Betancourt and Juan Gualberto Gomez.

On June 1, 1901, Maximo Gomez traveled to the Quaker village of Central Valley where he met with Estrada Palma and advanced the idea of his candidacy for president of Cuba. Estrada Palma accepted and Gomez began campaigning for the upcoming election. Estrada Palma had the backing of Alfredo Zayas, Martin Morua Delgado, and generals Jesus Rabi, Emilio Nunez and Jose Miguel Gomez. The campaign grew devisive and violent; not even the legendary heroes were spared. While campaining in Camaguey and Manzanillo, an angry pro-Maso crowd attacked Maximo Gomez with stones.[33] Most Cubans reacted with horror to the assault. It was a sign that for those intransigent zealots, there were no boundaries to the degree of violence they were capable of unleashing against their opponents, an unhealthy political trait that was to define the often violent reactions to debates so important in the civil life of a functional democracy.

The Republic's first election was traumatic. Maso claimed that the Central Board of Elections was controlled by his political adversaries and withdrew his candidacy. Estrada Palma won the elections without opposition while still living in the United States. It was not an auspicious beginning. The president elect did not campaign for office. In fact, the real winner was Maximo Gomez, who commanded great respect among the people and campaigned tirelessly throughout the island on Estrada Palma's behalf. The president elect landed in Gibara, Oriente, on April 20, met with Maso in Manzanillo where the two old patriots embraced each other in a symbolic gesture of unity. A few weeks before their arrival in Havana on May 11, 1902, Palma met in Washington with Secretary Root and Governor Wood to work out the details for the transfer of government from the United States to the people of Cuba. May 20 was set as the birthday of the island's liberal Republic.

There was great excitement among the people as the date for the transfer of power grew near. Cubans understood the historical magnitude of the impinging events. On May 20, 1902, the process began to unfold. The official ceremony took place in the palace of the former Spanish captain generals, where Leonard Wood transferred the government of Cuba to the Cubans. After the Stars and Stripes of the American Union were lowered, Maximo Gomez raised the Lone Star of Cuba. At Morro Castle, Gen. Emilio Nunez raised the flag of the New Republic. With deep emotion in his eyes and his voice, Gomez, a steady hand throughout 30 years of heroism and immense sacrifice, stated: "I believe we have arrived."

## IT FAILED THE FIRST ROUND

With full freedom and a tenuous independence, Cubans began the long-awaited, difficult task of self-government that could provide the laws, economic infrastructure and services, such as free education, hospitals, roads and police security, that would promote and uphold a capitalistic market economy with the United States as main commercial partner and financial investor.

Just as the rest of the Caribbean, Cuba was at the time an impoverished enclave with certain noticeable differences. It had a well-developed sugar industry, a modern and efficient management group, an experienced labor force, available foreign capital and a long-standing partnership with the U.S. sugar market, all of which greatly improved Cuba's ability to generate wealth.

The challenge for Cubans was, therefore, not creating wealth, but how to distribute it, especially for the majority of impoverished Cubans who for centuries had been denied the most productive sources of wealth. The recently defeated Spaniards remained in control of the retail business, including food groceries and clothing. Banking, tobacco and mining were in foreign hands, mostly American, while the rest of agricultural production was hampered by a depressed national market that barely yielded the needed return for growth and development. Politics had become the best and fastest road to economic success and helped explain the ferocity of the struggle for power. What makes this issue truly remarkable is that within two generations, Cubans would recover control of the island's wealth.

From the beginning of his presidency, Estrada Palma put forward his administration's goal, which included an honest, efficient management of public funds, a sound educational system and a favorable commercial treaty with the United States. He succeeded in all three areas. This Cuban-American Quaker is remembered as the presidential paradigm of financial honesty. On his inauguration day, the treasury of the Republic had $539,994; two years later, it had more than seven million.[34] Under Estrada Palma, 25% of the budget went to education. The president's motto was: "more teachers than soldiers."

On May 22, 1903, a Reciprocity Treaty was signed, giving Cuba's sugar a 20% tariff preference over other sugar-producing countries. In return, Cuba granted certain U.S. manufactured products a tariff reduction of between 25% and 40%. This was a huge boost to the war-torn economy. The agreement helped Cuba establish a solid foothold in the largest sugar market on the planet. In 1904, the average American consumed 75 lbs. of sugar per year.[35] The Reciprocity Treaty encouraged capital investment in the big sugar factories or *centrales*, which rose from 50 million in 1896 to 205 million in 1909, while sugar production tripled between 1900 and 1903 to one million tons.[36]

As the 1905 race for the presidency got underway, the political environment on the island began to deteriorate. Estrada Palma was told by friends and supporters that he was needed for four more years. He agreed and announced his reelection bid. Hoping to partake of the spoils of government, the political opposition to Estrada Palma's reelection became a formidable challenge. The Liberal Party coalesced as a national political force led by Gen. Jose Miguel Gomez, the charismatic veteran leader from Santa Clara, and Doctor Alfredo Zayas, a corrupt, clever politician, who ran on the liberal ticket for president and vice president, respectively, to unseat the president.

## ESTRADA PALMA REQUESTED U.S. MILITARY INTERVENTION

The president's faction reacted by forming "the fighting cabinet," led by Gen. Fernando Freyre, who displayed a high-handed, intimidating behavior, dismissing employees from their jobs who supported the liberal candidates. The situation turned violent when news broke that Col. Enrique Villuendas, a popular opposition leader, had been murdered by a local chief of police. In protest, the Liberal Party withdrew from the presidential race, leaving Estrada Palma to win again without opposition. It was a brief and bitter victory when on August 16, 1906; the opposition led by regional leaders rose up in rebellion in what became the August Little War or *Guerrita de Agosto*. The small rural guard force was incapable of suppressing the uprising, and Estrada Palma requested U.S. military intervention.

The U.S. president, Theodore Roosevelt, did not welcome the request from the Cubans, but Estrada Palma insisted on landing 2,000 to 3,000 soldiers to restore order on the island.[37] Roosevelt tried to work out an accommodation between the rebels and the government. He wrote the Cuban ambassador in Washington: "Our intervention in Cuban affairs will only come if Cuba herself shows that she had fallen into revolutionary habit, that she lacks the self-restraint necessary to ensure peaceful self-government and that her contending factions have plunged the country into anarchy."[38] Roosevelt sent Secretary of War William Taft and Under Secretary of State Roger Bacon to Cuba to negotiate a solution. Estrada Palma again rejected a compromise solution and threatened to resign if the United States did not intervene militarily.

Roosevelt wrote Estrada Palma: "I most earnestly ask that you sacrifice your own feeling on the altar of your country's good and yield to Mr. Taft's request by continuing in the presidency a sufficient length of time to in his judgment inaugurate the new temporary government... I pray that you at least have sacrificed yourself for your country and that when you leave office you leave your country free."[39] The unyielding old veteran again stood his ground. For William Taft, Estrada Palma was "a good deal as an old ass...obstinate ... in their characteristic Spanish way"[40]; and he was probably right. On September 28, 1906, the first president of the Republic resigned, living the island without government. On the following day, 2,000 Marines landed in Cuba, initiating the the second U.S. intervention. What made this one different was that most of the government bureaucracy at the local and national levels remained in Cuban hands, and U.S. soldiers and Marines remained stationed outside major cities, and the Lone Star of Cuba was not replaced by the U.S. flag.

## *VIOLENCE AS AN ACCEPTED POLITICAL FORMULA*

For Cuba's national pride, the fall of the Republic was a terrible embarrassment; for months, critics of Cuba's ability for self-government had openly stated their case, but for many Cubans then, just as today, the real culprit of the Republic's failure was the American intervention in the war and the Platt Amendment. Seldom mentioned is the dysfunctional heritage with violence as an accepted political formula. It is evident that there were serious difficulties in installing on the island a democratic republic based on rule of law and leadership ability to find common grounds to settle political disputes without resorting to the use of violence. The bitter truth was that the liberal Republic failed in the first round.

Professor Aguilar stated on this issue: "The fact that the Cubans themselves had invited foreign rule provoked a wave of pessimism and disillusionment throughout every level of Cuban society. It was no longer possible to maintain even a pretense of faith in self-government."[41] For the gregarious Cubans, politics was a passionate struggle for power and the nation was a Balkan melodrama of intrigues, loyalties to local and regional political bosses, a share in the spoils of government, and, while outside of political power, a recurrent call for rebellion.

## CHARLES MAGOON AND THE SECOND U.S. INTERVENTION

On October 6, 1906, the U.S. governor, Charles Magoon arrived in Havana. He was a 45-year-old judge from Minnesota who was serving as governor of the Panama Canal Zone construction project when President Roosevelt appointed him to head the U.S. provisional government in Cuba. Soft spoken, friendly and accessible, Magoon's administrative skills resembled Gen. Brooke's. He worked closely and efficiently with the Cuban political leadership.

Among his first directives was the establishment of an Advisory Board that included many of the most talented and respected Cubans whom he would consult on relevant issues. He also initiated a major public works program that included improving and expanding aqueducts in many cities, building roads and railroad tracks, dredging harbors and constructing bridges. The project created badly needed jobs throughout the island.

In an effort to diffuse growing veteran discontent and

accommodate political factions, Magoon granted a number of bureaucratic sinecures known as *botellas*, which ended up depleting the carefully guarded budget surplus left by the Estrada Palma government. It was an unfortunate practice that would discredit his tenure in office.

The *botellas* issue caused Cuban historians to criticize Magoon's administration. "Greedy for despoilment. He fell like a buzzard on the treasury of Cuba and devours it"[42]; "His kindness in granting 'botellas' became a public scandal... the administration in general returned to the corrupt practice of colonial times."[43] In a virulent attack, it was claimed that "the American Governor ... profoundly corrupted the Cuban nation."[44] Later historians suggested a different perspective in regards to the corruption issue. The noted scholar Hugh Thomas wrote: "The argument of most Cuban historians, later copied by guilt-ridden North Americans, that Magoon taught the Cubans corruption are among the most hilarious examples ever of self-deception."[45]

During Magoon's administration and after a heated debate, the Cuban Permanent Army was established. Those who opposed the measure argued that the Army could eventually become the decisive factor in Cuba's political life, in the Spanish tradition of militarism or, even worst, in the Latin American model of brutal messianic "caudillos." Others believed it the key to securing government stability against armed rebellions such as those that toppled President Estrada Palma. Gen. Pino Guerra, the veteran who had led the August 1906 uprising, was rewarded by being given command of a 10,000-man army — a bad precedent. Just as the second intervention got underway, President Roosevelt stated U.S. priorities. "... to establish peace and order ... start a new government and then leave the island."[46]

## *ANNEXATION NO MORE*

By this time the idea of annexation was out among the main proponents of the U.S. expansionist agenda. One of the leading imperialist advocates, Senator Cabot Lodge, wrote: "Disgust with the Cubans is very general. Nobody wants to annex them."[47] Cuba's historical version of the issue of annexation tends to be presented as a manifestation of the imperialist need of a voracious neighbor to exploit the economic resources of the largest island in the

Caribbean. This is a distortion of the conceptual meaning of the word. Considering the Texas case as model, annexation is acceptance by the U.S. Congress of a formal request from an independent country to join the American Union as full partner with equal rights and responsibilities.

But by the time of the 1906 intervention, the old idea of annexing Cuba to the United States was no longer an issue among powerful politicians in North America. Now the preferred, more convenient, idea was for Cuba to be treated as a political and economic protectorate. It allowed for the naval bases at Guantanamo and Bahia Honda and for protection of financial interests on the island without granting full partnership in the American Union.

In Cuba, the idea of annexation had become moribund. It was especially abhorrent to the large population of African ancestry, who had felt the sting of discrimination of the white American soldier and had read and heard of the KKK's persecution of African-Americans in the South. Annexation was also rejected by the majority of Spaniards who remained in the island after the war and whose lives and properties were protected by the Cuban Republic. For centuries, Spaniards had controlled retail business as a quasi monopoly; annexation meant the arrival of well-financed open market competition. And for most Cubans inspired by Jose Marti's idea of a "Cuba Libre" and the heroic deeds during the 30-year struggle for freedom, it was not a welcome proposition.

Despite the bloody fight for independence, the Cubans were strongly attached to their Hispanic and African roots. "La Hispanidad" was felt in the language, religion and extended family loyalties, together with a relentless quest for the pleasures of life, vividly manifested in music, dance and relaxed sensual intercourse, all of which constituted unacceptable behavior in the dull, hypocritical, Calvinist American society of the turn of the Century.

It was obvious that by the second U.S. intervention, the idea of annexation was much less attractive for everyone involved. At this juncture, Magoon called for national elections in order to turn the reigns of power over to the Cubans.

To make a bid for the presidency, the Conservative Party (Conservadores) was created mostly from the ranks of the old

Estrada Palma political coalition. The Conservadores were led by Gen. Mario Garcia Menocal. Facing the challenge, the liberals united their various factions and won the November 1908 election. Their leader, Gen. Jose Miguel Gomez, became the second president of the Republic. On March 31, 1909, Magoon transferred the government to the Cubans, ending the second U.S. intervention in the island.

# CHAPTER XI

## *FROM INTERVENTION TO INTERVENTION*

[1] Hugh Thomas, op cit, 400

[2] Luis E. Aguilar. Cuba 1933: *Prologue to Revolution*. (The Norton Library, New York, 1974),15

[3] From Garcia to Estrada Palma, June 27, 1989. (Boletin Archivo Nacional de Cuba, 1936), 108-112

[4] Joaquin Llaverias and Emeterio Santovenia. *Actas de la Asamblea de Representantes y del Consejo de Gobierno durante la Guerra de Independencia*. (La Habana, El Siglo XX, 1932), 119-122

[5] New York Herald, September 25, 1898 and La Lucha, September 30, 1898

[6] Boletin Archivo Nacional 32 (1933) *De Gomez a Estrada Palma*. (October 28, 1898), 94-95

[7] Rubens. *Liberty*, op cit, 392-393

[8] Llaveria and Santovenia. *Actas*, Vol. 5, 43-61

[9] Robert P. Porter. *Special Report on the visit to Maximo Gomez and in Relation to the Payment and Disbandonment of the Insurgent Army*, Washington, 1899.

[10] Rafael Martinez Ortiz. *Cuba los Primeros Años de Independencia*, Vol. 3 (Editorial LeLivre, Paris,1929), 55-56

[11] Brooke cabinet: Jose Antonio Gonzalez Lanusa in Education and Justice; Pablo Desvervine in Finance; Adolfo Saenz in Public Work and Commerce and Domingo Mendez Capote as Interior Secretary.

[12] Herman Hagedorn I pg. 226

[13] Ibid, 236

[14] Samuel Gompers. *Imperialism: Its Danger and Wrongs*. (American Federationist, V (Nov. 1898), 182

[15] Elihu Roots to Paul Dana, January 1900, Roots Papers (Department of State)

[16] The New York Times. December 19, 1898

[17] Outlook 63: Cuban Character (December 23, 1899)

[18] Herman Hagedorn, J. pg. 371

[19] Ibid, 282

[20] Roosevelt, Letters, II 1005 (Department of State)

[21] Brooke to McKinley. Sept. 26, 1899 in McKinley's Papers (Department of State)

[22] Herman Hagedorn, Vol. 1, 261

[23] Civil Report of Wood 1901, Vol VII

[24] Irene A. Wright. *Cuba*. (New York 1910), 354

[25] Herman Hagedorn, op cit, Vol. 1, 329; Fitzgibbon, op cit, 31; Martinez Ortiz, op cit, Vol. 1, 427-38; Trelles, op cit, 5

[26] It refers to a tribal chief or, as in this case, to political bosses.

[27] Herman Hagedorn, op cit, Vol. 1, 302

[28] Hugh Thomas, op cit, 443

[29] Washington Evening Star, June 11, 1901 pg.1

[30] Herman Hagedorn, op cit, Vol. 1, 368

[31] Juan M. del Aguila, *Dilema of a Revolution.* (Westview Press, Atlanta, 1988),18

[32] Mary Katerine Crabb. *Cuban Communism: 1959 – 2003.* (Editors Irving Horowitz and Jaime Suchlicki, 2003). 11th Edition, 136

[33] Rafael Estenger. *Sincera Historia de Cuba,* op cit, 253

[34] R. Iznaga. *Tres Años de Republica: Folleto Político.* (Havana, Rambla y Bouza, 1905), 28

[35] Hugh Thomas, op cit, 469

[36] José Alvarez Diaz. *A Study on Cuba.* (Miami: University of Miami Press, 1963),.233

[37] Taft and Bacon, op cit, 207

[38] Roosevelt, Letters, V (William Taft Letters, Department of State), 411-13

[39] Ibid, 422

[40] H.F. Pringle. *Life and Times of William Howard Taft.* 2 vols (New York, 1939), Vol. 1, 310

[41] Aguilar, op cit, 28

[42] M. Lozano Casado. *La Personalidad del General José Miguel Gomez.* (1913), 17

[43] M. Ortiz, op cit, 243-244

[44] Telles, op cit, 9

[45] Hugh Thomas, op cit, 485

[46] Allan Reed Millet, op cit, 146

[47] Selections from the correspondence of Theodore Roosevelt and Henry Cabot Lodge. 1884-1918 Ed. H.C. Lodge (1925) pg. 233

# CHAPTER XII

# THE PROTECTORATE (1909-1934)

*THE PRESIDENCY OF JOSE MIGUEL GOMEZ – THE ARMY AS A DECISIVE POLITICAL FACTOR – THE MENOCAL PRESIDENCY – THE "DANCE" OF THE MILLIONS – THE COLLAPSE OF THE ECONOMY – THE PRESIDENCY OF ALFREDO ZAYAS – IT ENTERS GERARDO MACHADO, THE FIRST POLITICAL MESSIAH – THE ARRIVAL OF IDEOLOGICAL MADNESS.*

## THE PRESIDENCY OF JOSE MIGUEL GOMEZ

For the next 25 years and four Cuban presidencies, the island's internal affairs were to be closely monitored, heavily influenced and, in some instances, controlled by Washington. The first of the "Protectorate" presidents was Jose Miguel Gomez, a charismatic leader of the Independence War, congenial, tolerant, but corrupt. Gomez was probably the most popular of the Cuban politicians of this period. He presided over four years of economic growth in full compliance with the individual rights of a fragile democracy.

Gomez' presidency coincided with the election of William Howard Taft. The new U.S. president was quite familiar with Cuba's political conflicts, and upon taking office, stated his administration's goals for the island: "to maintain peace but to keep the U.S. out of Cuba." What did Taft mean? Was it a small, swift military operation against specific rebellions? The answer was soon to come. During Gomez' administration, Havana grew into a cosmopolitan city with more than 300,000 residents who could turn noisy, crowded days into magical, bohemian, memorable nights. Cuba was also undergoing an extraordinary, massive migration form Spain. In the 17 years that followed the birth of the Cuban Republic in 1902, more than 436,000 Spaniards made the transatlantic voyage and settled in the island.[1] The former colony, the beloved Cuba, was again for the Spaniards the island of hope and dreams. Fidel Castro's father, Angel Castro, a Galician, returned to Cuba with this wave of economic immigrants. He made his first trip with Gen.

Valeriano Wayler's troops; now he was returning to build a fortune in the northern Oriente province with close commercial ties to the powerful United Fruit Company.

A challenging crisis began to develop in 1907, when a group of radical black leaders founded the Independent Party of Color (Partido Independiente de Color)[2] whose members bitterly complained that Afro-Cubans had been betrayed by the new Republic and needed their own political organization to voice their rights and interests. Juan Gualberto Gomez and Martin Morua Delgado, the most influential and respected Afro-Cubans, rejected this option. Morua, at the time president of the Senate, led Congress in enacting a law that prohibited political parties based on race or religion. On the surface, the crisis seemed to have been defused, but it was not.

On May 20, 1912, several thousand Afro-Cubans in Oriente province launched a rebellion under the leadership of two war veterans, Evaristo Estenoz and Pedro Ivonet, which was felt throughout Cuba. The island-Protectorate was facing the horrors of a race war and the possibility of U.S. intervention. Secretary of State Philander Knox left no doubts in his message to the American Minister in Havana. "The *Nebraska* (a battleship) should arrive at Havana tomorrow... a gunboat would be ordered to Nipe (a bay near the United Fruit holdings)... you will inform the Cuban government that in the event of its inability or failure to protect the lives or properties of American citizens in Cuba, the government of the U.S. will land forces."[3] Cuba's president was prepared to face the rebellion.

## THE ARMY AS A DECISIVE POLITICAL FACTOR

Since taking office in 1909, Gomez had taken the necessary measures to reshape the Armed Forces by integrating the Rural Guard into the Army and appointing his close friend and war veteran, General Monteagudo, commander of the 10,000-man force. The president also created a coastal navy, with two light cruisers, the *Cuba* and *Patria*, as well as several gunboats. Gomez did not make the Estrada Palma mistake of not having an army to fight and so was able to survive recurrent Cuban rebellions.

Ordered to engage the rebels, the new Army advanced on their strongholds in Oriente. Washington would not wait much longer and landed a Marine detachment on Daiquiri Beach. Feeling the political pressure, the Cuban Army found the rebels and crushed them. Ivonet, Estenoz and more than 1,000 of their followers perished in the fight and criminal persecution. This tragic episode marked a milestone in the island's history. From this bloody insurrection, the Cuban military would play a major role in Cuba's political life. At first, the army served to protect the government and crush the frequent veteran rebellions, which could endanger the government's stability and precipitate a U.S. intervention; however, as the military tested their new-found power, the army began to evolve into a potent political machine capable of influencing or even deciding election results through intimidation, graft or simply by stuffing ballot boxes with the names of their candidates. The Cuban Army became even more assertive later on, including a direct assault on the office of the president. It is fair to say that from the Army of the Protectorate-Republic to the Rebel Army of Fidel Castro, the Cuban military has been a decisive factor of political power in the island — an unfortunate fact of history.

Political corruption became so widespread that it turned into a socially accepted pattern of behavior. Nicknamed the "Shark" (El Tiburon), Gomez shared the spoils of power lavishly. He was referred to as the shark that swims but shares in the splash (*El tiburón se baña, pero salpica*). During his time in office, large sums of money were made from government concessions to build roads, bridges, aqueducts, sewers and telephone networks, and for land speculation, including Havana's Villanueva railroad station and the dredging of the island's major ports. President Gomez reestablished cockfighting and the national lottery, both very popular among Cubans. The lottery was held every Saturday afternoon, with thousands of collection stations throughout the Island. It was an instant success, and the collection stations soon became one of the most corrupt tools of wealth and political influence.

During Gomez' tenure, the Cuban economy grew steadily thanks to sugar production, which reached the two million ton mark with the 1912-13 harvest. He did not run for reelection — a wise and uncommon decision. His Liberal Party, badly split, nominated Alfredo Zayas. A liberal faction joined the conservative candidate, Mario Garcia Menocal, who had secured the support of the Army Commander, Gen. Monteagudo, who professed a manifest dislike for Zayas. Menocal won and on May 20, 1913, became Cuba's third president.

## THE MENOCAL PRESIDENCY

Mayor Gen. Mario Garcia Menocal was a war hero, a Cornell University graduate, a landed patrician, a distinguished gentleman and probably the most aristocratic Cuban president of all. He was a partner at H.B. Hawley, a Cuban-American company that owned the "Chaparra" sugar mill, the largest in the world and which Menocal had successfully managed for a time. As a political leader, he was pragmatic and authoritarian, with a cunning sense of timing. Like Gomez, he was also corrupt, but unlike him, lacked the populist charisma and generosity. Menocal's first presidential term was good for the national welfare, including the creation in 1914 of the Cuban peso.

Since the birth of the Republic in 1902, the economy had suffered from a diversity of foreign currencies, including the Spanish peso and the U.S. dollar. Such diversity caused cumbersome financial stress on commercial and banking transactions. Menocal solved the problem by creating a national monetary system with the Cuban peso at par value with the U.S. dollar, the only foreign currency officially allowed to remain in circulation.

Another significant accomplishment of Menocal's administration was regulation and expansion of Cuba's banking system, greatly stimulated by the rise in sugar prices in the international market due to the economic impact of World War I. Thirty-seven new banking institutions were founded during his presidency. The Banco Nacional de Cuba underwent extraordinary expansion, with more than 194 million pesos/dollars in deposit and 130 branches throughout Cuba.[4]

The railway communication system was also improved. By 1919, there were 4,900 Km. of railroads, with 480 Km. under construction. The train became a major source of transportation linking most regions of the island. Fifty-five thousand passengers and 74,000 tons of cargo used the railways daily.[5] The airplane also came very early to Cuba. In 1913, ten years after the first flight of the Wright brothers at Kitty Hawk, a Cuban aviator, Agustin Parla, flew from Key West to Mariel, and in November 1920, Havana was connected to Key West by Aeromarine Airways, flying three hydroplanes and also carrying mail.[6]

## THE "DANCE" OF THE MILLIONS

During Menocal's presidency, the sugar industry flourished, reaching 2,608,000 tons in 1915, and increased its share of world production from 2.7% in 1900 to 15.4% in 1915. By this time, and protected by the Reciprocity Treaty that provided special tariff benefits, Cuba's sugar dominated the U.S. market, crushing the competition from the rest of the Caribbean islands. However, the biggest impact on the Cuban economy and its people came with the sudden, tremendous increase in the price of sugar at the outbreak of World War I.

### TABLE XIII
### Cuba's Sugar Mills, Production and Price from the Birth of the Republic to the Outbreak of World War I

| YEAR | ACTIVE SUGAR MILLS (CENTRALES) | TONS | PRICE |
|------|-------------------------------|------|-------|
| 1902 | 171 | 850,000 | 1.93 |
| 1905 | 174 | 1, 173,349 | 2.89 |
| 1910 | 175 | 1, 843,127 | 2.82 |
| 1912 | 172 | 1, 912,764 | 2.71 |
| 1913 | 171 | 2, 441,980 | 2.05 |
| 1914 | 173 | 2, 615,220 | 2.74 [7] |

As Table XIII shows, the price of sugar remained constant from 1902 to the beginning of the Great War. Prior to World War I, the financial benefits for mill owners and bankers came mostly from the steady increase in *central* sugar production. With the outbreak of war in August 1914, the price began to increase.[8] With Germany, Austria-Hungary and Russia, the three major European producers of beet sugar, locked in combat, England, their main client before the war, had to look elsewhere for sugar. Cuba was ready, willing and able to supply the British Empire its sugar needs.

## TABLE XIV
### England's Purchase of Cuban Sugar During WWI

| YEAR | TONS |
|------|------|
|  | 450,000 |
| 1915-16 | 550,000 |
| 1916-17 | 780,000 |
| 1917-18 | 883,000 [9] |

The economic future of the island looked bright as never before. When the United States entered the war in 1917, Cuba joined the Allies' war effort by entering in 1918 into a fixed price agreement of 4.6 cents per pound of raw sugar. With the prospect of excellent returns, American capital flowed into the island to buy land for cane production and to build new and larger *centrales*. During World War I (1914-18), 25 modern mills were built,[10] making Cuba once again the largest sugar producer in the world.

The war brought unprecedented prosperity, and moneylenders eagerly sought customers. Strict banking procedures were ignored. Many loans went unsecured. Jose Lopez Rodriguez, known as "El Gallego Pote," a prominent developer of the Miramar suburb, was given a $5 million unsecured loan to buy the majority shares of the Banco Nacional de Cuba, a private institution that became a leading lender during the sugar boom.

In this money-mad environment, Cubans were called to the polls in November of 1917. Menocal decided to seek reelection and had Gen. Emilio Nunez as his vice presidential running mate. The Liberals again nominated Alfredo Zayas, but this time with all the liberal factions allied with him, Zayas presented a united, liberal coalition. Intense violence erupted during the campaign, and many people were killed. Zayas won the election, but fraud overrode the will of the electorate. The fraud was so massive that 300,000 votes were counted above and beyond the 500,000 allowed. Menocal had stolen the election, and the liberals took up arms.

Former president Jose Miguel Gomez, joined by the Army Garrisons in Santiago de Cuba and Camaguey, led the fight. The rebellion is known in Cuban history as "La Chambelona" or the "Lollypop," taking its name from a popular conga sung at liberal political rallies. Menocal was not easily swayed, however. He was a courageous and able commander who equipped his loyal forces with modern machine guns and had the unrestricted support of the Woodrow Wilson administration.

U.S. endorsement of Menocal was evident in the many State Department notes to William Gonzalez., the U.S. minister in Havana who stated that Washington would only recognize "a legally established government." In support of this policy, the United States deployed warships into Cuban waters and landed Marine detachments in Santiago de Cuba, Guantanamo and Manzanillo.

The "Chambelona" had strong popular support but, lacked tactical cohesion and was defeated at Caicaje in central Cuba, where former President Gomez was captured and later sent into exile. So ended another of Cuba's many rebellions. It was also evident from Mr. Gonzalez' notes that Washington was willing to enforce its protectorate policy on Cuba's internal affairs.

Firmly in control of the presidency, Menocal's second term was a disappointment when compared with the achievements of his first. With widespread corruption a dominant feature of his presidency, the island's society was dazzled by the economic prosperity of the golden years. More than 50,000 *colonos* were among the Cubans who expanded their land holdings, paying off old debts, showing off their wealth and living the good life of financial success. Cuba was experiencing an economic bonanza as never before. The construction industry was thriving, with beautiful homes being built in the Vedado and Miramar suburbs. Wealthy Cubans recreated gothic, Italian Renaissance and French classic architectural style. The Country Club suburb had even larger mansions and was the preferred place to live for the Cuban upper class.

## THE COLLAPSE OF THE ECONOMY

In May 1920, the price of sugar reached 22.5 cents per pound and then abruptly, like an unexpected bolt of lighting, plummeted. By December 1920, it had fallen to 0.03 cents on the world market. The dance of the millions was over. Cuba was in a state of shock

Many mill owners, *colonos* and sugar speculators that had borrowed on the sale of the next harvest could not meet their bank obligations. In turn, the banks that had departed from sound loan procedures were now unable to collect on their loans and became insolvent. Fearing the worst, the people rushed to take out their savings. A run on banks took place, and panic took hold of the devastated Cuban financial system. The Menocal government tried different measures but to no avail. It was an economic catastrophe. By the summer of 1921, 18 banks had collapsed. Some bankers and sugar speculators fled the island; others like Pote Rodriguez hung themselves. The Cuban-owned banks were the hardest hit, while foreign banks, with their solid monetary reserves, were able to weather the storm. From this time on, foreign banks would begin assuming a dominant position within the island's economy.

## TABLE XV
## (In millions of dollars)

| | Loans | | | Deposits |
|------|------------------|----------------|------------------|----------------|
| Year | Foreign Banks | Cuban Banks | Foreign Banks | Cuban Banks |
| 1920 | 82.8 | 203.1 | 88.2 | 352.5 |
| 1921 | 85.8 | 19.1 | 55.2 | 24.8 |
| 1925 | 152.2 | 17.3 | 134.8 | 61.3 |
| 1926 | 201.3 | 26.5 | 107.7 | 61.7[11] |

Months before the financial debacle, President Menocal and the liberal opposition agreed to enforce a new electoral code. They invited Gen. Enoch H. Crowder, a West Point graduate, attorney and judge advocate general of the U.S. Army who had served in the Magoon administration of Cuba in 1906-08, to help draft the electoral code and mediate the frequent disruptive political disputes. Crowder was also to advise the Cubans on bureaucratic and financial reforms. The American envoy arrived in Havana's harbor on the battleship *Minnesota*, a powerful reminder of the island's protectorate status.

With the economy in shreds, Cubans went to the polls in 1920. The liberals nominated their old leader, Jose Miguel Gomez, but Menocal made a masterful political move and offered the candidacy to Alfredo Zayas, once more dividing the Liberal Party. The formula was a success and, on May 20, 1921, Alfredo Zayas became Cuba's fourth president.

## *THE PRESIDENCY OF ALFREDO ZAYAS (1921-1925)*

Alfredo Zayas was probably the most learned and intellectually enlightened of Cuba's presidents. An historian, attorney and poet, Zayas was also a savvy, corrupt politician. Imprisoned by the Spaniards during the war of independence, Zayas opposed the Platt Amendment as a delegate to the 1901 Constitutional Convention. His brother, Juan Bruno Zayas, one of the most courageous and beloved leaders of the rebel army, was killed in action.

Zayas took office during the economic crisis and the onset of a powerful nationalistic revival spearheaded by intellectuals and students. The 1918 University of Cordoba reforms in Argentina served as model for the Cubans who were impacted by the 1923 visit to Havana of Jose Arce, president of the University of Buenos Aires, a social reformer who on many occasions signaled the need for students' direct presence on the national political stage. The response of Cuba's youth was the creation of the "Federacion Estudiantil Universitaria" (FEU) or Student Federation, which immediately moved to the forefront of Cuba's rising demands for an end to the U.S. protectorate and honesty in government.

The mood of the Cuban students and intellectuals was changing fast. The call for direct participation was loud and clear and framed the political dimension of the dawning struggle. A variety of social and economic doctrines reached the island with the thunder of epic reforms. The young Cubans were heavily influenced by the Bolshevik Revolution in Russia, the Mexican Revolution and radical intellectuals led by the Peruvians Jose Carlos Mariategui and Victor Raul Haya de la Torre, Argentinean sociologist Jose Ingenieros, Mexican educator and philosopher Jose Vasconcelos, Colombian writer Jose Vargas Vila, and Nicaraguan Augusto Cesar Sandino, an anti-American leader.

The Latin American reformers were deeply engaged in finding answers to the miserable failure of their republics, looking not at the political dysfunction inherited from the decadent Spain, but at the all-pervasive, gigantic shadow cast by the colossal success of the United States. Standing up to the Yankees was the rallying call for action. But, blaming the Yankees for their mistakes and failures, was also a popular excuse.

The Cubans had specific grievances directly associated with the

Platt Amendment that was like the lighting rod of their growing nationalist feelings. Later, when the Platt Amendment issue had been favorably resolved, the Cubans became fixated with the notion that the Republic's failures were rooted in U.S. intervention during the Protectorate Republic period. It was a time of nationalistic fervor and dogmatic promises of social justice, but the Cuban intelligentsia, just as their Latin American peers, failed to search deep into the reasons of the Republic political miscarriage — a huge mistake.

Under the stress of a depressed economy, President Zayas was faced with diminishing sources of public funds to pay for his financial obligations. Zayas requested a $50 million loan from the J.P. Morgan Bank in New York. During the negotiations, the Cuban president saw the heavy hand of U.S. special envoy Enoch Crowder, who demanded as a requirement for the loan the formation of a new cabinet whose members were to be picked from a list of names prepared by Crowder himself. The U.S. envoy was afraid Zayas' cronies would dispose of the money in dishonest transactions.

In June 1922, Zayas agreed to the demands and named the proposed Cabinet, referred to by the press as the "honest Cabinet." A few months after receiving the $50 million loan and in open defiance of Crowder, Zayas dismantled the American-sponsored Cabinet. The U.S. pro consul was irate, but impotent to do anything. In view of growing anti-imperialist mood in Latin America, Washington had been implementing a more cautious foreign policy of less direct intervention in the region, including Cuba.

By 1923, the U.S. consumer market began to increase demand for sugar. Foreign investors purchased new land for sugar production, and new *centrales* sprang up, primarily in Camaguey and Oriente. In 1924, the United States bought 2,316 million tons of sugar from Cuba.[12] The total harvest topped four million tons. The vast expansion program impacted the island's land distribution, reinforcing growth of large land holdings or *latifundios* owned mostly by foreign corporations. The *latifundios* became a bone of contention among Cuban nationalistic advocates.

Historian Ramiro Guerra wrote: "Latifundism is so strong and powerful in our country that it is impossible to fight it without appealing to the government to intervene in defense of the nation...

It is the duty of the Republic to come to the rescue."[13] Many Cubans resented these huge land holdings in the hands of foreigners, fueling a growing, powerful nationalistic drive. But by the end of his presidency, Zayas was well engaged in corrupt dealings, oblivious to pressing national issues. Rejected by Menocal's conservative party in his bid for reelection, Zayas shifted his support to the liberal candidate, Gen. Gerardo Machado, a maverick and gregarious politician who defeated Menocal. On May 20, 1925, Gerardo Machado became Cuba's fifth president.

## IT ENTERS GERARDO MACHADO, THE FIRST POLITICAL MESSIAH

When Machado became president, the Cuban Republic was 23 years old and seemed to be moving in the direction of political stability and economic growth. Machado won the presidency on a platform of national regeneration under the slogan "water, roads and schools." He called for an end to the Platt Amendment and improved health care. Machado was a political crossbreed between Jose Miguel Gomez' charisma and Menocal's resilient, abrasive leadership style. He was a very popular and feared politician. The son of a war veteran turned cattle thief, his first job was that of a butcher in the town of Camajuani. During the War of Independence, Machado fought mostly in the Santa Clara region, where he rose through the ranks to brigadier. After the war, Machado briefly held various government positions and later became manager and vice president of the Cuban Electric Company, the largest utility company in Havana.

Machado's first three years in office were probably the most successful of the Cuban Republic. Several aqueducts were built to supply the water needs of major cities; a vast program of road construction got underway, creating thousands of jobs, and a modern communication system that opened new agricultural and industrial markets. Completion of the Central Highway finally linking Havana and Santiago de Cuba was the culmination of Machado's successful road network program.

Education improved with the addition of new classrooms in the public school system and several vocational-technical schools throughout the island. Teacher salaries were raised and the

University curriculum modernized, with an emphasis on science and engineering. The Machado administration also developed an urban renewal program, paving streets and improving the sewer system of major cities. Havana's Malecon (boardwalk) was widened and extended to its present splendor as a majestic waterfront boulevard. The *escalinata* or stairs leading to the University's Alma Mater square and Capitol building were constructed under Machado's first term. The president's words held a nationalistic message when he proclaimed, "Let us assure our political independence through economic independence."[14] Machado advocated the economy's "Regeneration" by breaking the one-crop sugar monopoly and diversifying agriculture.

The president was immensely popular, and in September 1926, the University of Havana conferred on him an honorary doctorate. During the first two years of his administration, he was named "favorite son" of 25 municipalities, and, in a shameless showing of adulation, journalists and politicians called him "El Supremo," "El Titan" and "El Egregio." Not until 34 years later would there be a leader who could again command such a frenzy of flattery, a guerrilla leader named Fidel Castro, who, by 1960, was being referred to as "El Caballo," (the Horse) "El Comandante" and "El Maximo Leader."

By 1927, Machado had stirred up nationalistic fervor and a sense of confidence in the ability of Cubans to govern themselves. Commenting on Machado's charisma, professor Aguilar said: "Considering the immediate past of Cuba and the spectacular programs and actions of the new government, it was no wonder that Gerardo Machado became, after a few months in power, the most popular president the island ever had." [15] It is difficult to measure the impact of the intense respect on the Machado sequel. By 1927, the president had decided to remain in power believing himself indispensable to Cuba's welfare.

## THE ARRIVAL OF IDEOLOGICAL MADNESS

The pro-Machado congress extended Machado's term in office (*la prórroga de poder*) for two more years, agreed to call elections for a Constituent Assembly to consider revising the 1901 Constitution and extend the president's term in office to six years without reelection. In April 1928, the newly elected Constituent

Assembly approved the reforms proposed by Congress and solemnly declared: "The Constitutional Convention does not hesitate to reaffirm that General Gerardo Machado y Morales, because of his commitments and his antecedents as founder of the Republic, is faced with the inevitable obligation of accepting a new presidential term."[16] Machado accepted and was reelected. His term, which began May 20, 1929, would run until May 1935. With enormous enthusiasm, the majority of Cubans had chosen to follow a charismatic leader into the grips of a dictatorship.

They were not alone, however, in this dysfunctional behavior. Elsewhere, charismatic leaders of different ideological persuasions were inspiring mass support and a frenzy of adulation: Benito Mussolini in Italy, Gertulio Vargas in Brazil, Mikolos Horthy of Hungary, Juan Domingo Peron in Argentina, Ion Antonescu in Rumania, Juan Vicente Gomez of Venezuela, Josef Pilsudski in Poland, Chian Kai-shek in China, Joseph Stalin in the Soviet Union and Adolph Hitler in Germany. Intolerant dogmas were sweeping the planet with zero tolerance for open pluralistic societies anchored in the fundamental rights of the individual citizen.

It was a time of ideological and racial aberrations that would cause millions of innocent people to be consumed by the horrific crimes of dogmatic intolerance, extermination camps, gulags and state-sponsored terror directed against their own citizens. With different cultural variants, the two main exponents of these global ideologies were fascism and communism. Since every nation has its quota of psychopaths, there has always existed a need for a criminal enforcer, individuals unfit to distinguish good from evil and able to inflict harm on other human beings without remorse. They became the vanguard of perverse popular dogmas.

By the 1920's, Spain had become a microcosm of the worldwide ideological struggle. Tens of thousands of impoverished Spaniards fled abroad. Cuba was a favorite destination. By 1928, more than half a million Spanish immigrants made the transatlantic voyage and settled on the island. Among the newly arrived Spaniards were a large number of anarcho-syndicalists. As they melted into Cuban society, they became a leading force among the labor movement's most influential leaders up until the early 1930s when the communists replaced them and took control of the workers' unions. However, as the struggle against Machado began to unfold, the anarcho-syndicalists turned their terrible skills into urban terrorism. This bloody legacy of political violence was to remain firmly entrenched among Cuban radicals. From this time on, dynamite and political assassinations were important tactical tools in the fight to control the island's government. Machado's extension of power had opened the doors for revolution. There was no turning back.

Death of a Dream

# CHAPTER XII

# THE PROTECTORATE (1909-1934)

[1] Compiled data contained in the Census of the Republic of Cuba from 1907 to 1919.

[2] Independent Party of Colored.

[3] *Foreign Relations*, 1912, 248.

[4] Alberto Arredondo, *Cuba tierra indefensa* (Havana: Editorial Lex, Havana, 1944), 193-4.

[5] Census of the Republic of Cuba. 1919.

[6] Joseph Nathan Kane. *Famous First Facts* (New York, The H.W. Wilson Co., 1950), 49.

[7] *Anuario Azucarero de Cuba, 195,*. Jose Alvarez Diaz, *A Study on Cuba, the Colonial and Republican Periods* (Coral Gables: University of Miami, 1965), 235.

[8] Phillip G. Wright. *The Cuban situation and our treaty relations* (Washington, D.C., 1931), 21.

[9] H.C. Prinsen Geerlings, *Cane Sugar and its Manufacture* (Altrincham, 1909), 10.

[10] Álvarez Díaz, op cit, 237.

[11] Álvarez Díaz, op cit, 232.

[12] Ibid, 245.

[13] Ramiro Guerra y Sánchez, *Azúcar y Población en las Antillas*, 3rd ed; Habana Cultural, 1944, 156.

[14] Machado, Gerardo, *Por la Patria Libre,* Havana: Imprenta de F. Verdugo, 1916, 9.

[15] Aguilar, op cit, 57.

[16] *Diario de Sesiones de la Asamblea Constituyente*, Havana, 1928, 12th session, 5.

Pedro Roig

# CHAPTER XIII

# *THE 1933 REVOLUTION*

*THE REVOLUTIONARY ORGANIZATIONS – THE SUMMER WELLES MEDIATION – MACHADO'S DOWNFALL – THE STUDENTS AND SOLDIERS ALLIANCE, A MARCH INTO CHAOS – ANTONIO GUITERAS – BATISTA RAISED TO POWER AND THE ARMY AS A POWER BROKER.*

The year 1933 was a momentous year for the Cuban people. It marked the beginning of a political and social revolution led by the expanding middle class. It included the end of the hegemony of the war veterans who, for 30 years, had dominated the Cuban government, and the rise to power of the first republican-born generation with an intense nationalistic commitment and a clearly defined emphasis on social justice and anti-imperialism. During this crucial year, the Army became Cuba's main power broker.

In 1933, the island's economic fabric began to fall apart as the U.S. economy sank into a depression. Hardest hit was the Cuban sugar industry whose share of the U.S. market dropped from 51.9% to 25.4% in 1933 sending over 240,000 heads of household into unemployment. By this time most opposition groups were engaged in urban terrorism and the use of explosives and political assassination became common practices. It was the model copied from the anarchist's terrorist manual. From this time forward killings among political factions and the use of explosives to deal with political grievances was acceptable social behavior. The pattern generated its quota of martyrs and heroes in a culture that glorified violence as a means of securing power and wealth. Such brutal behavior became the preferred revolutionary tactic that was to remain deeply entrenched among Cuban rival groups with destabilizing political consequences.

## *THE REVOLUTIONARY ORGANIZATIONS*

Among the better-organized groups fighting Machado was the ABC, made up mostly of middle class professionals who were integrated into secret layers of cells. By 1933, the ABC was a sophisticated, efficient revolutionary group led by some of Cuba's foremost intellectuals and business entrepreneurs. Historian Aguilar Leon believed ABC political doctrine to be "the most serious study of Cuba's problem written during this entire revolutionary period."

Another prominent group in the fight against Machado was the University Student Directorate — "Directorio" that also took the path of urban warfare. One of its leaders, Carlos Prio, eventually became president in the 1948 elections. The "Directorio" students believed themselves heirs of Jose Marti's unfinished revolution and champions of the anti-American stance to end Washington's Protectorate in Cuban internal affairs. As was the norm rather than the exception among revolutionary groups, the "Directorio" had split along ideological lines, resulting in the formation of the "Ala Izquierda" or left wing from which most members, including Raul Roa, Cuba's future Secretary of State during the Bay of Pig's invasion and the October Missile Crisis, drifted toward communism.

By 1933 Cuban labor unions were also flexing their political muscles. For Cuban workers the road to legal standing and bargaining rights had been long and difficult. By 1920 there were 400 separate unions in the Island. In 1925, labor leaders finally agreed to create the "National Confederation of Cuban Workers" (CNOC). At first, the labor confederation was controlled by the anarchists. They soon joined the fight against Machado, and, as a result of the regime's savage reprisal, the anarchist leadership within the CNOC was decimated.

The Communist Party in Cuba had a humble beginning. Founded in 1925, eleven Cubans and six foreigners answered to the first roll call. They were led by Julio Antonio Mella, the charismatic leader, and by Carlos Balino, former anarchist who helped Marti while working in a Key West tobacco factory. Among the foreigners was Yunger Semjovich (also known as Fabio Grobart) who in due time became the link with Jules-Oroz, Secretary General of the Latin American Department of the Commintern in Moscow. A short time later, poet Ruben Martinez Villena joined the Party and, after the death of Balino in 1927 and the assassination of Mella in 1929, became the most prominent leader of the Cuban Communist Party.

Pedro Roig

## THE SUMMER WELLES MEDIATION

As the level of violence increased in the island, the Roosevelt administration decided to send a political mediator to work out a peaceful settlement. Benjamim Summer Welles, an influential diplomat and close friend to the President, was appointed U.S. Ambassador in Havana. Welles was a graduate of Groton and Harvard. He had been a page at Franklin D. Roosevelt's wedding and had direct access to the White House.

Welles arrived in Cuba on May 8, 1933, and, within a week, was able to grasp the intensity of the public's rejection of the Machado government. In his first report to the State Department, he wrote: "If the present acute bitterness of feeling against the President persists or becomes intensified....it would in all probability be highly desirable that the present chief executive be replaced, at least during the electoral period."[1]

For Machado, the U.S. ambassador's mediation was a highly confusing affair. He strongly felt that Washington was friendly to his presidency and appreciative of his support for American financial interests on the island; however, his personality did not bear well with having to compromise with political enemies, and that was precisely the issue of Welles' mediation. Machado also understood that Washington's support of his presidency was essential for survival of the government. Therefore, he was faced with a vital question: how far to move into Welles' mediation without losing his grip on power. That was the old general's dilemma. The dictator went along on the initial negotiations trying to figure a way out of his predicament.

By the eighth week, after Welles' arrival in Havana, the first mediation meeting took place in the American Embassy. It was obvious that no one cared to dress up the hard evidence of U.S. meddling in Cuba's internal affairs and the fact that Cuba was for all practical purpose a U.S. protectorate. The ABC, the National Union and other small groups were present at this first meeting, Machado sent three delegates, but the more radical groups like the "Directorio" and the "Ala Izquierda" refused to join.

At first, Welles' efforts toward a peaceful settlement looked promising, but it soon became clear that the opposition was deeply split and the dictator not willing to yield power to his adversaries. The ambassador, however, believed that as long as the ABC, the most relevant political group, was at the negotiating table, there was a good chance of success. On this issue, he wrote: "Fortunately, the representatives of that organization (ABC) are both intelligent and well disposed."[2] The ABC was afraid of a radical revolution and went along with the mediation to secure an institutional transition that hinged on the rule of law, property rights, and individual freedoms.

They were vehemently opposed to the Platt Amendment, but were willing to accept Summer Welles' mediation as a political tool to accelerate Machado's downfall. As Martinez Saenz stated: "We tried to follow the pragmatic policy of doing what each circumstance allowed us to do. The ABC used every opportunity to act, within the margin of its possibilities, for the integral renovation of Cuba."[3] But pragmatic solutions were not options to a nation caught in a fiercely emotional political struggle and pulled by an intense nationalistic feeling. The island was ripe for dramatic social and political change. The U.S. Ambassador felt confident that he was moving closer to Machado's downfall, but waiting in the shadows was an unexpected turn of events: a social revolution. .

The formal mediation lasted for 27 days when Machado's unwillingness to compromise his control of Cuba's government became obvious. On July 27, the dictator addressed his rubber stamp Congress in a vitriolic anti-Yankee speech. In a fashionable nationalistic rapture, the old general rejected the U.S.-sponsored political mediation,[4] thus ending the slim chance of peaceful political transition.

Machado was gambling in the perception that Welles' support in Washington was weakening, and, despite his close relationships with the President, the American envoy had powerful adversaries in the State Department. This fact became evident in Secretary of State Cordell Hull's less than cordial letter to Welles: "Out of the mass of information which has been sent to the United States from Cuba, some misapprehension has arisen as to what you are doing, and there has been some adverse comments, both here and in Latin America, that the United States is attempting to coerce rather than to persuade."[5]

But Machado's gambling failed. The U.S. withdrew its decisive support and by August 1933 the regimen was doomed.

Pedro Roig

## MACHADO'S DOWNFALL

The end of the dictator was ignited by a minor labor dispute. On July 25, 1933, Havana bus drivers went on strike protesting a municipal tax increase. The strike turned into a political confrontation that escalated when streetcars operators (tranvias) and taxi drivers jointed the protest. Capital transportation came to a halt. By August 1, it had spread to other labor sectors and grown into a general strike.

With time running out, Machado called for a meeting with the communists perceived by the dictator to be the leaders of the strikes. Machado offered them legal recognition and state support. Ruben Martinez Villena, Joaquin Ordoqui and Jorge Vivo met with Machado and accepted the offer. The communists called off the strike but failed. It turned out to be the agreement of the impotents since neither party had the strength to control the mounting crisis.

On August 6, rumors that Machado had resigned swept the capital. Thousands of people went out to celebrate and were gunned down by the police. Twenty-two were killed and more than 70 wounded. It was obvious that the Machado's regimen was agonizing and the attention turned to the transition of power to avoid a chaotic situation. In the mist of this political confusion, Summer Welles turned to the Cuban Army and met with General Alberto Herrera. He assured the officer of a prominent role in a peaceful transition of power. Actually Welles offered the presidency to General Herrera.

On August 12, with the Army's support, the American Ambassador presented Machado with a plan for his resignation and a legal transition of power. A defiant dictator visited the Columbia Military barracks where he found that he had lost the support of the Army and had to resign.[6]    That afternoon Machado left the presidential Palace and flew to Nassau in the Bahamas.

With the dictator gone, the designation of General Herrera as provisional president was rejected by most of the leading organizations who accused him of being too close to Machado. Under pressure and looking for consensus, Summer Welles went with a safe alternative and named the non-partisan Carlos Manuel De Cespedes, son of the hero of the War of Independence, as the new provisional president. He was to last in power 22 days.

With the news of Machado's departure, the people went wild with enthusiasm and a large quota of revenge against those that had served the fallen regime. The "Machadistas" were hunted down, their properties vandalized, and a power vacuum began to develop throughout the island, but despite the breakdown of authority, Summer Welles was triumphant. He had won a great political victory, at least he thought he had. The economy was prostrate, and members of the revolutionary organization roamed the streets with weapons in hand. Army morale was low with officers' future uncertain and afraid to restore order. The old political parties were discredited and a new era of social justice and national sovereignty was dawning. The American Ambassador was in for a terrible awakening. The fall of Machado had unleashed a social and political revolution.

## THE STUDENTS AND SOLDIERS' ALLIANCE: A MARCH INTO CHAOS

This revolutionary period is among the most confused in Cuba's tragic history. It was framed within a severe economic depression, an urgent call for social justice, a break down of public order, an emotional need to wipe out the "Platt Amendment" and uncontrollable factional violence. The young republic's political institution simply collapsed.

With the blessing of the American Ambassador and the support of the ABC Party, the Cespedes government made a feeble effort at implementing political reforms and governing the island. It failed. They could not re-start the economy, nor keep the weapons-carrying factional groups under control. It was in this glooming setting that what could have been a minor grievance demand by the sergeants at Camp Columbia, for better boots and higher pay, turned into a rebellion that toppled the Cespedes presidency.

On the evening of September 3, the NCO's led by Sergeant Fulgencio Batista presented their grievances to their officers. The demands were rejected. It was at this time that in an embarrassing and inexcusable show of behavior, most officers left the base in the hands of the sergeants. Early on September 4, Havana was buzzing with rumors of an army mutiny. The sergeants were in control of Cuba's most important military base, not knowing what to do next.

Perplexed by their newly gained power and confused by the possible consequences of their illegal actions, the NCO's began looking for a way out. It came from the most unexpected place: the university students.

That day the young Cubans led by Carlos Prio, Justo Carrillo, Ruben de Leon, Manuel Antonio Varona and Rubio Padilla meet with the NCO's. Later they were joined by Ramiro Valdez Dausa, Santiago Alvares, journalist Sergio Carbo and university professor Ramon Grau San Martin. In a move of great audacity the students and the NCO's forged an alliance of convenience. They fired the U.S.-supported president Cespedes and announced the creation of a Provisional Revolutionary Junta of five members known as "la Pentarquia". This unexpected alliance of soldiers and students provided the "Directorio" with access to political power and gave the bewildered NCO's the needed legitimacy, turning a military mutiny into a revolution. Cespedes resigned the presidency and Ambassador Welles requested immediate U.S. military intervention. The Cespedes government had lasted three weeks. The ABC was out of power, bitter but heavily armed and ready for a fight, which was soon to come.

At the U.S. Embassy, Welles was reporting to Washington that "in all likelihood, there will be a complete collapse of government throughout the island."[7] The assessment was partly accurate since in many cities and rural areas, there had been a breakdown of public order with local officials and police units paralyzed by the confused political situation. In a telephone conversation with the Secretary of State, Cordell Hull, the U.S. Ambassador said: "I think that the situation is getting worst. I have had a conference with the political leaders of the Republic and they are of the opinion that it would be wise to land a certain number of troops from the American ships."[8] Washington turned down the request for direct military intervention, but several U.S. warships began to approach the island's harbors.

The "Pentarquia" had a short life and failed in its effort to govern the convulsed island. On September 9, a group of students barged into the Junta's meeting room in the presidential palace, where one of the governing members asked the students to leave immediately, at which point the 21-year-old student leader Carlos Prio, head of the "Derectorio", responded: "the Directorio" has withdrawn its vote of confidence in the "Pentarquia" and elected Dr.

Grau president."[9]   Ramon Grau San Martin, of the five Junta members, was the students' favorite due to his open defiance of Machado. On September 9, the students appointed him president of Cuba. Two days before, sergeant Fulgencio Batista had been promoted to Colonel and Army Chief. He was on his way to become Cuba's political arbiter for years to come.

On September 10, Grau took office, while at the U.S. Embassy, Welles was in shock. The "Pentarquia" had lasted less than 120 hours in power. The students and sergeants had broken established political rules and, throughout the island, there was great uncertainty and fear, but for the young student leaders energized by an all-embracing nationalistic sentiment, this was the time of redeeming the broken dreams of the War of Independence. It was Sergio Carbo that best defined the students' perception of that historical moment: "The Republic came of age and with cries of joy escaped from the American Embassy."[10] It was evident that the idealistic students and bewildered soldiers had broken away from the U.S. embassy patronage and, in the process, embarrassed the U.S. proconsul; but there were two terrible forces from which they could not escape: The economic depression and the bloody fight of the political factions. As the army and the police retreated to their barracks, public order broke down and violent groups took to the streets. In the bolchevick model, several small towns and sugar mills were taken over by radicals that raised the red flag and established "soviet" administrations. In the Central Mabay near Bayamo, strikers took control of the sugar mills for several weeks.[11] In the midst of the power vacuum and political confusion the newspaper *El Mundo* asked the obvious question: "Who is ruling Cuba?"[12] For the first time in the island's history, with unbounded pride and exalted emotions, the Cuban youths had marched directly into political chaos.

Twenty days into his student-appointed presidency, Grau had to face the challenge of the ABC and about 300 officers of the old army that had gathered at the Hotel Nacional. This had become the center of resistance against the students-sergeants' revolutionary government and a decision had to be made as to whether to end the rebellion outpost in the capital. On Oct 1, a council of war presided by now Colonel Batista, which included Sergio Carbo and Antonio Guiteras, ordered an attack on the entrenched officers at the "Hotel

Nacional". The following day, the fight began with shelling from the small cruiser *Cuba* and several artillery guns. The officers fought gallantly, killing 80 soldiers and wounding over 200, but eventually they were overwhelmed by the superior firepower. Batista offered terms to the officers and by mid afternoon they surrendered. But as the officers lined up and walked out of the Hotel Nacional, shots were fired and, in the confusion, a member of a political faction gunned down and murdered 11 of the officers, wounding 22. Divided by an internal power struggle, the ABC failed to join the rebellion. For the students-sergeants it was a tragic victory.

Finally on October 8-9, more than 2,000 ABC members launched its expected assault against the Revolutionary Government, capturing several small garrisons in Havana and taking control of the military airport and its five planes, of which one bombed Camp Columbia, but by midday Batista's forces had surrounded and captured the airport. The remaining rebels retreated to the colonial fortress of Atares. There they fought for several hours. Havana was shaken by the sounds of the artillery guns that were demolishing the old fortress. With defeat nearing one of the rebel leaders shoot himself and a white flag was raised but the troops were not in the mood of taking prisoners and murdered over 200 rebels that had laid down their weapons.[xiii] The ABC was defeated and its surviving leaders went into hiding or exile. Batista had by now become the most powerful member of the Provisional Government, but that night the students were celebrating what they believed was a revolutionary victory.

## ANTONIO GUITERAS

With the cry "Cuba for the Cubans" the soldiers and students gave Grau's presidency the support and momentum needed to enact the laws for political and social reforms. Antonio Guiteras Holmes, a Philadelphia born liberal-socialist was named the Interior Minister and became the folk hero of the revolution and the leader of Grau's government radical wing. Guiteras was the son of a Cuban who was a French teacher and of a Puritan American mother. The family moved from Philadelphia to Pinar del Rio when he was seven years old. He attended the University of Havana, joined the 1927 Student Directorate and earned a pharmacist degree.

Guiteras was a thoughtful and laconic man of action. He was a non-Marxist, social democrat, incorruptible, with strong nationalistic and anti-imperialist views. Guiteras wrote few articles, but led the implementation of the revolution's radical decrees. During the fight against Machado, "Tony" Guiteras and his followers, attacked the small army garrison of San Luis, Oriente, adjacent to the Sierra Maestra, where he was later captured and imprisoned, but despite the failure of the attack, his reputation as a revolutionary leader was well established throughout the island. It seems that Guiteras attack on the San Luis Garrison became a model for Fidel Castro's assault on the Moncada's barracks 20 years later.

For the communists, Antonio Guiteras was a dangerous demagogue. "Unlike many of his comrades, he had never been a communist, not even a member of the 'comunizante' ala izquierda estudiantil".[14] The fact was that the speed and depth of the social, political and economic changes led by Guiteras were simply breathtaking. A day after Grau was appointed president, the Revolutionary Colition announced the abrogation of the Platt Amendment. Ten days later, established a maximum work day of eight hours; lowered the utility rates by 40 percent; dissolved all political parties that had supported Machado; created the Department of Labor; gave women the right to vote; provided autonomy to the University and on November 8th, the revolutionary leadership enacted the Nationalization of Labor Decree, by which 50 percent of all employees in the island had to be Cuban natives, with the exception of technicians and managers that could not be substituted by Cubans.

For the communists, the "50 percent law" was "a new agency of hunger, misery and exploitation"[15] and Antonio Guiteras was a "socialist demagogue"[16] Despite the strenuous efforts of the Castro regimen to fabricate a communist profile in Antonio Guitera's radical thoughts, the facts were that he was a non-Marxist socialist, who fought for workers rights and individual freedoms within the market economic system. For a large sector of Cuban radicals, Antonio Guiteras was the revolutionary prototype, and his ideals became the model for the social, political and economic liberal reforms that later clashed into a fight to death with Castro's Marxist revolution.

Pedro Roig

## BATISTA RAISED TO POWER AND THE ARMY AS A POWER BROKER

By the end of 1933 the social democratic revolution was falling apart. There were multiple factors gathering against the Grau-Guiteras radical reforms. Within the students-soldiers coalition, the formers sergeants, now full fledge officers of the new army where looking more into their ranks and place within a transition government than into falling with the revolution. Colonel Batista knew that he held the key to power and the political alternative. Most people support for the Grau-Guiteras government was unreliable. Grau was acutely aware of the growing opposition led by colonel Mendieta; ex-president Menocal; the communist; Sumner Welles who had taken a personal animosity to the students liberal reforms; the Spaniards merchants enraged by the 50% decree; the pseudo-revolutionary gangs roaming the streets and above all, by the fact that the Cuban economy remained caught in the grips of the devastating world wide depression, a different economic scenario to be face 26 years later by the Castro led revolution.

Since the down fall of the Cespedes presidency in September 4, 1933, the U.S. had refused to recognize the de facto social democrat government of Grau San Martin. On November 20th President Franklin D. Roosevelt met with his friend and Cuba's envoy Welles in Warm Springs, Georgia, where the issue of non-recognition of the students-soldiers government was address. On November 23, Roosevelt declared in a press conference: "We are not taking side.... we haven't yet got a provisional government that clearly has the support of the majority of the Cuban people. What can we do? We can't do anything, the matter rest".[17]

On November 29, Welles returned to Cuba for the last time. He had been appointed Under-Secretary of State but before his departure he met with Grau and several opposing politicians to try to reach a transition of power, which failed. On December 12, Welles informed the State Department: "In view of the unexpected and complete collapse of negotiations this afternoon shall leave Havana by airplane Wednesday and arriving Washington, Friday morning".[18] Finally the U.S. proconsul was gone. He had openly intervened in Cuba's internal affairs and failed but Roosevelt rewarded his friend diplomatic career with an executive post in the

State Department. He was replaced by Jefferson Caffery.

On January 10, when asked on what had to be done to gain U.S. recognition Caffery deceivingly answered: "I will lay down no specific terms; the matter of your government is a Cuban matter and it is for you to decide what you will do about it"[19] but it was clear that Washington's policy towards the revolutionary government remained unchanged. The Americans had huge investments in the island. Fear of an economic collapse on the eve of the sugar harvest was ever present and even though the communist party strongly opposed the Grau-Guiteras radical reforms Caffery was concerned about "certain seemingly communistic tendencies in the present regimen."[20] Like his predecessor, the new U.S. envoy was elitist and viewed the Grau government with contempt: "I agree with former Ambassador Welles as to the inefficiency, ineptitude, and unpopularity with all the better classes in the country of the de facto government. It's support only by the army and the ignorant masses who had been misled by utopian promises."[21]

Batista and the sergeants turned colonels were unwilling to go down with the Grau-Guiteras revolution and began looking for a suitable presidential alternative, agreeable to Washington. On January 13, Batista met Grau and told him bluntly that the U.S. had refused to grant recognition to his government and that Colonel Mendieta could lead the new government with Washington recognition. Grau was willing to compromise but Guiteras threaten with an all out rebellion backed by the small Cuban Navy and a large segment of the police. Batista hesitated. On January 14 Guiteras entered and took control of the American owned "Compañía Cubana de Electricidad" but the following day Batista made his move to depose Grau. In a tumultuous meeting at the Columbia barracks Batista ended the social democrat revolution that he had helped to ignite with the sergeants' mutiny 127 days before. Carlos Hevia was named as provisional president and Antonio Guiteras went on his promised rebellion that failed within few weeks. Guiteras moved underground ready for a fight with Cuba's strong man, Fulgencio Batista. Grau departed for Mexico. In an emotional farewell embraced with Carlos Prio, the student leader that had led his presidential appointment, Grau told him: "Don't worry Carlos, we'll return to power soon."[22] Hevia failed to rally the Mendieta support and Batista rushed him out. He had lasted less than 48 hours as president.

On January 17, Batista told Caffery that he was placing Mendieta as provisional president. The American envoy was pleased with the choice. The next day the old war veteran Colonel Mendieta became Batista's surrogate president. On January 23, Washington extended a "formal and cordial recognition"[23] to the Cuban government and the American banks agreed to finance the upcoming sugar harvest. The guns of the battleship "Wyoming" anchored at Havana's harbor joyfully saluted the new government. The revolution was over but despite the appearance of normalcy Cuba's social and economic fabric had change forever.

# CHAPTER XIII

# THE 1933 REVOLUTION

---

[1] Foreign Relations of the United States, 1933 (Washington, D.C.: U.S. Government Printing Office, 1952), V, pg. 290

[2] Telegram, June 21, 1933, U.S. Department of State Papers (OS/3556), National Archives

[3] Aguilar, op.cit, 138

[4] Ibid, 140

[5] Foreign Relations, 1933, V pg. 154

[6] Diario de la Marina, (Agosto 23, 1933), 4

[7] Foreign Relations (1933), II, pg. 379

[8] Memorandum of telephone conversations between Secretary of State Hulls and Wells. 5 Sept. 1933, (837.00/837.00/3800, RG.59)

[9] Prensa Libre, 24 Mayo 1944.

[10] Ruby Hart Phillips. *Cuba Island of Paradise.* (New York, 1959), 66

[11] Thomas, op cit, 653

[12] El Mundo, Septiembre 23, 1933

[13] Thomas, op.cit, 669

[14] Thomas, op.cit, 650

[15] Ibid, 187

[16] Sheldon Blis. *Roots of Revolution: Radical thoughts in Cuba.* (University of Nebraska Press, 1987), 117

[17] Thomas, op.cit, 670

[18] Foreign Relations, 1933 II, pg. 539

[19] Foreign Relations, 1934 V, pg. 97

[20] Foreign Relations, 1933 V, pg. 544

[21] Foreign Relations, 1934 V, pg. 95

[22] Diario de la Marina, Enero 22, 1934

[23] Foreign Relations, 1934, pg. 349

Pedro Roig

## CHAPTER XIV

# THE CONSTITUTIONAL PRESIDENTS
# (1940 – 1952)

*THE 1940 CONSTITUTION – BATISTA'S BEST POLITICAL
PERFORMANCE – RAMON GRAU: THE FRENCY OF
CORRUPTION – EDUARDO CHIBAS, "UN LOCO GENIAL" –
FIDEL CASTRO AND THE "BOGOTAZO" – CARLOS PRIO:
THE "CORDIAL" PRECIDENCY – CHIBAS' LAST STAND AND
THE ARMY COUP D'ETAT.*

By 1940, the Cubans were exhausted from all the violence and were looking desperately to escape from massive unemployment and poverty. The leadership from the political spectrum understood the people's mood for stability as well as the need to develop a viable institutional frame, rooted in the vigorous nationalism and liberal thoughts that had blossomed during the previous decade. The PRC (Auténticos) and the Communists joined Batista in calling for the drafting of a new constitution that would focus on social justice and full individual freedoms. On November 15, 1939, elections were held for a "Constitutional Assembly". Over one million Cubans went to the polls and elected 76 assembly members. Batista's coalition elected 35 delegates and the opposition won 41 seats. The delegates came from all walks of life, rich and poor, blacks and whites, barons of industries, intellectuals, labor leaders. The best and the brightest.

It soon became evident that they transcended their political and ideological differences. It was a shinning moment for the Cuban people. A patriotic sense of solidarity settled among Assembly members. Were the Cubans learning to walk through the difficult path of democratic consensus, tolerance and compromise? During those months of magnificent cooperation, it seemed like a real possibility.

It took six months for the delegates to draft and approve the "New Constitution". It became the law of the land on the 10 of October of 1940. It was an outstanding liberal constitution that mirrored the ideals of the 1933 generation in which all the political and individual freedoms coexisted with a fairly intrusive state bureaucracy in charge of protecting and implementing the social legislation. Workers were provided with minimum wages, job tenure, and eight-hour day, a forty-four hour week, paid vacations and the right to strike. Freedom of the press and civil rights of minorities were granted and well protected by law. The President was to serve only one term of four years and the University of Havana's autonomy was legislated in the Constitution.

## BATISTA'S BEST POLITICAL PERFORMANCE

It was evident that the democratic process was gaining momentum on the island. On July 14, 1940, national elections were held. Batista took off his colonel uniform and with the backing of a large coalition that included the Communist Party, defeated Grau, the PRC's (Auténticos) candidate. Batista received more than 800,000 votes to Grau's 575,000. By all accounts it was a fair and clean election. The former sergeant was a popular figure, especially among the poor or "humildes". He became the first president under the new constitution. Two communist leaders, Juan Marinello and Carlos Rafael Rodriguez, soon joined Batista's cabinet and became prominent advocates of Fulgencio Batista's presidency. This close political alliance was more evident after Hitler's invasion of the Soviet Union in June of 1941. With the loss of the Ukrainian beet fields, Cuba began to supply the Russians with 70,000 tons of sugar per month and later the Cuban Secretary of State, Fernandez Coucheso, was received in Moscow by Joseph Stalin while the Soviet Ambassador in Washington, Maxim Litvinov, opened the first Soviet Embassy in Havana.

The war needs brought Cuba even closer to Washington. Batista traveled to the United States and was received by President Franklin D. Roosevelt and New York Major Fiorelo La Guardia. The Cuban government signed several military agreements with the U.S., including the construction of two air bases, San Julian and San Antonio, under U.S. operational administration to help in the war effort against the German U-boats that were creating havoc in the Caribbean waters.

During the first Batista administration, the daily newspaper *Prensa Libre* published its inaugural edition. Eduardo Chibas, a prominent opposition leader of the PRC (Auténticos), began his radio broadcast, which would evolve into Cuba's most popular and influential political platform, and the program "La Guantanamera" went on the air at CMQ Radio, recounting police reports on crimes of passion. It became an immediate success. There was an atmosphere of optimism. The pseudo-revolutionary gangs were virtually under control, with some sporadic acts of terrorism that were swiftly and harshly repressed by an efficient police force. Batista was among the first successful populist leaders in the confused Latin American term, including his "panache" for cronyism, graft and corruption. He effectively transferred power from the Columbia military barracks to the Presidential Palace, re-establishing civilian authority, but Batista's best performance, throughout his political life, was the peaceful transfer of power to Grau in the 1944 election where his candidate, Carlos Saladrigas, was defeated at the polls by the "Auténticos". He left the presidency a wealthy man and with Cuba moving forward on the difficult road to institutional democracy. Blas Roca, the Secretary General of the Communist Party, synthesized the strong relationship of the Cuban radical left with the outgoing president when he referred to Fulgencio Batista as "this magnificent reserve of Cuban democracy."[1]

### RAMON GRAU: THE FRENCY OF CORRUPTION

Ramon Grau was inaugurated on October 10, 1944. He was received by popular acclamation with church bells ringing, and huge political rallies throughout the island. The standard bearer of nationalism, a political messiah that best symbolized the cry of "Cuba for the Cubans". The repository of the Grau-Guiteras hundred days revolution that had been broken down by the U.S. proconsul eleven years before. It seemed that with Grau and the "Auténticos", Cuba was finally moving ahead on the road to decency and honesty in government, framed into a prosperous economy under the rule of law.

In his inaugural address, Grau synthesized the popular expectation. He stated: "It is not I who has taken office today, but the people."[2] Grau's presidency was to be the fulfillment of the revolutionary promise, but it failed again, and this time it was not broken as the result of the U.S. meddling in Cuba's internal affairs, but by the frenzy of corruption and gangsterism in Grau's government. A miserable charade of broken dreams.

A legion of hungry office-seekers from the old radical groups fell upon the government bureaucracy with voracious tenacity. It was a pitiful sight. A contemptible vision of graft and violence masquerading in a wave of revolutionary slogans. The ever present gravitation of the decrepit Hispanic political culture overflowed in meaningless rhetoric, turned Grau's presidency into a confused sham of theft and murderous gangsters, roaming the streets in the midst of public deception and a sense of shameful betrayal. The pseudo-revolutionary gangs fought among themselves demanding government jobs and embarrassing a President that truly did not care.

Corruption and violence walked hand in hand. The two most powerful gangs were the Socialist Revolutionary Movement (MSR) and the Insurrectional Revolutionary Union (UIR). They had their roots in the fight against Machado, with overlapping loyalties and frequent transfers of alliances among members.

The MSR was led by Rolando Masferrer, Mario Salabarria and Eufemio Fernandez.[3] Masferrer was a communist veteran of the Spanish Civil War, where he had been wounded in the leg during the Ebro River Battle. He was later nicknamed "El Cojo" or "The Cripple". Mario Salabarria was appointed Chief of Cuba's Secret Police with the rank of major. The UIR leader was Emilio Tro, a friend of Grau and veteran of the Pacific War, where he had fought with the American forces in WWII. He was appointed by President Grau as Chief of the Police Academy and also had the rank of major.

The University of Havana was a magnet for these rival groups that fought for control of the University Student Federation (FEU). It generated an environment of violence and fear where political rivalries were often settled at gunpoint. Due to the University's autonomy, the police was not allowed into the campus, creating a sanctuary for hiding weapons and criminal activities. The newspaper *El Mundo* wrote: "...violence holds sway at the University. Professors and students are nothing but the evident prisoners of a few groups of desperados who impose their will and pass their examinations at pistol point."[4] On October 1945, Fidel Castro with a high school diploma from the elitist Belen Jesuits School, enrolled as a law student, joining the ranks of those seeking leadership positions in the Student Federation. (FEU).

Castro entered the gang-ridden campus ready and willing to be part of this bloody mess. Soon he was carrying a gun and using it. He shot and wounded Leonel Gomez, a political rival and joined Emilio Tro's pseudo-revolutionary gang UIR. Several researchers have pointed to this issue: "Fidel Castro got involved in one of this group UIR while studying at the University of Havana".[5] Max Lesnix a friend of Castro is among those that have spoken on his gang involvement. In a 1991 interview, Lesnix stated: "Tro was converted into a "padrino" or godfather of Castro."[6] It should be noted that Emilio Tro's gang was a militant anti-communist faction, a contradiction in Castro's ideological resume.

On June 15, 1947, through CMQ Radio, the nation heard in horror how the Chief of the Secret Police, Mario Salabaria, one of the top leaders of the MSR gang, went with a judicial order to arrest Morin Dopico, Marianao's Chief of Police, at his home in Orfilas, neighborhood where he was meeting with Emilio Tro and several UIR members. A ferocious gunfight ensued. At the end, there where seven dead bodies including Emilio Tro, and the pregnant wife of Dopico. This terrible crime was filmed by Manolo Alonso "Guayo" and shown in Cuba's theaters. The Grau presidency continued to slide into shame while Castro lost his godfather.

### EDUARDO CHIBAS, "Un loco genial"

At this juncture, Eduardo Chibas, by now one of Cuba's most popular leaders, broke away from the PRC (Auténticos) and formed the Partido del Pueblo Cubano (Ortodoxo) to whose ranks rally the liberal left, willing to wipe out gangsters and corruption. For the disillusioned masses, Chibas' slogan was a call to action. "Verguenza contra dinero" (Honesty against money). It became a powerful message of decency and honesty in the administration of a future government. The roots of the "Ortodoxos" leadership were anchored among women activists and in the rebellious Oriente province. Conchita Fernandez, Consuelo Murillo, Emilio "Millo" Ochoa, Luis Conte Aguero, Roberto Garcia Ibanez, Alberto Saumell, and Chibas himself, a native of Santiago de Cuba, where his father owned the tramways and a sugar mill.

In his childhood, Chibas went to "Dolores" Jesuit School and, when his family moved to Havana, he continued his Jesuit education at "Belen" and joined Cuba's social elite at the Havana Yacht Club, but by 1947, this child of privilege was Cuba's foremost radical leader. Strongly anti-communist, Chibas attacked Blas Roca, the Secretary General of the Communist Party, with his bare fists and monopolized the revolutionary rhetoric of nationalism, honesty, social justice and individual freedoms. The idol of the new generation, the leader of the "Ortodoxo" Party, was a charismatic, sizzling communicator, a volatile and moody showman with a laser tongue that cut deep into his political adversaries' characters and agendas. Courageous, at times irrational and prone to depression spells; Chibas became the gospel of the revolution. From the depth of history, like a recurrent curse, the Cuban people looking for a political messiah had found "un loco genial" (a crazy genius).

Fidel Castro was soon to join Chiba's Party, but kept drifting into violent adventures. In the summer of 1947, Castro enrolled in the abortive invasion to overthrow Trujillo, the brutal Dominican dictator. The expedition was paid for by Jose Manuel Alemán, the arch-corrupt Secretary of Education, and led by the ex-communist and full-time thug Rolando Masferrer. The Dominican intellectual Juan Bosh was the symbolic head of the expeditionary forces that gathered at "Cayo Confite", a tiny island off the coast of Camaguey until Grau ordered the small Cuban navy to call off the invasion.

## FIDEL CASTRO AND THE BOGOTAZO

From the aborted "Cayo Confite" expedition, Castro traveled in March 29, 1948, to Bogota, Colombia, as a member of the Cuban student delegation in a gathering of regional students protesting the Ninth International Conference of American States where General George Marshal, U.S. Secretary of State, was meeting with the foreign Minister of Latin America to create the Organization of American States, OEA. The students, mostly sponsored by the Argentine fascist dictator, Juan Domingo Peron, was to host an anti-imperialist conference, demanding the return of the Falkland Islands (Malvinas) to Argentina, the independence of Puerto Rico and for the U.S. to turn over the Canal to Panama.

At this time, Colombia was in the grips of a highly contested election where the medieval-minded conservative party was facing the possibility of defeat at the polls by Jorge Eliecer Gaitan, the eloquent and charismatic liberal candidate. It was at a gathering of Colombia's social elite in the elegant "Teatro Colon" that thousands of anti-American leaflets were dropped from the balconies by the students including Fidel Castro. He was arrested by the Colombian police then released. Most of the anti-American leaflets had been printed in Havana.

On April 7, Gaitan met with Castro and del Pino at his law office in downtown Bogota to be briefed on the goals of the student protest. The two Cubans were invited to a second meeting two days later, but it was not to take place. On April 9, the hopes and dreams of the Colombian masses were shattered by a fanatic who shot and killed Gaitan. Bogota exploded in a cataclysmic outburst of fury and bloodshed. One third of Bogota was burned to the ground. Castro got hold of a rifle and joined the madness of revenge and killing. The "bogotazo" lasted for two terrible days. At the end, the Colombian Army smashed the spontaneous uprising. Thousands of people were killed in one of the bloodiest rebellions in America's history.[7] For Castro it was his first lesson in the need to direct the people's anger and frustrations to specific objectives and the effectiveness of a professional army in breaking down a popular rebellion. From this first-hand experience, Castro knew that in his quest for power, the Army of the Republic was an obstacle to be wiped out — a lesson that he never forgot.

## CARLOS PRIO: THE CORDIAL PRECIDENCY

Carlos Prio became president in 1948. For Cubans it was to be the last free and pluralistic election. The new president was a popular figure, forged in the 1930's generation as leader of the Directorio Estudiantil. At 45 he was still young and handsome with a charming smile and a sharp wit. Socially pleasant, it was difficult not to like him. He was a genuine nationalist and staunch democrat that truly believed in the right of his political adversaries to criticize his presidency without fear of reprisal, a shining accomplishment in a violent partisan and vindictive environment. Prio was to be known as "El presidente cordial".

But his presidency would be marred by scandals of gangsters and mismanagement. Prio brought some honest cabinet members, like Manuel Antonio de Varona, Justo Carrillo, Aureliano Sanchez Arango, Luis Casero and Jose "Pepin" Bosh, but there came also the corrupt bunch headed by the Vice President, Guillermo Alonso Pujol, and Ramon Vasconcelos, the Secretary of Communications, a thief and cold-blooded assassin who years before had murdered in Santiago de Cuba Alfredo Justiz Maspons, the 26-year-old son of Colonel Justiz, a hero of the War of Independence. Vasconcelos was the publisher of *Alerta* where Fidel Castro was a frequent columnist.

Prio's presidency gave Cubans the greatest volume of congressional legislation in both quantity and quality of the enacted laws. He pressed forward and got the approval of the National Bank, which provided a solid monetary system and consolidated the Cuban banking institution. Felipe Pazos, an outstanding economist, became its first director. The National Bank was one of the greatest achievements of the Cuban Republic. Next came the Agricultural and Industrial Bank, which provided loans to farmers and developing industries at low interest rates. Twenty-five percent of the national budget was invested in education, increasing the number of primary and high schools. Salaries of teachers and university professors were raised and two state universities were opened in Santiago de Cuba and Santa Clara.

Fiscal year 1950-51 showed a substantial budget surplus, allowing the president to grant a general salary increase for public service employees. During Prio's presidency, Cuba became the second Latin American nation with respect to its international monetary reserves. Retirement funds enacted into law for employees in commercial establishments, actors, architects, doctors and government employees. The president pushed legislation giving women civil rights equal to men and a court of Constitutional and social guarantees was established.

On October 24, 1950, Prio inaugurated the first TV channel on the island and Cuba became the second country in the world, after the U.S., to enjoy this new revolutionary entertainment media, generating a rush to buy television sets. By February 1951, a second TV station was opened at CMQ. During Prios' presidency, the island lived through a sustained period of prosperity, which impacted the growth of the middle class and improved the living standards of the Cuban laborers.

## CHIBAS' LAST STAND AND THE ARMY COUP D'ETAT.

In early June 1951, Chibas increased the tempo of his radio attacks against Prio and the leading members of his cabinet. His popularity was at an all time high and he seemed on his way to be Cuba's next president when he clashed with Prio's Secretary of Education, Aureliano Sanchez Arango, a seasoned debater and well-respected politician. On his Sunday radio broadcast, Chibas kept hammering at the need to eliminate corruption. It was the obsession of his life and became more than any other issue, the obsession of the revolution's generation.

The clash began in June, when Sanchez Arango called Chibas a Master of defamation,...a man of no honor, a fake apostle of the lie, the demagoguery and the calumny, accusing Chibas of being involved in dishonest coffee deals.[8] Chibas' response was swift. He accused Sanchez Arango of stealing money earmarked for the children's education to buy a lumberyard farm in Guatemala. For weeks, the Cubans were caught in the ferocious clash of these high rated debaters.

Chibas assured his audience that he had the evidence of Aureliano's corruption in his briefcase and that he was to show it in a public forum, but he was wrong as the Secretary of Education was an honest man and there was no evidence to show. Chibas had been misled into believing the evidence was forthcoming, a huge mistake that put in jeopardy his credibility. On the streets, people began shouting at him "Chibas, where is the briefcase?"[9] The leading presidential candidate was doomed. On Sunday, August 5, Chibas went to CMQ radio station, spoke for a few minutes and ended with a desperate farewell: "Sweep away the thieves in the government. People of Cuba, arise and walk! People of Cuba, keep awake! This is my last knock at your door [Mi ultimo aldabonazo]; Chibas then took a 0.38 pistol and shoot himself. He died the 15 of August 1951; the nation was shocked.

During Chiba's funeral, over 200,000 people walked with the fallen idol's casket through the streets of Havana. There was a terrible feeling of despair, anger, confusion, and political emptiness. It was during those tumultuous hours that Castro proposed to Pardo Llada the idea of marching with Chibas' casket to the Presidential palace to overthrow Prio's government. Pardo asked Castro: "to the palace, for what?" Castro answered: "to take power".[10] The idea was turned down. For Pardo it was crazy, "una locura," but it became obvious that Castro's audacity was beginning to surface, also his masterful ability to perceive the adversary's weakness and to take advantage of unexpected opportunities.

In the profound contradiction of a sick political culture, Chibas, an irresponsible demagogue was turned into a role model. He was given the honor of a Colonel killed in action. In his quest to save the Republic, he eventually poisoned its infant institution. Emotions were in full control of events. Illogical conclusions were the recurrent political thoughts. Miguel de Unamuno said it best: "we fill up the broken links of logic with rhetoric".[11] Chibas, the hopeful messiah, had fallen. The search for another "Loco Genial" began in earnest.

The fall of Chibas created a political vacuum with the "Auténticos" discredited, the Ortodoxos leaderless, and Batista with less than 10% of the support in the polls; elections became a run for the moral high ground. Desperate for credibility, the "Auténticos" nominated Carlos Hevia, an engineer of proven integrity who for a few hours was Cuba's president during the turmoil of the 1930's, while after some bitter infighting, the "Orthodox" chose the respected university professor Roberto Agramonte. The frontrunners had two things in common: both were honest and soon proved to be the antidote of charisma.

The elections were to take place on June 1, 1952, but on March 10, the Army headed by Batista overthrew president Prio in a swift, bloodless coup d'etat. It took the soldiers less than one and a half hours to wipe out the legitimate republic administration. Deeply disillusioned, the people did not react to this political crime that signaled the collapse of the 1940's Constitution and the return to power of the corrupt Army clique. Nobody attended the funeral of Cuba's democracy.

# CHAPTER XIV

# THE CONSTITUTIONAL PRESIDENTS

---

[1] Blas Roca, Carlos Rafael Rodríguez. *En Defensa del Pueblo* (1945), 41-43.

[2] Phillip, op.cit, 224.

[3] Enrique Ros: *Fidel Castro y el Gatillo Alegre* (Miami: Ediciones Universal, Miami, 2003), 61.

[4] As quoted in Suchlicki, op cit, 125.

[5] Samuel Farber, Revolution and Reaction in Cuba 1933-1960 (Middletown: Wesleyan University Press, 1976).

[6] Georgie Anne Geyer, *Guerrilla Prince* (Boston: Little, Brown and Company, 1991), 58.

[7] Ibid, 84.

[8] Lela Sanchez Echeverria, *La Polémica Infinita* (Bogoto: Quebecor World, 2004), 92.

[9] Ibid

[10] Geyer, op.cit, 90.

[11] Crow, op cit, 272.

# CHAPTER XV

# *FIDEL CASTRO: THE FORMATIVE YEARS*

## *RAUL: THE MARXIST BROTHER AND THE LINK TO MOSCOW – THE "MONCADA"– "EL DIRECTORIO" AND JOSE ANTONIO ECHEVERRIA.*

According to the Baptism Certificate from Santiago de Cuba's Cathedral, dated January 19, 1935, Fidel Castro was born on August 13, 1926 in Biran, Oriente. At his birth, and for the next seven years, his father, Angel, was married not to his mother, but to Maria Luisa Argote, a teacher and the mother of Fidel's two half siblings, Pedro Emilio and Lidia. During his early years, he was known as Fidel Ruz. His mother, Lina Ruz, had started working as a maid in Maria Luisa and Angel's household at the age of fourteen.

In 1896, Angel Castro, a native of Lanara, Galicia, joined General Valeriano Weyler's colonial army to fight against the Cuban rebels. After the Spanish debacle in 1898, Angel returned to Spain, but within a year, he was back in the Caribbean island of opportunities.

American bankers had invested heavily to develop the sugar industry in the area of Holguin, Puerto Padre, Banes and Mayarí. The United Fruit Company was interested in the large tracks of land for agricultural produce, especially bananas and sugar cane. This was where Angel Castro settled and began his rough and difficult quest for wealth.

Young Angel Castro's first job was construction of the United Fruit Railroad. The company was linking its immense land holdings, including the Boston and Preston Sugar Mills, with the new port of Antilles, in the Bay of Nipe, which became a trade center with New York and other eastern U.S. seaports. Later, Angel went into business for himself, walking the railroad tracks and selling water, lemonade and fruit to the cane cutters. It was a booming economy that allowed the enterprising Angel to save enough money to buy a farm at Biran near Mayari. The land was virgin, fertile and cheap, in a region that resembled the semi-savage, primitive and often violent settlements of the American Western frontier.

Angel was an illiterate immigrant out for himself. No one disputed his courage and violent nature. Riding a horse with a gun on his side, he called attention because of his implacable gaze and will power. This proud peasant soon made a fortune while remaining an ambitious, fierce loner. Among his few trusted friends was Fidel Pino Santos. A self-made man, wealthy and politically prominent in Orient, Angel, the solitary "Gallego", felt as if Fidel Pino Santos were his elder brother and actually named his third child with Lina, after him, Fidel. Pino Santos had also become Lina's confidant. In a moving letter dated December 8, 1938, Lina begged him to intercede with Angel so that he would officially recognize the paternity of their six children, and avoid the painful trauma of being known as the bastards from Biran.[1]

Fidel Castro was born into a dysfunctional family. His father was busy building a fortune. He spent the first three years of his life with his grandmother Dominga Ruz, a sorcerer from Artemisa, who practiced religious African rituals.[2] Dominga, Lina and the children lived in an adobe shack near his "Gallego" father and his wife Maria Luisa's principal household.

In 1930, Lina arranged with Angel to send Ramon, Angela and Fidel to Santiago de Cuba where they lived in the dilapidated house of the Haitian Consul, Hippolyte Hibbert, all expenses paid by Angel through Pino Santos. Fidel was three years old; his future godfather was an unscrupulous, distant and often violent character. Castro told Carlos Franqui that he remembered been physically abused by Hibbert.[3] He was to spend over two-and-a-half years in Hibbert's foster home. Growing up in this wrenching environment, void of family love and care, the child began to exhibit disturbing behavior such as frequent outbursts of violence, recurrent used of foul language and difficulty establishing friendship bonds with his peers. By the time he was six years old, Fidel Castro had developed an intense aggressive personality.

Castro's formal schooling began in first grade at La Salle, an excellent Christian Brothers school where he was enrolled through Pino Santos influence although he had not yet been baptized. At the school, he found that the students enjoyed outings to a beach house at "Rente" across the bay that the Christian Brothers owned. It had baseball fields and other sports facilities. Castro knew immediately that the way out of the misery of Hibbert's house was to be a boarding student. To achieve this, he staged a violent in-house rebellion. In his interview with Franqui, he said, "I proceeded to rebel and insult everyone... I behaved so terribly that they took me straight back to school and enrolled me as a boarder. For me it was a great victory."[4] Early in his life, Castro had discovered that violent behavior could pay off. From this time on, he became a bully.

As he grew taller, Castro became more confident of his physical strength and fought more frequently with his peers. He even clashed with a teacher and was expelled from school. Lina took her troubled son back to Biran where he threatened to set the house on fire if he was not sent back to school in Santiago.[5] Pino Santos' influence was used again, and Castro was enrolled at Dolores Jesuits School, where the old Santiago families sent their boys. It was a turning point in the young adolescent's life. Among Ignacio de Loyola's enlightened and highly disciplined followers, Fidel Castro discovered a surrogate family.

For the towering historian Will Durant, the Jesuits had been "the most successful educational order in history"[6] and their graduates would become outstanding leaders in almost every walk of life. This close-knit, ascetic organization was vitally concerned with discipline, obedience and loyalty. Founded as a military order, members had to be always ready to fight as the best soldiers of Christ. "Ad Majorem dei Glorian"—"To the Greater Glory of God." Loyalty became an essential trait reinforced through spiritual exercises in which for several days of meditation and training, the individual found the strength to remain loyal to the apostolic mission. In 1941, Castro transferred to the Belen Jesuits in Havana where he continued this rigorous education and attended daily mass.

In this elite school, Castro learned the Aristotelian logic, which establishes the relationship between premise and conclusion, and that of the Socratic Method where the individual is trained to argue for and against the same issue. The troubled adolescent accepted as a matter of faith the supremacy of the Jesuit dogma. It seems as though the militant influence of the Jesuit training framed in young Castro the need to be always secure within the safety of a righteous dogma. Catholic or Marxist, Castro was to remain until the end firmly entrenched as an intolerant, fighting for a dogma. In their enlightened teaching, the Jesuits could mold the liberal genius of a Voltaire or the fierce dogmatism of a Castro.

In the Spanish Jesuit years, Castro was heavily influenced by a Fascist-Falangist bias, and supported the Roman concept of civic virtue rooted in manliness, discipline, and courage, as well as a strong resentment of Anglo-Americans for the centuries of military humiliation inflicted upon Spain. In this militant environment, Castro excelled in sports and oratory. Professor Brian Latell writes in his incisive analysis of the Castro brothers that the time spent with the Jesuits was for Fidel "the happiest years of his life."[7]

During the period with the Jesuits, Fidel's role model was the charismatic fascist leader Jose Antonio Primo de Rivera, who founded the "Falange Espanola" (Spanish Phalanx). This superlative communicator proposed the fascist ideology of a Corporate State, which advanced a mild socialist doctrine organized by corporations in the fascist assembly. It also advocated a militant nationalism. Jose Antonio believed in the power of the masses to forge the rebirth of Spain's glorious days by rallying all Spanish-speaking countries to stand up against the Anglo-Saxon hegemony. Fascism was Fidel's first step into the dogmatism of totalitarian doctrines. His anti-Yankeeism was also rooted in the "Falangist" priest grievances against the U.S. for the 1898 disaster and loss of the beloved Cuban colony. Adolph Hitler was another inspiring Castro model. At the University, "he walked soberly around campus with a copy of 'Mein Kampf'" (Mi lucha) under his arm.[8]

By the time Castro entered the University in 1945, he was 19 years old, void of democratic ideals and growing in the belief of an all-intrusive militaristic state, where soldiers rein supreme. Castro walked into the university ideological milieu as a proto-Fascist and left four years later with a law degree, a wife, a son and powerful attraction to Marx and Lenin's ideological doctrines.

## RAUL: THE MARXIST BROTHER AND THE LINK TO MOSCOW

At this stage and for many years to come, Fidel Castro denied being a Marxist, but he did encourage his brother Raul to join the communist ranks. The younger brother went from reading American comic magazines to Engels and Marx. Years later, Raul recalled that his first contact with the communist literature was Engels' *The Origin of the Family, Private Property and the State*. In that press conference, Raul said: "I read it twice. It was not a difficult book to understand."[9]

Fidel knew he had to conceal his Marxist preference from the Cubans, but he could use Raul as a trusted link with the Kremlin. He had just turned 22 and was eager to please his older brother. It was fitting to send Raul on this important assignment. In March 1953, four months before the attack on the Moncada army barracks, Raul traveled to Vienna to attend the World Youth Conference. The main speaker was Vladimir Semichastry, the future chief of the KGB, the soviet intelligence service. Afterwards he went to Bucharest, Budapest and Prague. Raul liked what he saw and turned into a militant communist.

He returned to Cuba on the Italian passenger liner Andrea Gritti. On board, Raul met Nikolai Leonov, a young Marxist on his way to Mexico and with whom he established a long lasting friendship. It was to be the best link with Moscow. Young Leonov eventually became a top-ranking KGB espionage chief and always remained very close to Raul. Upon his arrival, and with Fidel's blessing, he joined the Cuban Communist Party. Raul recalled that from that moment on, he was "ready to die for the communist cause."[10] Recent declassified KGB documents offer evidence that Fidel "deliberately made a Marxist of Raul, giving him books to read and sending him on the famous youth conference trip."[11]

## THE MONCADA

During the first year of Batista's regime, the opposition split into two major camps. There were those who believed in a peaceful return to a constitutional democracy, and those who were seeking a violent revolution. Grau led the politicians that looked for the electoral solution, while Carlos Prio headed and financed the groups seeking violent overthrow of the dictator. On the island, Aureliano Sanchez Arango, who had recently returned from exile, was actively carrying the banner of rebellion, Batista's intelligence forces failed to perceive the threat to the regime posed by Cuba's younger generation. The police focused mainly on the older revolutionary groups. This proved to be a mistake.

From the minute Batista took power, Castro knew that the doors for a violent revolution were open and did not waste any time forging what members simply called "the movement".[12] It was to be a disciplined vanguard, willing to obey Castro's command to the death. The members were committed to the ultimate sacrifice and behaved like monastic soldiers. To die a heroes death was a welcome outcome. Castro was a persuasive communicator; his discourse was to remain always an apocalyptic call to death. "Patria o Muerte" (Fatherland or Death).

The movement was organized in small self-sufficient cells. Secrecy was mandatory. Most members came from the ranks of the "Ortodoxos" youth. Castro's trusted inner circle was small and included the Leninist sympathizer, Abel Santamaria, a Pontiac car dealer, his sister Haydee, affectionately called "Yeye", Boris Santa Coloma, Renato Guitart and Pedro Miret. By the time of the Moncada assault, the movement had over 250 hard-core members, mostly from Pinar del Rio and Havana. They had raised $15,000 for weapons and materials to carry on the attack.[13]

The Moncada barracks in Santiago de Cuba was the base for the Maceo regiment, with over 1,000 men. Castro targeted this army base believing that his small force of around 130 men and 2 women (the exact number of men remained impossible to verify) could take the fortress by surprise. The attack was to take place at dawn on July 26, the last day of Santiago's Carnival. Castro was counting on the fact that the soldiers should have been sound sleep after three days of drinking and dancing. This immensely popular carnival was a syncretism festivity where Catholic saints and African deities came together at the sound of the "Conga" drums and the city exploded in a memorable festival of rum and music.

The equipment of Castro's poorly trained groups where a myriad of different arms, mostly small caliber rifles, shotguns, a few machine guns and pistols. Their goal was to assault a force ten times larger and with better weapons. For security reasons, most of Castro's men were not aware that their final destination was the Moncada barracks, and went to Santiago believing they were on a training exercise at a farm rented by Renato Guitart on the road to Siboney Beach, 20 miles east of the city. Guitart belonged to Santiago's close-knit bourgeoisie family and was the only "Santiaguero" in Castro's assault group.

On the eve of the attack, those about to die had chicken fricassee for dinner. It was at this time that the small militant group learned they were to assault and capture the Moncada Garrison. Castro told them: "We will attack at dawn...when the guards are only half awake and the officers are still sleeping off their drunkenness... It will be a surprise attack and should not last more than ten minutes."[14] For a moment, there was complete silence. The specter of death had entered the room. For many, this was to be their last supper. The silence was broken and Gustavo Arcos challenged the wisdom of the operation. Castro responded with a direct question. "Are you afraid"? the "Máximo leader" was establishing a behavioral pattern among his followers. Even in a clearly suicidal mission, only those willing to die had a place in the "Movimiento". With his manhood directly in question, Arcos went along on the attack. He was badly wounded.

The other criticism of the plan came from the group's physician, Mario Munoz: "Fidel, I am ready to die for Cuba, but to think that we can take the Moncada barracks with a few more than one hundred men, when they have a garrison of more that a thousand soldiers, is to send these boys to sure suicide... I will be in the vanguard, but I repeat that this plan seems to be madness even a crime."[15] Munoz also went on the attack; in few short hours he was dead. It is evident that Castro had found the key to motivate reasonable people into becoming willing martyrs. He would repeat this pattern over and over again.

At 5:00 A.M., they left the farm on their way to the Moncada. Renato Guitart was in the lead car. Castro drove the second one. As they reached gate #3, Guitart jumped from the car, wearing an army sergeant uniform and shouting: "Attention...The General is coming". It worked. The three sentries were captured and disarmed, but suddenly an unexpected roving guard detachment discovered the intruders and the shooting began. The surprise was lost. Guitart and his six men vanguard fought their way into the camp where, due to the soldier's quick response, four of them were killed. Renato Guitart was among the death. In just a few minutes, the attack was crushed; however, Castro managed to escape. The repression was brutal. From the assault group, eight died in the fight and 56 were tortured and murdered. The Army suffered 22 dead.[16] The first chapter of Castro's apocalyptic sense of mission had been opened. It was to be repeated for over half a century of violence, ruin and death.

On August 1, Castro and two companions were captured by a

16-man patrol led by Lieutenant Pedro Sarria while they were sleeping in the area of "La Gran Piedra" nearby Santiago. Some of the soldiers called for Castro and his men's immediate execution, but Sarria recognized one of the prisoners as a fellow Mason and spared their lives. This fateful event was immediately followed by the arrival at the mountain site of the Archbishop of Santiago, Enrique Perez Serante, who had secured from Batista the guarantee of Castro's life. The enraged soldiers insisted on killing Castro on the spot, but were controlled by the Archbisho's valiant intervention. An irony of destiny, the life of the future Marxist dictator was saved by the Church.

On September 21, 1953, Castro and the survivors of the attack were brought to trial in Santiago's courthouse. Castro spoke in his own defense and that of his men. The prosecutor, Francisco Mendieta, asked the maximum sentence of 26 years in prison. Castro took the stand and spoke for two solid hours, making reference to the Ortodoxo's program, the *Bible*, equality, Jean-Jacques Rousseau, and the Latin American war of independence, and made a weird comment about the devil's rebellion, the need for social justice, agrarian reform, insisting that his revolution was inspired in the ideals of Marti and Chibas. Castro ended his speech with a quote from Adolph Hitler's "La Historia me Absolvera" –History will absolve me—. "There is no question that Fidel's last words came from his careful reading of Hitler's' Rathaus speech."[17] At the end, he was sentenced to 15 years in prison. The other survivors of the Moncada fiasco received lesser sentences. It was also evident that a political pattern was being established in Castro's discourse: the absence of any mention of communism. In the long Moncada speech there was never a reference to the Marxist ideology. Cuba would have to wait seven years for Castro's confession that, since the beginning of the struggle, he was a communist.

The "Presidio" or prison was on the Isle of Pine and they were treated well and as "political prisoners" separate from the common criminals. In the "Presidio," Castro was allowed to receive books and establish the "Abel Santamaria Ideological Academy". There he ran a close-knit, disciplined group, loyal to his authority. On May 15, 1955, Batista pardoned Fidel Castro and the other Moncada survivors, the next day, they marched out of the "Presidio". On July

7, Castro left Cuba and settled in Mexico.

Castro´s brother in law Rafael Diaz Balart, a courageous and brilliant thinker from a patrician family in Oriente, knew Castro from their university days and was among the few members of the Cuban Congress that opposed Batista's pardon. He stated in the House Chamber: "Fidel Castro and his group wanted only one thing: power, but total power…I believe that this amnesty, so imprudently approved will bring many days of mourning, of pain, of blood and poverty to the Cuban people."[18]

A few months before Castro's release from prison and secured in the Presidential Palace, Batista called for a bogus national election. They were held in November 1954. Running unopposed, the military dictator won the electoral farce. Immediately the political opposition demanded new and transparent elections. The specter of Machado's bloody rebellion was looming as a terrible option.

Cosme de la Torriente, an 82-year-old veteran of the War of Independence who called for a "civic dialogue" framed by the non-partisan "Friends of the Republic Society" SAR, attempted a serious peaceful settlement. Batista, obsessed with remaining in power until the end of his illegitimate term, failed to see the advantages of the political compromise offered by the SAR. It was another fateful mistake.

The years of luxurious living had changed the humble ex-sergeant's taste and perception of his social and political needs. Gone was the populist leader, always re-inventing himself and expanding his political base. By the time of his return to power, Batista was obsessed by money. Illicit profits were everywhere as before, in the dredging of the island's harbors, in the national lottery and "bolita" stands, in highways, bridges, tunnels, real estate transactions and "mafia controlled" gambling casinos.

## *"EL DIRECTORIO" AND JOSE ANTONIO ECHEVERRIA*

In November 1955, the fight to overthrow Batista began to coalesce into a formidable, fighting organization, the student directorate, "El Directorio", founded by Jose Antonio Echevarria to lead the struggle in the tradition of the 1933 generation of urban warfare. On December 2, Jose Antonio Echeverria led a demonstration against the dictator. Hundreds came running down the Havana University campus stairway "La Escalinata" waving the Cuban flag in "San Lazaro" street. There the police was waiting. They fought with stones and fists. In the melee, Jose Antonio was wounded and had to be hospitalized. The T.V. news recorded the street fight and brought it inside people's homes. It was a shocking story and Jose Antonio Echeverria became the symbol of the rebellion.

On December 4, during a baseball game, 18 members of the "Directorio" jumped into the field displaying anti-Batista banners. The game was being broadcast live on TV, thousands of viewers witnessed in anger the bloody beating given to the demonstrators. The year ended with a nationwide student strike that lasted over three weeks. The military regime was shaken.

By the end of the year, the student's rebellion burst into a formidable display of courage and determination. It was overwhelming. Batista's savage repression could not and would not defeat their heroic stance. As professor Suchlicki aptly stated; "A generation break stronger perhaps that any other one in Cuba's history was taking place in the 1950's –a break that thrust the leadership of the anti-Batista movement upon the young. The students were still willing to follow a leader, but one from their own ranks. Echeverria thus emerged as the representative of Marti's and Chiba's ideals. He, more than any one else, commanded the admiration of the students and as time went by, of the Cuban people."[19]

While in Mexico, Castro was highly disturbed by the news of the student's rebellion, and above all, by the fact that Jose Antonio was leading the fight. In October, with a State Department visa, Castro traveled to several U.S. cities, to raise funds among the Cuban exiles. In New York's Palm Garden theatre, he told a cheering audience that he was preparing an invasion of Cuba[20] and later in Miami's Flagler theatre he promised that he would never betray the revolution by receiving moneys that had been stolen by dishonest politicians. In his Miami speech, Castro said: "It is not a revolutionary movement when you have to accept money from the thieves"[21] It was a promise of high ethical standards. By doing so, Castro had closed the doors to receiving "money from thieves". Would he keep his promise? Would Castro stand on this moral commitment? Time would tell.

# CHAPTER XV

# FIDEL CASTRO: THE FORMATIVE YEARS

[1] Serge Raffy. *Castro el Desleal*. (Santillana USA, Doral, 2006), 44.
[2] Ibid, 34.
[3] Carlos Franqui. *Vida, Aventuras y desastres de un hombre llamado Castro*. (Editorial Planeta, Barcelona, 1988), 27.
[4] Ibid., 27.
[5] Ibid, 29.
[6] Durant, op.cit, 910.
[7] Brian Latell. *After Fidel: The Inside Story of Castro's Regime and Cuba's next Leader*. (Palgrave McMillan, New York, 2002), 62.
[8] Geyer, op.cit., 42.
[9] Lattel, op. cit., 125.
[10] Ibid., 130.
[11] Ibid., 127.
[12] Raúl Castro. *Fundamentos*. (FAR, Habana, Junio-Julio 1961), 11.
[13] Duarte, op cit, III, 290.
[14] Geyer, op.cit, 115.
[15] Ibid, 117.
[16] Raffy, op.cit, 121.
[17] Geyer, op cit, 132.
[18] Rafael Diaz Balart. Cuba: Instrahistoia, una lucha sin tregua. (Ediciones Universal, Miami, 2006), 66-68.
[19] Suchlicki, op cit, 146.
[20] Raffy, op cit, 159.
[21] José Duarte Oropesa. *Historiología Cubana*. (Ediciones Universal), 372

# CHAPTER XVI

# *THE 1956 GENERATION: THE HEROIC*

*THE "GRANMA" SHIPWRECK – HERBERT MATTHEWS AND THE "NEW YORK TIMES" – THE ATTACK ON THE PRESIDENTIAL PALACE – FRANK PAIS: THE FIRST DISSIDENT – WASHINGTON SHIFTS FROM BATISTA TO CASTRO – THE PEOPLE'S REBELLION – THE REBEL ARMY: THE INSTRUMENT OF TOTAL POWER – BATISTA'S MILITARY FIASCO – THE PEOPLE'S VICTORY?*

There are times that try peoples' will to be free ... the determination to get rid of a corrupt government ... the humiliation of foreign intervention in ones internal affairs ... the time for courage and heroism ... the time for revolution ... when a whole generation fights for a dream of redemption and justice. For the Cubans the time was 1956, the year when Batista in his infinite greed, closed the option for a peaceful political transition.

The ancients believed that fate, more than human actions, mark the path of historical drama. The 1956 generation fought with utmost courage, searching for a bright tomorrow of justice, liberty, and full sovereignty looming in the horizon. Sometimes it looked as if it had been conquered, touched, felt, but always vanished like a terrible nightmare. The 1956 generation's destiny was to fight for the vanishing quest.

They came from all walks of life, from different economic, social and ideological backgrounds, but with a common ideal of honesty, social justice and full sovereignty for which they were willing to die. It was their destiny to spend half a century in the trenches, and those still alive are still carrying on the struggle at the dawn of the Twenty-First Century. They are the heroic symbols of the unreachable dream. Frank Pais, Pedro Luis Boitel, Gustavo Arcos, Renato Guitart, Hubert Matos, Rogelio Gonzalez Corzo, Jorge Mas Canosa, Manuel Artime, Virgilio Campaneria and Jose Antonio Echeverria synthesize the legendary struggle. This generation more than any other before symbolizes the Cuban tragic search for freedom.

As the rebellion grew in intensity, Castro felt he was being left out of the fight. The students were not waiting for him to lead the struggle. His excellent political instincts told him that he was turning into a marginal figure. Frank Pais, the charismatic teacher from Santiago, was heading the clandestine operation of the "26 of July Movement" and Jose Antonio Echeverria was becoming a national hero. Castro knew that his quest for power was vanishing. He had to return, and soon. According to Jorge Valls, one of the founders of the "Directorio": "Fidel's first and most implacable war was not against Batista at all, but against any competitive revolutionaries. Under no circumstances was he about to be preempted."[1]

On April 4, 1956, Batista's military intelligence service, SIM, discovered a plot by army officers seeking to overthrow the regime. It was headed by Colonel Ramon Barquin, the military attaché in Washington. The "Secret Service" infiltrated the conspiracy and all plotters were arrested, courts-martial and sentenced to prison.

The officers' plot was known as the "Conspiracy of the Pure" in contrast with the discredited high command headed by General Francisco Tabernilla who wasted no time in promoting his friends and family members into the command structure. Two of his sons were appointed to head the air force and tank regiment. With few exceptions, the higher echelons of the officer corps was filled with the Tabernilla clique of corrupt and incompetent commanders. The issue of Tabernilla's manifest incompetence was brought to Batista's attention by some concerned associates but to no avail. Batista stuck to the bitter end by his friend masquerading as a general. The result was a lowering of the Army's moral and leadership capabilities, with disastrous consequences for their illegitimate government.

On April 29, a group of "Auténticos" led by Reynold Garcia and funded by Carlos Prio attacked the barracks of the "Goicuria" regiment in Matanzas. The Army had been tipped off; several machine guns and hundreds of soldiers were ready and waiting for the attack. It turned out to be a killing field. But it so happened that a photographer from *Life* magazine was also aware of the impending attack and took pictures of the shocking massacre. American public opinion was outraged by the terrible images. In Cuba, *Bohemia* magazine also published the photos. The nation was outraged. Throughout the island a deep sense of rejection against Batista began gaining momentum and the ever-rebellious Oriente turned into a tinderbox.

In Mexico, Castro's group was trained by Alberto Bayo at the "Santa Rosa" ranch near Chalco. Bayo was a Cuban-born officer of the Spanish Foreign Legion. Like Castro, his parents were Spaniards and Bayo joined the Civil War on the side of the Republic. Also at the ranch was Argentinean Ernesto Guevara "Che", a communist with a passion for motorcycles — a curious ideological combination. "Che" struck up a close friendship with Raul Castro and forged a commitment to create a Marxist society in Cuba.

On August 5, and running out of time for his announced invasion by year's end, Castro crossed the Rio Grande. As a wetback, he slipped into the U.S. and went to MacAllen, Texas, for a pre-arranged meeting with former president Carlos Prio at the hotel "Casa de las Palmas".[2] In MacAllen, Castro broke his moral commitment and asked a triumphant Prio for money. He was given $50,000. He went back to "Santa Rosa" with Prio's cash.

In September, Frank Pais traveled to Mexico for a final briefing on Castro's invasion. The plan called for a combined landing of 82 men at "Playa Colorada" near Niquero, and a large uprising of the Oriente underground. Frank proposed scaling down the operation.[3] He believed that the movement was short on weapons and was not ready for a fight of that magnitude. An alternative option was for Castro to slip into Oriente with a few men, move undetected into the thick forest cover of the Sierra Maestra where the underground could reinforce him with men and equipment. Castro insisted on the original plan, however, and prevailed. Frank returned to Mexico in October for the final briefing on the invasion, November 30 chosen as the landing date.

The secret infiltration option did not fit the pattern of marketing a persona — a kind of MacArthur "I shall return" to the Philippines propaganda stunt. A quiet infiltration was out of the question. Always a master showman, Castro was looking for a spectacular comeback; therefore, he was to land in a miniature invasion with the propaganda effect of a glorious return.

In Havana, "The Directorio" was stepping up the fight. On Saturday, October 28, Rolando Cubelas led a commando team into the Montmatre Night Club and killed the Chief of Army Intelligence, Colonel Antonio Blanco Rico. The following day, in a fierce gunfight at the Haitian embassy, the "Directorio" killed General Rafael Salas Canizares, Batista's chief of police, a brutal, cold-blooded assassin.

## THE "GRANMA" SHIPWRECK

In Mexico, Castro was on the move. In the early morning of November 25, the overloaded yacht *Granma* sailed from the north of the Tuxpan River in Yucatan. Eighty-two men with heavy infantry weapons crammed into the 12-meter boat. Battered by huge waves and strong winds, the invasion was on. Forty-one men were sailing to their death or to be captured. The next day, Frank Pais received a cipher note with instructions that *Granma* was at sea on its way to "Playa Colorada" beach. Frank got in touch with Celia Sanchez, head of the movement in the landing zone, to ready the welcoming group and went on to alert the Santiago underground of the approaching uprising. With the landing just a few hours away, Celia left her home to meet with Crecencio Perez, a powerful outlaw of the mountains. The reception network was placed on high alert. Several fishermen were on the lookout from Niquero to Cape Santa Cruz. Several trucks had been secured to move the invaders into the hills as quickly as possible. A group headed by Guillermo Garcia was at "El Plátano" near the Toro river ready to dispatch the rebels to "El Puriel" where "Mongo" Perez, Crecencio's brother, was to lead Castro and his men up the impenetrable mountains. It was Celia, the ever-efficient planner, at her best.

Celia Sanchez was among the most outstanding fighters of the 56's generation, slim, dark-haired, the daughter of a highly respected doctor from Manzanillo, who spent a lot of time taking care of sick farmers in the mountain. She grew up in that environment of community service and was able to establish a solid network with the peasants of the region; she was especially close to Crecencio Perez, the most powerful chieftain or "cacique" of the "Sierra Maestra". Celia, the committed revolutionary, was also highly, disciplined and courageous. Her role after the landing disaster was to be spectacular and decisive in Castro's survival.

As scheduled, on November 30' Frank Pais led the Santiago uprising. Taken by surprise, the Moncada Garrison hesitated and the rebellion spread into the city streets. Dressed in green fatigue uniforms with red and black armbands, the movement took control of the downtown area. Jorge Sotus occupied the maritime police station and burned it down. They cut power lines, sabotaged railroad tracks and bridges, but by mid afternoon, the army began retaking the city and crushed the uprising. Frank Pais barely escaped and fled underground.

Finally on December 2, the *Granma* reached Oriente and ran aground at "Los Coyuelos". Not only was it late but landed at the wrong place. Out of the shipwreck,[4] the men jumped into the shallow waters, ankle deep in mud and began the desperate march to shore. Within a week, 21 would be killed, 20 captured. Twenty-three managed to slip into the surrounding towns, while 18, including Castro, were found by Celia's underground network and hidden safely in a peasant's house. Soon "Mongo" Perez got the beaten invaders up into the mountains sanctuary. Celia's superb organization made the difference between survival and oblivion. It was evident that Crecencio Perez's help was a turning point after the landing disaster. Castro had survived and was safe under the protection of the legendary "Godfather" of the "Sierra Maestra".

## HERBERT MATTHEWS AND THE "NEW YORK TIMES"[5]

Inspired by Antonio Guiteras' revolutionary ideals, the Cuban middle class, as in the 1933's fight against Machado, was once again leading the struggle. There were daily acts of sabotage in the cities to which Batista's police responded with terrible ferocity. It was becoming evident that despite the economic upswing, Batista's power was slowly fading. Also the two principal opposition parties, the "Orthodoxos" and the "Auténticos" were by now pitifully irrelevant. The Cuban youth were on the march to revolution. The cities or "El Llano" — the Plains — had turned into the main fighting front. In her book, Georgie Ann Geyer, addressed this issue: "In fact, the fight in the cities was far more dangerous and brutal than anything that was happening in the relatively 'Peaceful' Sierra… in the cities Batista launched his most scourging reign of terror."[6]

In February, Crecencio's network sent supplies and ten fighters, among them Celia Sanchez who joined Castro in his forest hideout, altogether, 30 guerrillas.[7] That was the size of Castro's skeleton force when he pulled a huge propaganda stunt. With Echeverria in Havana and Frank in Santiago leading the bloody struggle, Castro felt the urgent need to get in the news to regain his leadership status. The fact that the army claimed to have killed him made it more pressing to take center stage without delay. There were lingering doubts as to whether Castro was dead or alive.

But Castro moved swiftly. By early February, Rene Rodriguez, one of *Granma*'s survivors, was already in Havana, with specific instructions to find and bring into Castro's mountain sanctuary an American journalist. Rodriguez met with the underground leader and it was decided to assign this superbly important task to Javier Pazos, a 21-year-old student and son of Felipe Pazos, former president of Cuba's National Bank. The Pazos were highly regarded in Havana society and intellectual circles. The elder Pazos knew Ruby Phillys, *The New York Times* correspondent in Havana; he agreed to help his son Javier and called Phillys to arrange the meeting. Felipe Pazos met with the American journalist at the *Times* office on Refugio street.

Phillys was told that Castro had survived the landing fiasco and was alive. A few days later, a secret meeting was arranged with Castro's personal envoy, Rene Rodriguez. Phillys believed the story and knew she was into a sensational piece of news. A veteran journalist, she wasted no time in calling the paper's foreign editor Emanuel R. Friedman with a cryptic request for Herbert Matthews, war correspondent and editor, to fly to Havana as soon as possible. The biggest propaganda scoop in Cuba's history was in the making.

Herbert Matthews was 57 and in delicate health, with heart problems. Fluent in Spanish, he had covered the Ethiopian conflict and the Spanish Civil war on the leftist Republican side and had met there with several well-known writers, including Ernest Hemingway. He was a graduate of Columbia University, played the piano and had an intellectual preference for classical literature and history. In 1922, he began working at *The New York Times*, by 1931 had married Edith Crosse, who was called Nancie by her friends. For years, Matthews headed the London desk and later became an expert in Latin America as well as a member of the *Time*'s Editorial

Board. Upon receiving Friedman's call, Matthews agreed on the Havana trip on condition that Nancie go along at the *Time*'s expense.[8]

On February 9, the couple arrived in Havana and checked in at the elegant Hotel Seville. The next day, Matthews met with Phillys and learned that Castro was alive, hiding in the Sierra Maestra's mountains and waiting for a *New York Times* journalist. In a later meeting with Felipe and Javier Pazos, he was asked if *Times* was sending a correspondent to cover the Castro story, to which Matthews swiftly answered that he was going himself. In his well-written book *The Man Who Invented Fidel*, Anthony De Palma wrote: "He did not intend to allow anyone to stand in the way of this story..."[9]

On February 15, Javier Pazos, Faustino Perez, another survivor of the *Granma*, and Lillian Mesa, an Havana socialite, picked the couple at the hotel and drove all night to Oriente. They ran into several military roadblocks, but with Matthews and Nancie dressed as rich American visitors traveling with Cuban friends, they were allowed by the soldiers to go through. Early on Saturday, Matthews and his party reached a safe house set up by Celia Sanchez near Manzanillo. Nancie was to stay there while Matthews and the others led by Felipe Guerra Matos drove in a jeep to the rendezvous point at the foot of the mountains. There a trusted Crecencio scout guided them as they walked up the difficult terrain. Matthews was tired, but thrilled. He was about to make history.

At dawn, they reached a clearing where the interview was to take place. De Palma described the moment when Castro appeared for his press meeting. "He wore fresh army fatigues, an olive-green cap and carried a long rifle with a sharpshooter's telescopic lens. We can pick them off at a thousand yards with these guns, he (Castro) boasted to Matthews soon after greeting him, brandishing the rifle as though it were a trophy."[10]

Matthews came to this meeting with his own ideological baggage. He had had a falling out with the Spanish Republic and was searching for a revival of the revolutionary flame. He deeply felt the nostalgia of Hemingway's lost Spanish cause and was immediately fascinated by Castro's overpowering personality, political ideals and the perception that the tall, bearded rebel was leading a well-armed guerrilla force of more than 500 men and women and was in full control of the "Sierra Maestra". It was a good show. Always a great communicator, Castro easily won over the willing journalist of the most powerful newspaper in the United States. With the *Times* as his propaganda stage, Castro and his 30 fighters could reach the world.

On February 24, the first of three articles was published on the front page of *The New York Times* under the headline: "Cuban Rebel is Visited in Hideout". The leading story read: "Fidel Castro, the rebel leader of Cuba's youth, is alive and fighting hard and successfully in the rugged almost impenetrable fastness of the Sierra Maestra." In his historic article, Matthews told his readers that Castro was anti-communist, with strong democratic ideals, fighting for free elections and the Constitution. Raptured by the young rebel's performance, Matthews called Castro the Cuban Robin Hood.[11] In his diary "Che" Guevara wrote, "Matthews, according to what Fidel told me, because I was not at the interview... showed himself to sympathize with the revolution.[12]

Batista's Minister of Defense denied the veracity of Matthews's story. On the 28, the "Times" responded with a front page photo of Castro and Matthews. Cuba was in shock. Ten weeks after the "Granma's" bloody disaster, Castro had returned from the shadows of death. It is evident that on the day of the story Castro was barely surviving in Crecencio's mountain sanctuary and controlling the reduced area under his own boots but Matthews rescued the failed leader and turned him, like a thundering lightening, into an unconquerable Robin Hood. In one stroke, the awesome power of the "New York Times" had propelled Castro into the top leadership of Cuba's revolution and a popular figure in the U.S., especially within the State Department. It was a masterful propaganda resurrection.

## THE ATTACK ON THE PRESIDENTIAL PALACE

Late in February, while Castro had regained center stage through Matthews front page, José Antonio Echeverria, Menelao Mora and Carlos Gutierrez Menoyo, assembled over one hundred men for a decisive blow to the head of the regime, an attack on the Presidential Palace to kill Batista. Two generations, driven by a proud nationalism, had joined forces to find a way into constitutional legitimacy, honesty and civil rights. The

"Directorio's" youth and a group from the old guard rebels, united their forces to carry on this daring mission. They were among the best and most experienced urban guerrillas in Havana.

It was to be a direct and final assault on the regime. A forty two men vanguard led by Menoyo and Mora were to fight their way into the palace. Menoyo was a veteran of the Spanish Civil War, and Mora an "Auténtico" former congressman. Both were known for their courage in combat. A support group was to take control of the buildings around the Palace to shoot at the defenders through the doors and windows so as to create confusion within the Palace. This important support group was to prevent the arrival of reinforcements and ensure there were no chances of an escape route for the dictator. José Antonio's group was to take over the CMQ Radio Station and announce to the nation that the dictator had been executed. The assault groups were armed with sub-machineguns, M1 carbine riffles, pistols and grenades. The date for the attack was March 13.

At 3:20 P.M. the first group came in fighting through the Palace gate at the "Zayas Park" entrance. Mora and Menoyo led the vanguard into the ground floor, shooting their submachine guns all the way into Batista's dining room and executive offices on the second floor where two officers were killed right by Batista's desk. The support group did not arrive. Their absence from the attack on the Palace turned it into a fatal failure. After the initial shock, the guards put up a stiff defense. Inside the building there was a fierce gunfight but Batista escaped in a lift to the third floor and the rebels were unable to reach and execute the dictator.

As scheduled, Jose Antonio's group took over the CMQ Radio Station and broadcast what came to be known as his last political will or farewell to the Cubans: "!People of Havana! The revolution is in progress. The Presidential Palace has been taken by our forces and the dictator has been executed in his den... we are confident that the purity of our intentions will bring us God's blessings so that we may bring the rule of justice to our nation...If we fall, may our blood signal the road to freedom." It was a hero's message. A devout Christian Jose Antonio had the heroic vision of a martyr.

Inside the palace, the fight continued for over an hour but without the crucial participation of the second group. Batista's reinforcement soon began to arrive on the scene and were able to recapture the palace grounds and save the shaken regime. By late evening the fight was over. Thirty-five men died in the assault, including Menoyo and Mora. Their bullet-ridden bodies lay on the palace marble stairs. Jose Antonio Echeverria was shot and killed by the police in a gunfight while approaching the University of Havana campus. On Echeverria's body, the police found a paper with the name of Pelayo Cuervo. It was his death sentence. That night a group of Batista assassins went to Cuervo's home, took him and murdered the prominent "Orthodoxo" political leader. By an stroke of destiny, both the dictator's life and Castro's quest for power had survived. The death of Jose Antonio Echeverria eliminated one of the principal challengers to Castro's hegemony in the revolutionary struggle.

That afternoon, in his mountain sanctuary, Castro heard the news of the attack to kill Batista. A Directorio victory meant the end of his quest for power. With 80 men[13] Castro was doomed and could not control his rage when he label the Directorio's attack "a useless waste of blood"[14] — an outrageous statement from the promoter of the "Moncada" and bloody "Granma" disaster.

In Havana, survivors of the assault were hunted down. On April 20, following the betrayal of Marcos (Marquito) Rodriguez, a Batista informer and active member of the Communist Party, the police stormed the Humbolt Seven apartment and killed Fructuoso Rodriguez, Joe Westbrooke, Juan Pedro Carbo and Jose Machado. The Directorio's leadership was virtually crushed in the capital. The Humbolt 7 informer was a protégée of Joaquin Ordoqui, one of the co-founders together with Julio Antonio Mella of the Cuban Communist Party. Ordoqui was always a disciplined and obedient agent of Moscow. In 1964, in the mist of the internal crisis known as the "micro facción" Castro brought charges of treason against Marcos Rodriguez and later arrested Ordoqui.

## FRANK PAIS: THE FIRST DISSIDENT

Frank was now 23 years old and had played a crucial role in Castro's survival by developing a highly efficient underground which included Crecencio Perez' mountain peasants, who had rescued the other 18 survivors of the *Granma* ship wreck. Frank's network was the main component for the safety of Herbert

Matthews' arrival in the Sierra Maestra, the decisive propaganda stunt that propelled Castro to the center stage of the revolution's leadership. Oriente's underground was fighting in Santiago, Guantanamo, Holguin, Bayamo, and Manzanillo as well as in many other towns and villages. Among the rebel youth, Frank's courage and wisdom was rapidly becoming a legendary model. While in his mountain sanctuary, Castro was the thunder but Frank had turned into the light and soul of the revolution.

The day before Matthews' interview with Castro, Frank led the top-ranking underground fighters up the mountain for a meeting with Castro. Attending this meeting was "Che" Guevara. The Argentinean Marxist wrote: "Frank Pais was one of those men that dominate on the first interview; his appearance is more or less similar to the actual pictures, but he had eyes of extraordinary depth", Guevara added on Frank's leadership abilities: "He gave us a silent lesson in order and discipline, cleaning our dirty rifles, counting the bullets and putting them in order so that they will not be lost".[15] At the February meeting, Castro requested and Frank agreed to send reinforcements to the small guerrilla group. On March 15, 1957, Castro received a group of 50 men led by Jorge Sotus, one of Frank's must trusted fighters and a veteran of the November 30 uprising, where he captured and burned the Maritime Police Building. Hubert Matos, a teacher from Manzanillo, took them part of the way in several trucks. "Che" Guevara indicates that with Sotus' reinforcement ... "our army had 80 men."[16]

But from the beginning, there was tension between Sotus and Guevara on the issue of command.[17] To avoid a dangerous split within his small force, Castro reacted swiftly and named Jorge Sotus as one of the three captains of his army. The other two captains were his brother Raul and Juan Almeida.[18] A four-man vanguard was led by Camilo Cienfuegos and Efigenio Almejeira in the rearguard with three men but this was a temporary arrangement. Castro would not allow his total control of the movement to be challenged.

Early in his struggle for power, Castro held a clear idea of his role as supreme leader of the rebellion. In Agosto 1954, he wrote: "Conditions that are indispensable...ideology, discipline and authority...all three are essential, but authority is basic.[19] Castro was not about to share command with anyone. In the Hispanic political tradition, he was the undisputable revolutionary "Caudillo". The clash with Frank was unavoidable.

The issue of total control of the rebellion by one leader was of great concern to Frank Pais and others risking their lives in the cities. Cuba's history was well documented on the malady of "Caudillismo". From the "Lagunas de Varona", where a faction of the Cuban Independence Army took over the "government in arms," to the 1934 "sergeant's revolt", where Batista emerged as the "Caudillo" and ruled the island for over 17 years, the issue of a "Máximo Lider" was important and disturbing. Guevara points to this deep political and strategic difference: "Practically there were two different groups…that months later would risk the unity of the movement, but it was obvious that the concepts were different."[20] The Argentinean Marxist was right. There were deep differences between Castro and Frank Pais.

Powerful and intelligent, Frank was a healthy synthesis of wisdom and courage. A faithful Christian and a militant anti-communist, Frank had something of the Spartan and the Puritan. He would have fought with Cromwell and died with Leonidas at the Thermopylae. The political difference between the new Cuban "Caudillo" and the young libertarian widened. On July 7, Frank informed Castro that the M-26-7 leadership was to be a six-member executive council and Castro with less than one hundred men in the mountains, was to be granted one delegate.[21]

Guevara wrote in his diary: "What failed throughout was a complete connection between the plain and the mountain side due to two fundamental factors: the geographic isolation of the mountains and the differences of tactics and strategies between the two groups of the Movement. This last phenomenon stemmed from a different social and political conception." [22] Castro's answer was to ignore Frank's letter and issue, without consulting with the M-26-7 National Council, the "Sierra Maestra Manifiesto." The new Cuban "Caudillo" was sending an unequivocal message. Castro was "The Máximo Lider".

Days before the letter to Castro, Frank attacked a small army post at the "Miranda" sugar mill, where the rebels under his command captured much needed weapons, but Frank's joy was cut short by the news that his younger brother, Josue, had been killed during a gunfight with Batista police in Santiago. Frank was terribly sadden and wrote that the death of his beloved brother "has left an emptiness in my heart and a very personal sorrow in my soul."[23] At this time, Frank was completing the final preparations to open a second guerrilla front at the Sierra Cristal in North-Central Oriente Mountains.

How could a second guerrilla front led by Frank Pais have changed the course of the Cuban drama? The question will always remain unanswered because on July 30, 22 days after his challenging letter to Castro, Frank was found by Batista's men and killed. Was he betrayed? Research by historians Rolando Bonachea and Marta San Martin has uncovered some startling evidence, which points directly to Vilma Espin, a Marxist from Santiago's upper class, who eventually married Raul Castro. The M-26-7 agents working at Santiago's Central telephone company were highly effective in gathering data on Batista police by monitoring their phone calls. On the other hand, Batista's men also listened carefully to the phone calls of Santiago's residents, which Vilma knew about since she was in charge of M-26-7 members that worked at the telephone company. The morning of his death, while hiding in the house of Raul Pujols, Frank received a strange and unnecessary phone call from Vilma. A short time later, Frank was found by Batista's police and gunned down. At 23 years old, the young lion died betrayed. On his bullet-ridden body lay the unfulfilled promise of liberty.

Santiago was overcome with sadness and anger. Thousands joined Frank's funeral procession through the city's narrow streets. It was a huge march of defiance. The Cuban flag covered the casket as the people sang the national anthem… "que morir por la Patria es vivir"—"to die for the Fatherland is to live." Cuban democracy had lost its best champion. The light of freedom was gone. In his mountain sanctuary, Castro knew that the most serious challenge to his leadership had been killed and the road to total power was finally secured.

## WASHINGTON SHIFTS FROM BATISTA TO CASTRO

The years following the end of WWII were marked in the State Department by inconsistent points of view, rapid and often complete changes in policy and by frequent misunderstandings of international conflicts. By 1947, the "Cold War" was beginning to dominate U.S. foreign policy, focused on Moscow's intent of spreading communism throughout the world. The Soviet Union's powerful Army was a permanent threat to Western Europe, and Stalin had consistently stated that no peaceful order was possible between Marxism and capitalistic societies. The "Cold War" was to last for over 40 years and become the centerpiece of U.S. foreign policy until the collapse of the Soviet Union in 1989.

When in 1952 Batista and the army returned to power, Washington was concentrated on the defense of Europe, the Korean War and the rise of China as a communist threat in Asia. The Cuban crisis was a marginal issue handled by second level bureaucrats in the State Department, the Central Intelligence Agency (CIA) and within the U.S. Embassy in Havana[24]. But the perception among Cubans was of solid support at the highest level in Washington fuelled by the stream of weapons sent to the Cuban army and the friendship displayed between the U.S. Ambassador, Arthur Gardner, and Batista[25]. The ambassador often appeared in newspaper photographs embracing Batista and his top generals, which reinforced the image of a strong alliance with Washington.

Matthews' interview with Castro had a devastating impact on Washington against Batista and produced a monumental shift away from the military regime. Mathews' writing was high drama. In *The New York Times* he called Castro "the most remarkable and romantic figure to arise in Cuban history since Jose Marti."[26] Gardner was removed and replaced by Earl Smith, a West Palm Beach socialite, friend of Senator John Kennedy and his wife Jackeline and Chairman of the Florida Republican Committee during Eisenhower's re-election campaign. Smith believed that Matthews' interviews had a profound influence in changing the support of the Washington establishment to Fidel Castro[27].

Before assuming his ambassador post in Havana, Smith met at lunch with Matthews and found that his strong support for Castro matched those of the bureaucrats on the "fourth floor" of the State Department. Even Herbert Matthews acknowledged the great impact of his *New York Times* report. He said: "the article on Fidel Castro and the Cuban situation which I did in February have literally altered the course of Cuban history."[28] Just before going to Havana, Smith met with Robert Hill, The U.S. Ambassador to

Mexico. Hill told Smith: "Sorry you are going to Cuba... you are assigned to Cuba to preside over the downfall of Batista... the decision has been made that Batista has to go." [29] The dictator was running out of time. The "fourth floor" in the State Department was shifting its support to Fidel Castro.

## THE PEOPLE'S REBELLION

By the summer of 1957 and despite the economic bonanza, the majority of Cubans began to turn against Batista. At this stage of the deepening crisis there was still a good chance for a peaceful settlement. The formula was a free and transparent election, but the greedy dictator kept postponing the electoral solution while the urban underground grew in strength and audacity. There were also signs of discontent among the military.

On the 5th of September, as part of a larger military conspiracy, a section of the Navy in Cienfuegos turned their weapons against the dictator. Poor planning prevented other naval units from joining the mutiny. By 5:30 A.M., the base was in rebel hands and hundreds of armed civilians joined the officers and sailors. It was a joyful and brief embrace of freedom. That afternoon, tanks and armed cars moved into the city while B-26 bombers attacked the rebel's defenses. The fight was fierce, by nightfall the rebellion was crushed.

By year's end, Castro with less than 300 guerillas, was still holding on in Crecencio's "mountain sanctuary" while the urban civic resistance of the "26 of July Movement," headed by engineer Manolo Ray, increased its clandestine activities throughout the island. Despite the ferocity of the police repression, bombs, drive-by shootings, sabotage, harbor and warehouse fires continued unabated. The eastern half of Cuba was in a virtual Civil War while at the capital, bombings and kidnappings became more frequent and daring. Professor Suchliki believed that: "The urban underground developed into the backbone of the anti-Batista struggle. It was the work of the urban underground more than anything else that brought about the downfall of the regime." [30]

On February 13, a "Directorio" expedition led by Rolando Cubelas and Armando Fleites landed at Playa Santa Rita, near Nuevitas. In three days they made their way into the Escambray

Mountains and began a guerrilla operation in Central Cuba. The Esso oil storage depot was blown up, damaging the capital water main, and on February 23, Argentine racecar champion Juan Manuel Fangio was kidnapped by the underground. This was a super propaganda stunt which captured international press headlines. On February 24, deep in the "Sierra Maestra", Radio Rebelde began its broadcasting of short wave transmissions under the direction of Carlos Franqui. On March 10, at the head of 50 men, Raul Castro left the Sierra Maestra and in six days reached the Sierra Cristal Mountains near his mother's land holdings at Biran. There Raul Castro took under his control several small forces, establishing a well-organized and disciplined command structure that became the embryo of the rebel army leadership in the 1960s. The growing power and intensity of the fights and rebellions in the cities led Fidel Castro to believe that the people were ready for a national uprising. He was to be proven wrong. On April 9, 1958 the "26 of July Movement" called for a general strike. It was broadcast on several ratio stations. The urban leadership, led by Manolo Ray, Faustino Perez and Marcelo Salado explicitly spoke against any communist involvement in the upcoming fight. Faustino Perez wrote in a manifesto: "The present revolutionary movement is far from being communist... the provisional government will hold national elections within the shortest possible time."[31] Marcelo Salado led the urban uprising in Havana. Several electric sub stations were destroyed cutting power off in old Havana and in Vedado, buses were overturned, schools and banks closed. Santiago joined the fight, but by mid-afternoon, the strike had failed. It was a bloody day, over 140 men, most of them young, including Marcelo Salado, were killed in the aborted strike.

## THE REBEL ARMY: THE INSTRUMENT OF TOTAL POWER.

The failure of the April strike had several significant consequences. The hopelessly corrupt regime felt that they could finish the rebellion by launching a final offensive against Castro. The inept army command believed that within six weeks several battalions could be ready to wipe out the mountain guerrillas. Another result of the failed strike was a shift in perception of the revolutionary prestige to be gained by joining the rebel army as a "Sierra" guerrilla. The issue was reinforced by the fact that the urban underground had become extremely dangerous, generating a flow of those wanting to join the more secure mountain sanctuary, which, according to Che Guevara, were in relative peace. "Che" wrote: "We were in an armed peace with Batista, his captains would not go up the *Sierra* and our troops were not allowed to come down"[32]

At this juncture, the Cuban communist party saw an opportunity to approach Castro by sending several leading Marxists to join the Rebel Army in the Sierra Maestra. They were led by Carlos Rafael Rodriguez, a former minister in Batista's 1940 cabinet. A brilliant thinker and cunning politician, Carlos Rafael gave Guevara the writings of Mao Tse-tung, which "Che" handed to his officers as mandatory reading. From this time on Carlos Rafael Rodriguez became one of Castro's most trusted advisors, but at first he was kept at the Las Vegas Camp, two kilometers away from Castro's headquarters.[33]   To further conceal his political objective of a Marxist regime, Castro stated to the press: "Never has the 26 of July, talk of socialism or nationalizing industries…We have proclaimed from the first that we fought for the full enforcement of the Constitution of 1940 which establishes guarantees, rights and obligations for all elements who have a part in production, including free enterprise and invested capital."[34]

Another significant repercussion of the failed April strike was the end of the bitter leadership struggle between the "Llano" (plane) and the "Sierra" (mountains). On this issue, "Che" Guevara wrote: "In the bosom of our own movement, two marked different tendencies flowed, which we have called the "Sierra" (mountain range) and the "Llano" (cities)…these two tendencies had representations in the National Directives of the Movement, which was changing during the course of the fight"[35] and "Che" added: "The comrades from the "Llano" represented the majority and their political ideology which had not been influenced greatly by the revolution's maturity process, were inclined to certain opposition to the Leader, they feared Fidel and the militarist faction which represented the people from the "Sierra".[36] After the failure of the April strike, Castro gained full control of the '26 of July Movement" throughout the island, and the guerrilla officers directly under his personal command became the leaders of the revolution, with Raul Castro and "Che" Guevara at the top of the strict hierarchy, immediately below Fidel Castro, both full-fledged Marxists.

Then, aware that the failed strike had reduced the perception of his ability to overthrow Batista by force, Castro began to reach out and make commitments with other political organizations. He was willing to share the revolutionary civil leadership by giving control of the future provisional government to civilians, mostly liberals, as long as he kept for himself military command of all the organizations fighting the hated dictator. He knew that the army was the arbiter of power. By becoming commander in Chief, Castro positioned himself for control in any future government. Castro's formula was to build up the "Rebel Army" where loyalty to the "Máximo Lider" became the essential pre-requisite even over ideological creeds. On July 20, most of the opposition leaders met in Caracas, Venezuela, and establihed the "Frente Cívico Revolucionario Democrático" known as "El Pacto de Caracas". The distinguished attorney, Jose Miro Cardona, was nominated as civil coordinator and Fidel Castro Commander in Chief of all the fighting organizations in the Island. Judge Manuel Urrutia was designated "President of Cuba in Arms". Jose Llanuza signed on behalf of Castro, who had created his own army. A masterful stroke.

## BATISTA'S MILITARY FIASCO

On March 1958, Washington publicly announced an arms embargo against Cuba and suspended shipment of 1,950 Garand rifles that had already been paid. According to Ambassador Smith, the psychological impact on the Batista government was devastating, especially the Army and labor movement.[37] It was a clear message. The U.S. had gotten tired of Batista's inability to pacify the island and was looking for a change. The dictator had been abandoned by its old friends in Washington. The perception was of doom and defeat, but the former sergeant turned general was ready for a last stand.

On May 24, Batista launched his expected military offensive in the dense forests of the "Sierra Maestra" mountains. The Army placed on the field 14 infantry battalions, and several tank companies with both aerial and naval support. Castro had recalled his small guerrilla bands and concentrated them in the secluded area of "La Plata". He had 280 fighters.[38] They placed dozens of mines, posted their best sharp shooters and few machineguns in the narrow trails of the almost impenetrable mountains and waited. Hubert Matos, a teacher from Manzanillo and one of the top "comandantes" of the revolution, wrote: "The trenches, correctly camouflaged, allowed the mobility of the men and protected us from an enemy thirty times superior. The mine and the cables that connect the detonators were disguised by the vegetation."[39]

What came next was Batista's failed campaign, a tactical blunder that touched the     nadir of incompetence. It started at the top of the command structure with General Francisco Tabernilla, a narrowly educated Army Chief who made up for in greed and corruption what he lacked in understanding guerrilla warfare. Tabernilla headed a demoralized army, which with the exception of some competent and courageous men, had been built throughout the years following the Sergeant's revolt of 1933 on favoritism and political loyalties.

At first, the army began to move up the narrow trails from several directions. The advance was fiercely disputed and bloody, but by the 25th day, Castro was almost encircled within four square miles. The Rebel Army's historic publication stated: "Our territory was reduced and reduced until we could not reduce any further."[40] Carlos Franqui, the "Radio Rebelde" director, wrote: "Fidel Castro is now taking into consideration the last possibility; that is, abandon the fronts and move into the abrupt zones of the Turquino, with small guerillas such as at the beginning of the war."[41] The situation was critical, Castro told Hubert Matos, "they are strong columns. We have to resist all that we can but if our positions are unsustainable, we will have no alternative but to dismantle the command post of La Plata and take it to the Pico Turquino."[42]

In those crucial moments as he arrived at the rebel command post, Hubert Matos recalled:  "Fidel was waiting for me and immediately described very graphically how the army penetrates the Sierra with various columns, with the intention of converge and attack the camp at La Plata...soldiers supported by the aviation advance to take over the Sierra from us. The army has forced the Che to retreat."[43]

On June 19, the elite battalion of Colonel Sanchez Mosquera, a brave and experienced officer, was ambushed and decimated in the narrow trails as he neared La Plata. Matos wrote: "At 10 AM, we have the enemy close to us, just five minutes off the ambush... the front of the vanguard is a group of some 30 men that advance while shooting... we opened fire at the same time that the mine explodes and the group is practically wiped out".[44] It was a desperate fight but the battalion advance was checked by the highly mobile guerrillas. Huber Matos said: "During the night of the 28 of June, the firing does not stop. Prisoners are captured and armament and ammunition are recovered, but it is difficult to subdue these people, even though they are surrounded. It is a valiant troop, motivated by an astute leader".[45] That was not the case with Major Quevedo's battalion, which on July 18 surrendered to Castro. This officer later joined the Rebel Army, a turning point in a bitter fight. At the end, Batista failed to dislodge the guerrillas from their mountain stronghold or to capture Fidel Castro. The consequences of this military failure were devastating to the regime.

## THE PEOPLE'S VICTORY ?

During these critical weeks, Castro exhibited his political audacity by daring to provoke the U.S. Government, ordering his brother Raul to kidnap American citizens that were in his area of operation. On June 26, in the midst of the fight in "Sierra Maestra", Raul kidnapped a busload of 49 American citizens including 24 Marines as they traveled back to Guantánamo. It made worldwide front-page news. There was outrage in Washington. The Pentagon recommended an immediate landing of a division in Oriente, but the State Department opposed it.[46] The Eisenhower administration, afraid to see Americans killed with U.S.-made weapons, requested a truce and demanded those weapons not be used in future operations. Batista's High Command was now totally demoralized. Some officers began to seek negotiations with Castro.

In August, Castro again displayed his extraordinary predatory instinct. Knowing that Batista's regimen was mortally wounded, he sent Che Guevara with 148 men and Camilo Cienfuegos with a column of 82 to march westward to the Escambray Mountains in Las Villas province, where the "Directorio" under Rolando Cubelas had been leading the guerrilla campaign. "Che" was instructed by Castro to take direct command of all rebel forces in that region of central Cuba. Hubert Matos with 129 men was ordered to link up with Raul forces, cut across the Central Highway and the Santiago Garrison. By mid-October, Guevara and Camilo Cienfuegos were secure in the Escambray Mountains and Castro was now in control of all the guerrilla operation fronts. The November elections were a fiasco and by the middle of December, Tabernilla told Batista that the officers were refusing to fight and that General Cantillo was negotiating with Castro.

On December 9, businessman William Pawley met with Batista and offered a transitional formula by which he was to resign and transfer the government to a "Junta" led by Colonel Barquin, General Diaz Tamayo, Jose Bosh of the Bacardi family and Colonel Borbonet. The offer was suggested by the State Department.[47] Batista rejected it. On December 17, Ambassador Smith told Batista that he could no longer maintain effective control over the island and should resign. In the early morning of January 1, 1959, Fulgencio Batista escaped to the Dominican Republic. Castro who was near Santiago heard the news and ordered Hubert Matos to enter the city, which had led the fight and buried the heroic symbol of the "56's generation", the beloved Frank Pais.

Five months before, Castro had been fighting for survival with 280 men in a four- mile perimeter; now he was victorious. The people were ecstatic with hope and joy. As in a classical drama, a terrible tragedy was unfolding.

# CHAPTER XVI

# THE FINAL STRUGGLE
# THE 1956 GENERATION: THE HEROIC

---

[1] Entrevista con Jorge Valls para Television Marti. Documental sobre Jose Antonio Echeverria, 2007

[2] Geyer, op cit, 139.

[3] Claudia Furiati, *Fidel Castro: La Historia Me Absolverá* (Barcelona: Plaza Janes, 2003), 254.

[4] Ibid, 250.

[5] Anthony De Palma. *The Man who Invented Fidel* (New York: Public Affairs, 2006).

[6] Geyer, op cit, 173.

[7] Furiati, op cit, 282.

[8] De Palma, op cit, 40.

[9] Ibid, 41.

[10] De Palma, op cit, 79

[11] Herbert Matthews. *The New York Times*, February 24, 1957.

[12] Ernesto Guevara "Che". *Pasajes de la Guerra Revolucionaria* (Habana: Ed. Txalaparta, 2001), Second Edition, 53.

[13] Ibid, 69.

[14] Suchlicki, op cit, 148.

[15] Guevara, op cit, 52

[16] Ibid, 60.

[17] Hugo Gambia. *El Che Guevara.* (Editorial Stockcero, 2002), 115.

[18] Guevara, op cit, 66.

[19] Ibid

[20] Ibid, 51.

[21] Geyer, op cit, 177-178.

[22] Guevara, op cit, 185

[23] Geyer, op. cit.,177

[24] Geyer, op cit,178

[25] Earl E.T. Smith, *El Cuarto Piso* (Mexico: Editorial Diana, 1963), 26

[26] De Palma, op cit, 133

[27] Smith, op cit, 14

[28] De Palma, op cit, 119

[29] Thomas, op cit, 949

[30] Suchlicki, op cit, 151

[31] Jules Dubois. Fidel Castro: Rebel – Liberador or Dictador? (Indianápolis, 1959), 249

[32] Guevara, op cit, 187-188

[33] Furiati, op cit, 137

[34] Dubois, 263

[35] Guevara, op cit, 193

[36] Ibid., 193.

[37] Smith, op cit, 52

[38] Furiati, op cit, 327

[39] Huber Matos. *Como llegó la noche*. (Barcelona: Tusquets Editores S.A., 2002), 142

[40] Obras Revolucionarias. Noviembre 1961, pg. 12

[41] Franqui, op cit. 112

[42] Matos, op cit, 161

[43] Ibid, 139

[44] Ibid, 143

[45] Ibid, 151

[46] Thomas, op cit, 1001

[47] Smith, op cit, 168

# CHAPTER XVII

# *THE WEALTH PRODUCING REPUBLIC*

It is extraordinary for a country to be able to sustain economic growth in the midst of a violent and bloody rebellion. That was the case of a large segment of the Cuban population who carried on the difficult task of creating wealth while political institutions were collapsing. A remarkable story indeed! During the last decade of the Republic (1950-1959), the Cuban economy grew steadily in the manufacturing of consumer goods, food and services, construction, tourism, transportation and communication. However, sugar, the dominant factor in the economy, faced enormous difficulties due to the increase in production from other countries, which created a sugar surplus that undermined the market price and precluded further growth. This became the biggest economic challenge facing Cubans on the eve of Castro's Marxist revolution.

By the 1950's, cattle and beef products were Cuba's second industry. Imports of pure-bred animals in large quantities contributed to improvements in both beef and milk cows. The most prominent beef cattle were the Zebu, which adapted best to the Island's soil pasture and climate and, when crossed with the "criollo," produced a large, sturdy animal. The Zebu and the mixed "criollo" accounted for 90% of the six million head of cattle in 1958.[1] Cuban cattle ranchers were modern managers who ran an efficient industry, which produced some of the best "tropical" cattle in the world with a meat yield of 54% per head.[2] The industry employed over 100,000 workers in steady well-paid jobs, and Cubans ranked fourth in Latin America in meat consumption (surpassed only by Argentina, Uruguay and Paraguay) with a yearly per capita estimated at 78.8 pounds[3] and a weekly per capita equal to a pound and a half of good quality meat, and at a low price.

The excellent growth in quantity and quality achieved by the cattle industry brought about a remarkable increase in the production of milk, which hastened the manufacture of butter, cheese, and evaporated and condense milk serving the national market. In 1952, Cuba imported over 2 million pounds of butter and produced 1.5 million pounds; by 1958, the import of butter was reduced to less than six hundred thousand pounds and Cuban production toppled the 4 million pounds of butter per year.[IV] During this period, there were seven industrial plants for evaporated and condensed milk and 59 ice cream factories serving the needs of the market. In 1958, with 6,563,000 inhabitants, Cuba was the fifth producer of fresh milk in the region.

## TABLE I
## LATIN AMERICA MILK PRODUCTION (1958)
## (1,000 METRIC TONS)

| | | | | | |
|---|---|---|---|---|---|
| 1. | BRAZIL | 4603 | 7. URUGUAY | 672 | |
| 2. | ARGENTINA | 4481 | 8. VENEZUELA | 387 | |
| 3. | MEXICO | 4205 | 9. ECUADOR | 375 | |
| 4. | COLOMBIA | 2085 | 10. PERU | 372 | |
| 5. | CUBA | 828 | 11. PARAGUAY | 132 | |
| 6. | CHILE | 764 | 12. GUATEMALA | 128 [5] | |

With ample food supplies, the Cubans were among the best-fed people in Latin America. The Island ranked third in daily per capita consumption of calories.

## TABLE 2
## LATIN AMERICA:
## PER CAPITA FOOD CONSUMPTION
## (CALORIES PER DAY)
### (Latest data available for 1954-57)

| | | | |
|---|---|---|---|
| 1. ARGENTINA | 3100 | 6. MEXICO | 2420 |
| 2. URUGUAY | 2960 | 7. CHILE | 2330 |
| 3. CUBA | 2730 | 8. HONDURAS | 2260 |
| 4. PARAGUAY | 2690 | 9. ECUADOR | 2130 |
| 5. BRAZIL | 2540 | 10. COLOMBIA | 2050 [6] |

The tobacco industry was a reliable source of year-round income for over 120,000 workers.[7] There were several factories that manufactured popular cigarette brands and tobacco to serve the huge national demand. Cubans were among the highest numbers of smokers in the world with a domestic consumption of 624 million cigarette packages[8] produced in Cuban factories and 22.7 million packages imported from the U.S.[9] The largest profit in the tobacco industry came from tobacco leaf exports and the best leaves came from the Vuelta Abajo region of Pinar del Rio. The combination of that region's soil and climate produced perfect leaves and, in turn, production of the best cigar in the world. Between two thirds and three quarters of tobacco production was exported as leaf, mostly to the U.S.

In 1958, Cuba had over 160,000 cars, with a regional per-capita second only to Venezuela.

## TABLE 3
## LATIN AMERICA:
## PASSENGER CARS PER CAPITA
## (CARS PER 1000 INHABITANTS)

| 1. VENEZUELA | 27 | 6. COSTA RICA | 3 |
|---|---|---|---|
| 2. CUBA | 24 | 7. MÉXICO | 11 |
| 3. URUGUAY | 22 | 8. BRAZIL | 7 |
| 4. ARGENTINA | 19 | 9. CHILE | 7 |
| 5. PANAMA | 16 | 10. PERU | 7 [10] |

The Cuban road network was a first class system with a central highway running through the entire island and numerous secondary roads branching into cities and towns along the coast that was used by a fleet of over 4,000 inter-cities buses.[11] Establishing an effective connection among the island's urban centers, the Santiago-Havana route had a daily service of ten air-conditioned buses — a prime transportation system equal to the U.S. at the time. The "Omnibus Aliados" was the largest and most successful company formed by bus owners and operators themselves, which served the Cuban capital at a cost of 0.08 per passenger.[12]

The principal airline was Cubana de Aviación created in 1930 as a subsidiary of Pan American Airways. That began life in 1927 with a route from Key West to Havana.[13] Cuban investors created Cubana de Aviación, and Pan American Airways retained 25% of its capital stocks. From the Havana "Jose Marti International

Airport", "Cubana" flew to New York, Madrid, Miami and Mexico City and served 19 airports in Cuba. As a well-managed operation, Cubana grew from 7,800 passengers in 1933 to 337,415 in 1958.[14]

At the dawning of the Republic, Cuba had an outstanding health care system with the lowest infant mortality in Latin America, at a ratio of 32 per 1,000 lives and the 13th lowest in the world. Cuba ranked over France, Italy, Spain, Japan and West Germany.[15] In 1957, Cuba's health care system had 72 large hospitals with more than 21,000 beds plus 250 privately owned medial centers and clinics, most of which operated similar to the present day HMO's in the United States at a cost of $5.00 pesos per month.[16]

It is a fact that Cubans did remarkably well in terms of the health care system. The University of Havana Medical School was rated among the best in the Western Hemisphere, and, in 1957, Cuba ranked third in Latin America with the ratio of 128 physicians per 100,000 people, equal to the Netherlands and better than the United Kingdom.[17] Each of the country's 126 municipal governments had emergency clinics or "Casas de Socorro", which provided urgent care and free medicine in poor neighborhoods. Including all medical facilities, Cuba had some 35,000 beds for 6.6 million inhabitants; an impressive ratio of one for every 190 inhabitants.

With splendid white sand beaches, excellent music, memorable bohemian nights, modern hotels, fine cuisine and great rum for "Mojitos" and "Daiquiris", Cuba was a tourist Mecca that ranked second in Latin America, behind Mexico, as a tourist destination with 350,000 visitors in 1958. The principal tourist attractions were Varadero beach and Old Havana. Many Hollywood stars and writers, like Ernest Hemingway, fell in love with the splendor of the enchanted Island.

The financial experience gained in the early years of the Republic pointed to the need for creating a National Bank to support and regulate the monetary system and provide the country with a solid financial instrument to accelerate its economic development. On December 1948, President Carlos Prio signed a bill establishing the National Bank of Cuba to regulate money and credit matters. The National Bank was an autonomous institution with the authority to centralize the nation's monetary reserves and regulate the credit system. The Cuban government held fifty-one percent of the capital of the Bank, while the rest was held by private commercial and savings banks.

During the 1950's, and encouraged by financial conditions created by the National Bank, the Cubans increased their investment in the Island by 12 percent and gained control of the banking system with 60% of all deposits held in Cuban banks.[18] During this period, several autonomous credit institutions were formed to promote industrial diversification outside of the sugar industry. The Agricultural and Development Bank (BANFAIC) was instrumental in the success of rice production, one of Cuba's most promising industries. The BANFAIC provided low interest loans and financed hundreds of agricultural investments throughout the Island. The Mortgage Insurance Institution lent money for low-cost housing development in East Havana and several welfare-related projects.

Rice is Cuba's favorite dish, especially when combined with chicken or black beans. In 1940, of a total consumption of over 411 million pounds of rice, Cubans imported 95.5%, mostly from Indochina, Thailand, Burma and India, but WWII cut this low-price supply source and encouraged domestic production. In 1956, of a total consumption of over 665 million pounds of rice, Cuban production accounted for 55.5%, while imports dropped to 44.5%.[19] In 1958, Cuba ranked fourth in Latin America's rice production.

## TABLE 4
## LATIN AMERICA:  RICE PRODUCTION (1957)
## (1,000 METRIC TONS)

| 1. BRAZIL | 3829 | 5. MEXICO | 240 |
|---|---|---|---|
| 2. COLOMBIA | 378 | 6. ARGENTINA | 217 |
| 3. PERU | 285 | 7. ECUADOR | 176 |
| 4. CUBA | 256 | 8. CHILE | 102 [20] |

By the end of the 1950's, the value of U.S. investment in Cuba was $861 million, equivalent in 1998 dollars to 4.3 billion,[21] greater than U.S. direct investment in Mexico, Argentina, France or West Germany.[22]  American investors moved into chemical plants, mining, transport, communication, pharmaceutical and food processing. Sears and Woolworths ("dime stores") opened several retail stores throughout the Island while Firestone and Goodyear built modern tire factories and Coca Cola began manufacturing, processing and bottling its world famous soda in Cuba.[23]

The textile industry developed substantially during this period. Founded in 1931 at Bauta, near Havana, the cotton-spinning "Textilera Ariguanabo" was the largest non-sugar factory in Cuba with 72,000 spindles, 2,000 looms and over 2,500 employees. In 1948, this highly successful industry opened a second textile plant in Matanzas. The "Companía Rayonera Cubana" had a large rayon factory with over 3,800 workers. It produced 5 million pounds of high tenacity rayon cordage, of which 85 to 95 per cent was exported.[24] Other textile factories were established, including the "Jarcias de Matanzas" that manufactured rope, cord and string of henequen. By 1958, the textile industry had become one of the most important economic activities in the Island.

One of Cuba's industrial prides is the Bacardi Company, founded on April 12, 1862, by Facundo Bacardi Masso, in the indomitable city of Santiago de Cuba. This is the story of determination, hard work and business acumen, guarded in a family tradition that brought Bacardi from its humble beginnings to the number one premium rum in the world. The Bacardi rum was first associated with two of the most famous cocktails, invented by North Americans serving in Cuba. By the time of the Spanish-American War in 1898, Jennings Stocton Cox, while working in the mining town of Daiquiri, created the first rum cocktail by mixing limejuice, crushed ice and sugar with Bacardi "Carta Blanca" or light rum. The "Daiquiri" became a worldwide success.

Two years later, with General Leonard Wood as Military Governor of the Island, a group of American soldiers drinking at a popular bar on "Neptuno" street saw a customer named Russell mixing Bacardi rum with Coca Cola. The soldiers tasted and liked the mix and gave a toast to "Cuba Libre" or a "Free Cuba" and the world's number one cocktail was born.[25] In 1960, the Company was confiscated by Castro's communist revolution, but the family and associates left the Island and with daring vision developed a formidable international operation that placed Bacardi as the number one alcoholic beverage company in the world.

Bacardi beer was first produced in 1927 in Santiago de Cuba

under the brand name "Hatuey" in memory of the "Taino" tribal chief who fought the Spanish "Conquistadores". A second plant was opened in Manacas, and a third, the "Modelo" brewery, in "El Cotorro" outside Havana. These plants were built with the latest technology, from temperature-controlled climate to stainless steel equipment. By 1958 the "Modelo" brewery was producing 22 million liters of good quality lager beer.[26] There were also the "Cristal," the "Polar" and the "Tropical' brewery companies in Havana. Altogether, the beer industry employed over 10,000 workers.

In 1958, Cuba had three cement plants in operation to serve the growing demand of the construction industry, "el Morro" cement in Mariel, "Titan" in Santiago de Cuba, and the "Santa Teresa" in Artemisa. As shown in the table, cement imports fell off after 1957 as a result of increased domestic production.

## TABLE 5
## CUBAN CEMENT IMPORTS AND DOMESTIC PRODUCTION
## (IN THOUSANDS OF BARRELS)

| YEAR | IMPORT | DOMESTIC PRODUCTION |
|---|---|---|
| 1951 | 1019.1 | 2246.8 |
| 1955 | 1515.4 | 2526.0 |
| 1957 | 957.3 | 4194.8 [27] |

Since the American Civil War in 1860-1865, canned and packaged food was industrially produced and became available for market consumers. In Cuba, the canning industry developed slowly until the outbreak of WWII when the canning of fruits and vegetables acquired real importance. The largest activity was the canning of pineapple, which by 1957 was exporting over 16 million pounds.[28] Other fruits and vegetables were canned for export and local consumption including tomatoes, pepper, coconut, guava and mangos. Meat-packing also became an important component of the industry with over 32 plants in full production.

In 1957, the leather industry was employing 27,000 workers,

with 70 tanneries. There were several large shoe factories, including Ingelmo, Amadeo and Bulnes, and over 1,500 smaller shops, which produced over 10 million pairs of shoes a year.

## TABLE 6
## CUBA: EXPORTS OF LEATHER PRODUCTS (1957)

|  | Thousands of Kgs | Thousands of Dollars |
|---|---|---|
| Cattle hides salted | 3266.0 | 922.9 |
| Cuttings | 415.2 | 33.1 |
| Shark Skin Cured | 46.2 | 10.5 |
| Ladies Handbags-Leather | 57.2 | 14.0 |
| Ladies Handbags-Alligator | 65.2 | 465.4 |
| Other Leather Manufacturers | 19.2 | 116.7 |
| Men's Leather Shoes | 6.8 | 37.2 |
| Ladies Leather Shoes | 0.4 | 2.4 [29] |

The North American carbonated beverage industry, like Coca Cola, Pepsi Cola, Canada Dry, and Orange Crush, had Cuban dependencies. The domestic production of soda or "refrescos" and mineral water was a major enterprise. Cuban production included "Ironber", the lime flavor "Cawy", the orange flavor "Green Spot", the pineapple flavor "Jupina", "Materva" and several smaller carbonated beverage companies. Coca Cola came in 1906 and later opened a bottling plant in Havana. In 1951, Cuba was producing over 24 million cases of carbonated beverages.[30]

Cuba had a large soap and detergent industry with two major U.S. – Cuban owned companies: "Crusellas", a subsidiary of Colgate, and "Sabates," a subsidiary of "Proctor and Gamble". There were two other all-Cuban factories, "Gravi" and "Jabon Tornillo," and several smaller plants. In the 1950's, the production of soap topped 100 million pounds per year. Over half of the soap output was so-called "yellow soap" for laundry and household cleaning purposes. Production of detergent began in 1952 when "Fab" was placed on the market by "Crusellas". In 1958, Cuba's production of detergent was almost equal to domestic demand.[31]

The degree of development reached by the Cuban radio and television industry was indeed extraordinary. In 1958, some 160 radio stations were transmitting to nearly one million radio receivers for a ratio of one radio set per every six persons, ranking Cuba as the first country in Latin America in per capita radio sets[32] and eighth in the world ahead of France and Great Britain.[33] In 1948, CMQ, owned by Goar Mestre and his brothers, Abel and Luis Augusto, inaugurated a ten-story building in the beautiful style of New York's Radio City Music Center, with eight modern studios, two auditoriums for live broadcast, and an elegant theater. There were other major national radio networks, including "RHC, Cadena Azul".

Television came to Cuba in October 1950, on Channel 2, placing Cuba among the first countries in the world to enjoy this entertainment marvel. On August 1951, the CMQ powerhouse entered the television broadcast industry on Channel 6 and soon was the top-rate operation in the Island. In 1952, Cuba was the first country in Latin America to broadcast TV in color.

During the 1954 baseball "World Series", a Douglas C-46 plane flying near the city of Cardenas linked a Miami TV station with a main receiver antenna in the Island that sent the signal into CMQ TV sub-stations in Central and Western Cuba, including Havana. The signal reached the homes of thousands of Cubans who were able to see the games live from Yankee Stadium. The CMQ plane was a forerunner of today's satellites.[34] In 1958, Cuba had 23 television stations and approximately 400,000 television sets for a per capita of one TV set for every 15 people.[35]

In 1958, there were 287 mines in Cuba, with nickel accounting for 31.2 percent of the total value of the mineral export. During WWII, the largest nickel deposit located in the northeast region of Oriente was transformed into a modern industrial complex at Nicaro and Moa Bay, making Cuba a major world supplier of nickel.[36] Copper was the second source of mineral income, with most production coming from the mines at Matahambre in the province of Pinar del Rio. Cuba was the fourth copper-exporting country in Latin America.[37]

During this period, there were also several manganese, chrome, lead, zinc, tungsten and cobalt mines, along with other smaller mining operations. The U.S. invested wisely in the mining industry and bought 98.28% of all minerals exported from the Island. Cuba held first place in production of nickel and cobalt, among all Latin

American countries.[38]

The extraordinary growth of the construction industry led to the development of numerous factories for the production of bricks, cement blocks, laminated iron and steel, corrugated iron roads and pre-stress structural parts. Due to the construction boom, several concrete mixing plants were created, equipped with modern concrete trucks to service the market demand.

During this period, there were over 500 pharmaceutical laboratories, thousands of retail and food stores (bodegas), restaurants and small eateries (fondas), over 600 cinemas and 58 newspapers.[39] At the start of Castro´s Marxist Revolution, Cuba had a national per capita income of $356 per year, and ranked third in Latin America, ahead of Mexico, Argentina, Chile, Brazil and Colombia.[40]

The eighteen years between 1940 and 1958 were the most important in Cuba's financial development, sustaining an increase in the standard of living of the people in the Island. Even Anibal Escalante, a communist leader and ideologue, acknowledged this fact. Escalante stated: "Cuba is one of the countries (of Latin America) where the standard of living was particularly high."[41] From 1942 to 1958, the Cuban "peso" remained at par with the "U.S. dollar" and bank deposits increased despite the political violence and institutional crisis; 1957 was the year of greatest financial achievement, which placed Cuba's economic development in the "take off" stage.[42] In 1958, there were about 50 banks with nearly 20 branches throughout the Island. By the time of Castro's Marxist victory, Cuba ranked third in total monetary reserves in Latin America and was first as to money in the hands of the people.[43] The wealth-producing Republic was swiftly and tragically crushed by Castro's communist revolution.

# CHAPTER XVII

# THE WEALTH PRODUCING REPUBLIC

[1] Study on Cuba. The Cuban Economic Research Project under the Chairmanship of Dr. Jose Alvarez Diaz. (University of Miami, Coral Gables, Florida, 1965), 526.

[2] Ibid., 528.

[3] Ibid.

[4] Ibid., 574.

[5] Source: UN 1966, 136; UNFAO 1997 b, 216-7.

[6] Source: UN 1960, 312-6; UNFAO 1998.

[7] Study, op.cit., 555.

[8] Ibid, 532.

[9] Ibid.

[10] Source: UN 1966, 332-3.

[11] Study, op.cit., 579.

[12] Ibid.

[13] On-Line Reference: "Pan American World Airways – History." http://www.panam.com/newhist1.asp.

[14] Ibid., 577.

[15] Kirby Smith and Hugo Llorens. From the paper *Renaissance and decay. Cuba in Transition.* ASCE 1998,248.

[16] Ibid.

[17] Ibid.

[18] Study, op.cit., 467.

[19] Ibid., 536-537.

[20] Statistical Year Book. United Nations, New York, 1959.

[21] Smith and Llorens, op.cit., 255.

[22] Ibid.

[23] Ibid., 256.

[24] Ibid., 560.

[25] Mari Aixala Dawson, Publisher. Facundo and Amalia Bacardi Foundation, Inc., Miami, Florida, 2006, 52-5.

[26] Ibid., 96.

[27] Study, op cit, 561-562.

[28] Ibid, 560.

[29] *Comercio Exterior* -1957. Finance Ministry, Cuba, 1959.

[30] *Cuba: Economía y Finanzas.* Editorial Mercantil Cubana, S.A. (November-December 1960), 4.

[31] Study, op cit, 562

[32] Ibid, 562

[33] U.N. Statistical Yearbook 1960, pg. 607

[34] Pablo Sirven. *El Rey de la T.V.* (El Clarín-Aguilar, Buenos Aires, 1996), 84.

[35] Study, op cit, 583

[36] Study, op cit, 574

[37] Ibid.

[38] Ibid.

[39] América en Cifras. Unión Panamericana, estadísticas culturales. (Instituto Interamericano de Estadísticas, 1960, Washington, D.C.)

[40] Study, op cit, 444

[41] Verde Olivo, Julio 30, 1961.

[42] Study, op cit, 421

[43] Ibid., 474

# CHAPTER XVIII

# *FREEDOM DEFERRED*

*"In vain will undisciplined spirits strive to achieve pure freedom.*
*For the master first reveals himself in limitations*
*and only law can give us liberty".*

*GOETHE*

*CASTRO AND THE REBEL ARMY – CASTRO AND*
*COMMUNISM – CASTRO: ICON OF THE AMERICAN LEFT –*
*"COMMON GOOD": THE SHINING BANNER OF TYRANNY –*
*WAS CASTRO PUSHED INTO THE SOVIET CAMP ? – FREE*
*PRESS DECAPITATED – BACK TO THE TRENCHES OF*
*FREEDOM – CASTRO'S DEEPENING CONFRONTATION*
*WITH WASHINGTON*

It was the first day of 1959 and the ever-emotional Cubans went wild with the news that the hated dictator had fled. The next day, Fidel Castro entered Santiago in triumph. The city that had led the fight welcomed the young bearded rebels as national heroes. In a large celebration rally at the "Cespedes" park, Castro rejected as slanderous the growing criticism that he was leading a Marxist revolution. He stated: "The Revolution is not communist."

## *CASTRO AND THE REBEL ARMY*

By January 5, the Rebel Army was in full control of the principal military bases in the Island and Castro was slowly moving towards Havana, consolidating his leadership role in a tumultuous victory march. On this date, Castro appointed the provisional government, with Judge Manuel Urrutia as president and several highly respected liberals and social democrats who were placed in key administration posts. They included Jose Miro Cardona as Prime Minister, Manuel Ray, Elena Mederos, Humberto Sori Marin, Justo Carrillo and Felipe Pazos. Pazos was the distinguished economist who had arranged for Castro's successful meeting with Herbert Matthews, *The New York Time's* editor who brought him back from the depths of disaster and into the supreme leadership role of the revolution, creating an international celebrity.

On January 8, in a theatrical parade, Castro entered Havana at the head of over 1,500 men of the Rebel Army; he was riding in full glory on top of a Sherman tank. A crowd of hundreds of thousands were lined up along the "Malecón" or seaside promenade in a historical welcome to Cuba's new messiah; by now, no other revolutionary group could challenge the Rebel Army and his leadership role. He was the revolution's master. At this early stage, Castro began to formulate his anti-American rhetoric. It turned out to be his most effective message. The deep and latent resentment against Washington's meddling in Cuba's internal affairs blossomed in Castro's fierce nationalistic stance. The people were delirious in their support for Cuba's sovereignty, thus "Nationalism" became the single most important issue of the revolution and turned into Castro's triumphal card, which he effectively used throughout the world. Years later, the nationalistic banner was still hanging by Castro's deathbed.

At first, the Cuban leader insisted that neither he, nor the "26 of July Movement," were Marxist. On January 12, at a huge rally in the old camp, Columbia, now renamed "Campamento Libertad", Castro again said: "I am not communist, neither the movement."[1] On February 7, five weeks after he entered victoriously in Havana, Castro made an audacious move: With a single stroke, he vested all legislative powers in the "Council of Ministers". From now on, fundamental laws of the revolution would have the Council's stamp of approval. In the frenzy to build a new Cuba, only a few people saw the terrible shadow of a tyrant growing rapidly in the sparks and glow of a proud nationalism.

Among those few, was the eminent attorney Miro Cardona, who the following day resigned as Prime Minister. He could not accept the flagrant constitutional violations imposed in the name of the revolution. It was a lonely stand for due process of law and freedom. Miro later wrote: "I resigned. Cuba did not protest; it accepted, it applauded.[2] Within 48 hours, Fidel became Prime Minister and his brother Raul, by now an outspoken radical Jacobin, was appointed Minister of the Revolutionary Armed Forces (FAR).

From Cuba's militaristic heritage, Fidel Castro knew that the Army's loyalty was the principal factor for political survival. Under that premise, he anchored his power base in the Armed Forces headed by his brother Raul and those officers that were totally committed to his personal and absolute leadership, above and beyond any ideological dogma. Castro and the Rebel Army were the revolution and the depository of the people's will. "Fidelismo" or complete loyalty to Fidel was firmly rooted from the very beginning as the supreme requirement to membership in the power elite circle.

Within 30 days of victory, most officers and soldiers of the defeated army were discharged, exiled, incarcerated or put to death. In some cases by grotesque, circus-like televised trials and executions. On January 13, five days after he had marched into Havana, Castro's Council of Ministers approved into law the death penalty, and the Interior Ministry, now headed by Ramiro Valdez, was turned into a deadly force capable of brutalizing the growing opposition with shocking levels of violence. In those delirious days of hopes and dreams, the terrible specter of fear entered the individual psyche and eventually framed the relationship of the people with the messianic leader of the revolution. The reign of terror was dawning.

On January 20, speaking from the presidential palace before a large multitude, Castro showed again his charismatic appeal to the masses. Standing in the balcony in full view of the mesmerized crowd, he asked a rhetorical and leading question. Should war criminals be shot? Yes, yes, shouted the exited crowd. What should we do with the enemies of the revolution? Should we send them to the wall? Yes, yes, and then in an emotional frenzy the crowd shouted: "paredon" or "the wall, the wall". A few minutes later, they were chanting rhythmically "Fidel, Fidel, Fidel". It was obvious that a living icon was in the making. Cuba's joyful and tragic embrace with a tyrant was just beginning while Castro was rehearsing what he later defined as "Direct Democracy".

On March 3, anxieties about the radicalization of the revolution were put to a decisive test as a result of the trial of a group of 43 pilots, bombardiers and mechanics of Batista's defeated forces, who were accused of war crimes. Presiding over the tribunal was "Comandante" Felix Pena, a courageous veteran of the Rebel

Army.   The Court found that the evidence presented by the prosecution was inadequate and they were acquitted.  Castro was outraged by the tribunal's verdict and immediately went on TV to accuse the Revolutionary Court of being mistaken.  He ordered a retrial.  He claimed that when a verdict was unjust, the revolution had the right to appeal.

A new tribunal was appointed.  Major Manuel Pineiro, known as "Barbaroja" or red beard, a trusted officer of Raul Castro's staff, was named to preside over the retrial.  The airmen were swiftly found guilty and sentenced to 30 years in prison and ten years of forced labor.  Felix Pena, overwhelmed by Castro's bitter criticism, killed himself.  In a national televised appearance, Castro moved one step closer to the Jacobin terror of the French Revolution.  He stated: "Revolutionary justice is based not on legal precepts but on moral convictions."[3]  If that was a valid premise, the question was then:  whose moral convictions?";  the answer seems obvious.  Revolutionary justice was to be based on Fidel Castro's values and moral opinions — a most tragic travesty of the judicial process.

## CASTRO AND COMMUNISM

There is a never-ending debate over whether by the time of his victorious march into Havana, Castro was a Marxist.  He had insisted that he was.  On December 3, 1961, Castro said: "I believe in Marxism Leninism...I believed it  the first of January."[4]

But in the early stages of his quest for total control of the government, he was saying the opposite, stating at every turn that he was not a communist.  Castro needed more time to find out how far the Soviet Union was willing to break in the U.S. sphere of influence in Cuba and challenge the Washington establishment by providing economic and military aid to the Cuban revolution, 90 miles from the American shores.

It seems that at the time Castro was influenced by the fashionable view that the Soviet Union was gaining momentum as a super power and, actually, moving ahead of the capitalist democracies.  In 1958, a few months before Castro's final victory over Batista, the Soviet Premier, Nikita Khrushchev, began bragging that Russian communism was going to "bury" America in economic competition.  In 1957, the Russians scored a great propaganda victory by beating the Americans into space with the sputnik, the first manned satellite, reinforcing the idea that by the 1970's the Soviet Union would be the leading economic power in the world and that Karl Marx had been proven right. Probably intoxicated by this Soviet statistic, Castro saw the opportunity of joining what was then perceived by many as a triumphant ideology.

On this issue, Castro was direct and to the point. He said: "The Soviet Union has entirely surpassed all of the capitalist countries...in the Soviet Union three times more engineers study than in the United Status. In the construction of homes, the Soviet Union is the first country in the world. That is, there are some things absolutely proven; the reality of history have completely proven the Marxist-Leninist doctrine."[5] At the end, Marxism turned out to be an ideological catastrophe. Castro was wrong. In the intense and confused ideological debate of that historical time, he chose to join the loser. Within thirty years the Soviet giant, the great Marxist Leninist miracle, would have collapsed in a colossal failure. Definitely Castro was not a successful visionary.

But in 1959 an alliance with the Kremlin was the optimum political and economic opportunity for Castro. Under the protection of the Soviet Union, he could radicalize the revolution while openly displaying his fierce anti-Americanism. On this issue, Brian Latell, one of America's foremost Cuba's analysts, said: "The last component in the decision to begin embracing communism openly fell into place by the end of his first months in power... Furthermore, allying himself and his revolution with Moscow would be the ultimate repudiation of the United States."[6]

## CASTRO: THE ICON OF THE AMERICAN LEFT

On April 15, Castro traveled to Washington as the keynote speaker of the American Society of Newspaper editor's annual luncheon. This was an unofficial visit to the U.S. — exactly how he wanted to go into the land of the Yankees. At the national airport, Castro was welcomed by Under Secretary of State, Roy Robotton. The Cuban leader arrived with a select group of advisors, mostly economists and leading upper-class businessmen like Jose "Pepin" Bosh, the powerful chairman of Bacardi Rum. Not a single communist was included in the Cuban delegation. In his keynote address to the American journalists, he again stated:

"This revolution is not communist."[7] The tall, charismatic Castro captivated the Washington editorial elite. Herbert Matthews was there, gleaming with joy; his "Robin Hood" was doing great. President Eisenhower decided not to meet with the irritating leader of the Cuban revolution and went to a golf match instead. A public relations mistake? Perhaps, but Castro was not looking forward to a meeting with the American President. He needed time to reinforce his growing image of champion of Cuba's nationalism. A high-level meeting with Eisenhower could tarnish that image; eventually he chose to meet with Vice President Richard Nixon.

It was a cordial encounter. Castro spoke about his vision for the common good of the people, while Nixon looked into the enigma of the probable ideological direction of Castro's revolution. Nixon was concerned with his findings, but nevertheless the administration made several attempts to provide financial assistance to Cuba. Rubotton tried to arrange a meeting between the Cuban economists and several officials from the Treasury Department and the Export Import Bank, but Castro refused to give his approval. The revolution was not willing to receive any economic assistance from the U.S. That was Castro's unshakable policy toward the Yankees.

From Washington, Castro went to Princeton and Harvard universities where hundreds of students and faculty gave him a cheering welcome. The embryonic radical student movements in the American universities were embracing a popular rebel leader that had dared to challenge the American bourgeoisie establishment. They were to recreate and cherish for years this image of the unconquerable heroe.

Castro became a symbol of the fight for social justice and when he turned into a brutal Marxist "caudillo" who crushed the civil rights of his own people, he was still remembered by the American radical left as the romantic icon of those early, happy days. A clear contradiction of Martin Luther King's "civil rights" noble ideal, and a tragic indictment of their double standards.

It was obvious that for Castro the U.S. trip was a monumental success. He proved once more a masterful and charismatic communicator who could win the hearts and minds of most Americans. Furthermore, Castro was able to confuse the Eisenhower administration, especially certain key intelligence officers, as to his ideological beliefs. Frank Bender, the CIA chief expert on communism for Latin America, met for three hours with Castro. Afterwards, Bender said to Cuba's Finance Minister, Lopez Fresquet: "Castro is not only not a communist; he is a strong anti-communist fighter."[8] Bender would later be a key organizer of the Bay of Pig's invasion.

But there were some who did not buy into Castro's anti-communist performance. Richard Nixon, the cunning vice-president, was one of them. In a memo dated April 25, 1959, he wrote on his meeting with Castro: "I urged him to state his position as being in favor of having elections at the earliest possible date." Castro going into considerable details, explained to Nixon, "The people did not want elections because elections in the past had produced bad government. He used the same argument that he was simply reflecting the will of the people in justifying the executions of war criminals and his overruling the acquittal of Batista's aviators. In fact he seemed to be obsessed with the idea that it was his responsibility to carry out the will of the people."[9] (Nixon) ... tried to impress upon him that there were certain individual rights which a majority should never have the power to destroy."[10] Castro gave Nixon some "rather confused arguments as to why industrial plants that were licensed and/or owned and operated by the government would serve the best interest of Cuba better than privately owned enterprises."[11] In summary, Nixon said: "The one fact we can be sure of is that he has those indefinable qualities which make him a leader of men. Whatever we may think of him he is going to be a great factor in the development of Cuba and very possibly in Latin American affairs generally... He is either incredibly naive about Communism or under Communist discipline..."[12]

## *"COMMON GOOD": THE SHINNING BANNER OF TYRANNY*

Castro was obviously a believer and disciple of French philosopher Jean-Jacques Rousseau, who preached the need to establish a new society in which citizens renounced their individual rights and devoted their efforts to the common good. On this issue, professor Susan Dunn, in her excellent analysis, stated: "For Rousseau, true freedom could belong only to citizens who were able to suppress their primitive wills, sacrifice their private, selfish, interest for the good of all.... Indeed, Rousseau's utopian..., includes no channels for expression of dissent or opposition... those who disagree with the general will are simply in error, expressing selfish particular interests that perversely thwart the common good of all... there can be no role for minority opinion. Neither dissenting individuals nor groups, political parties or factions can be tolerated by the cohesive whole."[13] That was all Castro needed in his quest for absolute power.

Jean Jaques Rousseau's doctrine did serve Robespierre's Jacobins and Lenin's Bolsheviks. It was now Castro's turn to raise the banner of the common good and himself as a man of destiny, chosen with the sacred duty to represent the "Will of the People". The defense of Rousseau's doctrine became a focal issue in Castro's brutal repression of individual rights. Terror became a psychological weapon, fear the expected response. Thanks to Rousseau's philosophy, Castro had from the beginning a doctrine to dress up his drive to rule Cuba as a "caudillo" in the decrepit Hispanic tradition. Above anything else, Fidel Castro "the Caudillo" was the shield and the sword of the "common good". Eventually, communism would become the facemask of "Fidelismo".

On May 14, Castro ordered the creation of the Agrarian Reform Institute "INRA" with him as President and Nunez Jimenez as director in charge of the day-to-day operations. Overnight, the INRA turned into the most powerful agency on the Island with the task to expropriate and redistribute private land, build roads, provide loans and form its own armed militia of over 100,000 men and women. Then on May 17, Castro signed the Agrarian Reform Law, which he had already promulgated in the Sierra Maestra while living in the shack that used to be his old headquarters at "La Plata".

The Agrarian Reform Law called for expropriation of latifundia (defined as estates larger than 402 hectares). Over 31,000 titled deeds of land were given to the peasants (28 hectares or less). The large sugar cane fields were confiscated and turned into 622 cooperatives, while the rice plantations and cattle ranches were converted into 263 cooperatives called "people farms". The peasants that received title land deeds could neither mortgage nor sell them and crop prices were set by the INRA, which overnight became Cuba's largest landowners. The Agrarian Reform law turned into the first major step in radicalization of the revolution. On June 13, Castro declared the critics of the Agrarian Reform to be "traitors" of the fatherland.[14]

In early summer of 1959, the first major crisis within the Armed Forces erupted when Air Force Chief Pedro L. Diaz Lanz accused Castro of having betrayed the liberal ideals of the revolution by embracing Marxist-Leninist dogma. Castro denied Diaz Lanz's charges and in a speech accused the Air Force Commander of being the Cuban Benedict Arnold. Diaz Lanz fled to the United States.

Next, came the character assassination of the loyal President Manuel Urrutia, who at a large rally delivered a powerful anti-communist speech. At this time, Urrutia did believe Castro's assertion that neither he nor the revolution was communist. The president was to receive a rude awakening when Castro appeared on television and charged Urrutia with being part of a conspiracy to fabricate a communist threat as to provoke foreign aggression. In a media blitz, Castro accused his hand-picked president of obstructing the revolution's forward march and, in a theatrical performance, resigned as Prime Minister. Urrutia was utterly confused.

On TV, Castro worked the crowds to a fever pitch and a multitude began gathering at the Presidential Palace chanting "Viva Fidel" and shouting for Urrutia to resign. Totally devastated by the torrent of insults and accusations, Urrutia lost his nerve and wept uncontrollably.[15] Hours later, disguised as a milkman, the good judge who had followed Castro's every command, except to embrace communism, sought asylum at the Venezuelan Embassy. Castro had inherited a vast media network with over 400,000 TV sets and used it to deliver his messages of fear and hope directly into Cuban living rooms. Urrutia was lynched on television.

The disastrous Urrutia's affair was followed by one of the most profound crises within the revolutionary leadership when Hubert Matos, a celebrated icon of the Rebel Army, announced his decision to resign as Commander of the Camaguey Military Garrison in protest for the communist takeover of the Armed Forces sponsored by Raul Castro and "Che" Guevara. It seems that Matos misread Urrutia's character assassination and opted for a peaceful confrontation with Castro on the issue of communism — a huge tragic mistake for the courageous believer in the civil rights of individual citizens.

Matos wrote Castro: "It is right however to recall to you that great men begin to decline when they cease to be just... I hope you will understand that my decision is irrevocable...allowing me to return home as a civilian, without having my sons, afterwards learn in the street that their father is a traitor or a deserter... I remain ever yours, comrade, Hubert Matos."[16] Castro's response was swift and furious. He ordered Camilo Cienfuegos to immediately arrest the highly respected "Comandante" who had led the Rebel Army into Santiago.

From his jail, Matos wrote: " The risk I run does not matter. I believe that I have the courage and serenity to face all contingencies".... very well, Fidel, I await calmly what you decide. You know I have the courage to pass twenty years in prision... I shall not order my soldiers...to open a single burst of fire against anyone, not even against the cut-throats you may send... I hope that...just as you once said, History will judge you too Fidel."[17] A man of strong convictions, and personal courage, Huber Matos misunderstood Castro's pathological need to be obeyed with unshakable loyalty and to be followed in the ideological path of his own choosing without hesitation. Matos was sentence to 20 years in prison.

## WAS CASTRO PUSHED INTO THE SOVIET CAMP ?

The theory that Castro was pushed into embracing communism due to the U.S. lack of support became fashionable among American journalist elite where Herbert Mathews was a leading pro-Castro advocate. This mistaken theory had partially survived despite powerful evidence to the contrary. On November 1959, ten months after taking power, Castro instructed a young Marxist, Hector Rodriguez Llompart, his Undersecretary of Commerce, to establish a direct link with Anastas Mikoyan, the first Deputy Chairman of the Soviet Union, who at the time was leading a scientific and technical exhibition in Mexico City. Rodriguez Lompart met with Mikoyan and arranged for a visit by the cunning Bolshevik to Havana. Castro's newspaper *Revolución* referred to the Cuban request on November 17.[18] Mikoyan accepted the Cuban "Caudillo's" invitation.

On February 5, 1960, Mikoyan opened the Soviet scientific exhibition in Havana. A concert was given in his honor at the Auditorium. Raul Castro and "Che" Guevara led the audience in a standing ovation for the veteran Marxist leader. On February 13, a commercial agreement was signed by Mikoyan and Castro under which the Kremlin would lend $100 million to Cuba, at 2.5 percent interest repayable in 12 years, to be used for machinery and technical assistance. But more important, Castro and Mikoyan announced that in 1960, the U.S.S.R. would purchase 425,000 tons of sugar at the world price and one million tons of sugar each year for the following four years.[19] The era of Castro's close economic and military links with communist Russia was dawning.

On January 4, 1960, a month before Mikoyan's visit to Havana, Aleksander Alekseev, a veteran KGB agent operating as a journalist of the Moscow newspaper

*Tass,* met with Fidel Castro, his brother Raul, "Che" Guevara and Nunez Jimenez. According to the declassified KGB-Presidium documents, Fidel Castro insisted on absolute secrecy of the meetings. Only those present were to know that the ideological model of the Cuban revolution was communism. Castro indicated that through INRA he was to end private property in Cuba.[20]

On January 17, Alekseev reported to the Kremlin that 1959 goals had been met most favorably and that Castro was accelerating the process in 1960. He also recommended implementation of large military aid to Castro's revolution and requested from Cuban intelligence an updated report of internal resistance to communism building up in the island.[21] The next day, Alekseev informed Moscow that Anibal Escalante, an old guard Cuban communist, was insisting on a major purge of those liberal members of the revolution that were actively opposing Marxism. Escalante pointed to Alekseev that the biggest threat was not the Americans, but those that fought against Batista, who believed in private property and Civil Rights and were not waiting for help from abroad.[22] On January 20, 1960, Alekseev recommended against a massive reprisal that could trigger a violent response and proposed a selective approach by imprisoning the most dangerous individuals while monitoring the people's reaction.[23]

## *FREE PRESS DECAPITATED...*

Freedom of the press is anathema to communism. Karl Marx's dogmatic gospel was to be protected against a free media capable of revealing to the public abuses of power, judicial violations and leadership mistakes. Therefore, the Cuban independent media had to be crushed. By April 1960, Cuba's radio and TV stations were virtually under government control. On May 11, the conservative newspaper *Diario de la Marina* was taken over by the revolutionary regime. A few brave journalists challenged Castro's outrageous order to silence the newspaper. A defiant Luis Aguilar Leon, one of Cuba's foremost intellectuals, wrote: "so it goes, the tour of unanimity has arrived in Cuba, the solid and impenetrable unanimity of totalitarianism".[24] *Prensa Libre* published it on May 13; it was to be among the last critical and free articles published in Cuba.

Three days later, *Prensa Libre* was confiscated. Humberto Medrano, a co-editor, wrote a courageous indictment of Castro's ferocious persecution of the free press: "No. Don't let them talk to you about communism, .... Everything is a lie. Hold on to what is yours, Cubans...hold on to your beliefs, to your principles, to the essence of your land and of your race, to your democratic traditions. Hold on to the truth. Hold on to Cuba."[25]

Neither Machado nor Batista had dared take total control of the Cuban media. Dogmatic intolerance was reigning supreme and protecting the Marxist dogma against the heresy of civil rights and individual freedoms. As Cuba's free press was crushed, a group of American intellectuals led by Waldo Frank founded the "Fair Play for Cuba Committee" to promote the Castro agenda in the U.S. Freedom of the "press" was dead. It was a lonely funeral.

Mikoyan's visit served to signal the beginning of the revolution's ideological realignment from the Western Market economies to the Soviet Marxist bloc and the first clash of Castro with a large segment of traditionally rebellious students. At Havana's Central Park, where Mikoyan was placing a wreath by Marti's statue, students staged a peaceful march against Castro's Soviet guest to protest Mikoyan's leadership role in the 1956 Hungarian massacre by Russian armored divisions.

Juan M. Salvat was among the march organizers and pointed to the students' grievances and the police's violent response. He said, "We believed that Mikoyan was one of the Soviet leaders that ordered the criminal repression of the Hungarian freedom fighters. Therefore, upon learning that Mikoyan was to place a wreath by Jose Marti's statue at Havana Central Park, a large group of high school and university students staged a peaceful protest march that was brutally repressed by Castro's police. For us it marked a turning point. It was clear that we were facing a new dictator and that he was turning Cuba into a Marxist State."[26]

## BACK TO THE TRENCHES OF FREEDOM

The destruction of the free press in Cuba signaled a call for action in the fight against Castro by those who believed in civil rights and individual freedoms. The same day *Prensa Libre* was confiscated, Mgr. Perez Serante, the priest who saved Castro's life after the Moncada disaster, issued a pastoral letter denouncing the communist threat to freedom. With his immense moral prestige, the beloved Archbishop of Santiago who led the Church in the struggle against Batista wrote: "The true Christian cannot live without freedom... "[27]. Castro was swiftly building a totalitarian Marxist state and the 1956's generation of Fank Pais and Jose Antonio Echeverria was answering the call to fight again for their Civil Rights and freedom.

Among the first to go into the fighting trenches was Jorge Sotus. A veteran of the "Rebel Army" who on November 30, 1956, captured and burned the Santiago Maritime Police Station, headed the first group of 50 men sent by Frank Pais to join Castro's small band in his mountain sanctuary and who led the first successful attack in the Sierra Maestra at "El Uvero".

Manolo Artime was a young Catholic leader with strong drive for social justice who briefly joined Castro's guerrilla movement and later headed the INRA in Manzanillo. They were part of a growing and effective underground being put together by veterans of the Batista struggle and new leaders just coming out of the high schools and university classrooms. Pedro Luis Boitel, Rogelio Gonzalez Corso, Manolin Gillot, Jorge Fundora, Virgilio Campaneria, Juanin Pereira, Manuel (Nongo) Puig, Porfirio Ramirez, Rafael Diaz Hanscom and Felipe Rodon, joined in the vanguard of the fight against Castro's Marxist state. They all died a hero's death.

## CASTRO'S DEEPENING CONFRONTATION WITH WASHINGTON

On May 17, the three large oil refineries in Cuba — Standard Oil, Texaco and Royal Dutch (Shell) — were ordered by the State to process a batch of Russian oil. The refineries refused on the grounds that they had previous refining agreements with Venezuela. With his cunning sense of timing, Castro saw the opportunity to press the Russians for a clear-cut commitment in the dangerous oil confrontations with the U.S. and Britain. Nunez Jimenez was sent to Moscow to find out where the Russians stood on this issue. Castro was pleased to learn that the U.S.S.R. was ready to challenge the Americans in their vital southern flank by becoming Cuba's major oil supplier. On June 29, 1960, Castro confiscated the three major oil refineries in the Island, and accused the U.S. of economic aggression, a successful cry that would turn out to be Castro's best excuse to later explain Cuba's economic failure. By the time the refineries were confiscated, he had been 18 months in power.

On July 6, and with Congressional approval, Eisenhower reduced the Cuban sugar quota by 700,000 tons. On July 9, Soviet Prime Minister Nikita Krushchev surprised the U.S. with a warning of possible retaliation on behalf of Castro's revolution. He said: "The U.S.S.R. is raising its voice and extending a helpful hand to the people of Cuba…speaking figuratively, in case of necessity, Soviet artillerymen can support the Cuban people with rocket fire."[28] In the cold war power play, it was the first time that the soviets were rushing to challenge the U.S. so close to their shores — a daring move.

At this time, Miguel Angel Quevedo, the publisher of *Bohemia*, one of the most successful and influential magazines in Latin America, accused Castro of betraying the nationalistic revolution. He wrote: "The deceit had been discovered… In order to carry out a purely national revolution there was no need to submit our people to the hateful Russian vassalage… this is a revolution betrayed."[29] Quevedo sought asylum in the Venezuelan embassy. *Bohemia*, the leading Castro supporter during the Batista struggle, was taken over by the government.

Now events began unfolding rapidly. On August 6, Castro confiscated several U.S-owned enterprises, including electricity and telephone companies and 36 large sugar mills. If there was any doubt as to the Marxist ideological path of the revolution, Ernesto "Che" Guevara dispelled the issue. Addressing the First Congress of Latin American Youth, Guevara said: "If I were asked whether our revolution is communist, I would define it as Marxist. Our revolution has discovered by its own methods the paths that Marx pointed out."[30] It was evident that Cuba was being transformed into a communist state. Washington was alarmed and confused as Castro's status grew in the Cold War confrontation between Russia and the U.S.

On September 18, Castro traveled to New York to attend the United Nations, but this time it was different. There were no cheering crowds waiting for the bearded leader, instead he was faced with a large group of hostile Cuban exiles. In New York he met for the first time with Khrushchev at the Hotel Teresa in Harlem. The Soviet Premier was very much impressed by Castro's charisma. The Russian diplomat Arkady Schevchenko recalled: "he was extremely pleased with the way things had gone. He told us he had found that Castro wanted a close friendship with the U.S.S.R. and had asked for military aid."[31]

On September 23, 1960, the Democratic presidential candidate John F. Kennedy, while in New York, addressed the Cuban issue and stated" "…we must make clear our intention…to enforce the Monroe Doctrine…and that we will not be content till democracy is restored in Cuba. The forces fighting for freedom in exile and in the mountains of Cuba should be sustained."[32] It was Kennedy's first public commitment to a free Cuba. As a true liberal, Kennedy felt until the end a profound rejection of Castro's totalitarian police state. The Cuban crisis was to be at the top of Kennedy's presidential agenda and would mark the darkest days of Camelot.

On October 18, 1960, Eisenhower recalled the U.S. ambassador from Havana and the next day imposed an embargo on all exports from the U.S. to Cuba except certain humanitarian items. Castro had achieved his goal: the total economic and political break with the Yankees. He understood that with the full economic aid of the U.S.S.R, the revolution could withstand the U.S. embargo and gain a significant advantage in his quest to become one of the internationalist leaders challenging America's capitalistic system. The U.S. embargo was an insignificant issue in Castro's vision of a world that was inexorably embracing communism. By the end of October, the revolution confiscated major Cuban corporations, including Bacardi, and all banks, the remaining sugar mills, the Nicaro nickel plant, Sears, Woolworth, Coca Cola, 61 textile mills, all restaurants, theaters, and hotels. It had taken Castro 22 months to bury capitalism in Cuba.

The Eisenhower administration was now ready to listen to the CIA's recommendation that military assistance be provided the daring Cuban underground and a group of young exiles trained in guerrilla war. The CIA believed that they had a winning model in the demise of the socialist president of Guatemala, Jacobo Arbenz, five years before.[33] It was a modest undertaking that exposed the CIA misunderstanding of Castro's enthusiastic support among the Cuban masses. Guatemala was the wrong strategic model. It seems that as the operational plan began to unfold, the Washington establishment never closed the gap between the final objective of overthrowing a Marxist state, 90 miles from the U.S. shores, and the resources made available to successfully achieve the task. The American diplomatic and political propensity of wishful thinking, arrogance and naivety was in full swing.

# CHAPTER XVIII

# FREEDOM DEFERRED

[1] *Revolución.* Enero 13, 1959
[2] *Diario de la Marina.* Miami, Noviembre 12, 1960
[3] Thomas, op cit, 1202
[4] Así lo dijo Fidel. Citas del Máximo Líder de la Revolución. (Colección Las Américas, Lider Maximo, 2006) 12
[5] Ibid, op cit, 17
[6] Latell, op cit, 150
[7] *Asi lo dijo Fidel,* op cit, 9
[8] Rufo Lopez Fresquet. *My fourteen months with Castro.* (New York, 1966), 110.
[9] Richard Nixon, Memo, Office of the Vice President, Washington, April 25, 1959. www.gwu.edu/~nsarchiv/bayofpigs/19590425.pdf
[10] Ibid, 2
[11] Ibid, 3
[12] Ibid, 4
[13] Dunn, op cit, 63
[14] Formes, Cuba, op cit, 208
[15] Geyer, op cit, 246
[16] Thomas, op.cit. 1244.
[17] Ibid, 1245
[18] *Revolución.* Noviembre 17, 1959.
[19] Robert S. Walter. *International Affairs*, Vol. 42 No. 1 (Jan 1966), 74-86.
[20] Aleksander Alekseev, KGB, Havana, January 4, 1960. Folio 3, Tomo 5, Lista 65 archive SVR (KGB).
[21] Semichastny, KGB, Havana, January 17, 1960. Folio 3, Tomo 5, lista 65, SVR (KGB).
[22] Ibid.
[23] Ibid.
[24] *Prensa Libre*, Mayo 13, 1960.
[25] Ibid, May 16, 1960.
[26] J.M. Salvat interview with the author.
[27] Thomas, op cit, 1282
[28] Geyer, op cit, 258
[29] Thomas, op cit, 1292
[30] Ibid.
[31] Geyer, op cit, 263
[32] Ibid, 1296.
[33] *New York Times.* June 13, 1961.

# CHAPTER XIX

# *THE BAY OF PIGS TRAGEDY*

*A DECREPIT SECRET OPERATION – THE BRIGADE – FROM TRINIDAD TO THE BAY OF PIGS: THE DISASTROUS CHANGE OF THE ORIGINAL PLAN – ON TO THE BAY OF PIGS – THE AIR ATTACK – THE DAYS OF COURAGE.*

By January of 1960, U.S. intelligence believed that Castro was moving swiftly to establish a communist state in Cuba closely associated with the Soviet Union. In the context of the Cold War, this was a dangerous challenge to the American people. To deal with this growing threat, the CIA created a Cuban Task Force led by Jacob Esterline, a veteran of the 1954 coup against the socialist president of Guatemala, Jacobo Arbenz.[1] Greatly concerned with the Soviet presence in Cuba, President Eisenhower issued a warning: "This nation cannot and will not tolerate the establishment of a Soviet satellite ninety miles from our shores."[2] On February 17, a CIA briefing to the National Security Council on Mikoyan's visit to Cuba, reported: "The U.S.S.R. had shifted from caution attitude to one of active support,"[3]

## *A DECREPIT SECRET OPERATION*

On March 17, 1960, the President authorized the CIA to develop a plan in order to deal with this threat to the national security. At the height of the Cold War, the Russian military presence in Cuba, especially the potential deployment of nuclear missiles, was unacceptable to the Americans. Castro had to be overthrown. The first option was direct U.S. military intervention. It was sure to solve of the problem, but it could also turn into a public relations nightmare as a reminder to many people throughout the world of the terrible Soviet intervention in Hungary.[4] The second option was to support the Cubans who were already fighting Castro by providing training and military supplies through covert operations. What was important for Washington was to end the growing Soviet threat to the U.S. mainland. This was the fundamental motive of the huge American involvement in the Bay of Pigs.

At the March 17 meeting at the White House, Eisenhower gave the green light for the CIA to plan for the creation of a Cuban exile military force to be trained for deployment in Cuba. It was to be a top secret operation that would not expose the U.S. involvement in its implementation. The official version was that the operation was financed by influential, wealthy individuals, mostly Cubans, seeking to depose Castro.[5] It was among the worst cover stories that could be conceived. Even after the CIA's direct participation ceased to be a secret, the Washington political establishment insisted to the end on framing the operation under the premises that the U.S. government was not involved. Hiding the U.S. active role and commitment in the invasion was wishful thinking at its worst. The magnitude of the operation made it impossible to fake the U.S. government's involvement. It was a pathetic masquerade that planted the seeds for a bloody disaster.

However, at the same time, Washington saw those Cubans willing to take up arms against Castro as their only viable alternative for eliminating the Soviet threat ninety miles from Key West. In the meeting, Eisenhower insisted "that the Cubans do most of what was required." He said: "Our hands should not show in anything that is done."[6] The Cubans never thought that they were being used as expendable tools in the Cold War confrontation. They truly believed that the Americans were their faithful allies in the fight for freedom.[7] On August 18, 1960, the Eisenhower administration approved a $13 million budget for the covert operation, with specific instructions that no U.S. military personnel be used in combat operations.[8] The Cubans were to do the fighting.

And fighting they did. In the long tradition of rebellion, the students and young professionals led the clandestine struggle. It was a most difficult fight against Cuba's "New Messiah". To face Castro's powerful discourse they needed strong convictions and faith in the ideals of civil rights, and despite the fierce repression headed by Ramiro Valdez, Cuba's Interior Minister, the rebellious youth created a large effective clandestine network. They fought with uncommon courage; their struggle was among the most heroic in Cuba's tragic political history.

## THE BRIGADE

Initially the American aid went to the underground resistance and the guerrillas. The strategy was predicated in the strength of the resistance movement and the veteran group fighting in the Escambray Mountains of Central Cuba. As the clandestine operation grew, the need to set up supply bases in the Florida Keys became clear as well as to provide extensive training to a hand-picked group of men in the complex skill of covert operations. On June 2, the first group was taken to Florida's West Coast, near Fort Myers, and transferred to the nearby island of Useppa, which Freddie Goudie, a prominent resistance leader had leased on behalf of the CIA. The men were told that everything was top secret. They received a physical examination and a serial designation starting with 2,500 so as to confuse Castro's intelligence services on the size of the forces being trained.

On June 22, 1960 the Useppa group was split up. Some men went to Fort Gullic in Panama for training in guerrilla warfare while the rest remained in the Florida Keys where they became part of the vitally important maritime crews and infiltration teams. Their principal task was to supply the resistance movement and to get into the island the radio operators and the experts in urban conflict. Sailing from the Florida Keys, these committed fighters brought small fast boats with their cargos of arms and men to the inlets and isolated beaches in Cuba. It was a most dangerous mission that took place for several years.

In late summer 1960, however, there was a radical change in U.S. strategy to overthrow Castro. As the U.S.S.R. began to increase their supply of weapons to Cuba, the Eisenhower administration decided to go for a powerful knockout punch with a well trained and equipped assault brigade that would establish and hold a beachhead for further operations.[9] The State Department arranged with the Guatemalan government for the use of a military base at Retalhuleu, in the mountains near the Pacific coast. On October 31, the CIA outlined an amphibious invasion plan with a 1,500 man brigade.[10]

A few days later, the American officers in Guatemala were ordered to begin conventional training including an airborne battalion. A group of 60 men was assigned to the infiltration and mountain guerrilla teams.[11]

The Guatemala base was used to train a force of several battalions of infantry supported by heavy weapons and tanks. A group of Cuban pilots were formed into a B-26 squadron and C-47 transport planes. The original landing target was not the Bay of Pigs, but the more suitable area of Casilda-Trinidad in south-central Cuba near the Escambray Mountains. This was an excellent landing site with an airfield, a deep water harbor, several piers, sandy beaches without nearby coral reefs and a paved road that led to the city of Trinidad, known as a hotbed of anti-Castro activities, where the Brigade could expect to be joined by several hundred men and women.

Originally there were four battalions. Alejandro del Valle headed the First Paratrooper Battalion. Hugo Sueiro was in charge of the Second Infantry Battalion. Erneido Oliva commanded the Armored Battalion and Roberto San Roman led the Heavy Gun Battalion. Eventually Erneido Oliva was named as the Brigade Second in Command and two more infantry battalions, the Fifth and the Six, were added to the Brigade order of battle. The Heavy Weapons Battalion had several 4.2 inch mortars and 75mm recoilless rifles. Each infantry battalion had their own light mortars for direct support. Five Sherman tanks provided the armored punch. Jose "Pepe" San Roman was named Brigade Commander.[12]

During the 1960 presidential campaign, Vice-President Richard Nixon and Senator John Kennedy held several televised debates. In fact, this was the first U.S. election in which television was used as a decisive political factor. During the debates, Kennedy criticized the Administration for being soft on Castro. Kennedy promised, if elected president, his full support in the fight for Cuba's freedom. "To strengthen the non-Batista democratic forces in exile and in Cuba itself, who offer eventual hope of overthrowing Castro... these fighters for freedom had virtually no support from our government."[13] In their last debate, Kennedy said to Nixon: "If you can't stand up to Castro, how can you stand up to Khrushchev."[14] Kennedy went on to win one of the closest elections in U.S. history. On November 18, 1960 CIA Director Allan Dulles and the Deputy Director of the Cuban Task force, Richard Bissell, briefed president-elect John Kennedy at Palm Beach on the "Trinidad" plan to end Castro's rule in Cuba.[15]

The Brigade's political view was mostly that of those with a middle class background, who since the 1930's had been at the forefront of Cuba's struggle for social justice and civil rights enshrined in the progressive Constitution of 1940. The men were mostly young professionals and students with an average age of twenty-nine. There were several officers of the regular and rebel army, but overall the men had little or no military experience. To make them into a efficient fighting force was the challenge facing the "Green Berets" who were in charge of the Brigade's training. They did accomplish their task and developed a solid bond of trust and respect with those young Cubans. The Brigade became an excellent fighting force. These proud men belonged to a generation forged during a long and bloody political crisis, strongly committed to institutional reforms, a generation convinced that Castro had betrayed the social-democratic revolution and was building a totalitarian Marxist state. As Kennedy pointed out, this democratic force represented the "hopes of overthrowing Castro." The Brigade was Cuba's best promise of freedom.

## FROM TRINIDAD TO THE BAY OF PIGS: THE DISASTROUS CHANGE OF THE ORIGINAL PLAN

By January 1, 1961, Castro had been in control of the Cuban government for two years, and John F. Kennedy was about to be sworn in as the thirty-fifth President of the United States. In Guatemala, the Brigade's strength was significantly increased and the CIA officers in charge of the "Trinidad" landing informed Washington that the success or failure of the invasion would hinge on the vital issue of air superiority. The CIA memo read: "It is considered crucial that the Cuban Air Force, capable of opposing the landing be knockout or neutralized before the amphibious shipping makes its final run into the beach."[16] This important document specifically outlined for the new administration the issue that control of the air was a fundamental premise for success. The personnel in charge of the invasion made it clear that it was crucial to destroy Castro's planes. Without air superiority, the invasion would not stand a chance.

On January 19, 1961, the day before the transfer of the presidency, Eisenhower met with Kennedy and stressed the point that the "Trinidad" invasion plan was now the new administration's responsibility.[17]  On January 28, Kennedy's leading team received their first briefing on the "Trinidad" operation.  The meeting was attended, among others, by the Vice President, Lyndon B. Johnson, Secretary of State Dean Rusk, Secretary of Defense Robert McNamara, National Security Advisor McGeorge Bundy, the Chairman of the Joint Chief of Staff and several CIA officers.  In the meeting President Kennedy authorized "a continuation and increase of the current CIA activities, including political as well as covert sabotage operations."[18]  Kennedy also reserved the right to call off the "Trinidad" invasion plan.[19]

On January 30, the Joint Chiefs of Staff gave approval to the landing operation.  Again control of the air was emphasized to be the crucial factor for success.  The Joint Chiefs of Staff concluded that the Brigade could hold the "Trinidad" beachhead as to permit the arrival of a Cuban provisional government.[20]  But by early February, barely four weeks into the new administration, top officials at the State Department and the National Security Council began raising objections to the need for the proposed invasion. In a memorandum to the president, McGeorge Bundy, Special Assistant to Kennedy in the National Security Council, wrote that he and Richard Goodwin "join in believing that there should not be an invasion adventure without careful diplomatic soundings which are similar to the State Department view."[21]

On February 11, Arthur Schlesinger, another close advisor to the President, warned against the landing on the grounds that there was no way to hide U.S. involvement in the military operation. He concluded that "at one stroke it would dissipate all the extraordinary goodwill which had been rising towards the New Administration."[22]  Four days later, Thomas Mann, the Assistant Secretary for Interamerican Affairs, wrote a memo to Dean Rusk opposing the "Trinidad" landing.  Mann advocated the idea of letting Castro's revolution fail and use it as a model of an ideological Marxist disaster.  He added: "I therefore concluded it would not be in the national interest to put this plan into execution."[23]  On February 18, McGeorge Bundy gave Kennedy the State Department's and Defense's opposing views on the proposed invasion and added his own opinion that included declaring a trade embargo, to allow the internal opposition to grow, and then launch "Bissell's battalion."[24]  It was obvious that Kennedy's top advisors held conflicting views as to the Russian military threat in Castro's Cuba and the urgency of eliminating it.

Several large Soviet bloc armed shipments had already arrived in Cuba with military personnel employed as instructors and technicians.[25] On January 27, the Joint Chiefs of Staff sent a message to the Secretary of Defense expressing their concern that the Castro revolution was becoming part of the communist bloc.[26] The Kennedy Administration inner circle was fully briefed and made aware of the Russian military build-up in the Island, but for the State Department and the NSC, the proposed plan to get rid of Castro and cancel the Soviet threat was overshadowed by the negative impact that such action could have on the new administration's international image.

It was in the midst of this heated debate that the first major decision in reshaping the Cuban plan was taken. On February 11, 1961, following the advice of Dean Rusk, the Brigade landing at "Trinidad" was cancelled on the grounds that it looked too much like a WWII invasion and it would be difficult to disguise U.S. involvement.[27] The CIA was ordered to find another site. Four weeks before the invasion, the Bay of Pigs was selected as the alternative landing site. It was to be a downsized operation to hide U.S. involvement. Suddenly the initial premise of a Soviet threat with the potential for establishing a missile platform in Cuba became less urgent. Therefore, the idea of keeping the appearance of a limited Cuban-exile military operation became the dominant policy of the Sate Department, which included the announcement that the planned B-26 attacks on Castro's airbases had been carried out by Cuban defectors.[28] It was a flagrant miscarriage of common sense. Well-educated, intelligent individuals were caught in an inexcusable charade, which brought shame and defeat to "Camelot". It seems that Robert Kennedy, with his outstanding strategic instinct, was among the few that never lost sight of the danger posed by Soviet military presence on the Island.[29]

## *ON TO THE BAY OF PIGS!*

It was early in April when an advance unit of the Brigade left Guatemala for Puerto Cabezas in Nicaragua from where the invasion would be launched, but at that time, the order to proceed had not yet been received. The Kennedy Administration was now facing a surge of Russian weapons in Cuba, including modern tanks and the imminent arrival of MiG fighter planes with trained Cuban pilots. Time was of the essence. Finally on April 4, in a meeting at the State Department, President Kennedy polled a dozen advisors on whether to order the invasion. With the exception of Dean Rusk, who abstained, and Senator William Fullbright, who opposed, the rest voted for allowing the Cuban Brigade into battle to establish a beachhead at the Bay of Pigs. The invasion date was set for April 17, 1961. Operation "Pluto," as the invasion plan was called in Washington, was on.

Official instructions arrived at "Puerto Cabezas" on the eve of the Brigade's departure. It read: Commencing at H-Hour of D-Day, the Brigade is to engage in amphibious and parachute landings, take, occupy and defend beachheads in the area of "Cochino Bay" and "Playa Groin".[30] The 2nd and 5th battalions were to land at "Playa Larga" called "Red Beach" up the northern most point of the Bay. The 4th and 6th battalions, the tank company and the heavy weapons were to land at "Gion" or Blue Beach; the 3rd battalion was to go ashore at "Green Beach" to cover the right flank of the beachhead. The first parachute battalion was to be dropped at San Blas and Palpite, two important road intersections at the edge of Zapata Swamp. There was an airfield nearby Giron.

The Zapata Swamps extended 65 miles east to west and 20 miles north to south and had two narrow roads of about six to eight miles that ran through the swamps. The first road linked the Australia sugar mill with Palpite and the second Covadonga with San Blas. Both Palpite and San Blas would become the two critical choke points of the beachheads. Castro's counterattack would have to advance through those two narrow roads — a most difficult and bloody affair. Palpite and San Blas, therefore, had to be taken and held.

At sunset, on Friday 14, 1961, the American officers said their farewells to the 1,474 men of the Brigade,[31] whom they had trained for the fight ahead. It was an emotional moment. As the ships steamed into the Caribbean Sea, the Cubans lining the railways waved their colored scarves and cheered with the joy of youth about to fulfill a cherished dream. Some of the Americans had tears in their eyes. Forward they went, proud of being the soldier of freedom.

## THE AIR ATTACK

Framed within the premise that air supremacy was essential for securing and holding the beachheads, the CIA's initial plan called for 22 B-26 medium bombers to attack Castro's airbases five times,[32] the last strike to coincide with the Brigade's landing. It was to be a massive blow but the State Department cut the number of B-26s from 22 to 16 in order to fit the cover story of an all-Cuban exile operation and to hide U.S. involvement. It was a significant reduction, but 16 B-26s could still deliver a powerful punch on Castro's airbases.

The time for action was at hand; the Brigade was on the move. The dice of destiny were rolling. It was at this crucial moment that the American political leadership became caught in the grips of doubt and paralyzing indecision. On April 14, on the eve of the initial air attack, President Kennedy called Richard Bissel, the CIA official in charge of operation "Pluto," and asked him how many B-26 were to be in the first mission and was told that all the 16 planes were committed in all the attacks. Kennedy then made a major decision and said to Bissell: "Well, I don't want it on that scale. I want it minimal,"[33] The all-important first strike, which had the advantage of surprise, was reduced from 16 to eight planes. In trying to hide its major involvement, the U.S. was now behaving like a clumsy giant. Still there was a slim chance of delivering a knock-out punch to Castro's small air force, with the five schedule attacks.

On April 15, at 2:00 P.M., the eight B-26 took off from Puerto Cabezas to attack Castro's airbases at San Antonio, Columbia and Santiago de Cuba.[34] At dawn, while waiting at his military headquarters known as "Punto Uno" or Point One in Havana, Castro heard the approaching planes and the blast of several explosions. "This is the aggression," he shouted.[35] Immediately he was told that the three bases were under attack. The raid was over in less than 20 minutes. Castro asked for damage assessment and was informed that only seven planes had survived the attack. Among them two T-33 jet fighters.[36] The Brigade lost two planes in the raid.

Immediately after the air strike, Castro ordered the arrest of more than a quarter of a million people throughout the Island suspected of being dissatisfied or in collaboration with the underground. There were not enough jails to hold them so they were rounded up and thrown into heavily guarded public halls, theaters, schools, warehouses and ball parks. A few weeks before the landing, the principal resistance leaders were arrested due to an unexpected random event while holding a meeting to coordinate urban operations.[37] Before the fight on the beaches was over, all of them had been executed by firing squad; they died young with the dream of freedom still warm in their hearts.

The returning B-26s landed at Puerto Cabezas and began preparing for the second mission scheduled for 1:00 P.M., but just before the planes were due to take off; the pilots received the shocking order that the next four air strikes had been cancelled. The decision would have incalculable consequences in the coming battle. Castro's remaining planes (seven) had survived to fight another day. On hearing the outrageous order, Gustavo Ponzoa, a pilot that had scored successful hits in the Santiago mission and was ready to fly again, said bitterly to the American officer: "This is the end of the invasion."[38]

General Rafael del Pino, a pilot in Castro's air force during those historic days, wrote: "We never understood why they did not strike our bases in the following days. If they had hit us by air on the 16 and 17, we would probably have succumbed."[39] The original CIA plan called for 22 B-26 planes to strike twice on April 15, twice on the 16 and once on the 17 of April, the fifth strike to coincide with the Brigade landing at the Bay of Pigs. However, with Washington politicians desperately trying to hide U.S. involvement, the decisive air attacks were finally reduced to one raid carried out by eight lonely planes. The order to cancel the remaining air strikes was a misjudgment of critical importance that verged on utter incompetence.

The reason for canceling all remaining air missions was rooted in the low credibility of the cover story, which by midday on April 15 had been blown apart by Raul Roa, the clever Cuban ambassador in the United Nations. The cover story called for a B-26 to fly from Puerto Cabezas in Nicaragua to the U.S. naval base in Key West, where with holes in the plane's fuselage, the pilot would impersonate a Castro defector who was part of a rebellion in the Cuban Air Force. A second B-26 seriously damaged in the actual attack had to make an emergency landing at Miami International Airport. But there was a crucial difference between the adversary's planes. The Brigade B-26 had solid metal noses, while the noses on Castro's B-26s were made of plastic. This major difference went unnoticed by the planners of the cover story — a huge mistake. At the U.N., Raul Roa accused Washington of direct aggression against Cuba.

In his answer, Adlai E. Stevenson, the distinguished U.S. Ambassador to the United Nations said: "These pilots and certain other crew members have apparently defected from Castro's tyranny"... "These two planes, to the best of our knowledge, were Castro's own air force planes and, according to the pilots, they took off from Castro's own air force fields." Then Stevenson raised a photograph of one of the Brigades' planes and said: "The Cuban star and initials F.A.R "Fuerza Aerea Revolucionaria" are clearly visible."[40] Unaware of the whole truth, Stevenson believed what his own government was telling him.[41] The fact is that the respected statement was lying. The Cuban Ambassador pointed to the clearly visible differences between the planes and blew open the cover story. For Stevenson it was perhaps the most embarrassing moment of his honorable career. In the ensuing confusion, Dean Rusk recommended to the President the cancellation of the remaining air missions. The President agreed.[42] It was a fatal decision for establishing and holding a beachhead at the Bay of Pigs.

## THE DAYS OF COURAGE

The frogmen team went first. Their job was to place beach marking lights. Soon the fourth battalion waded onto Giron (Blue Beach) and captured the airfield.[43] The second battalion got ashore at Playa Larga (Red Beach) and began to secure the landing site. There was some sporadic resistance from the militia garrison, which was swiftly overcome, but before the militia retreated north, a radio message was sent informing that a large force was landing at the Bay of Pigs. During the early stage of the slow and difficult night landing, Jose San Roman, the Brigade's Commander, received an important message. It read: "Castro still has operational aircraft — expect you will be under attack at first light. Unload all men and supplies and take the ship to sea."[44]

The third and six battalions were able to land on time at Giron beach, but at sunrise, in Playa Larga, the fifth battalion had not landed yet and was still on the ship *Houston*. The first battalion flew into the beachhead at 6:00 a.m. This was an elite unit of paratroopers, commanded by Alejandro del Valle, a leader of boundless courage. The paratroopers were dropped in two areas, San Blas and Palpite, at the entrance of roads that cut across the swamps. Tactically these sites were to be strongholds for the beachhead's defense. The first drop at San Blas was right on target, but the one on "Palpite" overshot the landing area and the men came down in the swamps, which meant that in the early hours of D-Day, "Palpite" had not been secured by the paratroopers.

At 3:15 a.m., Fidel Castro was informed that a major landing was taking place at the Bay of Pigs. After examining the strategic conditions of the area, Castro decided to hit the beachhead with all available forces. Time was of the essence. A 900 militia unit stationed at the Australia Sugar Mill, near Playa Larga, was ordered to attack. It was followed by the Matanzas Officer School, the Ameijeiras Police Battalion and the Rebel Army Special Forces.[45] At 4:45 a.m., Castro called the airbase at San Antonio and instructed the few planes (7) that had survived the April 15 air raid to be prepared for immediate action. At 5:20 a.m., two Sea Fury fighters and one B-26 took off with orders to attack the ships at daybreak.[46] On the ground, the sugar mills of "Australia" and "Covadonga" became Castro's staging area. At these sites, he would concentrate all available troops, tanks and artillery for the offensive on the beachhead. His tiny air force was enough to provide protection for the massive troop concentration. From the "Australia," his forces would advance to "Playa Larga" through "Palpite" while from "Covadonga they would hit 'Girón' by way of "San Blas,"[47]

The land battle began early in the morning of April 17. The Playa Larga front was led by Erneido Oliva, a charismatic officer of African descent, a man of great personal courage, who was second in command of the Brigade. He had few available men for the fight ahead. Without the paratroopers who were dropped on the swamps and the fifth battalion, which was still on board of *Houston*, Oliva could only count on the 200 men of the second battalion. This was a small, highly trained elite force, led by Hugo Suiero, a brave warrior and a gentleman. By mid-morning, the Playa Larga front erupted in gunfire. It was the first wave of Castro's militia moving on trucks. The action was swift and terrible; the lead truck went up in flames and exploded. The militia battalion made a hasty retreat.[48]

In the air, the three Castro planes came roaring in at sunrise. The first target was the *Houston* followed by the escort ship *Barbara J.* The pilots failed to score on the ships and lost a B-26 to anti-aircraft fire, but the second air attack was successful and hit the *Houston* with their rockets. The ship began sinking fast and the captain ran her up the sand bottom at the west side of the bay, opposite the beachhead landing. The fifth battalion was still on board and the men were strafed by machinegun fire from the overhead planes as the survivors waded ashore.

In the "San Blas" front, ten miles north of Giron, Alejandro del Valle paratroopers and Roberto San Roman heavy weapons dug in at Covadonga road. They also established another stronghold on the secondary road to "Yaguaramas". A company of the third battalion was covering their right flank. Since noon, the San Blas front was under heavy artillery fire and Castro's militia, supported by tanks, launched several attacks which failed to pierce the San Blas defenses, but in the air, the Brigade B-26 were no match for the swift Sea Fury and T-33 Jet fighters. For Castro these few surviving planes did make the difference in the outcome of the battle. At the end, the Brigade lost eight B-26, or half of their attacking force.[49] Even though the pilots knew the odds, they kept flying in. A most heroic sacrifice.

With air supremacy, Castro's pilots kept up the relentless attacks on the beachhead, shooting down the Brigade's planes and hitting the ships in the bay. By 11:00 a.m., the *Rio Escondido* was sunk at the Giron landing site. It had been hit by a rocket, exploding in a huge ball of fire. The two remaining merchant ships, the *Caribe* and *Atlantico*, still loaded with weapons, food and ammunition, were ordered to move 12 miles off the Cuban coast, waiting for nightfall to make a dash onto the beach and unload precious supplies, but the civilian captains and sailors had seen enough fighting and steamed into the open sea, out of harms way, never to return.

Abandoned at the beach, the Brigade kept fighting with a rapidly diminishing supply of anti-tank and mortar shells. Without air cover, they had to do with whatever they had brought in the first hours of their landing. On the Playa Larga front, the night battle was fierce. The Castro militia displayed a powerful emotional commitment with their new messianic leader and kept charging the

Brigade trenches with terrible loses.

Castro's Chief of Operations at the Bay of Pigs, General Jose Ramon Fernandez, wrote: "That night we were turned back at Playa Larga despite the efforts of the militia Officer's School Battalion and other units… the Officers School suffered heavy casualties and the enemy also suffered important losses."[50]  Hayne Johnson, a Kennedy apologist, praised the courage and skill displayed at those desperate hours. He wrote: "For the Brigade to hold on that first day against overwhelming odds…was a tribute to the men… only two elements were missing, air cover and sufficient ammunition, to keep going.[51]

That night the ships that had the supplies failed to return.  At sunrise on April 18, a Castro tank was severely damaged and the crew surrendered. As it turned out, the tank's commander knew Oliva and told him: "you have put up one hell of a battle, Erneido, you have whipped a very large force and have hurt them badly.  I salute you.  But I must warn you, there is an even larger force coming, and they are going to power their way through yours."[52] By now, Oliva's small elite force was almost out of ammunition. He informed San Roman of the critical situation and was told to fall back from Playa Larga and to establish a new line of defense three miles north of Giron.  There they would make their last stand.

On the second day, the fight raged throughout the front lines. Castro's militia began moving on Playa Larga and down the beach road to Giron where Oliva had deployed men from the Second, Fourth and Sixth battalions.  At "San Blas", the army artillery launched a massive bombardment followed by several militia attacks with T-34 and Soviet tank support; however, the paratroopers, heavy weapons and  third battalion held their ground. Again the militia failed to pierce the bloody strongholds at "San Blas," but short of ammunitions, Del Valle knew that the end was near.

In a desperate attempt to destroy the vital remnants of Castro's planes, President Kennedy ordered an air raid to be launched in the early hours of April 18. Before daybreak, six Brigade's B-26 flew into eastern Cuba to hit the air bases near Havana, but a heavy ground haze covered the target area and made it impossible for the pilots to find the airfields. Gonzalo Herrera, a pilot of unlimited courage, turned on the lights of his plane and even lowered his landing gear to draw the attention of the antiaircraft battery, but they held their fire. The raid failed and Castro's planes survived once again.[53]

Just after midnight of the third day, still dressed in black ties from a gala affair, President Kennedy and some cabinet members met at the White House with Admiral Burke and other military and CIA officers to discuss the use of American planes in those desperate hours to secure air supremacy over the beachhead. Again, Dean Rusk spoke against U.S. direct involvement, while Admiral Burke insisted in the use of Navy jets to gain control of the air over the beachhead. After a heated debate, Kennedy agreed to allow Navy fighters off the carrier *Essex*, on duty near the Bay of Pigs, to provide one hour of air cover for Brigade B-26 as they attacked Castro's forces near the beach. The time for the air cover was set from 6:30 to 7:30 a.m. What followed was a tragic mistake.

It appears that the CIA officer in charge of the Cuban Task Force, Jack Esterline, got confused with the time difference between Puerto Cabezas and the Bay of Pigs since they were in different time zones. In the confusion, the three Brigade B-26 arrived at the target area one hour ahead of the Navy jets air cover. Four American advisors that had volunteered to fly in two of the B-26 were shot down over Giron by Castro's jets. The only survivor was the undefeatable Gonzalo Herrera, who stroke the militia gathering at "San Blas". He returned to Puerto Cabezas with 38 bullet holes in his B-26 fuselage and one engine out. Gonzalo Herrera was the last Brigade pilot to fly into the Bay of Pigs.[54] His lone air strike at "San Blas" had a kind of a catharses effect on the almost beaten defenders. With defeat looming ever closer, the 22-year-old Alejandro del Valle, Commander of the paratroopers, got on top of one of his two remaining tanks and ordered his men and those of the Third battalion to attack. Without any hope of victory and few remaining bullets, they went forward. It was a hopeless heroic charge.[55]

The end was swift. For three days of courage, abandoned at the beachhead, the Brigade fought with great skill and boundless determination. San Roman's last message read: "Tanks closing on Blue Beach (Giron) from North to East. They are firing directly at our headquarters… out of ammunitions… I am destroying my radio now," [56] then silence. The tragedy at the Bay of Pigs was over.

Pedro Roig

# CHAPTER XIX

# THE BAY OF PIGS TRAGEDY

---

[1] Piero Gleijeses. *Ships in the Night: The CIA, The White House and the Bay of Pigs.* (*Journal of Latin American Studies*, Feb. 1995), 142

[2] Graystone Lynch. *Decision for Disaster* (Washington: Brassey's, 2000),14

[3] CIA, Briefing, Cuba, February 17, 1960.

[4] CIA, Memorandum for the Director, by Abbot Smith, Acting Chairman, Board of National Estimates, 2-11-96

[5] Haynes Johnson. *The Bay of Pigs* (New York: Norton Company, 1964), 37.

[6] Memorandum of conference with the President, 03-16-60; CIA, A Program of Covert Action against the Castro regimen, 03-16-60.

[7] Johnson, op cit, 27

[8] Gleijeses, "Ships in the Night...", 30.

[9] Gleijeses, op cit, 10

[10] CIA, Classified Message, Oct. 31, 1960.

[11] Gleijeses, op cit, 11.

[12] Lynch, opcit, 25

[13] Ibid., 24-25

[14] Lynch, op cit, 23

[15] Allen Dulles. Memorandum for General Maxwell Taylor, 06-01-61.

[16] CIA Memorandum for Chief WH-4, Policy Decision Required for conduct of strike operations against government of Cuba, 1-4-61.

[17] The White House, meeting in the cabinet room 9:45 A.M., January 19, 1961.

[18] Mc George Bundy. Memorandum of Discussion on Cuba, Cabinet Room, January 28, 1961.

[19] Ibid.

[20] R.O. Drain, Memorandum for Record 01-30-61.

[21] Mc George Bundy. Memorandum from the President's Special Assistant for National Security Affairs to President Kennedy, 02-08-61.

[22] Arthur Schlesinger Jr.. Memorandum from the President's Special Assistant to President Kennedy, 02-11-61

[23] Mann. The March 1960 Plan, 02-15-61.

[24] Bundy to JFK, 02-18-61.

[25] The Military build up in Cuba, 07-11-61.

[26] Joint Chief of Staff. Memorandum for the Secretary of Defense, U.S. Plan of Action in Cuba, 01-27-61

[27] Lynch, op cit, 38

[28] Ibid.

[29] Schlesinger, op cit, 471

[30] Johnson, op cit, 82

[31] Lunch, op cit, 65

[32] Lynch, op cit, 42

[33] Bissell, op cit, 183

[34] Eduardo Ferrer. *"Operación Puma"*, Miami, 1975, 154.

[35] Jonson, op cit, 90

[36] Rafael del Pino. *Proa a la Libertad.* (El Planeta, 1991), 86-87

[37] Ros, op cit, 215

[38] Gustavo Ponzoa. Interview for TV Marti Documentary "En Nombre de la Libertad: Historia de Bahía de Cochinos", 04-13-2005.

[39] Del Pino, op cit, 81

[40] Johnson, op cit, 92

[41] Lynch, op.cit., 76.

[42] Bissell, op cit, 184

[43] Lynch, op.cit., pg. 88

[44] Ibid.

[45] Quintin Pino Machado, *La Batalla de Giron* (Habana: Editorial Ciencias Sociales, 1983), 72-3.

[46] Ibid, 74-78

[47] There were other marginal and difficult tails to the target areas.

[48] Lynch, op cit, 101

[49] Ferrer, op cit, 216

[50] Fidel Castro y Jose Ramon Fernandez. *Playa Giron.* (Editorial Pathfinder, New York, 2001)

[51] Johnson, op cit, 127

[52] Lynch, op cit, 104

[53] Ibid, 126

[54] Ibid, 129

[55] Johnson, op cit, 157

[56] Lynch, op cit, 131

# CHAPTER XX

# *"I AM A MARXIST..."*

*Fidel Castro*

# *THE CUBAN MISSILE CRISIS*

*KRUSHCHEV'S MISTAKEN PERCEPTION OF KENNEDY'S METTLE – EXODUS AND EXILE – NIKITA'S DANGEROUS BLUFF: THE CUBAN MISSILE CRISIS – CASTRO'S SOCIAL ENGINEERING: "EL HOMBRE NUEVO" – CASTRO VS KENNEDY.*

## *KRUSHCHEV'S MISTAKEN PERCEPTION OF KENNEDY'S METTLE*

The defeat of the Cuban Brigade was a monumental failure for the Kennedy Administration, especially in the context of the Cold War confrontation. In Moscow, Nikita Khrushchev saw in the Bay of Pig operation a confused and hesitant superpower, led by an indecisive President who could cave in under pressure. Anatoly Dobrynin, the Soviet Ambassador to the United States, believed that Khrushchev's perception of Kennedy was shaped by the lack of resolve shown by the President during those crucial days in Cuba. The Soviet Ambassador, regarding Khrushchev's view of Kennedy, wrote: "That after the failure of the American backed invasion of Cuba by exile forces, the American president would yield to his pressure."[1]

On July 3-4, 1961, the leaders of the two superpowers met in Vienna. At the summit, according to Ambassador Dobrynin, Khrushchev displayed "an aggressive almost threatening tone..."[2] Kennedy was shocked by Khrushchev's behavior. For Professor Graham T. Allison: "Kennedy had worried both after the Bay of Pigs and after the Vienna meeting with Khrushchev, that the Chairman might have misjudged his mettle"[3] From then on, he believed that the threats were serious and a military confrontation with Russia was possible, but the Kremlin leadership was not seeking a war with the U.S. they knew they could not win.

Khrushchev was counting on Kennedy's indecisiveness under pressure as shown during the Bay of Pigs crisis. The Soviet leader was simply "bluffing"[4] — a most dangerous game which brought the world to the brink of a nuclear catastrophe.

In Washington, Robert Kennedy was acutely aware of the dangerous consequences to U.S.–Soviet relations, inherited from the Bay of Pigs disaster. On April 19, as the Brigade fought their last desperate hours, Robert Kennedy sent a memo to the President warning that "if we don't want Russia to set missile bases in Cuba, we better decide now what we are willing to do to stop it...the time has come for a showdown, for in a year or two years the situation will be vastly worse."[5] A brilliant and courageous character, Robert Kennedy was right on target. He understood the dangers posed by a Soviet miscalculation of their strategic options and saw the imminent threat of the deployment of nuclear missiles in Castro's Cuba — remarkable foresight.

On December 1, 1961, barely seven months after the defeat of the invasion, Castro announced to the World the defining ideology of his revolution. Glowing in his victory over Washington, the Cuban dictator stated: "I am a Marxist-Leninist and shall remain a Marxist-Leninist until the day I die."[6] Castro himself made it official. Cuba was a communist state. Lenin was the ideological inspiration and Stalin, the political model.

But with his statement "I am a Marxist", Castro confirmed Washington's fears that the Island, ninety miles from the U.S. shores, was moving ever closer into the Soviet military orbit and that the deployment of nuclear missiles could be in the Kremlin's secret agenda. The Kennedy Administration was facing basically the same threat and similar fear, which had led to the creation of the Cuban Brigade and which ended in a bloody tragedy, but now the Russians' presence in Cuba was perceived as a real direct threat to U.S. national security.

In February 1962, the Joint Chiefs of Staff established a first priority plan for completion of all contingency plans for military operations against the communist Island.[7] Robert Kennedy was placed in charge of overall supervision of the clandestine undertaking known as Operation Mongoose, drafted by General Maxwell Taylor, a World War II hero. Again, Cubans were to be used in the covert missions, including attempts to assassinate

Castro. Operation Mongoose was predicated on the premise that: "final success will require decisive U.S. military intervention." President Kennedy was briefed on the guidelines on March 16, 1962.[8]

## *EXODUS AND EXILE*

But as Castro moved swiftly to establish his communist state, the Cuban economy began to fail, creating the need to ration food and consumer goods, which would continue during the long years of Castro's unshakable grip on power. The Cuban revolution led by the Marxist Messiah was proudly on the march to a colossal economic disaster. Meantime, after the Bay of Pig's tragedy, most of the Cuban middle class went into exile. Between December of 1960 and October of 1962, more than 45,000 children were sent alone to the United States by their parents, on air flights known as "Operation Pedro Pan" (Operation Peter Pan). In October of 1965 more than three thousand Cubans flee through the Camarioca port in Matanzas. Between December of 1965 and April of 1973, the "Vuelos de la libertad" (Freedom Flights), the largest air bridge of immigrants in the history of the United States with 3,049 flights, helped 280,000 Cubans escape Cuba. In April, 1980, approximately ten thousand Cubans enter the Peruvian Embassy in Havana and solicit political asylum. An internal crisis engulfs the island nation which results in the exodus known as Mariel. More than 125 thousand people abandon the island by boat to the United States. Ten of thousands have fled the Island through the sea in precarious rafts and small boats. It is undetermined how many have perished in their attempt to escape during these years, but by the summer of 1962, over 200,000 Cubans had escaped Castro's communist debacle.

It was at this stage that the other Cuba began to blossom in South Florida as a source of economic success. The wealth producing Cuba was not crushed by Castro's revolution, but went on to U.S. shores and through many years of hard work created in South Florida a financial emporium. Under the leadership of Jorge Mas Canosa, the Cuban exile community also became a powerful presence among Washington's bipartisan political institutions. At the dawn of the Twenty First Century, the wealth producing Cuba, of nearly one million people, was generating 36 billion dollars a year as compared with Castro's communist state of 6 billion dollars[9] — a tribute to the fiercely enterprising and hardworking Cubans, who, given the right institutional environment, were able to become one of the most successful immigrations in U.S. history.

## NIKITA'S DANGEROUS BLUFF:
## "THE CUBAN MISSILE CRISIS"

The idea of placing nuclear missiles in Cuba dawned on Khrushchev while vacationing in the Crimea, across the Black Sea from Turkey, where the U.S. had deployed the "Jupiter" missiles[10]. Turkey occupies the Asia Minor region known in antiquity as "Anatolia" and a European enclave where Constantinople, present day Istambul, is located just across the Dardanelle Strait. Turkey is bounded by the Russian Republics of Georgia and Armenia, and shared with Russia the shores of the Black Sea. In 1953, during the Cold War, Turkey became a close U.S. ally and joined the North Atlantic Treaty Organization (NATO). It also deployed the "Jupiter" nuclear missiles right next to the Soviet Union. By 1961, according to Robert Kennedy: "The President had asked the State Department to reach an agreement with Turkey for the withdrawal of the "Jupiter" missiles in that country. They were clearly obsolete and the "Polaris" submarines in the Mediterranean would give Turkey far greater protection[11].

But, according to *The New York Times'* columnist, James Reston, the Soviet leader believed that Kennedy was "an inexperienced young leader who could be intimidated and blackmailed."[12] In his autobiography, Khrushchev wrote: "My thinking went like this: if we installed the missiles secretly and then if the U.S. discovered the missiles after they were already poised and ready to strike, the Americans would think twice before trying to liquidate our installations by military means."[13] Initially Mikoyan and Gromyko, two important politburo members, were hesitant but eventually they went along with deploying the nuclear missiles in Cuba.

Castro was approached by the newly appointed Soviet ambassador in Havana, Aleksandr Alexeyev. Castro welcomed the idea: "that is a very bold move...but if making such a decision is indispensable for the socialist camp, I think we will agree to the deployment of Soviet missiles on our island. May we be the first victims of a showdown with the United States imperialism."[14] The architect of the "Moncada" bloodbath was ready for a large audience. The world was now the stage for his glorious apocalyptic sacrifice. Castro was ready for the final showdown.

All together, the Soviets began the construction of several sites for medium-range missiles, capable of reaching urban American targets up to the Canadian border, dozens of heavy bombers, and a combat force of over forty thousand men. On October 14, a U-2 aircraft spotted and photographed the launching sites. Two days later, McGeorge Bundy informed the President that the Soviets were deploying missiles in Cuba. The most dramatic event of the Cold War began to unfold. On October 22, 1962, President Kennedy addressed the nation in a televised speech. He stated that the Soviet Union was deploying nuclear missiles in Cuba and announced as one of his first measures, a "strict quarantine of all offensive military equipment being shipped to the Island." The young President was standing firm and ready for a direct confrontation.

Professor Allison addressed several issues that hardened John Kennedy's resolve to stand up to Khrushchev's nuclear threat: "For this President, nothing short of forceful response would suffice. To fail to act forcibly would undermine the confidence of the members of this administration...destroyed his reputation with all but few members of Congress...created public distrust of his words and encourage friends and foes of the United States abroad to doubt his courage and commitments"[15] Khrushchev had misunderstood Kennedy's readiness to negotiate, with character weakness. A mistake.

The Soviet Premier knew that his boisterous claim of nuclear superiority was not based on facts. During the missile crisis, Khrushchev stated that Russia was producing nuclear rockets like sausages. On this point, his son Sergei, working at a rocket design project, later told this amusing story: He said that he asked his father "How can you say we are producing rockets like sausages...we don't have any rockets." To which his father answered: "that's all right. We don't have any sausages either."[16] The Russian leadership knew the facts too well. On this issue, Ambassador Dobrynin wrote: "at the time the balance of strategic forces favored the U.S....Khrushchev hoped to redress the nuclear balance by moving our intermediate range missiles to a point from which they could strike the U.S."[17] The Russian Ambassador believed that Khrushchev had been bluffing all along. He pointed to the fact that in Moscow "no one ever thought of the possibility of a military confrontation with the United States. That was absolutely excluded from our plans."[18]

But Khrushchev's bluff was dangerous. As Soviet ships began approaching the quarantine zone, 500 miles around the Island, protected by the American Navy with specific orders not to allow the Russians ships to reach Cuba, a violent clash became a distinct possibility. By the time of Kennedy's speech to the nation, on Monday, October 22, the ships were a few days away from reaching the quarantine line. On October 23, Khrushchev received a message from the American president requesting that the ships bound for Cuba not enter the quarantine zone in order to avoid a direct confrontation. Khrushchev replied: "any violations of freedom of the sea were to be considered as an act of aggression which pushes mankind towards the abyss of nuclear missile war."[19] That evening at a Russian Embassy reception in Washington, a high-ranking Russian General suggested that the ships' captains heading for Cuba were under orders to defy the quarantine zone.[20]

Early that night, in a televised speech addressed to the Cuban people, Fidel Castro denied the presence of offensive missiles in Cuba and went on to openly challenge President Kennedy's stated position that the deployment of nuclear missiles in Cuba was an unacceptable threat to U.S. national security. Castro said in defiance to Kennedy: "We will acquire the arms we feel like acquiring and we don't have to give an accounting to the imperialist."[21]

Late on Tuesday, October 23, as the Soviet ships continued to approach the quarantine zone, Robert Kennedy met with the Russian Ambassador in Washington, Anatoly Dobrynin. Kennedy was direct and to the point. The U.S. was ready to go into a major conflict on the issue of the deployment of nuclear missiles in Cuba. According to his memoirs, Dobrynin "conveyed all of Robert Kennedy's harsh statement to Moscow." Initially there was no reply from the Kremlin. The Soviet leadership was paralyzed and deeply confused. The Americans had called the bluff. The Soviet Ambassador described Kremlin's leadership as being enveloped in "total bewilderment".[22]   Next day, October 24, the Cuban Missile Crisis reached its climax.  The Russian ships were about to enter the quarantine zone and naval intelligence reported that a Soviet submarine had joined the ships.  The aircraft carrier *U.S.S. Essex*, a veteran of the Bay of Pigs, was ordered to make the first interception.  The showdown was fast approaching.  We know today that the Soviets were not going to war over Cuba, but at the time the outlook for a nuclear confrontation seemed very real.

The first sign that the Russian leadership was caving in began to appear by midmorning on Wednesday, October 24.  It came to the White House in an urgent intelligence message indicating that several Russian ships near the quarantine line had stopped.  At 5:15 p.m., a Defense Department spokesperson announced publicly that some of the Russian ships proceeding toward Cuba were changing their course and turning back.[23]   On hearing the first intelligence report, Dean Rusk said to McGeorge Bundy:  "We're eyeball to eyeball and think the other fellow just blinked."[24]   But still a negotiated settlement had not yet been resolved.  The Russian missiles were still on Cuban 90 miles from the U.S. and Kennedy wanted them out.

On Thursday, October 25, in a briefing at the White House, the CIA indicated that some of the missiles deployed in Cuba were operational.[25]   Kennedy ordered the loading of multistage nuclear weapons on aircraft in Europe.  Also military targets were identified in Cuba that included three massive air strikes per day until Castro's air capability was destroyed.[26]   The next Friday, October 26, Kennedy authorized the Sate Department to prepare for the establishment of a civil government in Cuba, after the invasion and military occupation of the Island.[27]

That night in Havana, Castro went to the Soviet Embassy and stayed there until 5:00 a.m. on Saturday, October 27.  He was deeply upset by the lack of information as to Khrushchev's stance in face of an imminent U.S. invasion.[28]  According to official Soviet documents and Nikita Khrushchev's memoirs, Castro sent a message in which the Cuban Marxist leader, in his recurrent apocalyptic conviction, requested a pre-emptive nuclear attack on the U.S. It was madness.[29]  In a letter to Khrushchev dated October 26, Castro stated: "The Soviet Union must never allow the circumstances in which the imperialists could launch the first nuclear strike…that would be the moment to eliminate such danger forever."[30] Khrushchev rejected Castro's nuclear war request. On this issue, Dobrynin said that "far from stiffening Khrushchev's resolve, this merely confirmed him in his determination to seek a compromise."[31]

But Castro was anxious for a fight and ordered Cuban anti-aircraft units to open fire on all U.S. reconnaissance planes flying over the Island. Around noon on Saturday 27, a U-2 plane was shot down over Cuba and its pilot killed. It is known today that the order was given by a Soviet general stationed in Cuba, but at the time it was viewed as a provocation to escalate the crisis.

Late Saturday night, Robert Kennedy went to see Dobrynin. It turned out to be the decisive meeting. With the urgency of preventing catastrophe, the American and the Russian worked out a formula for a peaceful negotiation of the crisis. The Soviet leadership was looking for a face-saving settlement. Under pressure of an imminent U.S. invasion of Cuba, Khrushchev told Politburo members: "Comrades, now we have to look for a dignified way out of this conflict."[32] Robert Kennedy put forward his brother's administration formula that proved to be the final solution. He proposed the gradual removal of American missiles in Turkey for the immediate withdrawal of all Russian missiles and bombers in Cuba. Dobrynin immediately informed Khrushchev. In his memoirs, the Soviet Premier stated that Robert Kennedy's offer was the turning point of the crisis.[33]

Dobrynin, a highly respected diplomat, wrote: "At 4 p.m. on Sunday, October 28, I received an urgent cable from Gromyko. It read: 'Get in touch with Robert Kennedy at once and tell him that you have couriered the content of your conversation with him to N.S. Khrushchev, who herewith gives the following urgent reply: the suggestion made by Robert Kennedy on the President's instructions are appreciated in Moscow. The President's message of October 27 will be answered on the radio today, and the answer will be highly positive'". Robert Kennedy insisted that the basis for exchange was to remain secret for several years. He also pledged not to invade Cuba.

It was evident that Nikita's bluff had failed and the nuclear missiles were removed from Cuba without consulting Fidel Castro. The Cuban Marxist dictator was publicly humiliated and his reaction against the Russian leader was violent and full of eschatological remarks. He cursed Khrushchev as a traitor and coward. The editor of *Revolution*, Carlos Franqui, recalled Castro screaming widely:"Son of a bitch, homosexual fagot"[34] He was out of control. The two super powers had relegated him to the marginal role of a disposable pawn, but at the end he would survive in power much longer than the two world leaders. Kennedy would be assassinated a year later and Khrushchev sacked as Prime Minister within two years. Unknown at the time, Castro was the winner of the missile crisis. As professor Suchliki aptly said: "It is ironic that the crisis, hailed as a U.S. victory, was nothing more than an ephemeral victory. In return for the removal of offensive weapons from the Island, the United States was satisfied to accept a communist regime only a few miles from its shores."[35]

## *CASTRO'S SOCIAL ENGINEERING:*
## *"EL HOMBRE NUEVO"*

Secured by the U.S. non-invasion commitment with Moscow, Castro began to implement his vision of a vanguard Marxist state to spearhead the struggle against American imperialism and the market economy. Under his watchful eyes, revolutionary Cuba became a dogmatic State in the Stalin model and Torquemada's tradition. In his quest for social engineering, Castro sought to sweep aside the pre-revolutionary influence of capitalism, as a source of individual greed and selfishness, so as to build a new individual," "El hombre Nuevo,"[36] re-educated in the Marxist-Leninist doctrine. Cuba's new messiah believed that the state could re-shape human behavior. It was social engineering with the inescapable horrors of unmitigated human suffering dressed up in the tragic myth of Marxism. An appealing and thoroughly dysfunctional dogma.

The new Cubans were to be non-materialistic, selfless, disciplined and obedient citizens meant to serve the common good. All other pleasures and desires for individual happiness and freedoms were to be repressed and silenced. The new Cubans were now soldiers of the State and servants of the revolution, ready to die in the struggle against capitalism and pluralistic democracy. According to "Che" Guevara, a good revolutionary had to hate the enemy. In his message to the "Tri-continental" meeting in Havana, Guevara said to the cheering crowd, "The hate as a fighting factor, the intransigent hate for the enemy, which goes beyond the human limitations and transforms it in an effective, violent and cold killing machine."[37]

In the new Cuba, only the "will of the people" framed within the state-oriented vision of the *Maximo lider* was to be accepted as the gospel of the revolution, the cult of redemption through violence and hate. In these circumstances there were many efforts to re-educate Cubans in Castro's Marxist regimen, among which the Military Units to Improved Production, UMAP, became the most terrible tool of the brutal application of social engineering to transform homosexuals and political dissidents into self-scarifying revolutionaries. Thousands of homosexuals were sent into[38] barbarian camps of forced labor.

Norberto Fuentes, one of the outstanding writers of the revolution and a close associate of Fidel and Raul Castro, up until the trial and execution of General Ochoa in 1989, wrote:...The government had at its disposition concentration camps and filled them with tens of thousands of bewildered young men who were sentenced to serve specifically because they were homosexuals... concentration camps is not used metaphorically; these concentration camps were pieces of land surrounded by electrified fences, watch towers, searchlights, and dogs, where famished slaves were forced to live in overpopulated barracks.[39]

The new communist Cuba was also full of grandiose commitments, some were impracticable, and others outrageous like the promise of milk production. In March 2, 1964, Castro said: "within ten years we will have milk production superior to that of Holland and cheese production superior to that of France."[40] By 1970 milk was strictly rationed and available only to children under seven years. There were empty promises and failed commitments. However, by 1970 there were still millions of Cubans who continued to be mesmerized by Castro's charismatic and emotional spell. It was a march into chaos and the Cubans went flag-waving and chanting revolutionary slogans, into an economic and institutional disaster, the worst in Cuba's history.

Pedro Roig

## CASTRO VS KENNEDY

They were the political antithesis of each other. While Castro proposed the collective veneration of the Marxist dogma, the total control of the State over individual rights, the use of revolutionary violence to protect his absolute power from the challenge of critics and dissidents, Kennedy was the exaltation of individual freedom, enshrined in his commitment for "Human Rights". The youngest president of the United States stated in his inaugural address: "The torch had been passed to a new generation of Americans... unwilling to witness or permit the slow undoing of those human rights to which this nation has always been committed, and to which we are committed today at home and around the world.". Kennedy was to become the champion of civil rights and individual freedoms, at home and throughout the world, while Castro was the essence of the Orwellian "big brother" totalitarian state. The clash was unavoidable.

On the issue of opening a dialogue with Kennedy's administration, Castro repeatedly said that his Marxist revolution was not negotiable. In his May 1, 1961 speech, Castro said: "No, sir...the Cuban people are charged with establishing the social, economic, and political regime which they see fit and they do not accept debate on this especially, with the government of the United States...therefore this is not open to discussion. They are deluded if they think we will debate these topics."[41]

On Christmas eve, December 24, 1962, after the Kennedy administration paid $53 million in food and medicine, the Cuban Brigade was freed from Castro's prisons and returned to Miami to a heroes' welcome. Two days later, a small group of the Brigade officers, led by Artime, Oliva and San Roman, drove from Miami to West Palm Beach for dinner with Kennedy and his wife Jacqueline. Later in the evening, the President and his guests held a press conference where it was announced that the President would go to Miami on December 29 to meet and talk with the men of the Cuban Brigade at the Orange Bowl.

During the Palm Beach press conference, Oliva, the courageous Executive Commander, announced that the President would be presented with the Brigade's gold and blue banner, which had flown at the beachhead during the three days of fierce fighting and which was smuggled out of Cuba by a survivor who avoided being captured and succeeded in reaching a friendly embassy in Havana. Oliva said at the press conference: "We will be giving President Kennedy the greatest treasure we possess at the present time."[42]

On a warm Saturday, December 29, 1962, the President and the First Lady entered the Orange Bowl stadium to a tumultuous welcome by over 40,000 cheering exiles. On the field the Cuban Brigade, dressed in khaki uniforms, stood at attention while a military band played the U.S. and Cuban national anthems. Then, "Pepe" San Roman went forward, saluted the President and said: "Mr. President, the men of the 2506 Brigade give you their banner". Kennedy unfurled the flag and made a promise to the Cubans. "I can assure you that this flag will be returned to the Brigade in a free Havana."[43] It was a promise of freedom cut short by the bullet of a self-professed pro-Castro assassin.

For John and Robert Kennedy, the Bay of Pigs tragedy became a personal issue. That day, in a public forum, the young American president committed himself to the freedom of Cuba. To the veterans of the Cuban brigade, he said: "Your conduct and valor are proof that although Castro and his fellow dictators may rule nations, they do not rule people; that they may destroy the exercise of liberty but they cannot eliminate the determination to be free."[44]

On January 2, 1963, Castro went on a rampage against Kennedy. Speaking at a rally at the Revolution's Plaza, Castro said in reference to Kennedy's promise to the Brigade: "what was the President of the United States demeanor, it was that of a pirate, this Kennedy is quite insidious" and again Castro addressed the issue that there was too much blood between his revolution and the Kennedy Administration for a dialogue. Castro said:. "Mr. Kennedy there is too much blood between us, there is an abyss of blood…but more that blood there is an abyss which separates our ideals".[45] Then, Castro went on with a threat that in a nuclear war, New York could be turned into Hiroshima. [46]

True to his promise, the President placed his brother, the Attorney General, in charge of the new plan to overthrow Castro, not to be confused with "Operation Mangoose," which was cancelled soon after the missile crisis. In January 1963, Robert Kennedy met privately with Oliva and Artime at his Hickory Hill Estate in Virginia. The *Miami Herald* journalist, Don Bohening, researched the Kennedy Administration's commitment to support the Brigade veterans in their fight for freedom. In April 2000, Bohening interviewed Oliva on the issue of the Hickory Hill meeting with the Attorney General and wrote: "The meeting was the genesis for Artime's $6 million program of paramilitary operations against Cuba from Nicaragua and Costa Rica. Oliva was until the end of the program, in charge of the military side...serving as liason with the Secretary of the Army, Cyrus Vance and his aid Alexander Haig. It was also agreed at the Hickory Hill meeting, said Oliva, to constitute a Cuban unit within the U.S. Army, bringing together all those Cuban-born soldiers, and then numbering several thousands, that would eventually work in collaboration with the Artime force to facilitate the liberation of Cuba."[47] In essence, the Kennedy brothers were fully engaged in the fight against the Castro regime and it is evident that Robert Kennedy was the point person in the struggle to get rid of the Cuban dictator.

The profound dislike between Castro and the Kennedy's was mutual. On September 8, 1963, ten weeks before Lee Harvey Oswald, a militant Castro supporter, murdered the President in Dallas, Fidel Castro spoke at a reception in the Brazilian Embassy in Havana: "We are prepared to fight them and answer in kind. The United State leaders must realize that if they assist in the terrorist plans to eliminate Cuban leaders, they themselves will be in danger." Then Castro added: "Kennedy is the Batista of our time".[48]

In 1966, journalist Georgi Anne Geyer interviewed Castro in Havana and after the meeting she wrote; "The picture he drew of how much he "liked" Kennedy was cynically calculated and far from true. Castro in truth hated John F. Kennedy. In his speeches, Castro made Kennedy into a monster. Billboards all over Havana derided and abused Kennedy and Castro had even threatened the American President."[49]

Today, the jury is still out on whether Fidel Castro planned and directed the death of John Kennedy, but there is too much evidence, including President Lyndon Johnson's certainty of Castro's involvement. In a TV interview with Howard K. Smith, President Johnson stated: "Well, Kennedy tried to get Fidel Castro, but Fidel Castro got Kennedy first".[50] For Oliva, the Afro-Cuban hero of the Bay of Pigs, Kennedy was: "The only President — excluding

Eisenhower — who did more than talk about getting rid of Castro".[51] Within a month after John Kennedy's death, President Johnson ordered Robert Kennedy to cancel the Cuban military program with the U.S. Army.[52] Never again would an American president try to implement a large scale exile operation to help liberate their homeland. The bullet that assassinated Kennedy also killed Cubans' best promise of freedom. The last major U.S. effort to free Cuba from Castro died with "Camelot".

# CHAPTER XX

## I AM A MARXIST...."    Fidel Castro

---

[1] Anatoly Dobrynin, *In Confidence* (New York: Random House, 1955), 44.

[2] Dobrynin, op.cit., 45.

[3] Graham T. Allison, Essence of Decision. (Harvard University. Little, Brown and Company. Boston, 1971), 194

[4] Ibid.

[5] Schlesinger, op.cit., 471.

[6] *Revolucion,* Deciembre 2, 1961

[7] U.S. CONARC, *Participation in the Cuban Crisis.* October 1963. pg. 17.

[8] Document G. Guidelines of Operation Mongoose, 03-14-62.

[9] Jorge Salazar Carrillo, "El Nuevo Herald". Septiembre 21, 2007, pg. 21ª.

[10] The Secret Cuban Missile Crisis Documents. CIA (Declassified). Introduction by Graham T. Allison. (Brassey's. New York, 1994), p VI.

[11] Robert F. Kennedy. *Thirteen Days: A Memoir of the Cuban Missile Crisis.* (Norton and Company. Paperback. New York, 1999), 71

[12] Geyer, op cit, 288

[13] Ibid .

[14] Dobrynin, op cit, 73

[15] Allison, op cit, 194

[16] Thomas C. Reed. *At the Abyss.* (Ballantine Books, New York, 2004), 95

[17] Dobrynin, op cit, 73

[18] Ibid, 45

[19] Ibid, 83

[20] *The Soviet Block Armed Forces and the Cuban Crisis: A chronology*, July-November 1962, 10-18-63, 50.

[21] Revolución, Octubre 24, 1961.

[22] Dobrynin. op, cit, 82-83

[23] Elie Abel. *The Missile Crisis* (Philadelphia, 1966), 153

[24] Document 36, McGeorge Bundy, Executive Committee Record of Action, 10-25-52

[25] Document 38, Mc George Bundy, Executive Committee Meeting Record Action, October 25, 1962, 5 P.M.  10-25-62

[26] The Air Force Response to the Cuban Crisis, 14 October-24 November 1962. ca. 1-63, 27-9.

[27] CINCLANT, Historical  Account of Cuban Crisis, 4-29-63, 56.

[28] Dobrynin, op cit, 85

[29] Document 45, Prime Minister Fidel Castro's letter to Premier Khrushchev, 10-26-62. Nikita Khrushchev, "Memorias", Vol. 2, Part 4, Guerra Fría, 521.

[30] The Cuban Missile Crisis, 1962. (Documents) Edited by Laurence Chang and Meter Kurnbluh. (The New Press, New York, 1992), 189

[31] Dobrynin, op cit, 85

[32] Ibid, 89

[33] Ibid.

[34] Franqui, "Retrato de Familia", op cit, 404

[35] Suchlicki, op cit, 169

[36] The New Men

[37] Ernesto Guevara, *Escritos y discursos* (Havana: Editorial de Ciencias Sociales, 1977), Vol. 9, 370.

[38] Raffy, op cit, 463

[39] Norberto Fuentes. *Dulces Guerreros Cubanos* (Barcelona: Editorial SEIX Barral, 1999), 322.

[40] *Hoy*, Febrero 3, 1964.

[41] *Revolucion*, Mayo 2, 1961

[42] Johnson, op cit, 343

[43] Ibid, 344

[44] Ibid, 345

[45] *Revolucion*, Enero 3, 1963

[46] Ibid.

[47] Don Bohening, *The Miami Herald.* April 16, 2000.

[48] Johnson, op cit, 354

[49] Geyer, op cit, 299

[50] Ibid, 301

[51] *The Miami Herald*, April 16, 2000.

[52] Ibid.

Pedro Roig

# CHAPTER XXI

# *CASTRO'S COMMUNIST AUTOCRACY: LIFE IN THE SHADOWS OF HOPELESSNESS*

*THE MINISTRY OF THE INTERIOR (MININT): THE MESSENGER OF FEAR – RAUL CASTRO AND THE ARMED FORCES' PYRAMID OF POWER – THE ARMY AND COMMUNIST PARTY – THE INTERNATIONALIST WARS – CASTRO AND TERRORISM – THE AFRICAN CAMPAIGN AND GENERAL ARNALDO OCHOA, "HERO OF THE REVOLUTION" – THE FAILURE AND THE BEGINNING OF THE END.*

Since 1959, Cuba was transformed into a nation at war. The American capitalistic empire was the enemy, and the fight was to the death. Under this premise, Cuba turned into a nation of soldiers, building a Marxist state led by Fidel Castro. With certain tactical variations, this political discourse was to be repeated until the end, when it became a meaningless exercise in futility, while all the while, the army remained the main source of power, stability and pride earned in the well-publicized internationalist campaigns. In an impoverished nation, exhausted by an endless war, controlled by the absolute will of one individual, it was a remarkable achievement that the army grew into an institution capable of surviving the failure of Castro's revolution.

## *THE MINISTRY OF THE INTERIOR (MININT): THE MESSENGER OF FEAR*

From his days in the Sierra Maestra, Castro knew that in the Cuban tradition, political power rested in the loyalty and control of the Army and the Security Forces. Within the first three months of his triumphal march into Havana, Castro wiped out the defeated army of the bourgeoisie republic and began the process of building his own Revolutionary Armed Forces. It is precisely here that we

335

see the profound differences with the Bolshevik Revolution where Lenin led the Communist Party to power and Stalin purged the Soviet army into submission. In contrast, Castro led his Rebel Army to power and turned the Cuban Communist Party into a political instrument of the Army and the Revolution.

On the issue of the decisive military influence in Cuba's political hierarchy of power, Professor Jorge I. Dominguez wrote: "Ruled in large part by military men who govern large segments of both military and civilian life, who are held up as paragons to both soldiers and civilians. Who are the bearers of the revolutionary tradition and ideology, who have politicized themselves by absorbing the norms and organization of the Communist Party and who have educated themselves to become professionals in political, economic, managerial, engineering and educational as well as military affairs."[1]

In October 1959, Raul Castro was appointed Minister of the newly created Revolutionary Armed Forces (MINFAR), and Fidel became Commander-in-Chief. From its inception, the new army was structurally integrated on a rigid hierarchical order, based on two fundamental requirements: loyalty and obedience to Fidel. The government had a pyramid structure, with Fidel at the top and his brother Raul a distant second. At the next level of power came the most trusted "comandantes" of the guerrilla war, proven by their unyielding obedience, "Che" Guevara, Ramiro Valdez, Camilo Cienfuegos and Juan Almeida among the select few.

From the very beginning, a repressive security apparatus was created under the Ministry of the Interior (MININT) to watch over the Armed Forces and the civilian population. The intelligence and security officers were trained by the East German Stassi and the Soviet KGB. MININT personnel served as Castro's enforcers and included several large units of elite troops. For the most part, they formed an efficient and brutal repressive force. The Minister of the Interior was a prominent member of Castro's inner circle of power. The MININT task was to capture, punish and destroy the enemies of the revolution. They were the messengers of fear.

Another important organization for vigilance, control and mass mobilization was the Committee for the Defense of the Revolution (CDR), a vital branch of the Ministry of the Interior, staffed mostly by members of the Communist Party. This paramilitary force was organized on every block of every city on the Island. Not even the Bolsheviks were capable of reaching that degree of vigilance and coercion at the street level. With over 4,800,000 members,[2] the CDRs effectively fulfilled their vigilance and mass mobilization duties. Fidel knew and praised the coercive value of the CDRs over civil society, especially their "vigilance duties." However, for Professor Horowitz, the "'Committee for the Defense of the Revolution' was a vicious and pernicious instrument of mass terror."[3]

The Territorial Militia Troops (MTT), under the MINFAR command, was a civilian paramilitary organization responsible for planning and deployment in defense of local areas. This force of part-time soldiers had been organized in several divisions with a total strength of one million men and women.[4] Poorly trained for combat, the MTT guns were never fired in anger and remained an expensive and wasteful tool in Castro's obsession with "The People's War".

## RAUL CASTRO AND THE ARMED FORCES' PYRAMID OF POWER

The MINFAR, led by Raul Castro, was the foundation of Fidel Castro's military dictatorship. Appointed in 1959, he was the longest-serving Minister of Defense in recent history. In February 2008, due to Fidel's deteriorated health, Raul Castro became the official Head of the Cuban Government. Until then, Raul Castro was perceived as a full-fledged Marxist, a harsh disciplinarian and a pragmatic administrator. Since the early revolutionary years, Raul looked up to Fidel with a mystic devotion and venerated him as a father figure, always willing to put up with Fidel's violent, abusive temper. During the difficult days of General Ochoa's trial and execution, Raul never flinched in his obedience to carry on Fidel's orders to kill General Ochoa, a highly respected front-line commander and "hero of the Revolution". Speaking to a gathering of generals in the MINFAR, on the issue of General Ochoa's execution, Raul said: "the most important symbol we have is named Fidel Castro... he is our father."[5]

It was impossible to be included in Cuba's military inner circle without Fidel's blessing. It is also a fact that Raul was recognized as the second most powerful leader of the Cuban revolution and his hold on the Armed Forces was a fundamental piece in understanding Fidel's narrow chain of command. In later years, a group of younger officers were added to the pyramid of military power: Abelardo Colome (Furry), Leopoldo Cintras, Senen and Julio Casas, Ramon Espinosa, Ulises Rosales del Toro, Joaquin Quintas Solá and Álvaro Lopez Miera. With the addition of these younger generals to the inner circle of power, MINFAR began the process of institutionalization and training in the professional model of the Soviet Armed Forces.

In essence, Cuba had been from 1959 a military dictatorship in a permanent state of war. For scholar Mark Falcoff, Castro's power "rests principally upon the loyalty and commitment of an officer class."[6] That became, in the words of Raul Castro: "The vanguard of the State."[7] Irving Louis Horowitz, Professor Emeritus at Rutgers University, wrote on the issue of the military rule: "The militarization of Cuba is a consequence of the inner history of the Cuban revolution; the personnel which made up the regime at the outset and continues to rule, has been military."[8]

## THE ARMY AND THE COMMUNIST PARTY

Fidel Castro rules Cuba as an autocrat with a fierce control over the Army, the Ministry of the Interior and the Communist Party. Under his messianic leadership, there was no room for dissent. There have been Cuban analysts who see the revolution as following the Soviet model of the Party in control of the government. However, in Castro's autocracy and a nation in a permanent state of war, the concept of an all-powerful party was unacceptable to the "Comandante en Jefe". Castro's Rebel Army officers brought him to power, grew in strength and professionalism with him and remained Castro's most trusted and loyal source of legitimacy and control of the Cuban government.

The Soviet and Cuban historiography offers profound differences between the roles of the Communist Party in both revolutionary processes. In 1917, Lenin led and established the Party as the center of power. After his death it took Stalin over eight years of a bloody internal struggle to gain total control of the Party and the government. Four leaders stood between him and absolute power: Trotsky, the founder of the Red Army; Kamenev, who ran the Moscow Party machinery; Bukharin, the most relevant ideologist; and Zinoviev, who led the Leningrad Party. By 1929, all of them had been executed or sent into exile. In contrast, Castro never faced a serious challenge from the Communist Party. From day one, he was the absolute ruler of Cuba and his power rested in the Armed Forces and not in the Party. Castro could have said like King Louis XIV of France, "I am the State".

Castro built the Cuban Communist Party (PCC) to manage the government bureaucracy, to serve in the Territorial Militia Troops (MTT) and to run the Committees for the Defense of the Revolution (CDR), but always under the watchful eyes of the Ministry of the Interior. One of the fundamental differences between the Cuban and the Soviet system— including the East European satellites — rested in the fact that from the beginning, Castro's inner circle of power was mostly made up of loyal members of the victorious Rebel Army and not from the Socialist Popular Party (PSP). Alvaro Alba, journalist and researcher of Soviet historiography, clearly points to the different roles of the Communist Party in the Soviet and Cuban revolutions. Alba said: "unlike the cases of Eastern Europe or the Soviet Union, in Cuba military power created political power, sustained it, substituted for it or eliminates it, as needed."[9] In Castro's Cuba, a nation at war, the Communist Party was established as a para-military institution in charge of administering the State's bureaucracy. As Alba notes: "The Communist Party was created by the governing elite in the mid 1960's... becoming to a great extent, the political instrument of the military."[10]

## THE AFRICAN CAMPAIGN AND GENERAL ARNALDO OCHOA. "HERO OF THE REVOLUTION"

From Bolivia to Ethiopia, from Angola to Viet Nam, from Nicaragua to Syria, the Cuban Army was engaged in most of the major conflicts of the last 40 years of the Twentieth Century, and it performed well. Actually the courage and skill displayed by the Cuban military in those missions are among the few sources of pride left to the failed Cuban revolution. For Fidel Castro, the internationalist campaign was his ticket to be able to forge a popular image in Third World countries, as a committed champion of the anti-colonialist struggle and a relevant player in the U.S.–Soviet confrontation during the final years of the Cold War.

Cuban soldiers were also surrogate fighters for the Kremlin and helped to pay, with their blood and sacrifice, the gigantic economic aid provided Cuba by the Soviet Union.

But at first, during the years 1962-1967, Castro displayed a policy independent from Moscow and followed his vision of turning the Andes Mountains into another Viet Nam, to fight the hated Americans in their own backyard. In open defiance to the USSR cautionary political approach, Castro actively supported the guerrilla movement in Latin America. During the First tri Continental Conference held in Havana in 1966, Castro re-affirmed his total commitment with the "War of Liberations". The Cuban leader believed that the time for a violent confrontation had arrived and he was to lead the international fight to final victory over the United States. "Che" Guevara shared with Castro his vision to create several guerrilla fronts in Third World counties. In Che's last message to the tri Continental, a few months before his death in Bolivia, he wrote: "How many Vietnams flourished throughout the World... Our every action is a battle cry against imperialism, and a battle hymn for the people united against the great enemy of mankind: the United States of America."[11] It was evident that the Cuban revolutionary leadership did share a pathological hatred of the United States. but by 1968, Guevara was dead and Cuba's sponsored guerrilla movement had failed.

Castro realized his mistake of trying to create an independent internationalist path and moved swiftly into the Soviet orbit. With the Cuban economy faltering, Castro realized the need for total realignment to fit into the perceived strength of the Soviets and Eastern European Marxist economies. The first sign of Castro's new "vision" of the path to victory was his public, passionate support of the 1968 Russian intervention in Czechoslovakia, to crush liberal changes implemented by Alexander Dubcek. It was a turning point in Castro's relation with the Soviets and they were pleased. By 1970, the Kremlin was providing massive economic and military aid to Cuba. This Moscow-Havana arrangement created the stage for Castro's army major intervention in Africa during the 1970's.

As a result of this close alliance, the Soviet Union began to train and modernize the FAR, improving its operational capabilities. By 1973, the Cuban Army was, according to Professor Phyllis Greene

Walker: "One of the most developed armed forces in the Third World."[12] That year, Castro broke off diplomatic relations with Israel and, as a show of defiance to the U.S. and Israel, sent a tank battalion to the Golan Heights in Syria during the Yon Kippur War.[13] By this time, Castro had turned into a militant supporter of Yasser Arafat. At the Non-Aligned movement meeting in Algeria, Castro denounced the "persecution and genocide being carried out by imperialism and Zionism against the Palestinian people,"[14] and later referred to Arafat as "a man we deeply love and admire and to whom we have always shown our solidarity."[15]

It is a well documented historical fact, the savage tortures inflicted upon American POW's in Vietnam by Cuban security officers. It all began in August of 1967[16] at a prison called "The Zoo", where Castro's interrogators established a program for testing new domination techniques so as to break down prisoners' will, into total submission.

In April 1999, the story of Castro officers' involvement in torturing American POW's in Vietnam came to light in the research book "Honor Bound".[17] Under the headline "Torture's aim was total surrender", *The Miami Herald* published the story on August 22, 1999. It read: "Almost daily for one year, the man the POW's called "Fidel" whipped them with strips cut from rubber tires until their buttocks hung in shreds… a Defense Department official has now reported that two North Vietnamese Army Colonels confirmed to him in 1992 that "Fidel" was indeed a Cuban and had tortured American POW's ."[18]

## CASTRO AND TERRORISM

The terrorist path was another venue for Castro's Internationalist War against the U.S. and was waged with fierce determination in every region of the World where the Americans and its allies appeared to be vulnerable. This warpath was in the context of his vision expressed during the "Sierra Maestra" guerrilla war. At the time, Castro said: "when this war is over, a much longer and greater war will begin for me: the war that I am going to wage against them (the Americans). I have come to realize that this is going to be my true destiny."[19] For Castro, the war against America was a lifelong commitment and Cuba became a sanctuary for terrorist training, supply of weapons and money.

Dariel Alarcón, known as "Comandante Benigno", a top-ranking officer in the FAR who fought alongside "Che" Guevara in Bolivia, escaped back to Cuba and later went into exile in France, said on the issue of foreign terrorists: "I had more than two thousand persons in training at the same time, in different parts of the country."[20]    Among the best-known terrorists that received training in Cuba was Ilich Ramirez Sanchez, known as "Carlos the Jackal".   He was trained at "Punto Cero," a school in urban terrorism.  By the time of his arrest in 1994, the "Jackal" had a long criminal career.  Jorge Masseti, a former Cuban intelligence officer, was with "The Jackal" at Punto Cero, training foreign terrorists in urban warfare.[21]  On July 11, 1975, *The New York Times* published the news that the French government had requested the expulsion of three Cuban diplomats because of their links with "Carlos the Jackal.[22]

From the 60's to the early 80's, Cuba was fully committed to supporting terrorist group: the "Tupamaros" in Uruguay, The Basque ETA in Northern Spain, the "Montonero" in Argentina, Yasser Arafat's "Al Fatah", the "Macheteros" in Puerto Rico, the Iranian surrogate "Hezbolah", and the Syrian forces in Lebanon and in Golan Heights.  In 1976, Raul Castro proudly said: "It is not a secret that in a time of danger and threat to the Syrian Republic our men were in Syria...[23]  On May 9, 2001, four months before the 9-11 terrorist attacks on New York and Washington, during a meeting with radical Muslim leaders in Iran, Fidel Castro stated; "The America regime is weak... the people of Cuba and Iran would put the U.S. on their knees."[24]

## THE INTERNATIONALIST WARS

In 1976, Castro decided to engage in the largest military action of his Internationalist Wars by sending over 36,000 troops to fight in Angola in support of the Marxist Popular Movement (MPLA). The Soviet leadership had approved the Cuban Army's involvement in Africa and provided the military hardware, including dozens of MiG-23 jet fighters and T-62 battle tanks.  In the African wars, Cubans earned a well-deserved reputation as a fine fighting force. By January 1978, with the full cooperation of the Soviet Union, Castro deployed several thousand troops to Ethiopia to turn back an invasion from Somalia.

General Arnaldo Ochoa, fresh from his successful campaign in Angola, was sent by Castro to lead the Cubans in Ethiopia. Ochoa fought a brilliant armored campaign, inflicting severe losses on the Somalian Army. The fact that some of Third World forces could be considered below the level of highly trained and disciplined military units did not detract from the professionalism and success achieved by the Cubans. According to Professor Juan del Aguila, "The Cubans did match up against the South African regulars in 1975-76."[25] For his military victories in Africa, General Ochoa was honored as a "Hero of the Revolution".

The "Internationalist Wars" dramatically increased Castro's image and political influence in the Third World. The late 1970's were the Cuban Marxist Dictator's best years. In 1976, a large Cuban army landed in Angola; in 1978, General Ochoa led the Cubans in Ethiopia. In 1979, the Marxist Maurice Bishop gained power in Granada and, with Castro's massive support, the Sandinistas took control of Nicaragua. That year Castro became the leader of the Non-Alignment Movement. It was a costly war — Cuba lost over 5,000 soldiers and wasted much needed economic aid from the Soviets. But they served to fulfill Castro's ambition for a major role on the global political stage. For professor Bethell, "The Cuban revolution burst on the world from a small Caribbean island to one of the central players in international affairs."[26]

Under Castro's vision of a nation at war with the United States and its allies, Cuba built the third largest army in the Western Hemisphere, after the U.S. and Brazil. It was well equipped by the Soviet Union and its Officer Corpse was trained in Soviet military doctrine at the Frunzen and Voroshilov Academies. It was a large army indeed. According to professor Bethell, "Relative to Cuba's population, the overseas army represented a larger deployment than that of the U.S at the peak of the Vietnam war."[27] A remarkable achievement, for a poor under developed country.

But the victories were short lived. By the late 1980's, the military and political success of the "Internationalist Wars" had vanished. The countries where the Cuban armies fought had turned away from communism. Especially bitter for Castro were the political changes taking place in Angola and Nicaragua which by the 1990's had evolved into multi-party democracies. It turned out to be a sad story in which the hero of the African campaign was courts-marshaled and sentenced to death. On July 1989, General Arnaldo Ochoa was labeled by Castro a traitor and executed — a tragic end to the "Internationalist Wars".

## THE FAILURE AND THE BEGINNING OF THE END

In 1960, Castro had freely chosen the communist system as a model to build a prosperous Cuba. His vision was predicated on the premises that in the Cold War confrontation, the USSR was to prevail over the United States and bury the market economy. In December 1975, at the First Congress of Cuba's Communist Party, Castro said: "The bankruptcy of the capitalistic economy had been confirmed by the inexorable prediction of Carl Marx,"[28] and at the Third Party Congress, he stated: "For its position as the first socialist country, for its enormous economic potential, its undoubted military might and its loyalty to the Marxist-Leninist principles and the proletariat internationalism, the USSR is a decisive contemporary force."[29]

But he was mistaken. Castro's ideological vision was faulty. It all came crashing down between 1989 and 1991, when the Soviet Union disintegrated. The fall of the Berlin Wall signaled the end of the Cold War and the historical victory of the U.S. and the market economy. What Castro had perceived as being on the wining side of the Cold War was now an unequivocal mistake. Communism had fallen into the abyss of its own fallacies. From the very beginning Castro was wrong fighting for a decrepit and dysfunctional dogma. The Cuban Revolution was a colossal failure and Cubans paid dearly for Castro's mistakes.

On July 31, 2006, Cubans were told that Fidel Castro was gravely ill and on February 24, 2008 Raul Castro took full control of the Cuban government. For over forty seven years, Fidel wielded total power as head of the Council of States, President of the Council of Ministers, First Secretary of the Communist Party and Chief of the Armed Forces. He had ruled the island with an iron fist, led a Marxist revolution ninety miles from the U.S., survived all attempts to overthrow his government and was dying in power. Indeed, a major personal victory. But, as Fidel began to fade into history's judgment, Raul was dutifully taking control of a nation in moral and economic ruins.

On July 26, 2007, the lack luster Raúl addressed the issue of Cuban workers' salaries and referred to the wages earned by the Cubans as "clearly insufficient"[30] which was quite an understatement. It is a fact that at the time of Fidel Castro's transfer of power to his brother, the average wage of a Cuban worker was 50 cents per day[31]. After nearly half a century implementing Castro's Marxist economic system and despite the massive non-military Soviet subsidy of $20,848 million and, more recently, Venezuela's $3,532 million[32], the revolution turned out the lowest per-capita salary in the Caribbean basin, even lower than Haiti's, the poorest country in the region.

## TABLE 7

### Yearly Salary  (in U.S. dollars) [33]
Haiti $ 473.00        Cuba $180.00

In 1959 as Castro was riding in triumph into Havana at the top of a Sherman tank, Cuba's cattle and beef products were the Island's second industry with six million livestock to feed six million people. The industry employed 100,000 workers and the Cubans ranked fourth in Latin America in meat consumption surpassed only by Argentina, Uruguay and Paraguay[34] Forty six years later, the state-control economy has less than four million heads of cattle to feed over 11 million Cubans.[35] In 1958, Cuba was the fifth producer of fresh milk in Latin America after Brazil, Argentina, Mexico and Colombia[36].

In December 1966, Fidel promised to a cheering crowd: "There will be so much milk that it will be possible to fill Havana Bay with milk"[37] By the time Raul inherited power, milk was still rationed and available only to children up to their seventh birthday.

In 1999, United Nations ranked Cuba as the second from last poorest country in Latin America.[38] The inefficiency of the Marxist system had created the conditions for a growing Black Market where people look for needed food at a higher price while limiting their buying power and encouraging corruption. On October 2, 2006 the BBC news reported from Havana: "with the state salary here about $15 per month and many essentials such as cooking oil and soap only available in hard currency (dollars), many people regard skimming off what they can from their jobs as necessary, even as a legitimate supplement to their incomes.[39]

Sugar, which has been the mainstay of Cuba's economy, has fallen to the production level of one hundred years ago. In 1906 the sugar industry, devastated by the War of Independence, produced 1,230,000 tons[40] while in 2006 the sugar production was 1,200,000 tons.[41] In the same year, the non-sugar agricultural industry reported a production decline of 20%[42] which explained why on February 2007 the Ministry of Economics stated that Cuba needed to import 84% of their food supply[43]. Indeed, a major system failure in an island with a fertile soil and a large peasant population. Castro's dysfunctional management performance has also reached other basic infrastructure such as housing and transportation.

On the issue of whether the revolution brought racial equality to the island, it is obvious by the hard facts that the top members of Castro's leadership structure remained dominated by white males. In a recent investigated report it was found that, while the Cubans of African descent represents over 60% of the population,[44] only four recognizable black faces sit on the party's 21 member Political Bureau and only two sit on the government's top body, the 39 member Council of Ministers"[45]

Several economic indicators point to the inefficiency of the Marxist system as the principal cause of Cuba's misery. In 1959, Cuba's per capita GNP was $850. In 2007, under a market economy, adjusting for inflation, it should have been, at least, the equivalent of $5100, placing Cuba above all Latin American countries, except Mexico. Today, the per capita GNP is $250. Indeed, a staggering drop from the outset of the Marxist revolution in 1959[46]. The hard currency debt is another indicator that negatively impacts the Cuban state controlled economy and severely impaired its ability to find new sources of international loans at low interest rate. In the years between 1989-1998, "the hard currency debt jumped from $6.2 billions to $11.2 billions, and about three-fourth of the debt has matured by 2001"[47]. By 1959, with a population of a little over 6 million, Cuban per capita foreign debt was less than $50. In 1996, with over 12 million people, the per capita debt reached $3180[48].

On the sensitive debate over the U.S. Embargo, a segment of Castro's apologists blamed Washington for the abysmal results of over 50 years of Cuba's Marxist economy. On this issue, we should let Fidel Castro answer the critics of the embargo. In December 1975, at the First Congress of the Communist Party in Havana, Castro said: "We don't want them (the U.S.) for anything, neither in our commerce, nor in the supplies"...[49] By this time the embargo had been in effect for over 14 years.

In April 1985, at a Playboy interview, Castro emphatically stated that the Cuban communist economy did not need to trade with the U.S. He said: "If we could export our products to the U.S. we would need to make plans for new lines of production.... because everything that we produce now and in the next five years had already been sold to other markets. Should we deprive our socialist countries of these products to sell them to the U.S.?"[50]

From 1960 to 1990 the U.S. Embargo was for Fidel Castro a side show. The Kremlin gave Cuba over $20 billion in economic aid[51] and Castro was not interested in trading with the hated Yankees. That was contrary to his vision of crushing capitalism. Castro was sure to be on the winning side of the Cold War, and the Cuban Revolution did not care to open the American market. The embargo became an issue of debate in the U.S. after the collapse of the Soviet Union which left Castro entrenched in the colossal disaster and misery of the failed communist dogma.

When the $20 billion of Soviet aid to Cuba is compared to the 13 billion dollars of the Marshal Plan for the reconstruction of Western Europe after the World War II, it tells the magnitude of the failure of Castro's revolution. Western Europe recovered from the terrible destruction of a major war against Nazi Germany with much less than the amount the Soviets gave Cuba. Where did the money go? The answer will remain hidden in Castro's mismanagement of Cuban centralized economy and in his secret accounting system.

In the U.S., Castro's image is at the bottom of the pit. From the dazzling welcome on his visit to the U.S. in 1959, Castro's popularity had plummeted among the American people[52]. In those early years the young Cuban leader was viewed as the embodiment of national sovereignty and freedom, the builder of a new Cuba under the frame of a just distribution of the nation's wealth and the respect of civil rights and individual freedoms, but as he turned Cuba into an impoverished Marxist autocracy, the radiance of those early hopes died.

Throughout the years, the Castro regime has been condemned by the Human Rights Commission of United Nations. At times, the resolutions were sponsored by Latin American nations such as Costa Rica, Uruguay and Peru. Later, they were joined by countries from the former socialist bloc, such as Poland, the Czech Republic and Hungary who have co-sponsored the resolutions to condemn the Cuban regime for its human rights violations. In the international ambit, Non Governmental Organizations (NGOs) such as Amnesty International and Human Rights Watch kept the Cuban dictatorship under permanent scrutiny.

Many of the original revolutionaries, already disenchanted, followed the path of dissidence and opposition joined by a growing number of young men and women borne under the revolution. Gustavo Arcos, Ricardo Bofill and Vladimiro Roca, among others, joined shoulder to shoulder with Oscar Elias Biscet, Martha Beatriz Roque, Oswaldo Paya, Guillermo Fariñas, Angel Polanco and Jorge Luis García Pérez "Antunez" to denounce the violations of the fundamental rights of the Cubans. All of them have suffered repression and incarceration.

Meanwhile, future events will continue to take us by surprise, like the defiance of the new generation raised in the grip of a shattered economy, alienated from the decrepit discourse of the gerontocracy, in which the average age of the ruling elite is 75 years old. Every day of their life, the younger Cubans had to face the ruins brought about by Fidel Castro's revolution. Without faith in the future, they live in the shadows of hopelessness.

A painful ritual that surface in the anger of the Cuban rap music and the courage of the "bloggers" that used the internet to express their independent thoughts, critical of the disastrous dogma that Fidel Castro imposed on the Cubans. This younger men and women may hold the key to freedom and prosperity. Perhaps a questionable probability, in light of their inexperience in dealing with tolerance, an essential pre-requisite to a healthy democracy.

Nevertheless, the revolution is dead and the Cuban youth is on the march, carrying on their shoulders the decaying corpse, still searching for a burial place. Sooner or later, they will find it and will bury this horrible madness. A new historical era is downing in the tragic island with no certainty of a happy end; only a recurrent search in the elusive quest for freedom.

Pedro Roig

# CHAPTER XXI

# CASTRO'S COMMUNIST AUTOCRACY:
# THE GLORIOUS ROAD TO FAILURE

[1] Jorge I. Dominguez. *The Civic Soldier in Cuba: In Armies and Politics in Latin America.* (eds. Abraham F. Lowenthal and Samuel Fitch), (rev ed. New York: Holmes and Meier, 1986), 263.

[2] Horowitz, op cit, 8

[3] Ibid.

[4] Raul Castro, speech in Sancti-Spiritus, May 1, 1985; Havana Television, May 3, 1985; cited in FBIS, Vol VI, 10 May 1985, Q1-8.

[5] Latell, op cit, 121

[6] Mark Falcoff. *Cuba the Morning After* (Washington D.C.: The AEI Press), 103.

[7] Quote in "Cuba en el Mes" (April 1995), 44

[8] Horowitz and Suchlicki, op cit, 403

[9] Alvaro Alba. *Militarización de la Sociedad Cubana.* Un-published manuscript. (Miami, 2000), 8.

[10] Ibid, 1

[11] George Galloway. *Fidel Castro Handbook.* (MQ Publications Ltd., 2006,), 207

[12] Horowitz, op cit, 354

[13] David J. Kopilow, Castro, Israel and the PLO. Cuban American National Foundation Report, 1984, 6.

[14] Galloway, op cit, 307

[15] Ibid, 308

[16] Stuart Rochester and Frederic Kiley. *Honor Bound. American Prisoners of war in Southeast Asia, 1961-1973* (Annapolis, Maryland: Naval Institute Press, 1998), 394.

[17] Rochester and Kiley, op cit,

[18] The Miami Herald, August 22, 1999.

[19] George Galloway, op cit, 152

[20] Video TV Marti. Interview with Dariel Alarcon on TV Marti, July 2003.

[21] Jorge Masseti

[22] The New York Times, July 11, 1975, 1.

[23] Verde Olivo, La Habana, No. 1, 1976, 97.

[24] Associated Press (AP), May 9, 2001.

[25] Suchlicki and Morris, op cit, 43

[26] www.cubaeuropa.com/historia/datos,htm.

[27] Ibid, 144

[28] Asi lo Dijo Fidel, op cit,18

[29] Bohemia, Febrero 14, 1986.

[30] Granma, Julio 26, 2007.

[31] University of Miami. Cuba Transition Project, Cuba Facts, and March 20, 2006

[32] Ministerio del Trabajo y Seguridad Social de Cuba. Resolución No. 30/05. — U.S. Department of State, June 1995, report on Haiti.

[33] Carrillo, op cit, 21A

[34] Study, op cit, 528

[35] Oscar Espinosa Chepe. *Cuba: Revolución o involución*. (Aduana Vieja Editorial, Valencia, España 2007), 131

[36] United Nations 1960 pgs. 312-316.

[37] Fidel Castro's speech at the Federation of Cuban women, December 1966.

[38] La Nueva Cuba. Edicion Digital, septiembre 3, 2002.

[39] BBC News, Oct 2, 2006.

[40] Study, op cit, 235

[41] Asociación de Economistas Cubanos. ASCE – release N 302-05-25-07.

[42] Espinosa Chepe, op cit, 129

[43] Granma. Febrero 26, 2007

[44] University of Miami, Institute of Cuban and Cuban American Studies. (Cuba Facts, Issue 11, April 2005)

[45] The Miami Herald, June 20, 2007 p 10 A.

[46] Carrillo, op cit, 21A

[47] Carmelo Mesa-Lago. *Cuban Communism;* Horowitz and Suchlicki, op cit, 105

[48] Salazar, op cit, 21A

[49] Así lo dijo Fidel, op cit, 25

[50] Ibid, 26

[51] Carmelo Mesa-Lago, Problemas Sociales y Económicos en Cuba. Revista CEPAL. Agosto 1, 2005.

[52] The Miami Herald, February 8, 2007, p 13A.

# BIBLIOGRAPHY

CHAPTER I
**A THEOCRACY IS BORN**
- Boorstein, Daniel. The Discoverer (New York: Vintage Books, Random House, 1983)
- Castro, Américo. España en su Historia (Barcelona, 1983) –Cristianos, Moros y Judíos—- Comella, Beatriz. La Inquisición Española (Madrid: Ediciones Rialp, 1999)
- Crow, John A. Spain (Berkeley: University of California, 1985)
- Durant, Will. The Reformation. A History of European Civilization from 1300-1564 (New York: Simon and Schuster, 1957)
- Johnson, Paul. A History of the Jew (New York: Harper and Row, 1985)
- Le Riverand, Julio. Historia Económica de Cuba (Barcelona: Ediciones Ariel, 1972
- Nadal, Jordi. España en su Cenit (Barcelona: Critica, 2001)


CHAPTER II
**SPAIN: THE GLORY AND THE RUIN**
- Herren, Ricardo. La Conquista Erótica de las Indias. (Barcelona. Editorial Planeta, 1991)
- Marrero, Leví. Cuba, Economía y Sociedad. (Madrid. Editorial Playor, 1974)
- Masó, Calixto. Historia de Cuba. (Miami. Ediciones Universal, 1976)
- McNeil, William. The Pursuit of Power. (University of Chicago Press, 1982)
- Ortega y Gasset, José. La España Invertebrada. (Madrid. Editorial Espasa Calpe, 1921)
- Schama, Simon. History of Britain. (New York: Miramar Book. Hyperion, 2000)
- Thomas, Hugh. Cuba: The Pursuit of Freedom. (New York. Harper and Row, 1971)
- Tuñón de Lara, Manuel. Estudios sobre el siglo XIX español. (Madrid. Editorial Siglo XX de España, 1984)


CHAPTER III
**CUBA IN ECONOMIC AND POLITICAL TRANSITION**
- Carr, Raymond. Spain, a History. (New York. Oxford University Press, 2000)
- Davis, David Brion. Inhuman Bondage. The Rise and Fall of Slavery in the New World. (New York. Oxford University Press, 2006)
- De Arango y Parreño, Francisco. (Havana, 1888)

- De la Pezuela, Jacobo. Diccionario Geográfico, Estadístico. Historia de la Isla de Cuba. (Madrid, 1863)
- Dunn, John. The Political Thought of John Locke. (Cambridge University Press, 1995)
- Dunn, Susan. Sister Revolutions. French Lighting, American Lighting. (New York. Forber and Forber Inc., 1999)
- García de Arboleda, José. Manual de Historia de Cuba. (Havana, 1859)
- Guerra, Ramiro. Manual de Historia de Cuba. (Madrid. Editorial Playor, 1975)
- Knight, F.N. Origino f Wealth and the Sugar Revolution in Cuba. 1750-1850. (Hispanic American Historical Review, 1957)
- Thomas, Hugh. The Slave Trade. (New York. Simon and Schuster, 1997)

## CHAPTER IV
### SUGAR, SLAVERY AND THE BIRTH OF CUBA'S NATIONAL CONSCIENCE

- Agramonte, Roberto. José Agustín Caballeros y los Orígenes de la Conciencia Cubana. (Universidad de la Habana)
- Durant, Hill. The Story of Philosophy. (Simon and Schuster, Touchstone. New York, 1961)
- Estenger, Rafael. Sincera Historia de Cuba. (Medellín, Editorial Bedout, 1974)
- Martí, José. Obras Completas. (Editorial Lex, La Habana)
-- Menocal, Raimundo. Orígenes y Desarrollo del Pensamiento Cubano. (La Habana. Editorial Lex, 1945)
- Moreno Fraginals, Manuel. Azúcar, Esclavos y Revolución. (Revista Casa de las Américas, 1968) Número 50.
- Suchlicki, Jaime. Cuba: From Columbus to Castro. New York. Charles Scribnes' sons, 1974)
- Valdés, Gerónimo. Gobernador y capitán General de Cuba. Habana 1842. Bando de Gobernación y Policía de la Isla de Cuba. Reglamento de Esclavos, Artículo 6.

## CHAPTER V
### SPAIN: THE ARMY AS ARBITER OF POWER

- Casanova Codina, Juan. O Pan o Plomo. (Madrid. Editorial Siglo Veintiuno, 2000)
- De la Sagra, Ramón. Historia Económica, Política y Estadística de la Isla de Cuba. (Havana, 1831)
- Fusi, Juan Pablo and Palafox, Jordi. España: 1808-1996. El Desafío de la Modernidad. (Madrid. Editorial España, 1997)
- Moore, John Basset. A digesto f Internacional Law. (Washington, 1906)

- Morales y Morales, Vidal. Iniciadores y Primeros Mártires de la Revolución Cubana. (Havana, 1931)
- Porter Vilá, Herminio. Historia de Cuba en sus Relaciones con los Estados Unidos y España. (Miami. Mnemosyne Publishing Inc., 1969)

## CHAPTER VI
### THE TEN YEARS WAR

- Bacardí Moreau, Emilio. Crónicas de Santiago de Cuba. (Madrid. Editorial Brogan, Segunda Edición, 1972)
- Casasús, Juan J. Calixto García. (Miami. Editorial Moderna Poesía, 1981)
- Cautelar, Emilio. La España Moderna. Crítica Internacional. (June 1893)
- Delgado, Octavio. The Spanish Army in Cuba, 1868-1898: An International Study. (Colombia University, 1980)
- Forner, Philip S. La Guerra Hispano-Cubano-Americana y el Nacimiento del Imperialismo Norteamericano. (Madrid. Akal Editor, 1975)
- Gallego, Tesifontes. La Insurrección Cubana. (Madrid. Imprenta Central, 1897)
- Gómez, Máximo. Diario de Campaña del Estado Mayor General Máximo Gómez. (Ceiba del Agua. Talleres Centro Superior Tecnológico, 1941)
- Handrick, Daniel R. Ejército y Política en España: 1868-1898. (Madrid. Editorial Tecnos, 1981)
- Howard, Philip A. "Changing History. Afro-Cuban Cabildos and Societies of Color in the Nineteenth Century". (Baton Rouge. Lousiana State University Press, 1998)
- Pirala, Antonio. Anales de la Guerra de Cuba. (Madrid, 1896)
- Roa, Raúl. Aventuras, venturas y desventuras de un Mambí en la lucha por la independencia de Cuba. Mejico. Editores Siglo XXI, 1970)
- Sedano y Cruzat, Carlos. Cuba desde 1850 a 1873. (Madrid, 1873)
- Soto Paz, Rafael. Los Verdaderos Generales. Habana. Revista Bohemia. Febrero 24, 1950)

## CHAPTER VII
### BETWEEN THE WARS (1868-78)

- Aidaud de la Sastre, Juan M. La Primera República Española. Historia y Vida. (Madrid. Extra 3, 1974)
- Bizcarrondo, Martha y Elorza, Antonio. Cuba y España. El Dilema Autonomista 1878-1898. (Madrid. Editorial Colibrí, 2001)
- Boorstin, Daniel. The Nacional Experience. New York. Vintage Books, 1965)
- Castellanos, Isabel y Jorge. Cultura Afrocubana. (Miami. Ediciones Universal, 1992)
- De la Concha, José G. Memorias sobre el Estado Político, Gobierno y

Administración de la Isla de Cuba. Madrid, 1853)
- De la Torre, José María. Lo que Fuimos y lo que Somos. O la Habana
Antigua y Moderna. (La Habana, 1857)
- De la Torre, Mildred. Autonomismo en Cuba. 1878-1898. (La Habana.
Editorial Ciencias Sociales, 1997)
- Barcía, María del Carmen. Elites y Grupos de Presión; Cuba 1868-1898.
(La Habana, 1997)
- De Polavieja, Marqués. Relación Documentada de mi Política en Cuba. Lo
que ví, lo que Hice y lo que Anuncié. (Madrid. Emilio Minuesan, 1898)
- Estevez y Romero, Luis. Desde el Zanjón hasta Baire: Datos para la
Historia Política de Cuba. (La Habana. Tipografía "la propaganda literaria",
1899)
- Franco, José Luciano. Antonio Maceo: Apuntes para una Historia de su
Vida. (La Habana, 1951)
- García de Arboleda, José. Manual de la Isla de Cuba; Compendio de su
historia, geografía, estadística y administración. (La Habana, 1859)
- Gonzalez del Valle, Francisco. "Antecedentes y Consecuencias de la
Dominación Inglesa". Cuaderno de Historia Habanera número 12. (La
Habana, 1937)
- Guggenhein, Harry F. The United Status and Cuba, a Study in Internacional
Relations. (New York, 1934)
- Madden, Richard R. The Island of Cuba: Its resources, Progress and
Prospects. (London, 1849)
- Martí, José. Nuestra América. Selected Writings.
- Montoro, Rafael. Discursos y Escritos. (Miami. Editorial Cubana, 2000)
- Ortiz, Fernando. Cuba, Martí and the Race Problem. (Pilón III, 3rd Quarter,
1942)
- Papeles de Maceo. Edición del Centenario. Introducción de Emeterio
Santovenia. (La Habana. Académia de la Historia, 1948)
- Ramos, Marco Antonio. Panorama del Protestantismo en Cuba. (San José.
Editorial Caribe, 1986)
- Roig de Leuchsenring, Emilio. Antonio Maceo: Ideología Política, Cartas y
Otros Documentos. (La Habana, 1950)
- Rubens, Horatio. Liberty: The Store of Cuba. New York. Brewer, Warren
and Putman Inc., 1932
- Sanguily, Manuel. La Lucha Política en Cuba. Los Unos y los Otros. (La
Habana. Imprenta de Soler Alvarez y Cía., 1889)
- Sanguily, Manuel. Defensa de Cuba. (Oficina del Historiador de La
Habana, 1948)
- Scott, Rebecca J. Slave Emancipation in Cuba. The Transition to Free
Labor: 1860-1899. (University of Pittsburg Press, 1985)
- Smith, Angel y Dávila, Emma. The Crisis of 1898. (McMillan Press LTD,

1999)
- Smith, Robert F. The United States and Cuba; Business and Diplomacy, 1917-1960. (New York, 1961)
- Stubbs, Jean. Tobacco on the Periphery. A Case Study in Cuba Labor History. 1860-1958. (England. Cambridge, 1985)
- Taylor, John Glanville. The United States and Cuba. Eight Years of Change and Travel. (London, 1851)
- Tuchman, Barbara W. The Proud Tower: 1890-1914. (New York. Ballentine Books, 1996)

## CHAPTER VIII
### THE WAR OF INDEPENDENCE: (1895-1898). THE FIRST PHASE: SECURING THE EASTERN PROVINCES (1895)

- Fee, Emory W. Ten Months with the Cuban Insurgents. Century Magazine, June 1898)
- Gamazo, G. Maura. Historia Crítica del reinado de Don Alfonso XIII. (Madrid, 1925)
- Ibáñez Marín, José. General Martínez Campos. (Madrid, 1908)
- London Times. March 1, 1895.
- Miró Argenter, José. Cuba: Crónicas dela Guerra. (La Habana. Editorial Lex, 1945)
- Ollero, Andrés. Teatro de la Guerra. (Madrid, 1898)
- Roig de Leuchsenring, Emilio. Ideario Cubano: Antonio maceo. (La Habana, 1946)
- Souza, Benigno. Ensayo Histórico sobre la Invasión. (La Habana. Imprenta Ejército, 1948)

## CHAPTER IX
### THE WAR OF INDEPENDENCE (SECOND PHASE 1896-1897). THE INVASION OF THE WESTERN PROVINCES

- Beck, Henry H. Cuba's Fight for Freedom and the War with Spain. (Philadelphia. Glove Publishing Company, 1898)
- Boza, Bernabé. Mi Diario de Guerra. (La Habana, 1947)
- Cardona, Gabriel y Lozada, Juan C. Weyler. Nuestro Hombre en La Habana. (Barcelona. Editorial Planeta, 1997)
- Carrasco García, Antonio. En Guerra con los Estados Unidos. (Madrid. Ediciones Almena, 1998)
- Castellano, Gerardo. La Trocha de Mariel a Majana. (Habana, 1947)
- Cleveland, Grover. Fourth Annual Message. December 4, 1896 FR. US. 1897.
- Correspondencia Diplomática de la Delegación Cubana en Nueva York durante la Guerra de Independencia de 1895 a 1898. (La Habana, 1943-

1946)
- Davis, Forrest. The Atlantic System. New York. Reynal Hitchcock, 1941)
- Diario de la Marina. La Habana. August 12, 1895.
- Diario de la Marina. La Habana. December 30, 1895.
- Economist, The. London, October 5, 1895.
- Estrada Palma, Tomás. Editor. La Invasión de Occidente. Partes Oficiales. (New York. Imprenta América, 1898)
- Goicochea, Luis. Diario (La Habana, 1921)
- Gómez, Fernando D. La Insurrección por Dentro. (La Habana. M. Ruiz y Co., 1897)
- Halstead, Murat. Our Neighbors and Their Struggle for Liberty. (Review of Reviews, April 1896)
- Heraldo de Madrid. September 5, 1897.
- Journal. February 23, 1896.
- Kissinger, Henry. Diplomacy. (New York. Simon and Schuster, 1994)
- Literary Digest, The. New York. April 30, 1895.
- Musicat, Ivan. Empire by Default. (New York. Henry Holt and Company, 1998)
- Ortega Rubio, Juan. Historia de la Regencia de Doña María Cristina. (Madrid, 1905)
- O'toole, G. J. The Spanish War; An American Epic, 1898. (New York. Norton and Company, 1996)
- Piedra Martell, manuel. La Campaña de Maceo. (La habana, 1967)
- Reina Cossío, René E. El Lazo de la Invasión. 24-31 de Diciembre, 1895. (Estudios Histórico-Militares. La habana: Oficina del Historiador de la Ciudad, 1956)
- Romano, Julio. Weyler. El Hombre de hierro. (Madrid. Espasa-Calpe, 1934)
- Time, The. London, 1895.
- Weigley, Russel F. The American Way of war. (Bloomington. Indiana University Press, 1977)
- Weyler, Valeriano. Mi Mando en Cuba. (Madrid. Imprenta de F. Gonzalez Rojas, 1910) May 17, 1896.

CHAPTER X
## THE WAR OF INDEPENDENCE: THE THIRD PHASE (1898). THE U.S. ENTERS THE WAR

- Cervera y Topeta, Pascual. From the English translation to "La Guerra Hispano-Americana. (The English Collection of Documents was issued by the Government Painting Office in 1899, Washington DC)
- Coblentz, Edmond D. and Hearst, William Randolf. A Portrait in his Own Words. (New York. Simon and Schuster, 1952)

- Collazo, Enrique. Los Americanos en Cuba. (Habana. Editorial de Ciencias Sociales, 1972)
- Durnat, John and Alice. The Presidents of the United Status. (New York. Gache Publishing Co., 1966)
- Foreign Relations. January, 1898
- Fuller, J. C. Decisive Battles of the U.S.A. (New York. Da Capo Press, 1993)
- Gould, Lewis L. The Spanish American War and President McKinley. (University of Kansas Press, 1982)
- Hernández, José M. Política y Militarismo en la Independencia de Cuba: 1868-1933. (España. Editorial Colibrí)
- Long, John Davis. America of Yesterday: As Reflected in the Journal of Davis Long. (Boston. Atlantic Monthly Press, 1923)
- Millet, Allen Reed. Th Politics of Intervention; The Military Occupation of Cuba, 1906-1909. (Columbus, 1968)
- Spanish American War, The: A collection of documents relative to the Squadron Operation in the West Indies, arranged by Rear Admiral Pascual Cervera y Topete. Washington, Navy Department, 1899.
- State Department Archives. Woodford-Sherman. December 7, 1897
- U.S. Navy Court of Inquire. (The Maine Explosion)
- White, Trumbull. United States in War with Spain. (Chicago. International Publishing, 1899)
- Wissan, Joseph. The Cuban Crisis as Reflected in the New York Press, 1895-1898. (New York. Columbia University Press, 1934)

CHAPTER XI
## FROM INTERVENTION TO INTERVENTION
- Aguilar, Luis. Cuba 1933: Prologue to Revolution. (New York. The Norton Library, 1974)
- Alvarez Díaz, José. A Study on Cuba. (Miami. University of Miami Press, 1963)
- Archivo Nacional, Boletín 32 (1933). De Gómez a Estrada Palma. (October 28, 1898)
- Crabb, Mary Catherine. Cuban Communism: 1959-2003. (Editors, Irvin Horowitz and Jaime Suchlicki, 2003) 11th Edition.
- Del Aguila, Juan. Dilemma of a Revolution. (Atlanta. Westview Press, 1988)
- From García to Estrada Palma, June 27, 1989. (Boletín Archivo Nacional de Cuba, 1936)
- Gompers, Samuel. Imperialism. Its Dangers and Wrongs. (American Federationist. November 1898)
- Iznaga, R. Tres Años de República. Folleto Político. (Havana. Rambla y

Bouza, 1905)
- Llaverias, Joaquín and Santovenia, Emeterio. Actas de la Asamblea de Representantes y del Consejo de Gobierno durante la Guerra de Independencia. (La Habana. El Siglo XX, 1936)
- Lodge, Henry Cabot. Selections from the correspondence with Theodore Roosevelt. (1884-1914 Ed H. C. Lodge, 1925)
- Lozano casado, M. La Personalidad del general José Miguel Gómez. (1913)
- McKinley, William. Papers. Department of State. (Brooke to McKinley. September 26, 1899)
- Martínez Ortiz, Rafael. Cuba, los Primeros Años de Independencia. (París. Editorial LeLivre, 1929)
- New York Times, The
- Porter, Robert. Special Report on the visit to Máximo Gómez and the relation to the payment and disbandonment of the Insurgent Army. Washington, 1899
- Pringle, H. F. Life and Times of William Howard Taft. (New York, 1939)
- Roosevelt, Theodore. Letters, V (Department of State) to William Taft.
- Roosevelt, Theodore. Letters. (Department of State) II, 1005
- Roots, Elihu. Papers. (Department of State) to Paul Dana. January 1900.
- Washington Evening Star.
- Wright, Irene A. Cuba. (New York, 1910).

CHAPTER XII
**THE PROTECTORATE**
- Anuario Azucarero de Cuba.
- Arredondo, Alberto. Cuba, tierra indefensa. (La Habana. Editorial Lex, 1944)
- Census of the Republico f Cuba. 1919
- Foreign relations. State Department. 248 (May, 1912)
- Geerlings, H. C. P. Prinsen. Cane Sugar and its manufacture. (Altrincham, 1909)
- Guerra, Ramiro. Azúcar y Población en las Antillas. (3rd Ed., Habana Cultural, 1944)
- Kane, Joseph Nathan. Famous First Facts. (New York. The H. W. Wilson Co., 1950)
- Machado, Gerardo. Por la Patria Libre. (Habana. Imprenta de F. verdugo, 1916)
- Diario de las Sesiones de la Asamblea Constituyente. 12th Session. Habana, 1928.
- Wright, Phillip G. The Cuban situation and our treaty relations. (Washington DC, 1931)

CHAPTER XIII
**THE 1933 REVOLUTION**
- Blis, Sheldon. Roots of Revolution: Radical Thoughts in Cuba. (University of Nebraska Press, 1987)
- Foreign Relations of the United states, 1933. (Washington DC, U.S. Government Printing Office, 1952)
- Phillips, Ruby Hart. Cuba: Island of Paradise. (New York, 1959)
- U.S. Department of State Papers. (05/3556). National Archives. June 21, 1933.

CHAPTER XIV
**THE CONSTITUTIONAL PRESIDENTS**
- Farber, Samuel. Revolution and Reaction in Cuba 1933-1960. (Middletown. Wesleyan University Press, 1976)
- Geyer, Georgie Anne. Guerrilla Prince. (Boston. Little, Brown and Company, 1991)
- Rodríguez, Carlos Rafael. En Defensa del Pueblo. (1945)
- Ros, Enrique. Fidel Castro y el Gatillo Alegre. (Miami. Ediciones Universal, 2003)
- Sánchez Echevarría, Lela. La Polémica Infinita. (Bogotá. Quebecor World, 2004)

CHAPTER XV
**FIDEL CASTRO AND THE FORMATIVE YEARS**
- Castro, Raúl. Fundamentos. (FAR, Habana. Junio-Julio, 1961)
- Díaz Balart, Rafael. Cuba: Instrahistoria, una lucha sin tregua. (Miami. Ediciones Universal, 2006)
- Duarte Oropesa, José. Historiología Cubana. (Miami. Ediciones Universal)
- Franqui, Carlos. Vida, aventura y desastres de un hombre llamado Castro. (Barcelona. Editorial Planeta, 1988)
- Latell, Brian. Alter Fidel: The inside store of castro's regime and Cuba's next leaders. (New York. Palgrave McMillan, 2002)
- Raffy, Serge. Castro el Desleal. Santillana U.S.A. Doral, 2006)

CHAPTER XVI
**THE 1956 GENERATION: THE HEROIC**
- De Palma, Anthony. The Man who Invented Fidel. (New York. Public Affairs, 2006)
- Dubois, Jules. Fidel Castro: Rebel, Liberator or Dictator? (Indianapolis, 1959)
- Furiati, Claudia. Fidel Castro: La Historia me Absolverá. (Barcelona. Plaza

James, 2003)
- Gambia, Hugo. El Che Guevara. (Editorial Stockcero, 2002)
- Guevara, Ernesto. "Ché". Pasajes dela Guerra. Revolucionaria. (Habana.
Ed. Txalaparta, 2001)
- Matos, Húber. Cómo llegó la Noche. (Barcelona. Tusquets Editores S.A.,
2002)
- Matthews, Herbert. The New York Times. February 24, 1957.
- Smith, Earl T. El Cuarto Piso. (México. Editorial Diana, 1963)

## CHAPTER XVII
### THE WEALTH PRODUCING REPUBLIC
- América en Cifras. Unión Panamericana, Estadísticas Culturales.
(Washington DC. Instituto Interamericano de estadísticas, 1960)
- Bacardí. Mari Aixala Dawson. Publisher: Facundo and Amalia Bacardí
Foundation, Inc., Miami, Florida, 2006.
- Comercio Exterior. 1957. Finance Ministry, Cuba, 1959.
- Cuba: Economía y Finanzas. (Editorial Mercantil Cubana, S.A.
(Noviembre-Diciembre, 1960)
- Sirven, Pablo. El Rey de la T.V. (Buenos Aires. El Clarín-Aguilar, 1996)
- Smith, Kirby and Llorens, Hugo. Renaissance and Decay. Cuba in
Transition. (ASCE, 1998)
- Statistical Year Book, 1959. United Nations, New York.
- Statistical Year Book, 1960. United Nations, New York.
- United Nations, 1960. 312-6, U.N.F.A.O., 1998.
- United Nations, 1966. 136; U.N.F.A.O., 1997 b, 216-7
- United nations, 1966. 332-3
- Verde Olivo. Julio 30, 1961.

## CHAPTER XVIII
### FREEDOM DEFERRED
- Alekseev, Aleksandr. KGB. Havan. January 4, 1960. Folio 3, Tomo 5, Lista
65. Archive SVR (KGB)
- Así lo dijo Fidel. Citas del Máximo Líder de la Revolución. Colección Las
Américas, Líder Máximo, 2006)
- Diario de la marina. Miami. Noviembre 12, 1960.
- López Fresquet, Rufo. My Fourteen Months with castro. (New York, 1996)
- New York Times, The. June 13, 1961.
- Nixon, Richard. Memo. Office of the Vicepresident. Washington. April 25,
1959.
- Prensa Libre. Mayo 13, 1960
- Revolución (Newspaper). Enero 13, 1959.
- Revolución (Newspaper). Noviembre 17, 1959.

- Semichastny. KGB. Havana. January 17, 1960. Folio 3. Tomo 5. Lista 65.
SVR (KGB)
- Walter, Robert S. International Affairs. Volume 42, No. 1. (January 1966)

## CHAPTER XIX
### THE BAY OF PIGS TRAGEDY

- Castro, Fidel y Fernández, José Ramón. Playa Girón. (La Habana. Editorial
Ciencias Sociales, 1983)
- Bundy, McGeorge. Memorando of Discussion on Cuba. Cabinet Room.
January 28, 1961.
- CIA Brifing. Cuba. February 17, 1960.
- CIA, Classified Message. October 31, 1960.
- CIA Memorandum for the Director, by Abbot Smith, Acting Chairman.
Board of National Estimates. 2-11-96.
- CIA Memorandum for Chief WH-4. Policy Decision Requested for conduct
of strike operations against government of Cuba. 1-4-61.
- Del Pino, Rafael. Proa a la Libertad. (El Planeta, 1991)
- Dulles, Alln. Memorandum for General Maxwell Taylor. 06-01-61.
- Ferrer, Eduardo. Operación Puma. (Miami, 1975)
- Gleijeses, Piero. Ships in the Night: The CIA, the White House and the Bay
of Pigs. (Journal of Latin American Studies. February 1995)
- Johnson, Haynes. The Bay of Pigs. (New York. Norton Company, 1964)
- Lynch, Graystone. Decision for Disaster. (Washington. Brassery's, 2004)
- Memorandum. The White House , meeting in the Cabinet Room. 9:45,
January 19, 1961.
- Memorandum of conference with the President, 3-16-60; CIA, a program
of covert action against the Castro regime. 3-16-60.
- Pino Machado, Quintín. La Batalla de Girón. (La Habana. Editorial
Ciencias Sociales, 1983)
- Ponzoa, Gustavo. Interview for T.V. Marti. Documentary "En Nombre de la
Libertad" (History of Bahía de Cochinos) 04-13-2005.
- Schlesinger Jr., Arthur. Memorando for the President's Special Assistant to
President Kennedy. 2-11-61
- U.S. Joint Chief of Staff. Memorandum for the secretary of defense. U.S.
Plan of Action in Cuba. 1-27-61.

## CHAPTER XX
### I AM A MARXIST... (Fidel Castro). THE CUBAN MISSILE CRISIS

- Abel, Elie. The Missile Crisis. (Philadelphia, 1966)
- Allison, Graham T. Essence of Decision. (Boston. Harvard University.
Little Brown and Company, 1971)
- Bohening, Don. The Miami Herald. April 16, 2000.

- Air Force Response to the Cuban Crisis. October 14-November 24, 1962. ca 1-63, 27-9
- Chang, Laurence and Kurnbluh, Meter. (Documents) The Cuban Missile crisis. (New York. The New York Press, 1992)
- Cinclant. Historical Account of Cuban Crisis. 4-29-63.
- Dobrynin, Anatoly. In Confidence. (New York. Random House, 1955)
- Document 36. McGeorge Bundy. Executive Committee Record of Action. 10-25-62
- Document 38. McGeorge Bundy. Executive Committee Record of Action. 10-25-62
- Document 45. Prime Minister Fidel Castro's letter to Premier Khruschev. 10-26-62
- Fuentes, Norberto. Dulces Guerreros Cubanos. (Barcelona. Editorial Seix Barral, 1999)
- Guevara, Ernesto. Escritos y Discursos. (Habana. Editorial de Ciencias Sociales, 1977)
- Kennedy, Robert F. Thirteen Days: A Memoir of the Cuban Missile Crisis. (New York. Norton and Company. Paperback, 1999)
- Reed, Thomas C. At the Abyss. (New York. Ballantine Books, 2004)
- Revolución (Newspaper). Mayo 2, 1961.
- Revolución (Newspaper). October 24, 1961.
- Revolución (Newspaper). December 2, 1961.
- Revolución (Newspaper). Enero 3, 1963.
- Salazar Carrillo, Jorge. El Nuevo herald. Septiembre 21, 2007.
- The Secret Cuban Missile Crisis Documents. CIA (Declassified) Introduction by Graham T. Allison. (New York. Brassey's, 1994)
- The Soviet Block Armed Forces and the Cuban Missile Crisis: A chronology. July-November 1962. (10-18-63)
- U.S. CONAR. Participation in the Cuban Crisis. (October 1963).

CHAPTER XXI
## CASTRO'S COMMUNIST AUTOCRACY: LIFE IN THE SHADOWS OF HOPELESSNESS

- Alba, Alvaro. Militarización de la Sociedad Cubana. Un-published manuscript. (Miami, 2000)
- Asociación de Economistas Cubanos. ASCE Release No. 302-05-25-07
- Associated Press. (AP) May 9, 2001.
- BBC News. October 2, 2006.
- Bohemia. Febrero 14, 1986.
- Domínguez, Jorge. The Civic Soldier in Cuba: Armies and Politics in Latin America. (New York. Eds. Abraham F. Lowenthal and Samuel Fitch) (rev. ed. New York. Holmes and Meier, 1986)

- Espinosa Chepe, Oscar. Cuba: Revolución o Involución. (España. Aduana Vieja. Editorial Valencia, 2007)
- Falcoff, Mark. Cuba, the Morning After. (Washington DC. The AGI Press)
- Galloway, George. Fidel castro Handbook. (MQ Publication Ltd., 2006)
- Granma (Newspaper). Febrero 26, 2007.
- Granma. Julio 26, 2007.
- Kopilow, David J. Castro, Israel and the P.L.O. (Cuban American National Foundation Report, 1984)
- Mesa Lago, Carmelo. Cuban Communism. (Ed. Horowitz and Suchlicki)
- Mesa Lago, Carmelo. Problemas Sociales y Económicos en Cuba. Revista CEPAL. Agosto 1, 2005.
- Miami Herald, The. February 8, 2007.
- Miami Herald, The. June 20, 2007.
- Ministerio del trabajo y la Seguridad Social de Cuba. Resolución No. 30 / 05.
- Nueva Cuba, La. Edición Digital. Septiembre 3, 2002
- New York Times, The. July 11, 1975.
- Rochester, Stuart and Kiley, Frederic. Honor Bound. American Prisoners of war in Southeast Asia, 1961-1973. (Annapolis, Maryland. Naval Institute Press, 1998)
- United nations, 1960.
- University of Miami. Transition project. Cuba Facts. March 20, 2006.
- University of Miami. Institute of Cuban and Cuban American Studies. (Cuba Facts, Issue 11. April, 2005)
- U.S. Department of State. Report on Haiti. June 1995.
- Verde Olivo (Magazine) La Habana. Noviembre 1976.

# INDEX